SWORD ART ONLINE

GIRLS' OPS

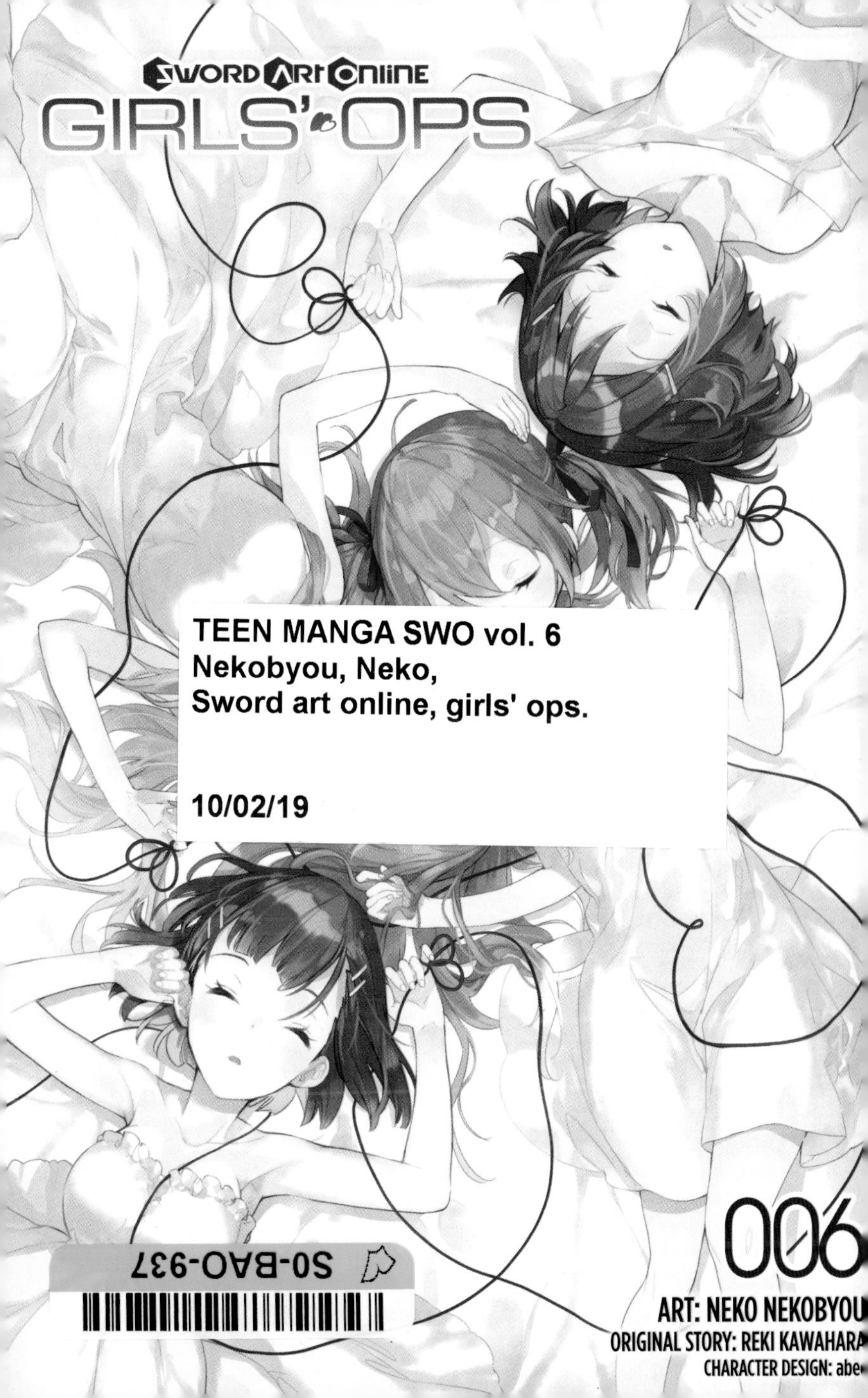

006

ART: NEKO NEKOBYOU
ORIGINAL STORY: REKI KAWAHARA
CHARACTER DESIGN: abec

006

SWORD ART ONLINE
GIRLS' OPERATIONS

art: Neko Nekobyou
original story: Reki Kawahara
character design: abec

C o n t e n t s

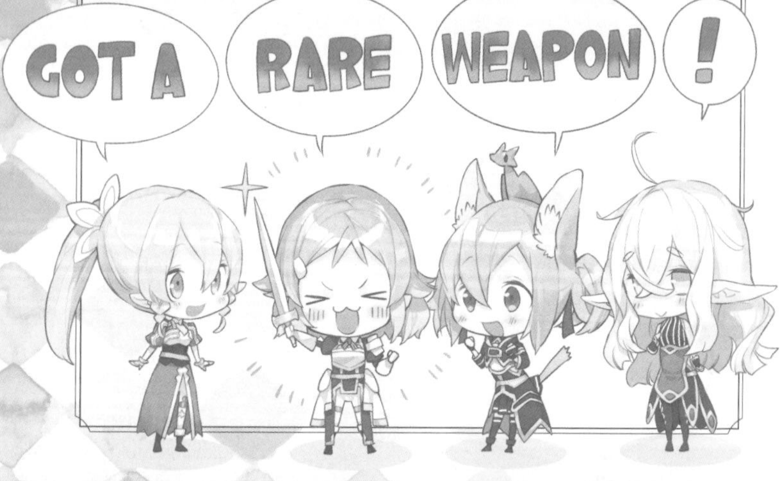
GOT A
RARE
WEAPON
!

SWORD ART ONLINE
GIRLS' OPS 006

SWORD ART ONLINE
GIRLS' OPERATIONS

ART: NEKO NEKOBYOU
ORIGINAL STORY: REKI KAWAHARA
CHARACTER DESIGN: abec

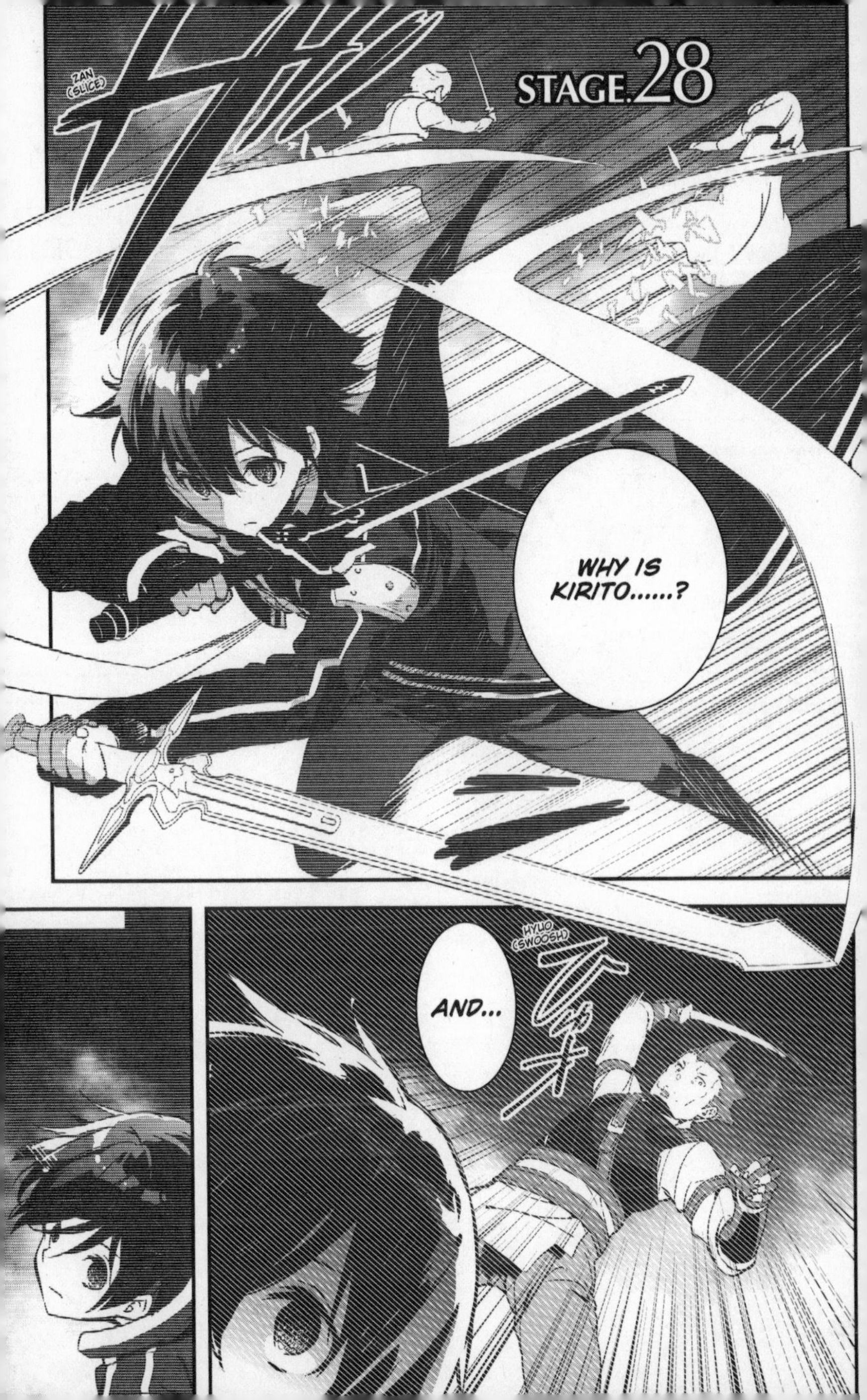
STAGE.28
ZAN (SLICE)
WHY IS KIRITO......?
HYUO (SWOOSH)
AND...

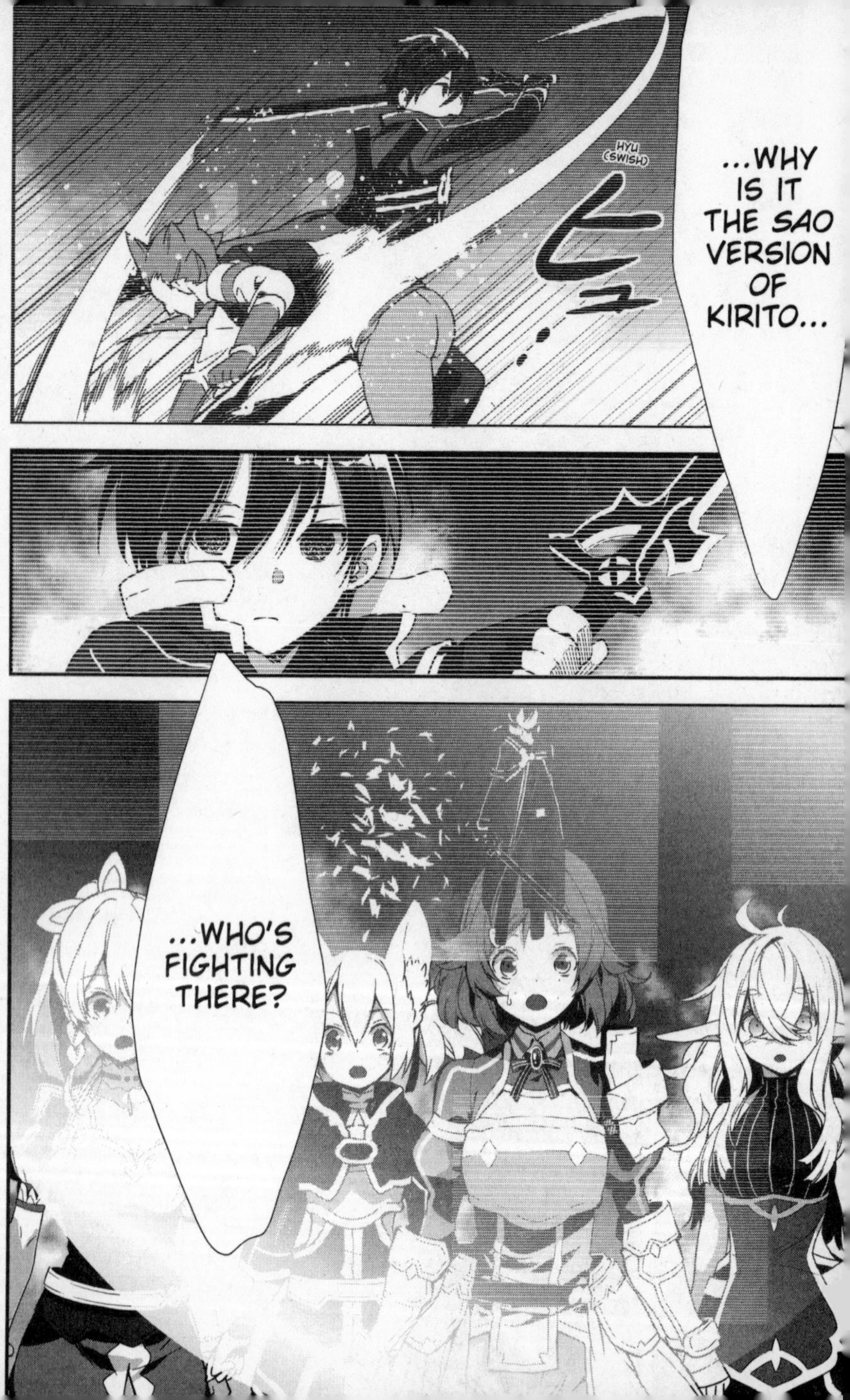
...WHY IS IT THE SAO VERSION OF KIRITO...
HYU (SWISH)
...WHO'S FIGHTING THERE?

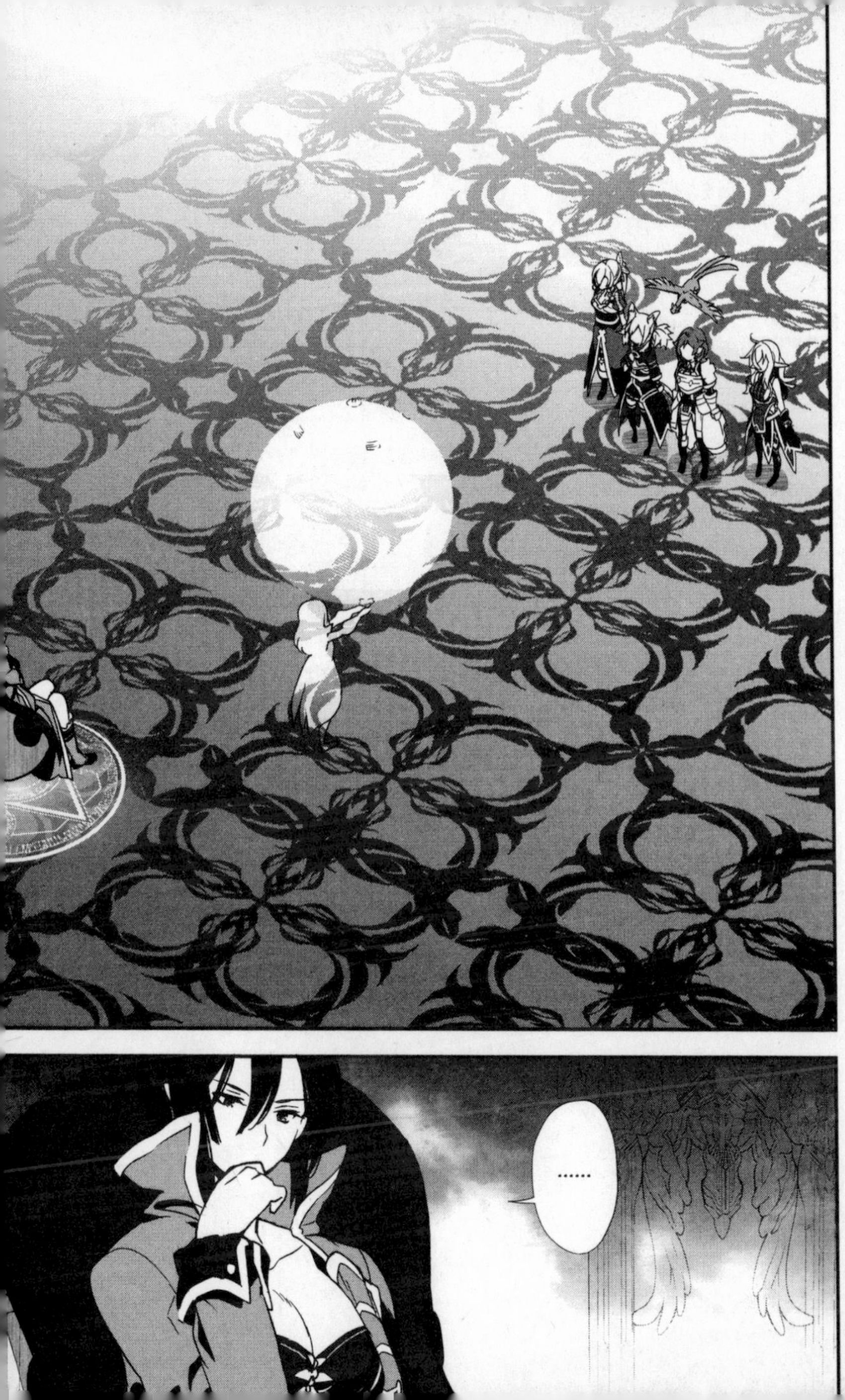
……

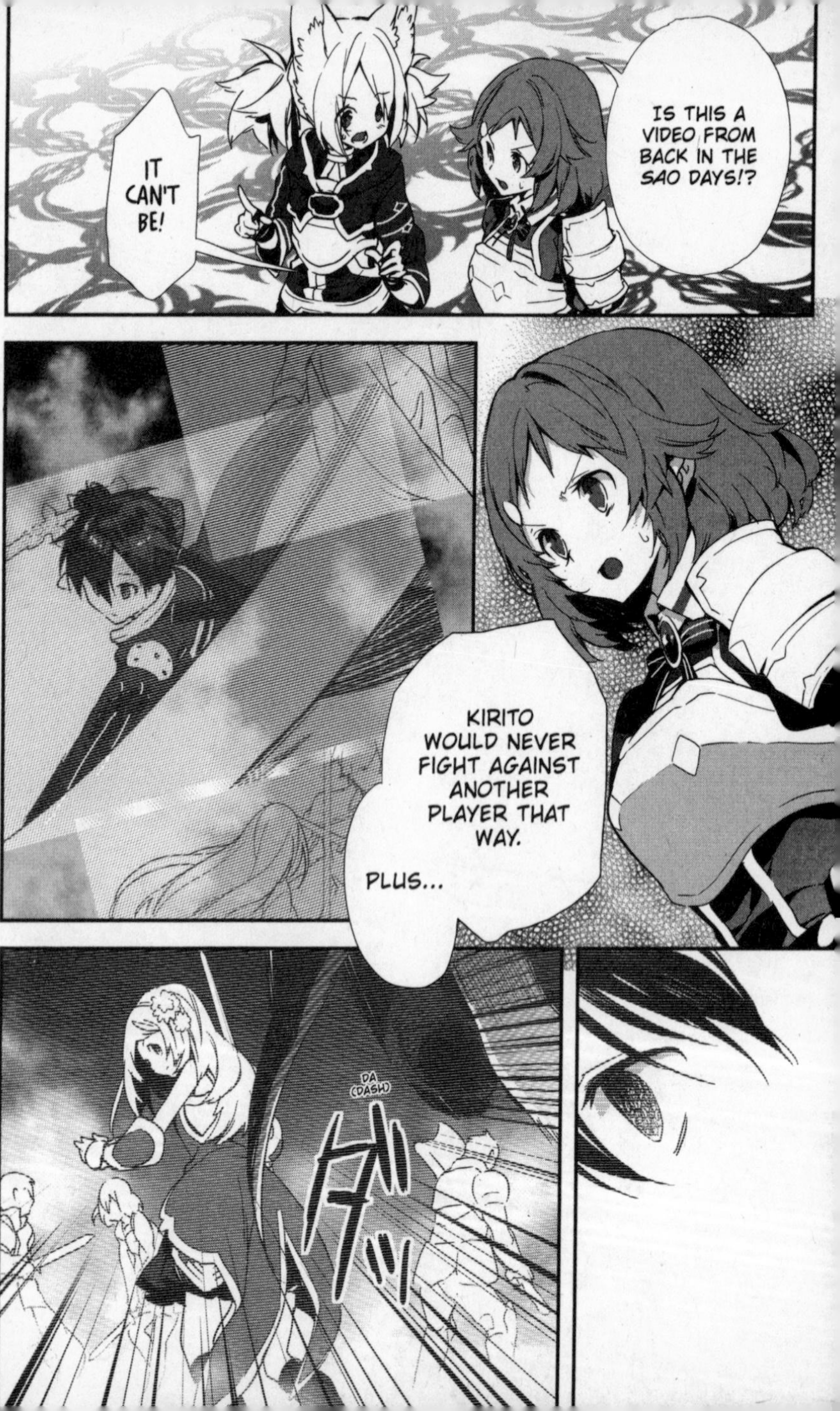
IS THIS A VIDEO FROM BACK IN THE SAO DAYS!?
IT CAN'T BE!
KIRITO WOULD NEVER FIGHT AGAINST ANOTHER PLAYER THAT WAY.
PLUS...
DA (DASH)

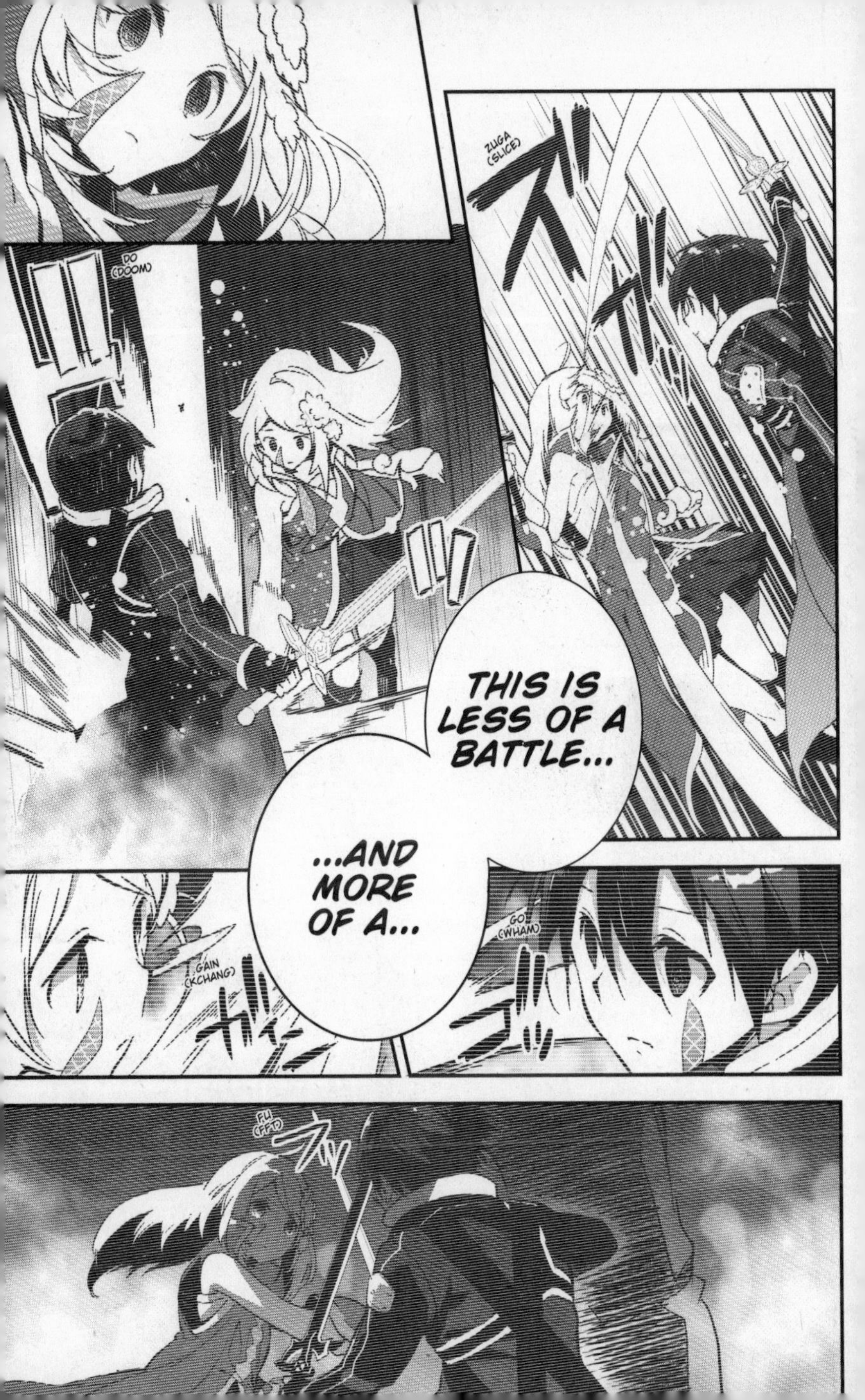
ZUGA (SLICE)
THIS IS LESS OF A BATTLE...
DO (DOOM)
GO (WHAM)
...AND MORE OF A...
GAIN (KCHANG)
FU (FFT)

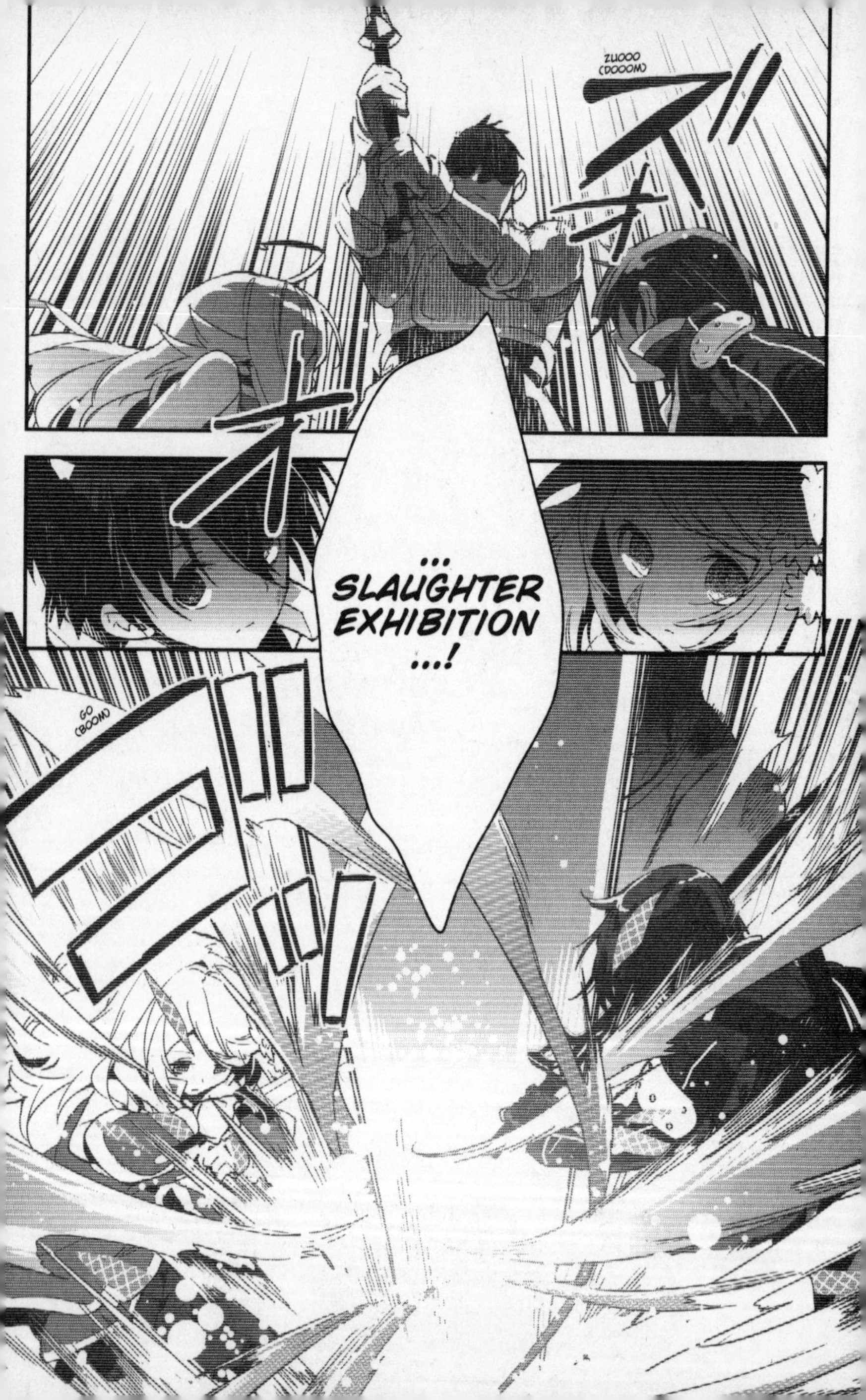
ZUOOO
(DOOOM)
...SLAUGHTER EXHIBITION ...!
GO
(BOOM)

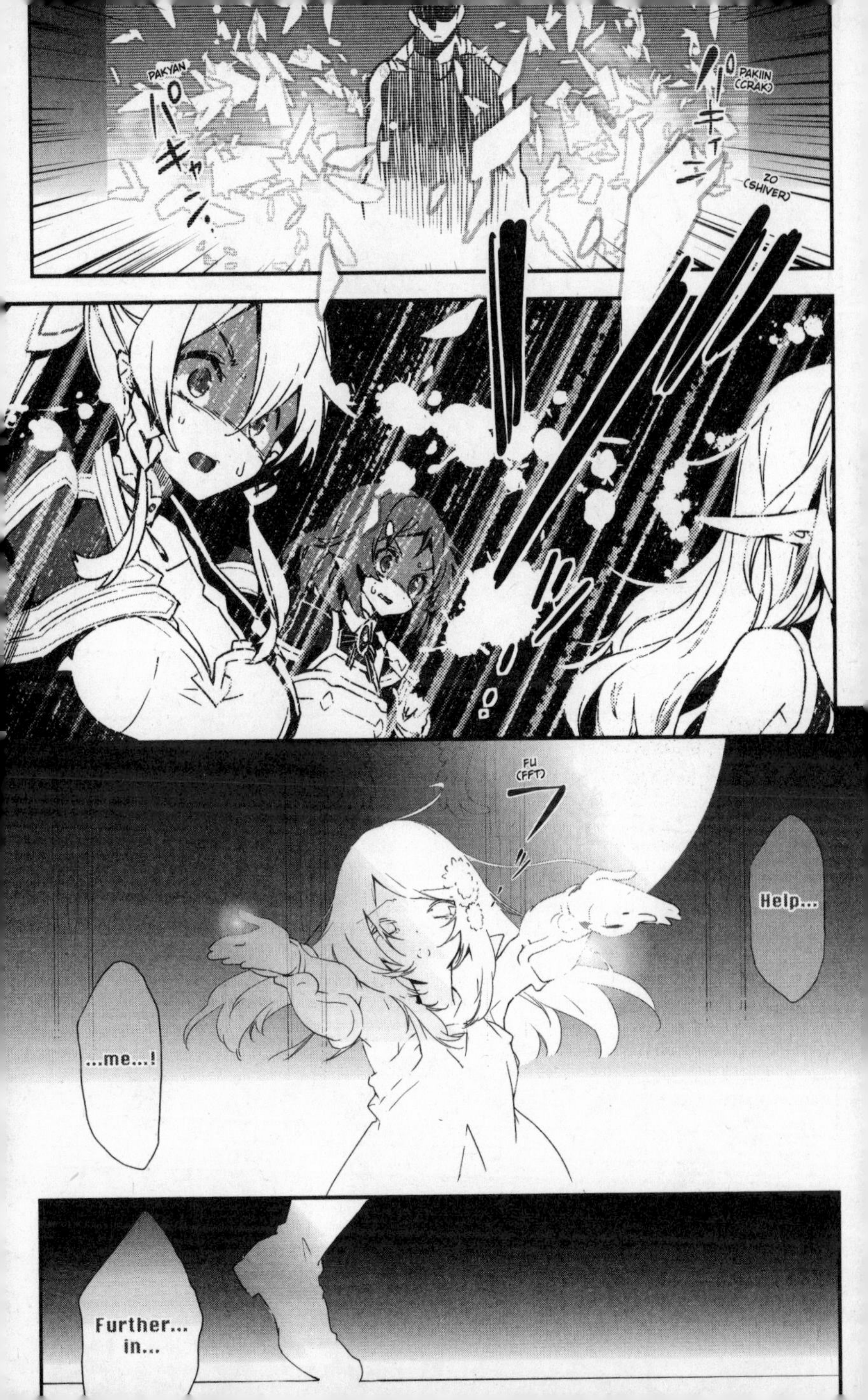

PAKIIN (CRAK)
ZO (SHIVER)
PAKYAN
FU (FFT)
Help...
...me...!
Further... in...

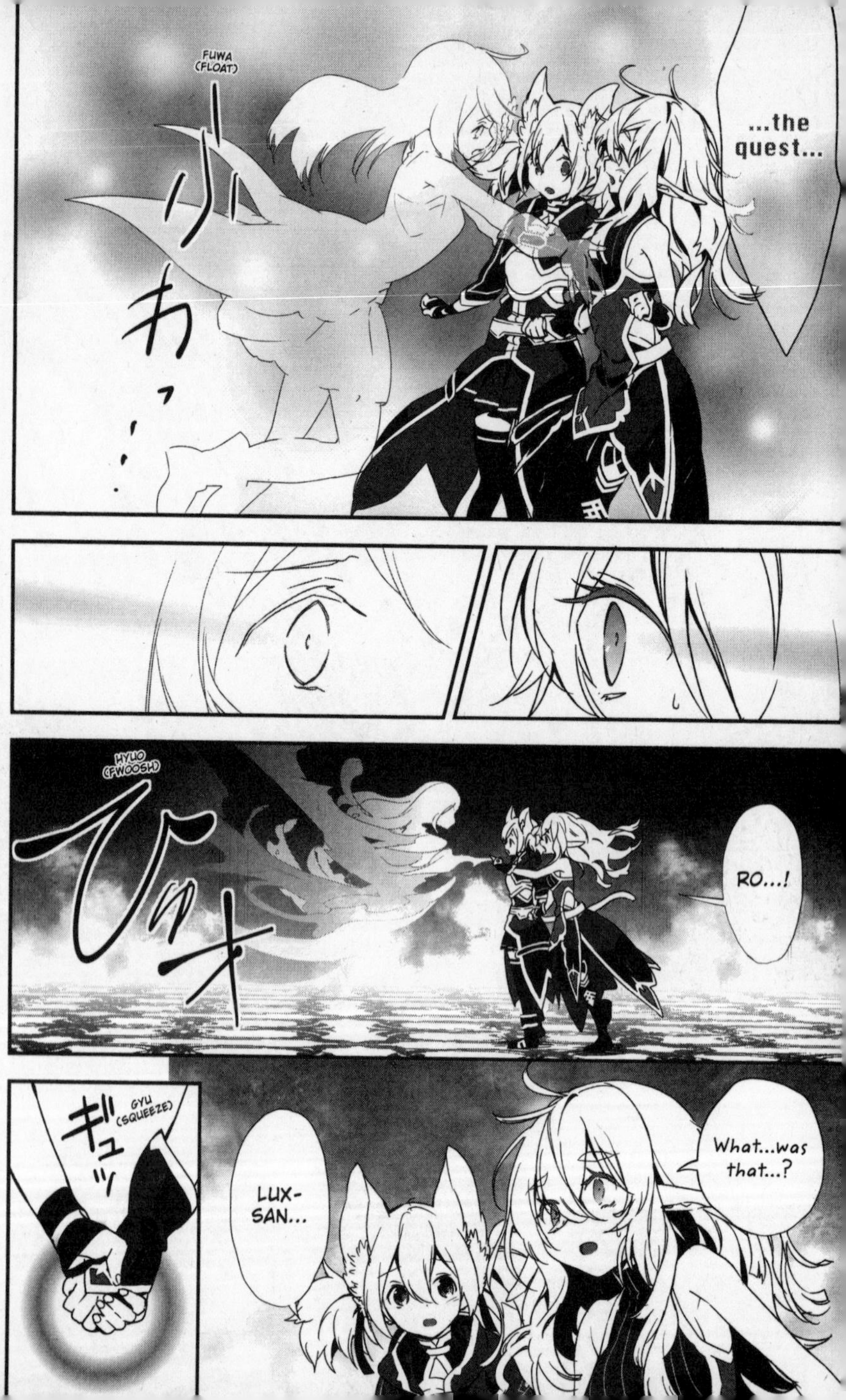
...the quest...
FUWA (FLOAT)
ふわっ...
RO...!
HYUO (FWOOSH)
What...was that...?
LUX-SAN...
GYU (SQUEEZE)
ギュッ

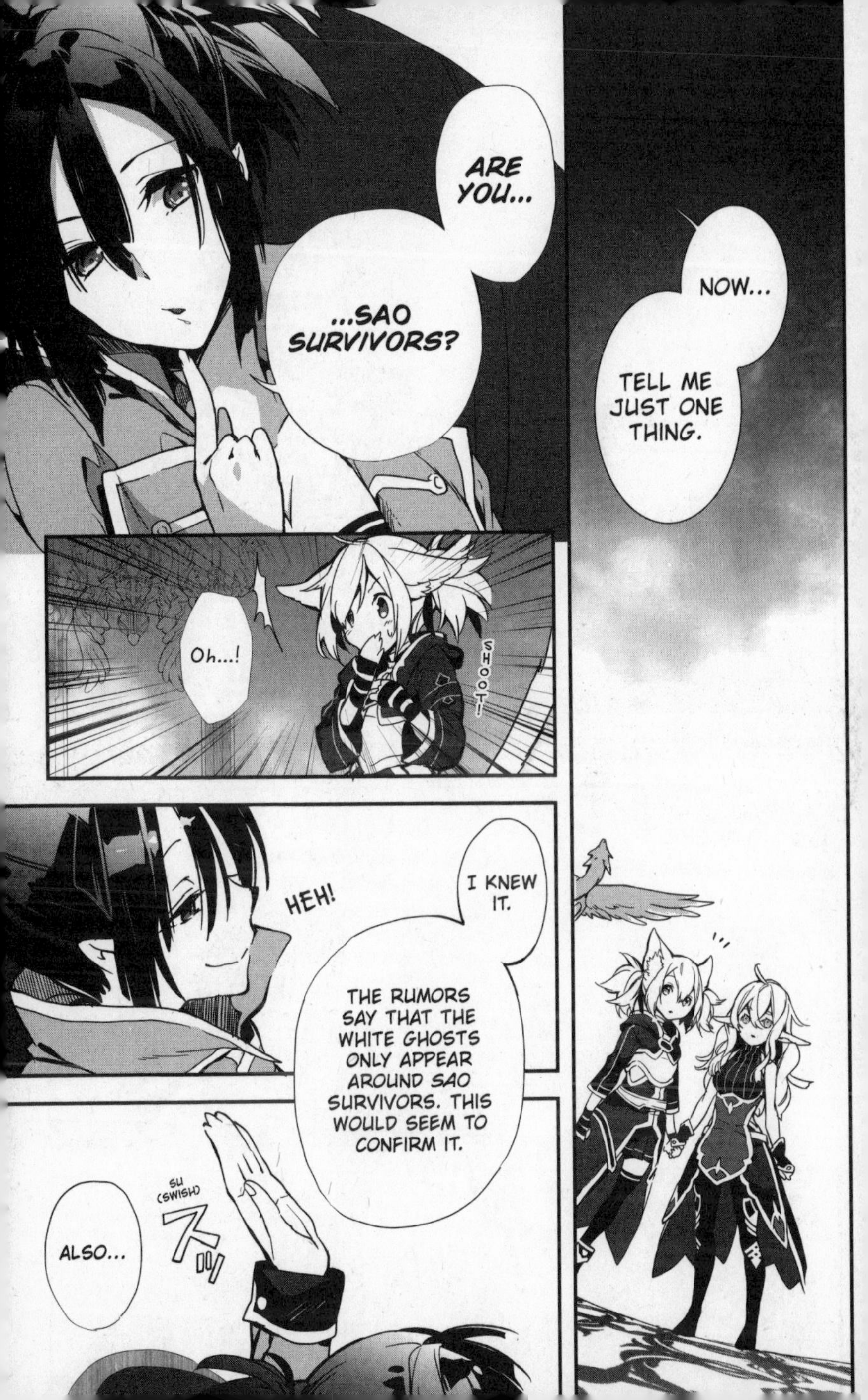
NOW...
TELL ME JUST ONE THING.
ARE YOU...
...SAO SURVIVORS?
Oh...!
SHOOT!
HEH!
I KNEW IT.
THE RUMORS SAY THAT THE WHITE GHOSTS ONLY APPEAR AROUND SAO SURVIVORS. THIS WOULD SEEM TO CONFIRM IT.
SU (SWISH)
スッ
ALSO...

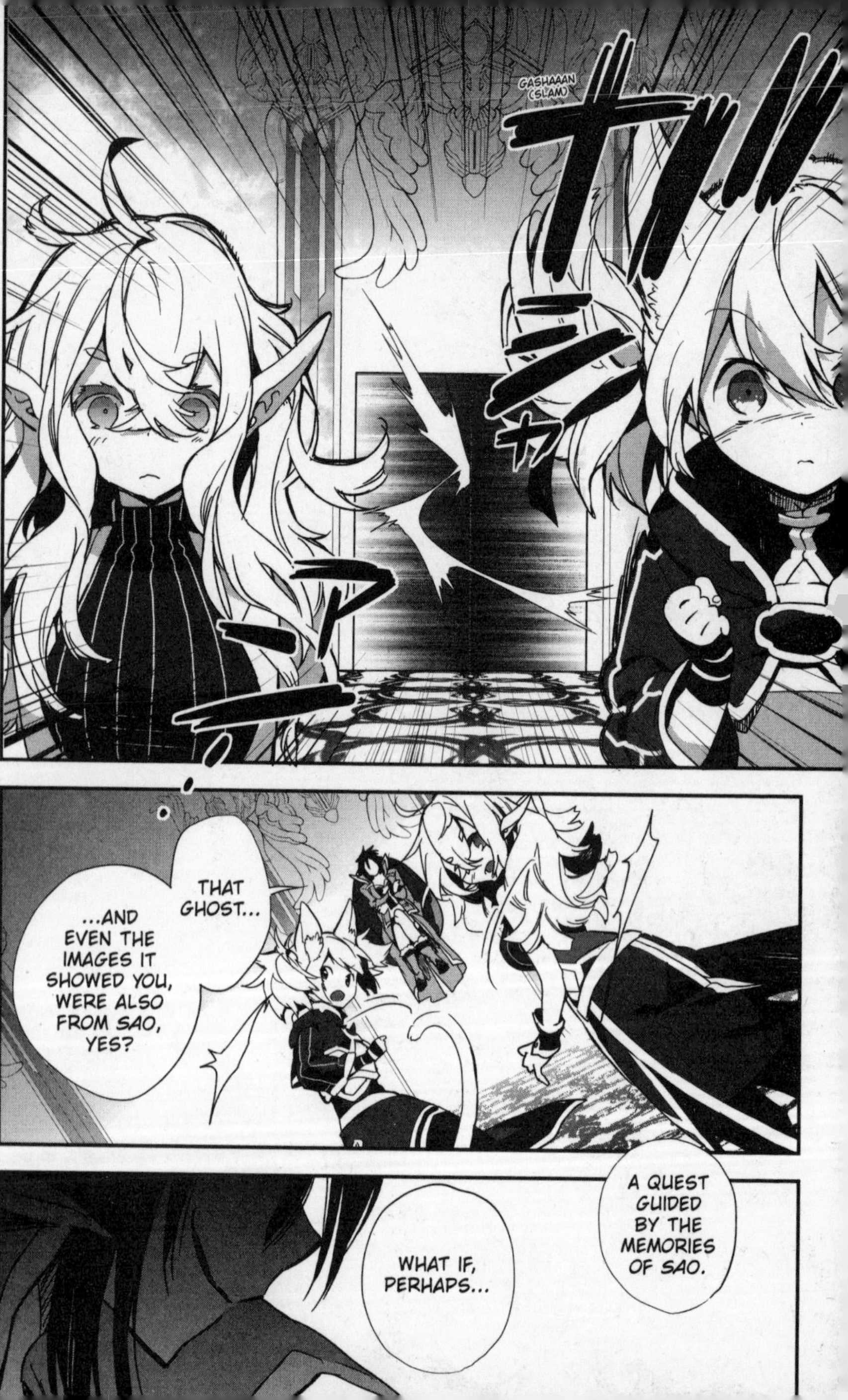
GASHAAAN (SLAM)
THAT GHOST...
...AND EVEN THE IMAGES IT SHOWED YOU, WERE ALSO FROM SAO, YES?
A QUEST GUIDED BY THE MEMORIES OF SAO.
WHAT IF, PERHAPS...

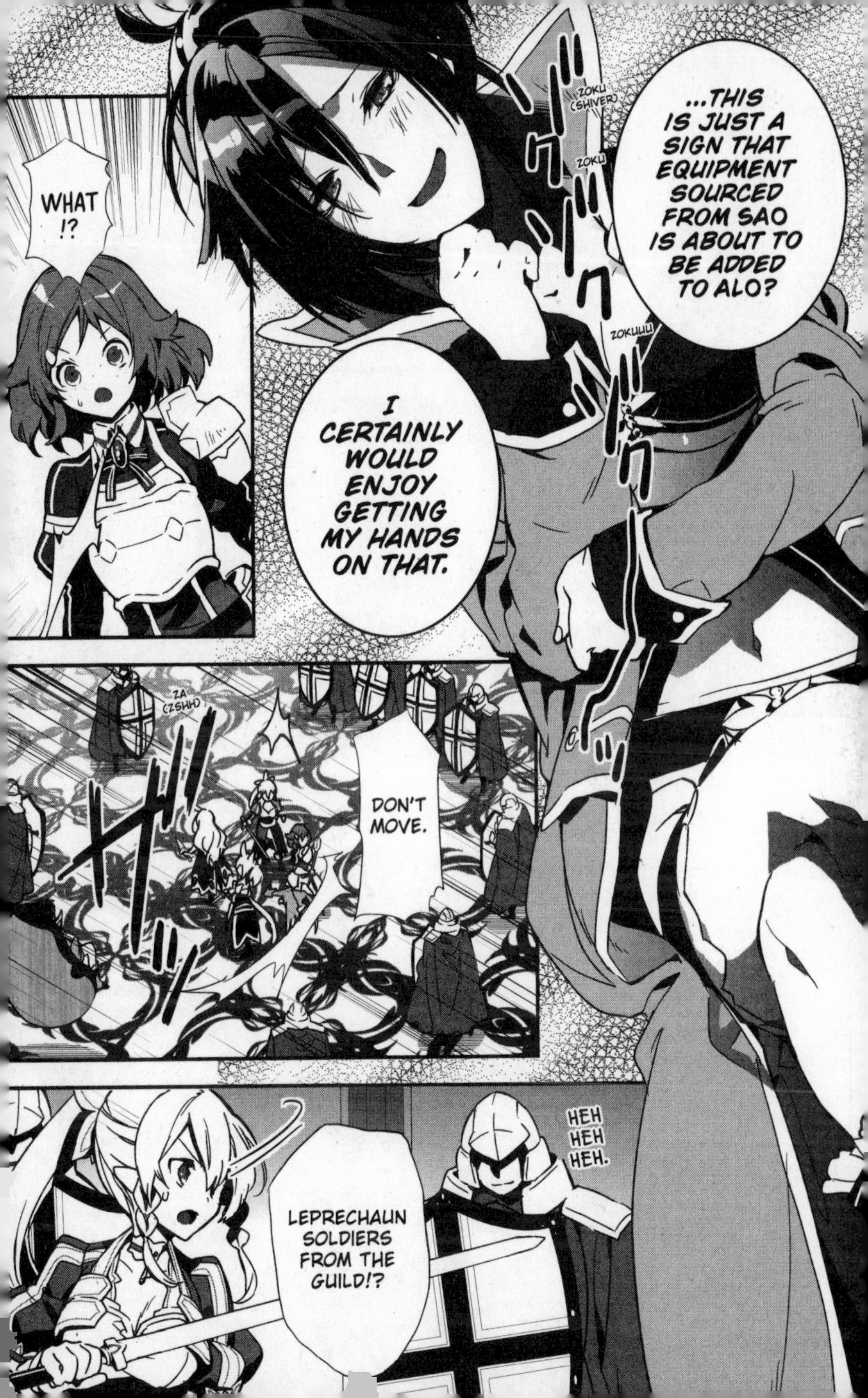
ZOKU (SHIVER)
ZOKU
...THIS IS JUST A SIGN THAT EQUIPMENT SOURCED FROM SAO IS ABOUT TO BE ADDED TO ALO?
ZOKUUU
I CERTAINLY WOULD ENJOY GETTING MY HANDS ON THAT.
WHAT !?
ZA (ZSHH)
DON'T MOVE.
HEH HEH HEH.
LEPRECHAUN SOLDIERS FROM THE GUILD!?

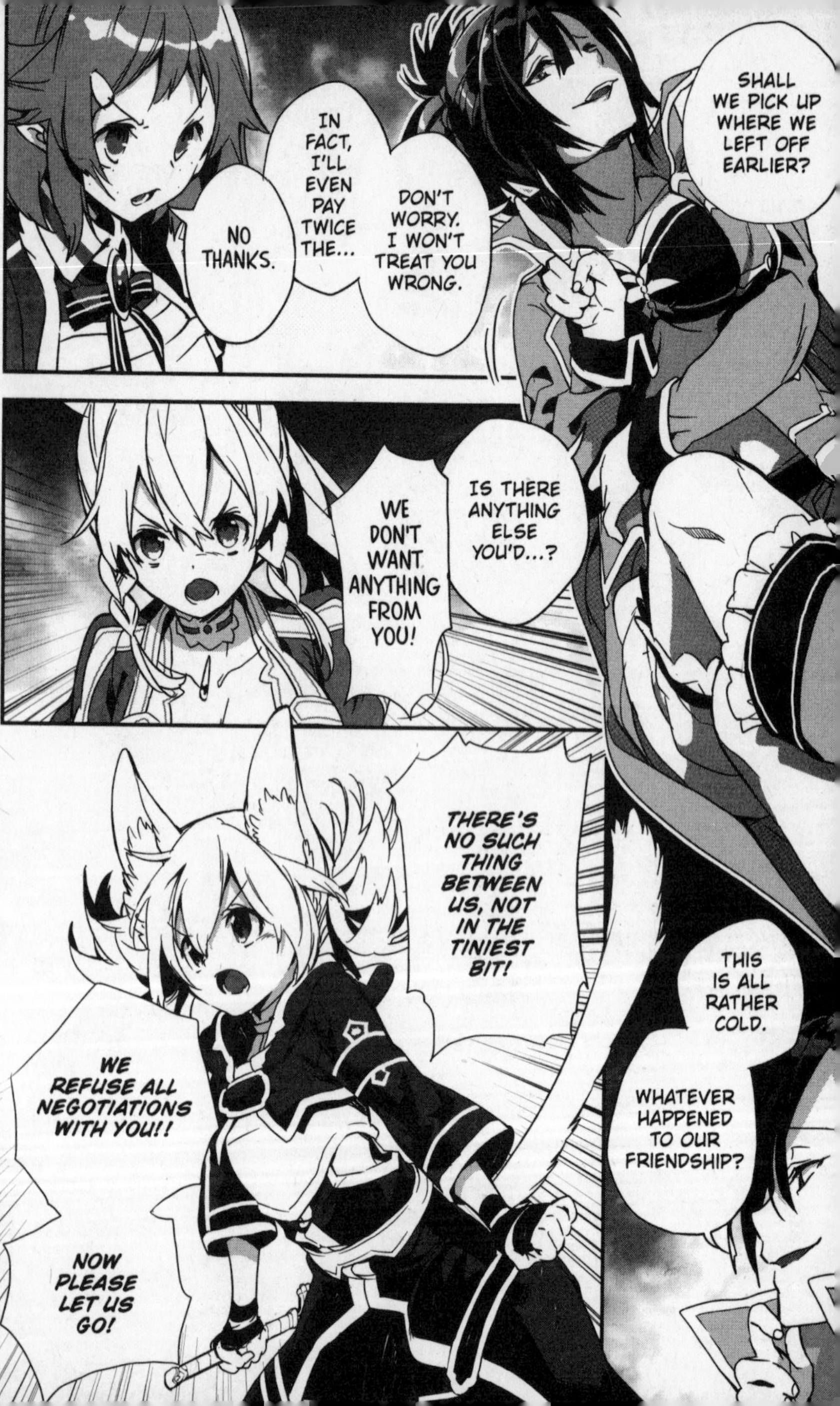
SHALL WE PICK UP WHERE WE LEFT OFF EARLIER?
DON'T WORRY. I WON'T TREAT YOU WRONG.
IN FACT, I'LL EVEN PAY TWICE THE...
NO THANKS.
IS THERE ANYTHING ELSE YOU'D...?
WE DON'T WANT ANYTHING FROM YOU!
THIS IS ALL RATHER COLD.
WHATEVER HAPPENED TO OUR FRIENDSHIP?
THERE'S NO SUCH THING BETWEEN US, NOT IN THE TINIEST BIT!
WE REFUSE ALL NEGOTIATIONS WITH YOU!!
NOW PLEASE LET US GO!

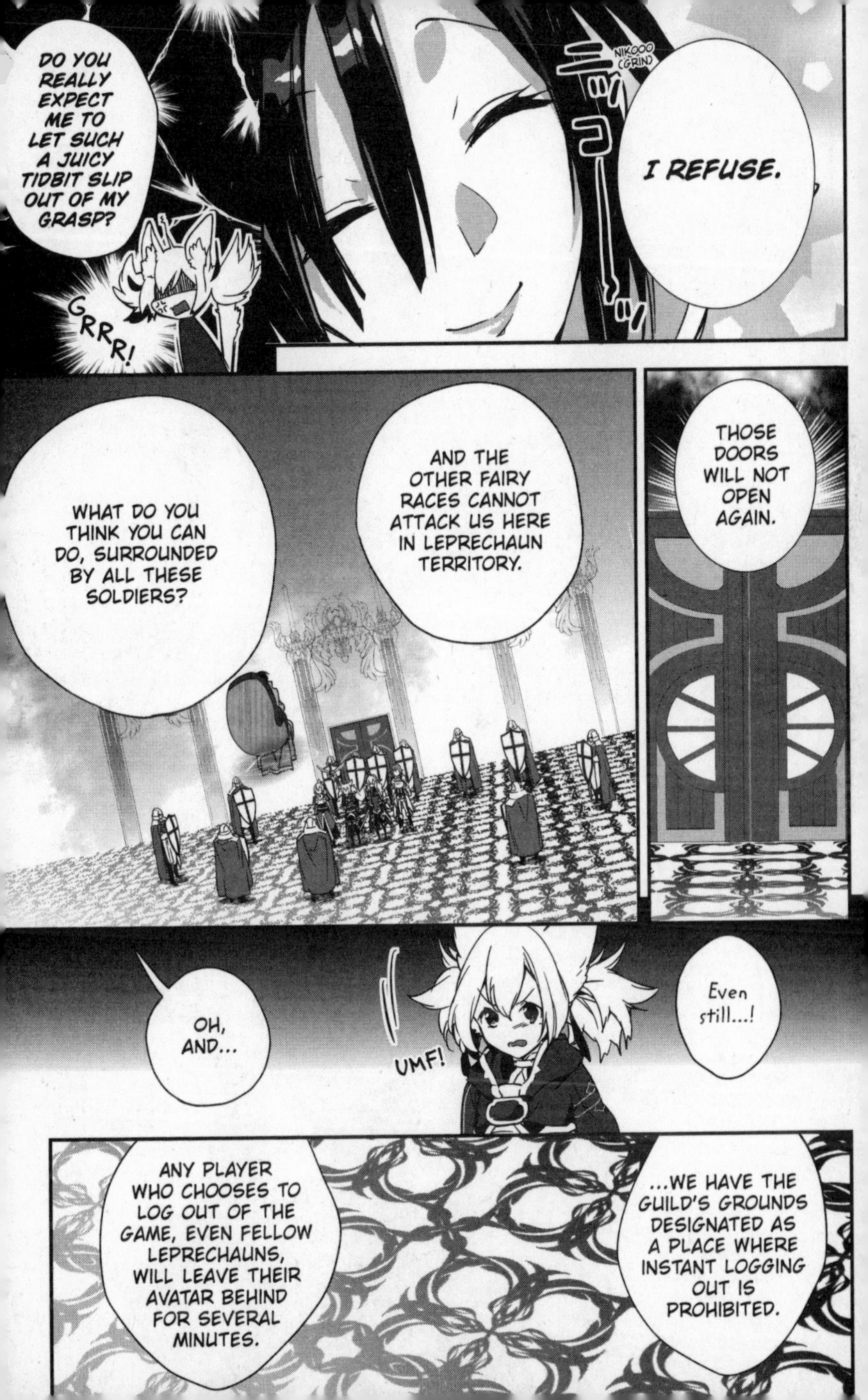
NIKOOO (GRIN)
I REFUSE.
DO YOU REALLY EXPECT ME TO LET SUCH A JUICY TIDBIT SLIP OUT OF MY GRASP?
GRRR!
THOSE DOORS WILL NOT OPEN AGAIN.
AND THE OTHER FAIRY RACES CANNOT ATTACK US HERE IN LEPRECHAUN TERRITORY.
WHAT DO YOU THINK YOU CAN DO, SURROUNDED BY ALL THESE SOLDIERS?
Even still...!
UMF!
OH, AND...
...WE HAVE THE GUILD'S GROUNDS DESIGNATED AS A PLACE WHERE INSTANT LOGGING OUT IS PROHIBITED.
ANY PLAYER WHO CHOOSES TO LOG OUT OF THE GAME, EVEN FELLOW LEPRECHAUNS, WILL LEAVE THEIR AVATAR BEHIND FOR SEVERAL MINUTES.

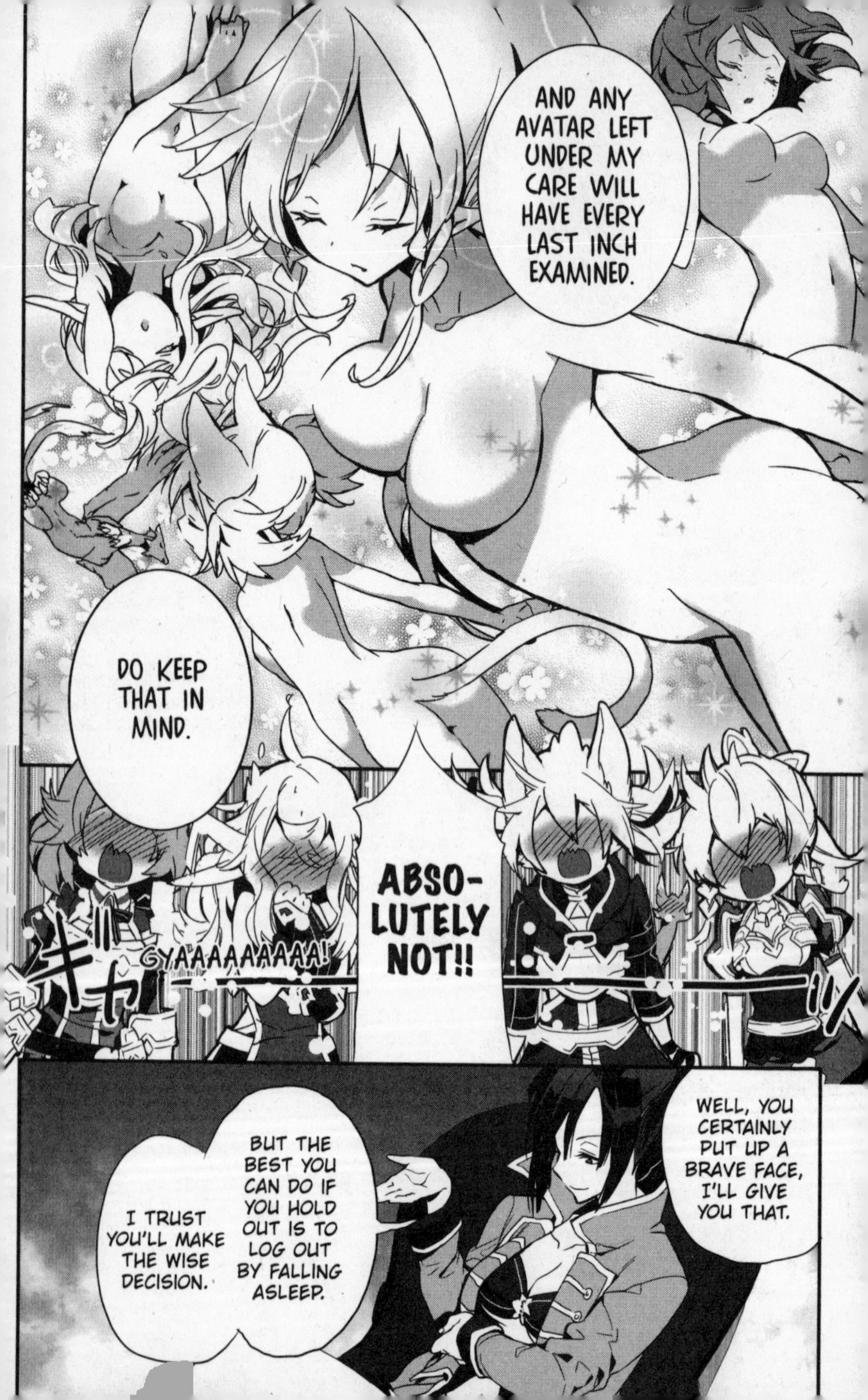
AND ANY AVATAR LEFT UNDER MY CARE WILL HAVE EVERY LAST INCH EXAMINED.
DO KEEP THAT IN MIND.
ABSO-LUTELY NOT!!
GYAAAAAAAAA!
キャ
WELL, YOU CERTAINLY PUT UP A BRAVE FACE, I'LL GIVE YOU THAT.
BUT THE BEST YOU CAN DO IF YOU HOLD OUT IS TO LOG OUT BY FALLING ASLEEP.
I TRUST YOU'LL MAKE THE WISE DECISION.

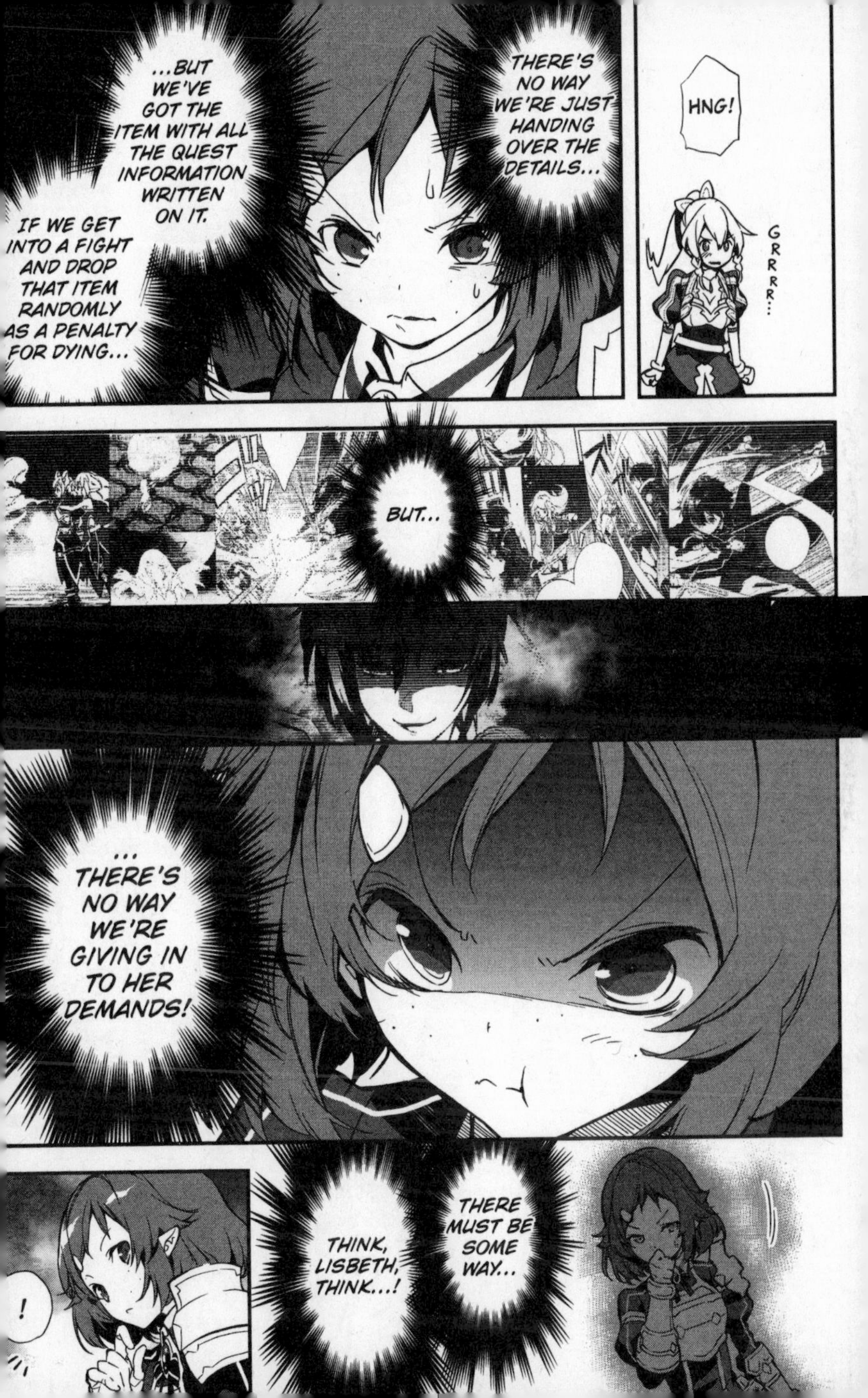
HNG!
GRRRR...
THERE'S NO WAY WE'RE JUST HANDING OVER THE DETAILS...
...BUT WE'VE GOT THE ITEM WITH ALL THE QUEST INFORMATION WRITTEN ON IT.
IF WE GET INTO A FIGHT AND DROP THAT ITEM RANDOMLY AS A PENALTY FOR DYING...
BUT...
...THERE'S NO WAY WE'RE GIVING IN TO HER DEMANDS!
THERE MUST BE SOME WAY...
THINK, LISBETH, THINK...!
!

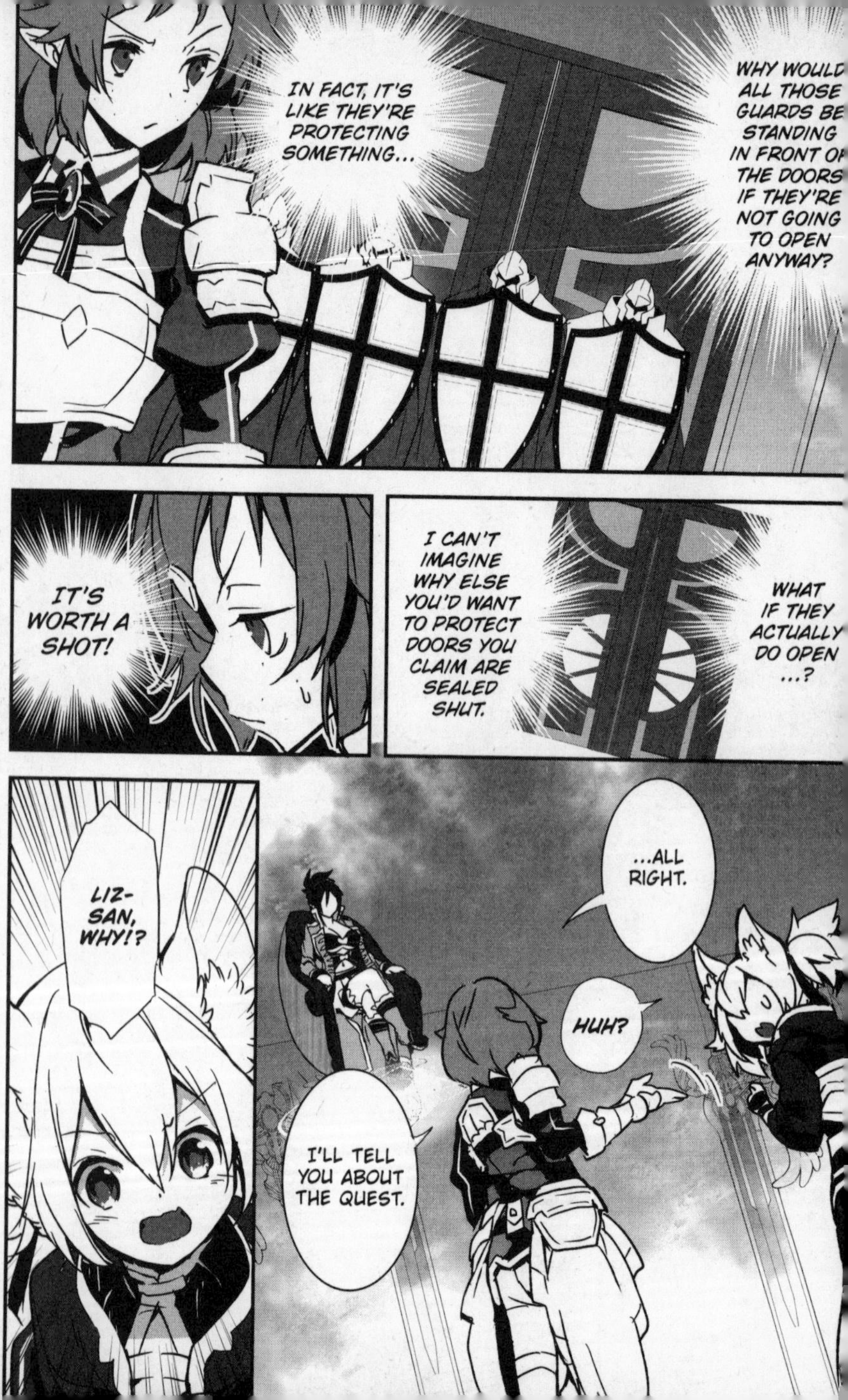
WHY WOULD ALL THOSE GUARDS BE STANDING IN FRONT OF THE DOORS IF THEY'RE NOT GOING TO OPEN ANYWAY?
IN FACT, IT'S LIKE THEY'RE PROTECTING SOMETHING...
WHAT IF THEY ACTUALLY DO OPEN ...?
I CAN'T IMAGINE WHY ELSE YOU'D WANT TO PROTECT DOORS YOU CLAIM ARE SEALED SHUT.
IT'S WORTH A SHOT!
...ALL RIGHT.
HUH?
I'LL TELL YOU ABOUT THE QUEST.
LIZ-SAN, WHY!?

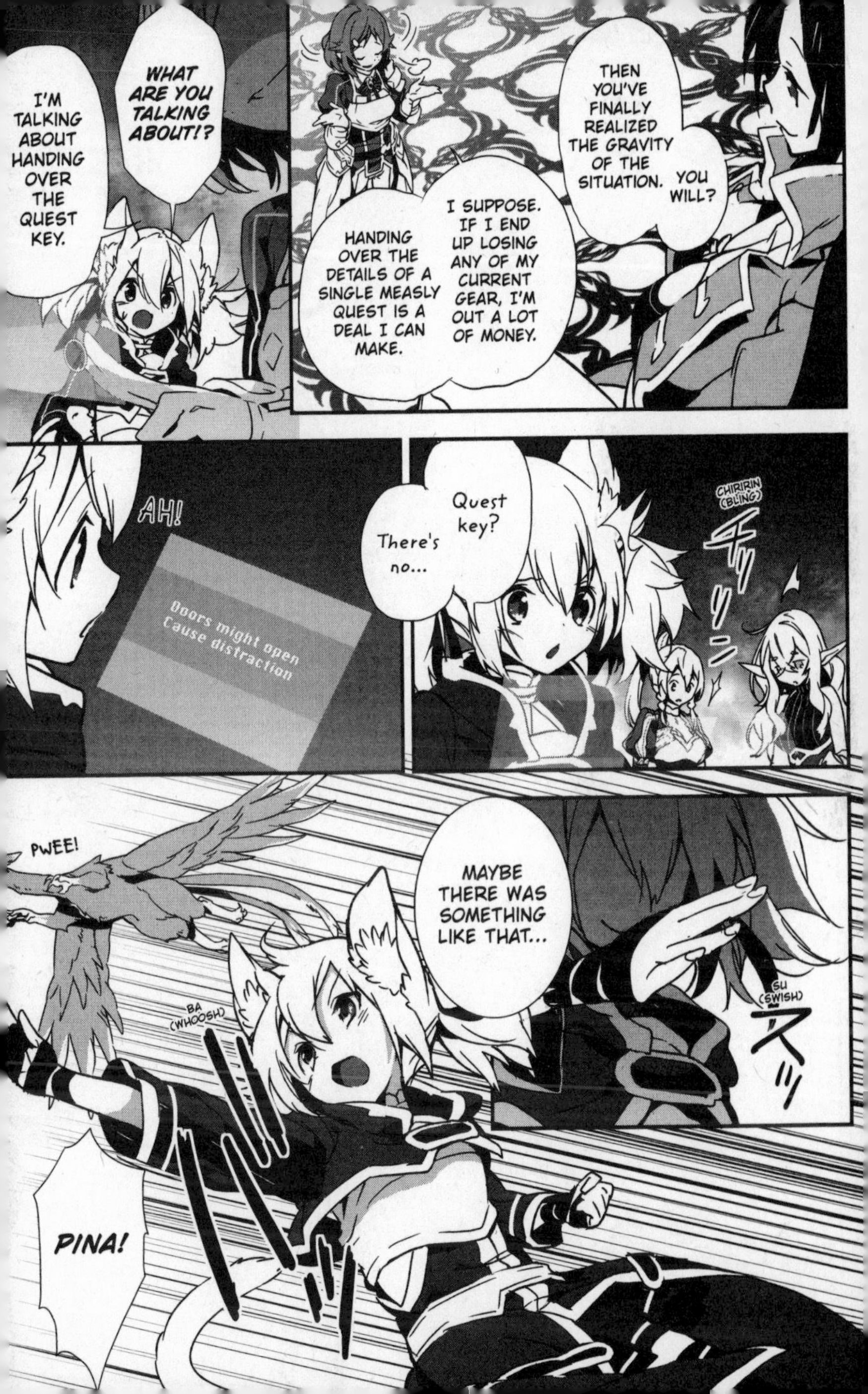
THEN YOU'VE FINALLY REALIZED THE GRAVITY OF THE SITUATION.
YOU WILL?
I SUPPOSE. IF I END UP LOSING ANY OF MY CURRENT GEAR, I'M OUT A LOT OF MONEY.
HANDING OVER THE DETAILS OF A SINGLE MEASLY QUEST IS A DEAL I CAN MAKE.
WHAT ARE YOU TALKING ABOUT!?
I'M TALKING ABOUT HANDING OVER THE QUEST KEY.
CHIRIRIN (BLING)
Quest key?
There's no...
AH!
Doors might open
Cause distraction
MAYBE THERE WAS SOMETHING LIKE THAT...
SU (SWISH)
BA (WHOOSH)
PWEE!
PINA!

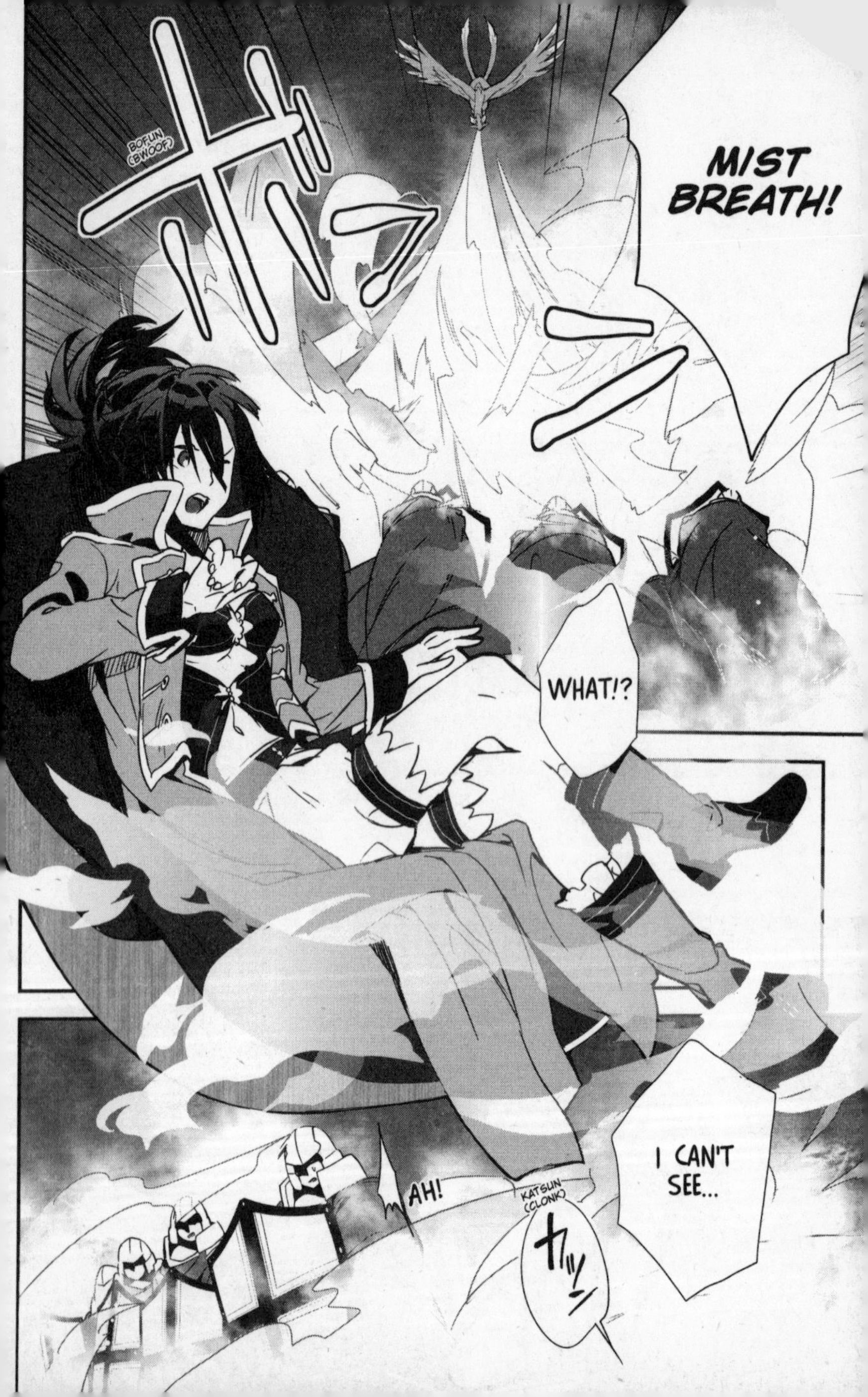
MIST BREATH!
BOFUN (BWOOF)
WHAT!?
I CAN'T SEE...
KATSUN (CLONK)
AH!

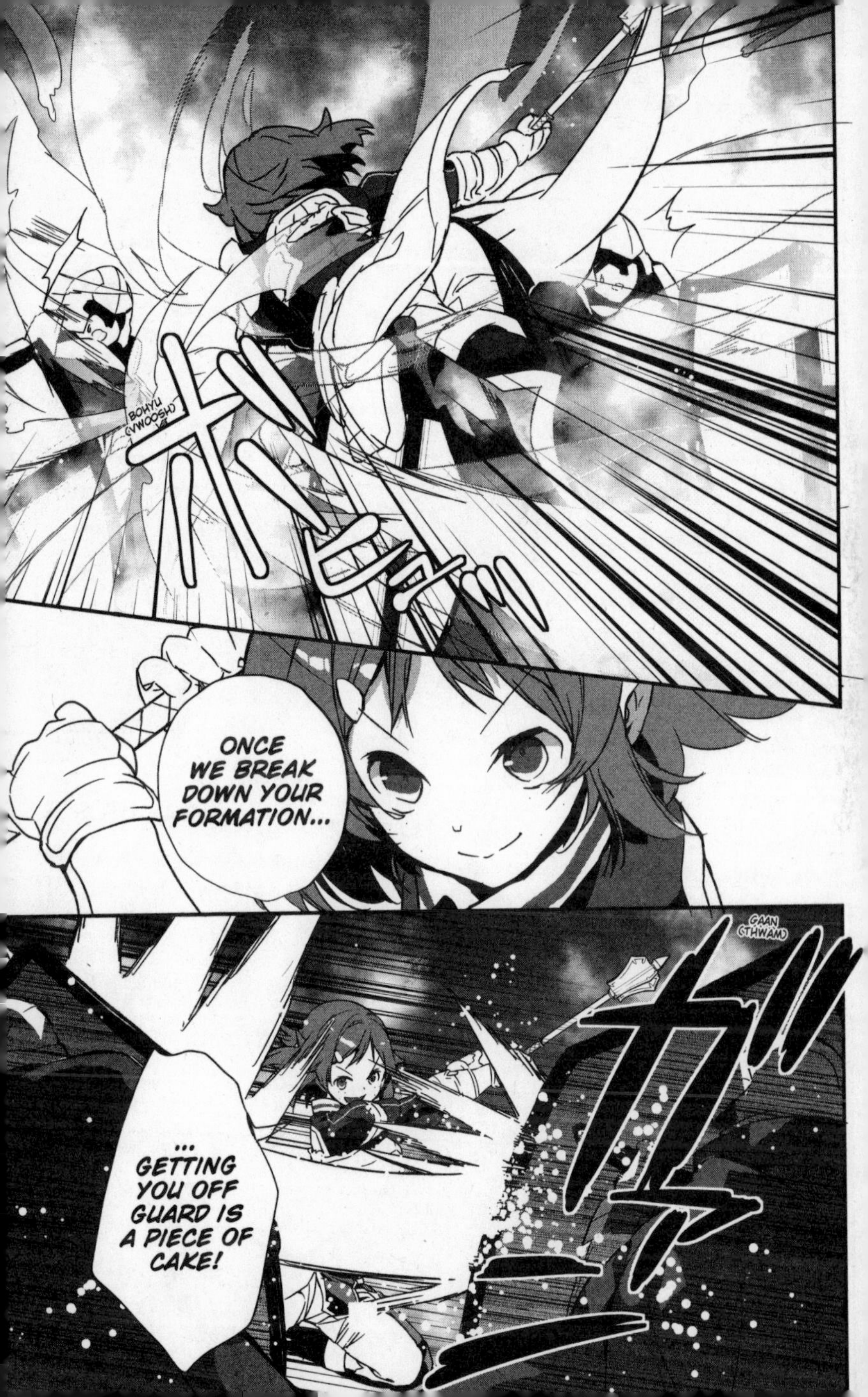
BOHYU
(VWOOSH)
ONCE WE BREAK DOWN YOUR FORMATION...
GAAN
(THWAM)
...GETTING YOU OFF GUARD IS A PIECE OF CAKE!

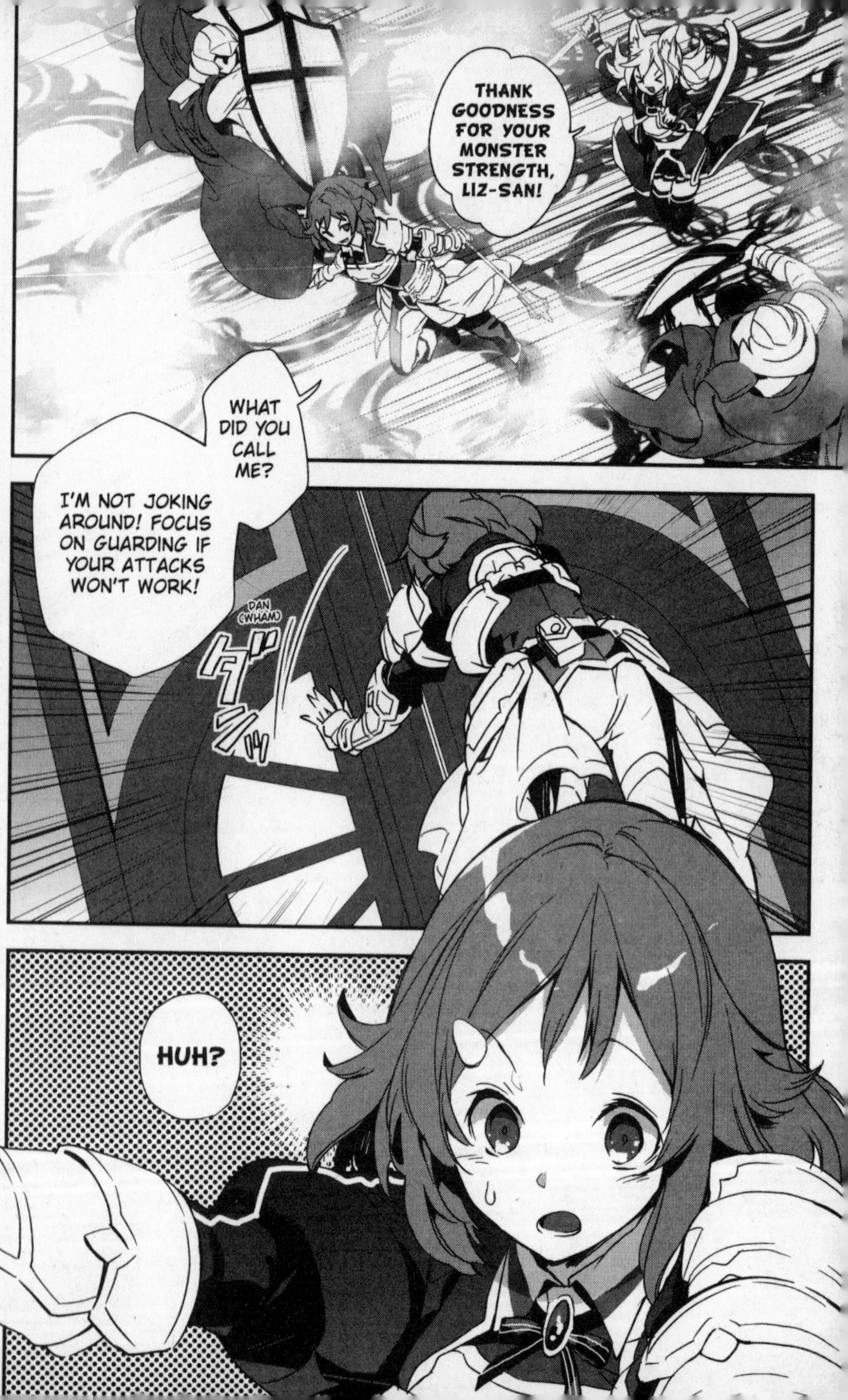
THANK GOODNESS FOR YOUR MONSTER STRENGTH, LIZ-SAN!
WHAT DID YOU CALL ME?
I'M NOT JOKING AROUND! FOCUS ON GUARDING IF YOUR ATTACKS WON'T WORK!
DAN (WHAM)
HUH?

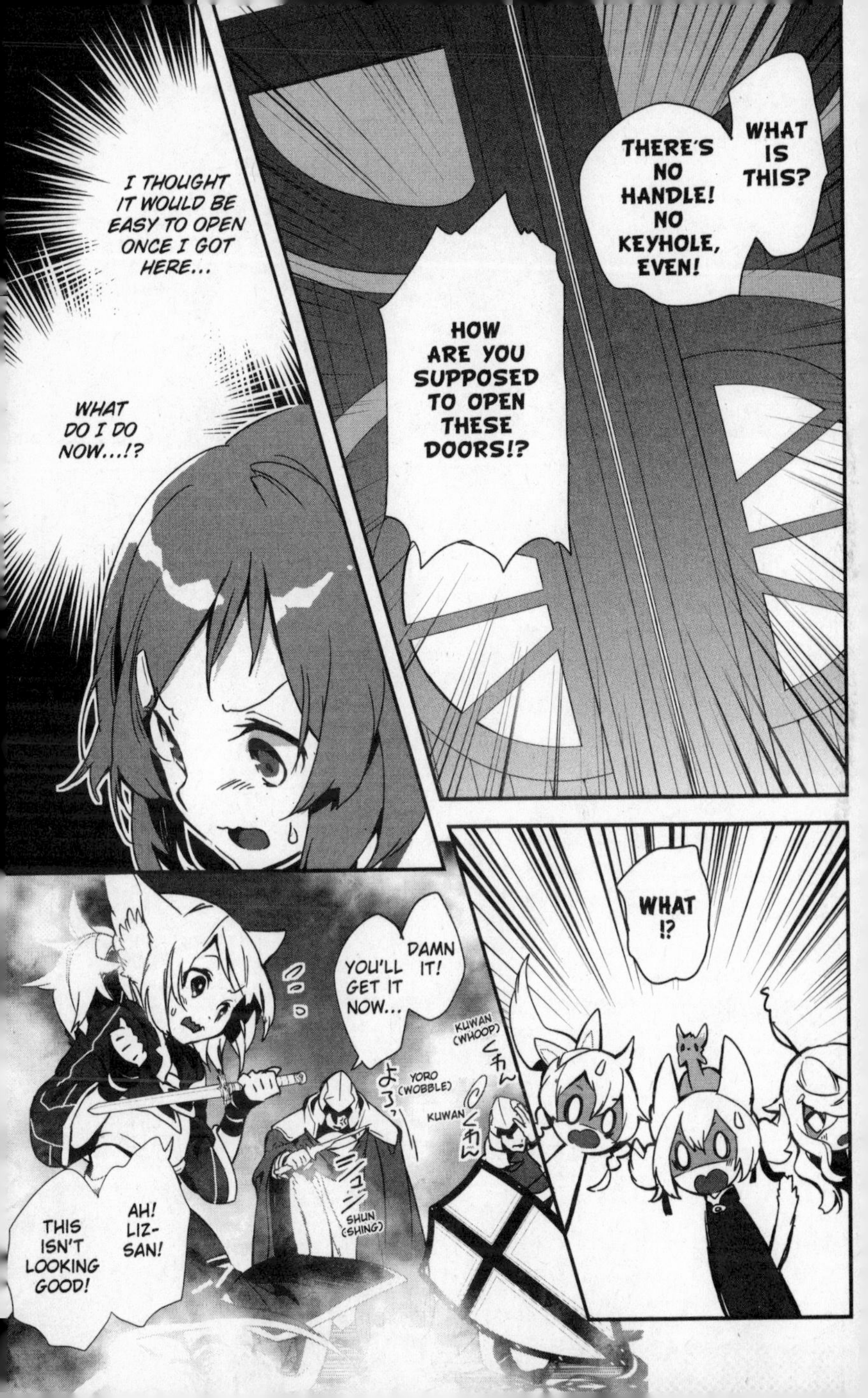
WHAT IS THIS?
THERE'S NO HANDLE! NO KEYHOLE, EVEN!
HOW ARE YOU SUPPOSED TO OPEN THESE DOORS!?
I THOUGHT IT WOULD BE EASY TO OPEN ONCE I GOT HERE...
WHAT DO I DO NOW...!?
WHAT!?
DAMN IT!
YOU'LL GET IT NOW...
KUWAN (WHOOP)
YORO (WOBBLE)
KUWAN
SHUN (SHING)
AH! LIZ-SAN!
THIS ISN'T LOOKING GOOD!

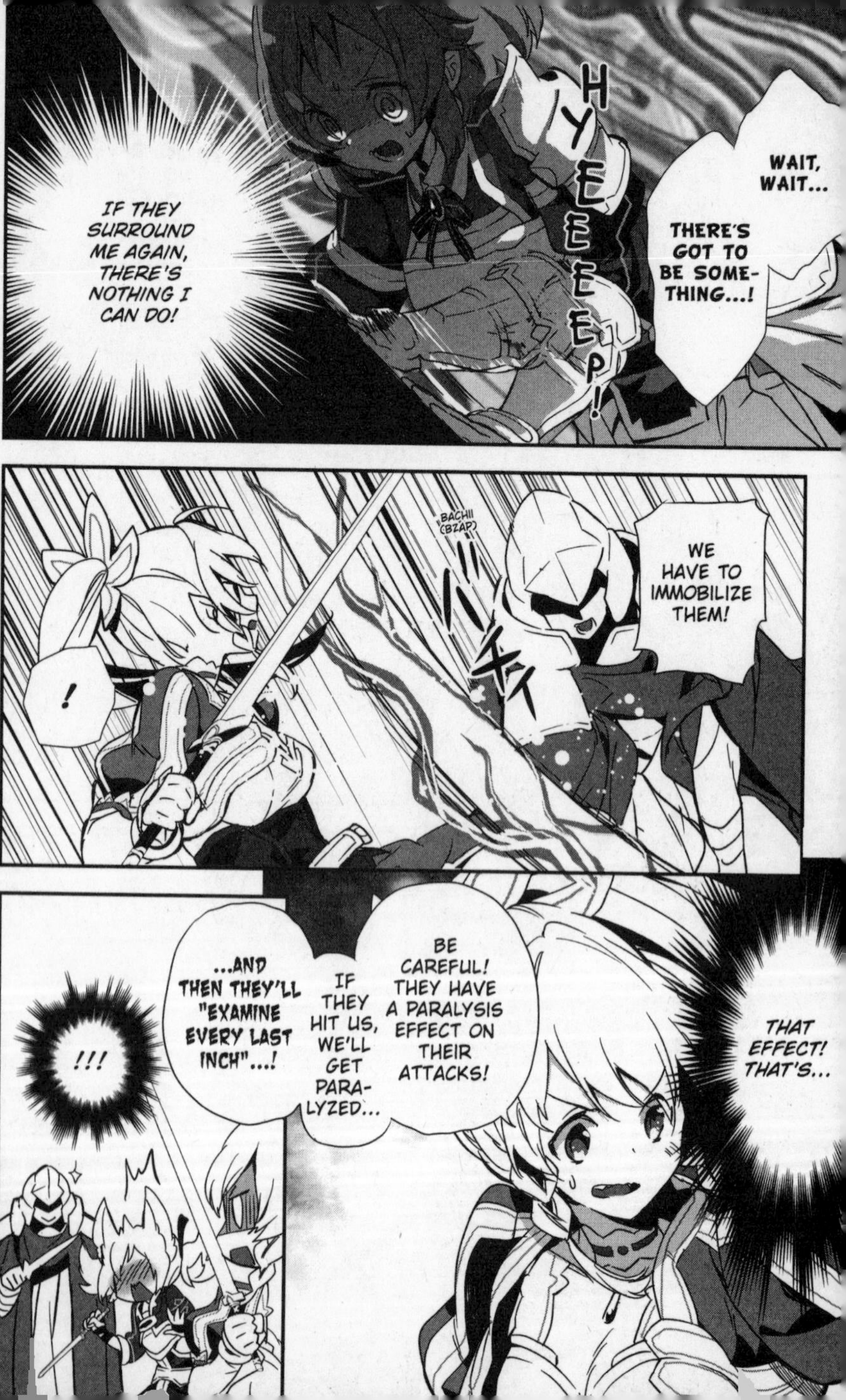
WAIT, WAIT...
THERE'S GOT TO BE SOME-THING...!
HYEEEEP!
IF THEY SURROUND ME AGAIN, THERE'S NOTHING I CAN DO!
WE HAVE TO IMMOBILIZE THEM!
BACHII (BZAP)
!
THAT EFFECT! THAT'S...
BE CAREFUL! THEY HAVE A PARALYSIS EFFECT ON THEIR ATTACKS!
IF THEY HIT US, WE'LL GET PARA-LYZED...
...AND THEN THEY'LL "EXAMINE EVERY LAST INCH"...!
!!!

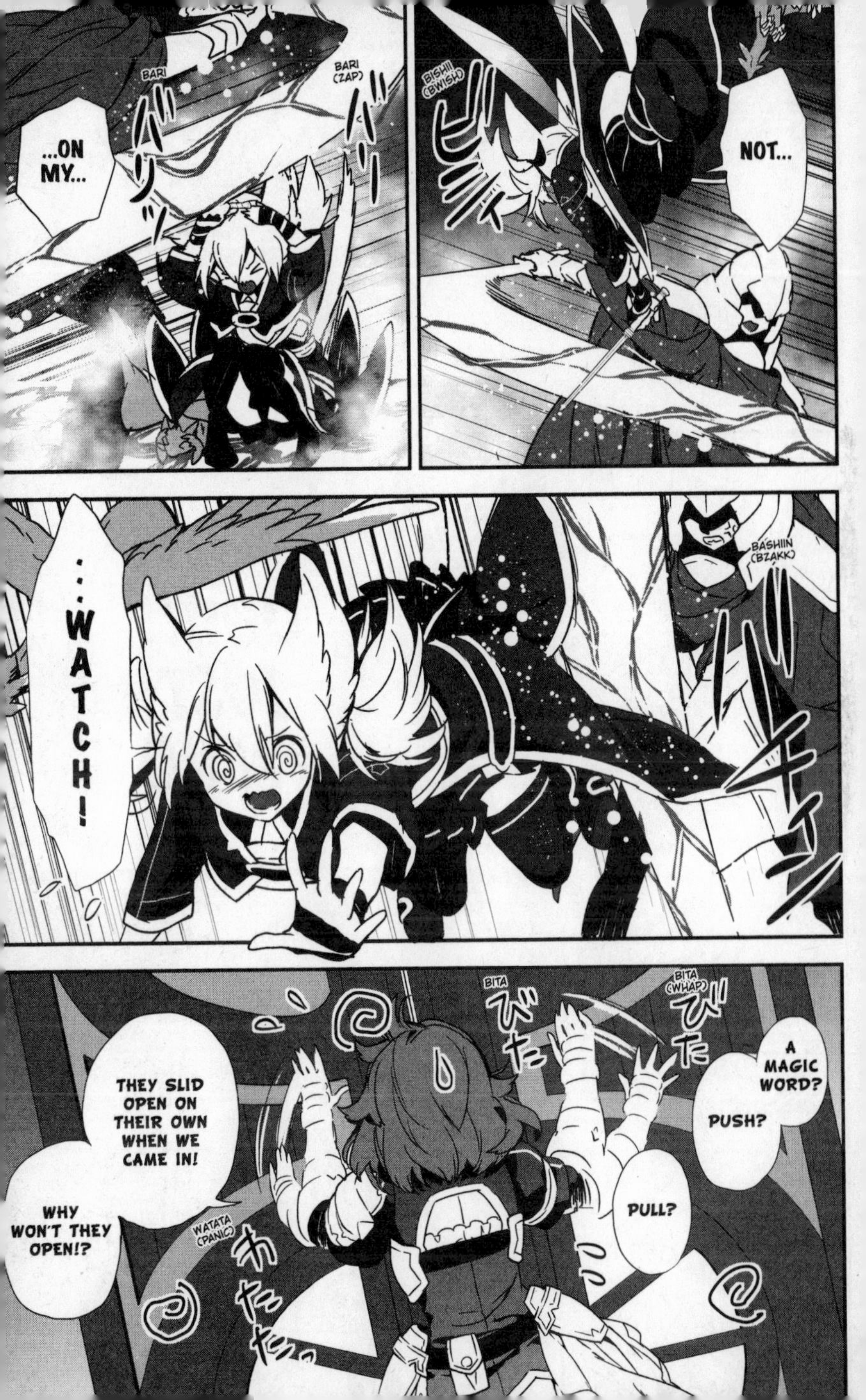

NOT...
BISHI!
(BWISH)
BARI
(ZAP)
BARI
...ON MY...
BASHIIN
(BZAKK)
...WATCH!
BITA
(WHAP)
BITA
A MAGIC WORD?
PUSH?
PULL?
THEY SLID OPEN ON THEIR OWN WHEN WE CAME IN!
WHY WON'T THEY OPEN!?
WATATA
(PANIC)

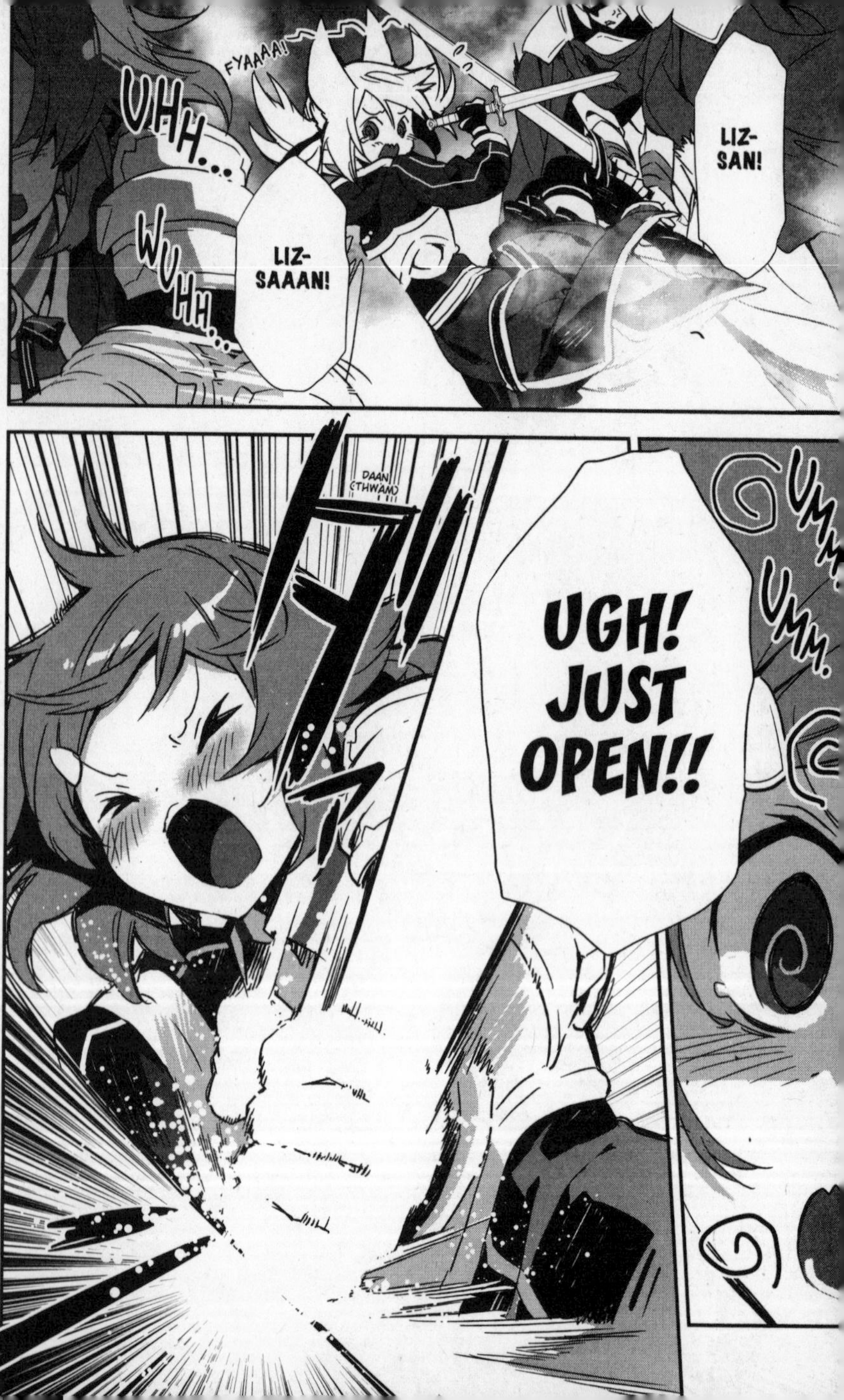
LIZ-SAN!
FYAAAA!
UHH...
LIZ-SAAAN!
WUHH...
UMM... UMM.
UGH! JUST OPEN!!
DAAN (THWAM)

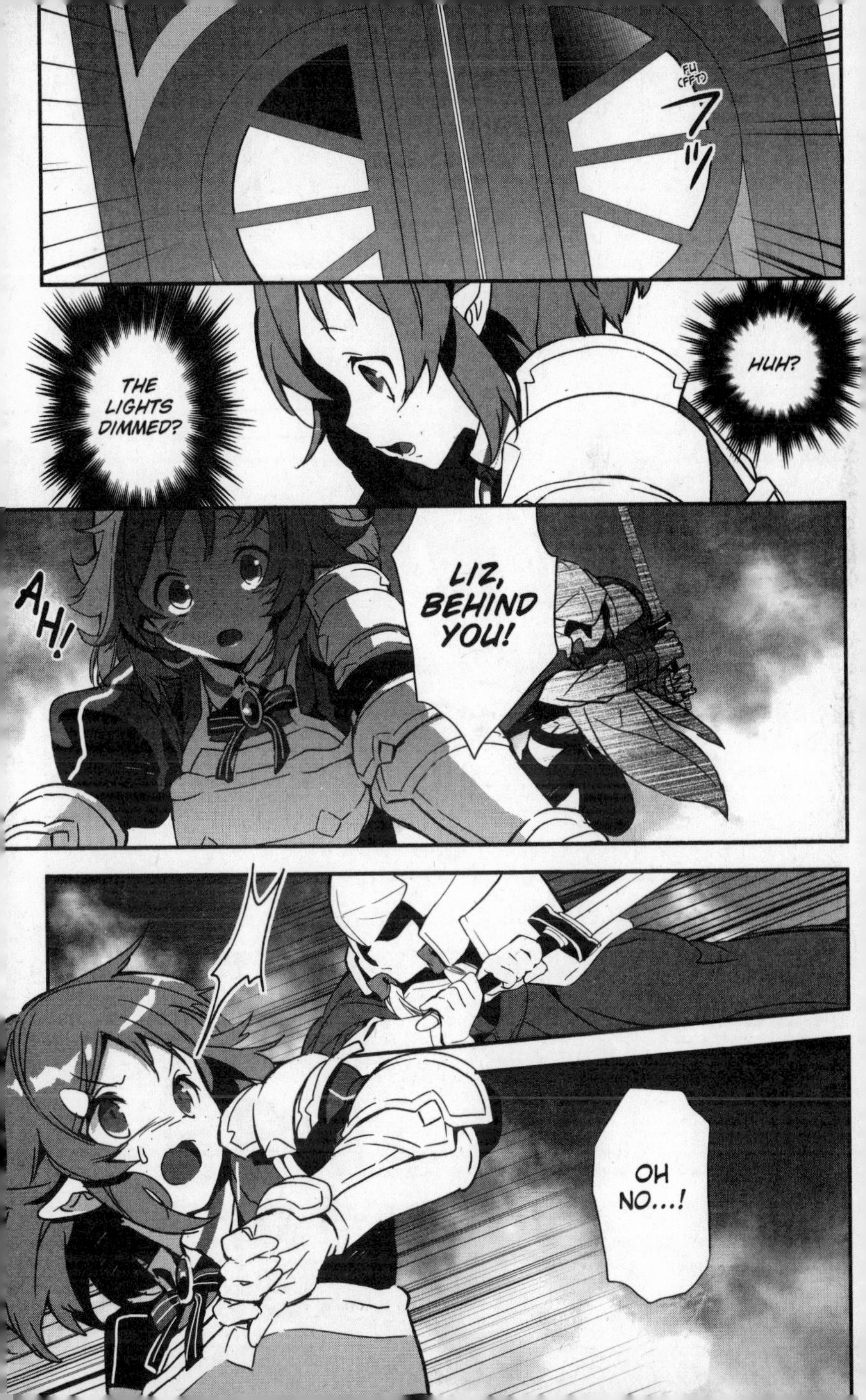
FU (PFFT)
HUH?
THE LIGHTS DIMMED?
LIZ, BEHIND YOU!
AH!
OH NO...!

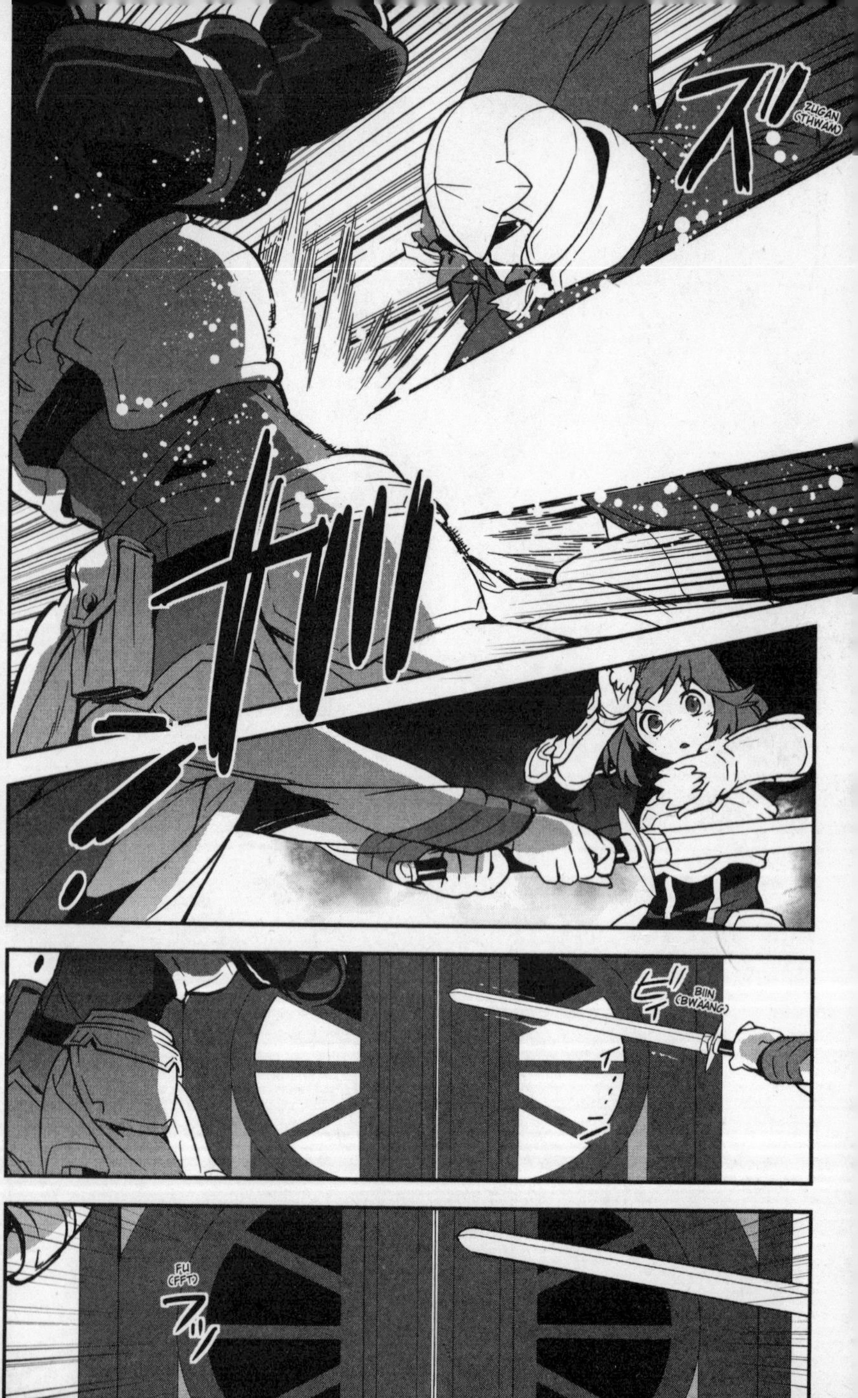
ZUGAN (THWAM)
BIIN (BWAANG)
FU (FFT)

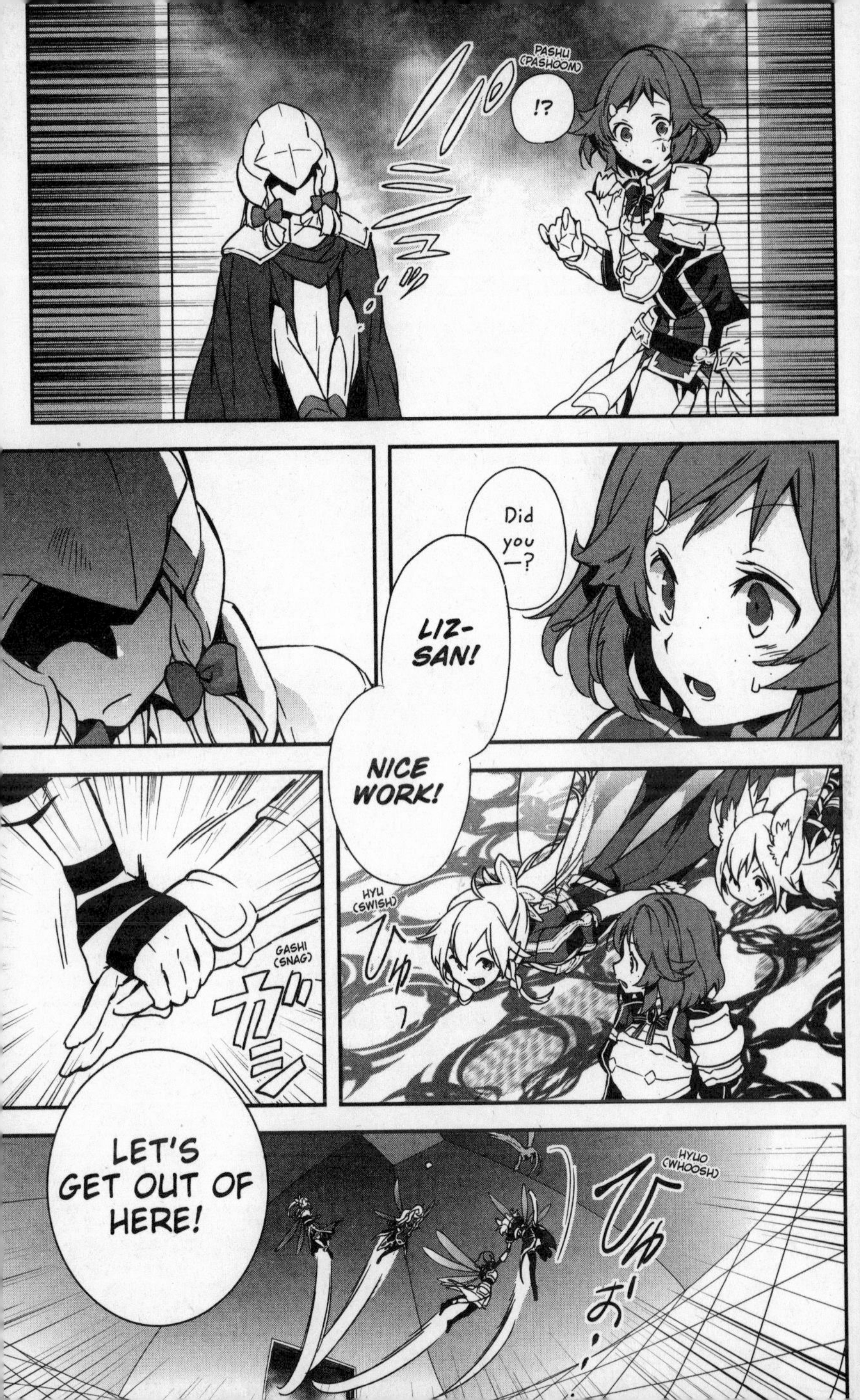
PASHU (PASHOOM)
!?
Did you—?
LIZ-SAN!
NICE WORK!
HYU (SWISH)
GASHI (SNAG)
HYUO (WHOOSH)
LET'S GET OUT OF HERE!

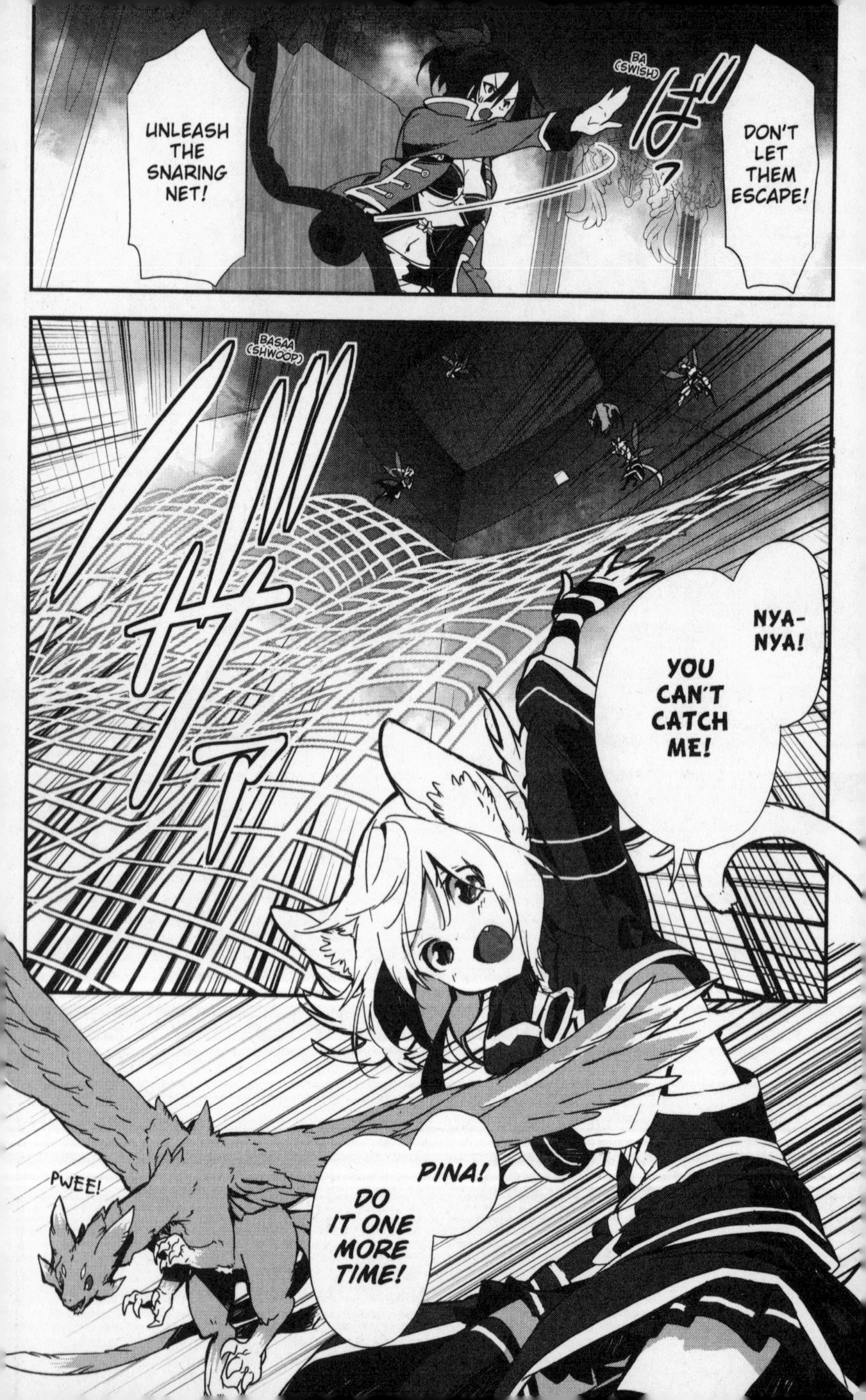
DON'T LET THEM ESCAPE!
BA (SWISH)
UNLEASH THE SNARING NET!
BASAA (SHWOOP)
NYA-NYA! YOU CAN'T CATCH ME!
PINA! DO IT ONE MORE TIME!
PWEE!

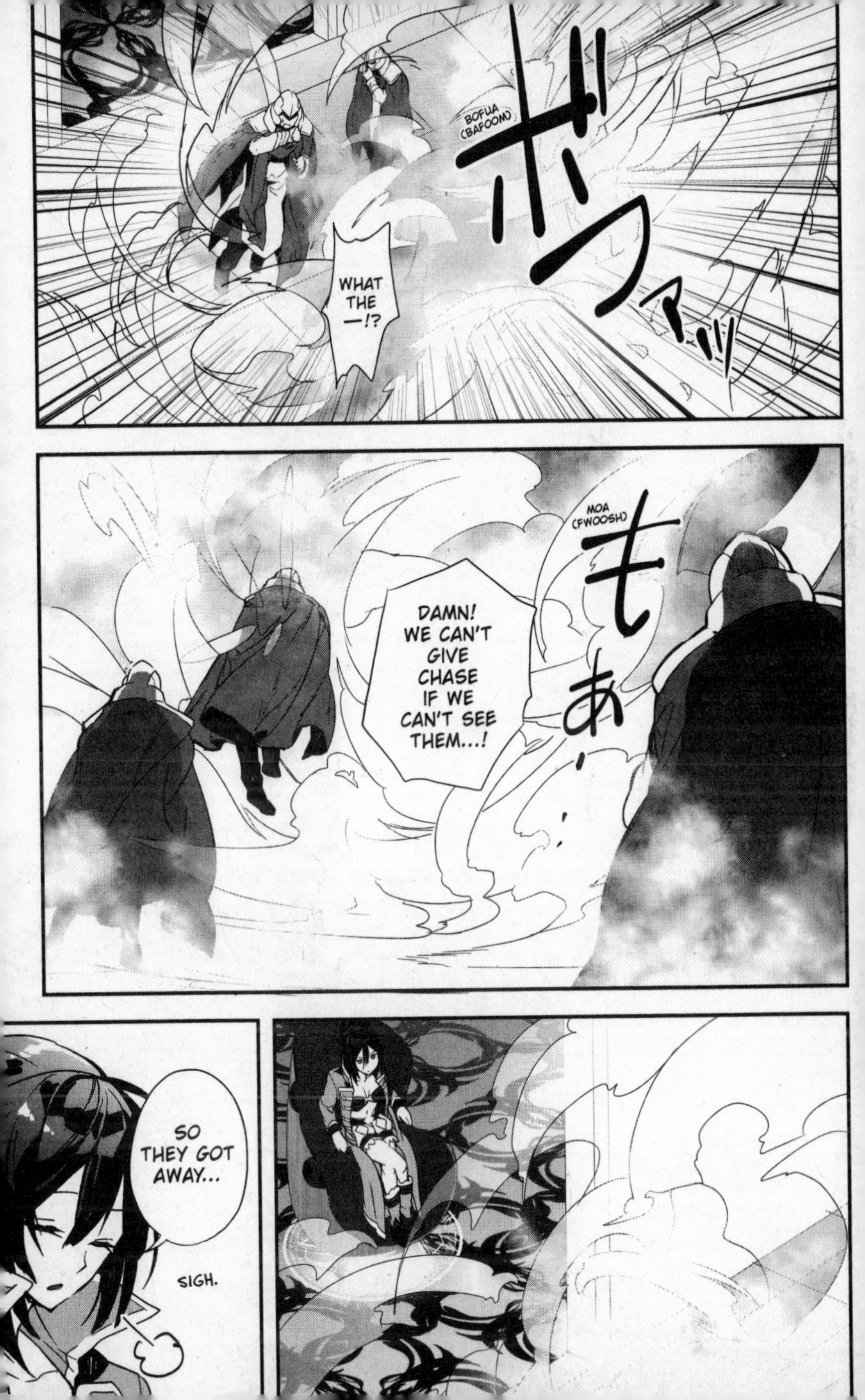
BOFUA (BAFOOM)
ボフアッ
WHAT THE—!?
MOA (FWOOSH)
もあ…!
DAMN! WE CAN'T GIVE CHASE IF WE CAN'T SEE THEM...!
SO THEY GOT AWAY...
SIGH.

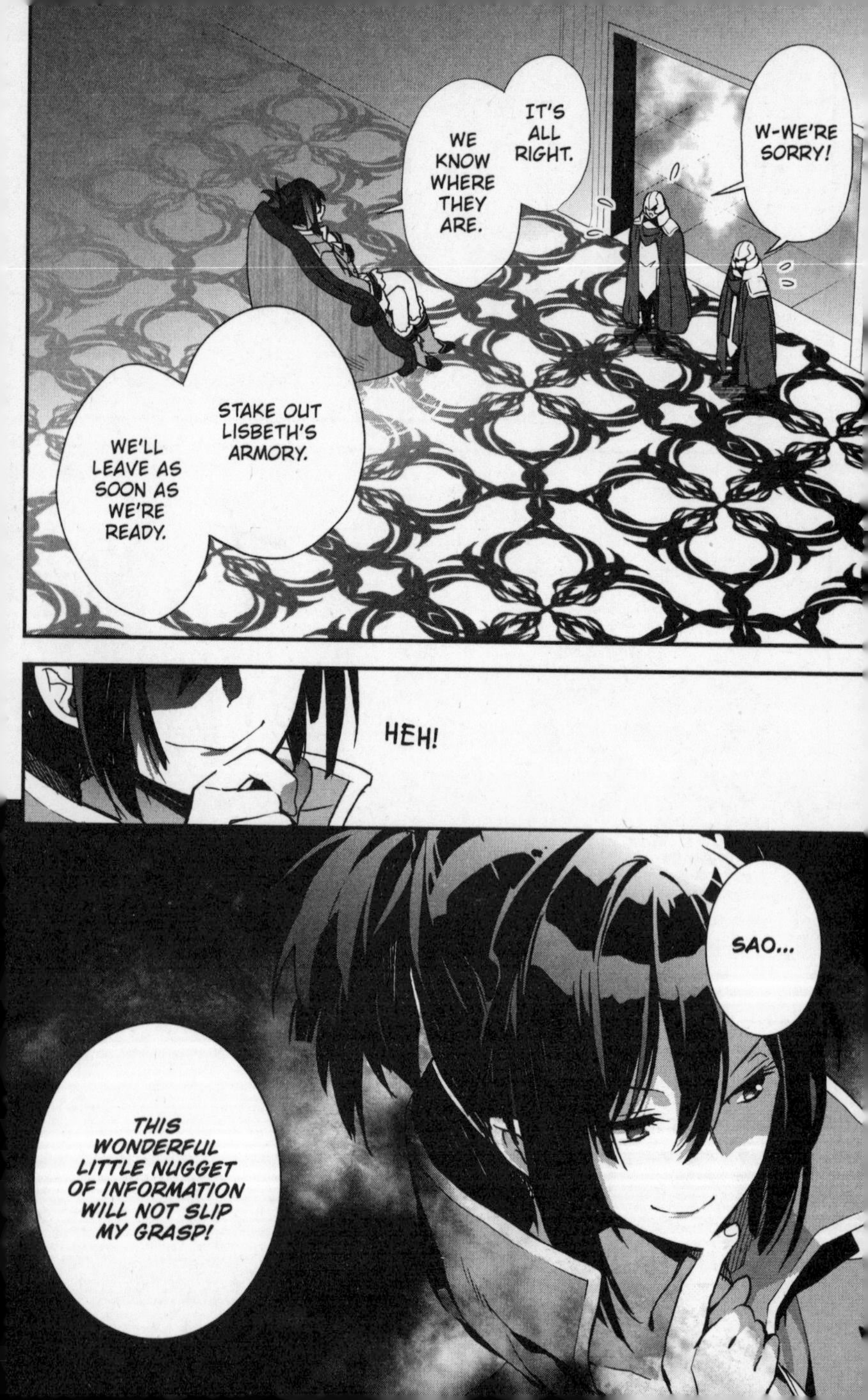
W-WE'RE SORRY!
IT'S ALL RIGHT.
WE KNOW WHERE THEY ARE.
STAKE OUT LISBETH'S ARMORY.
WE'LL LEAVE AS SOON AS WE'RE READY.
HEH!
SAO...
THIS WONDERFUL LITTLE NUGGET OF INFORMATION WILL NOT SLIP MY GRASP!

SWORD ART ONLINE
GIRLS' OPS

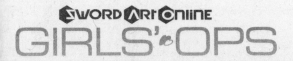

JUST
LIKE
PINA
♪

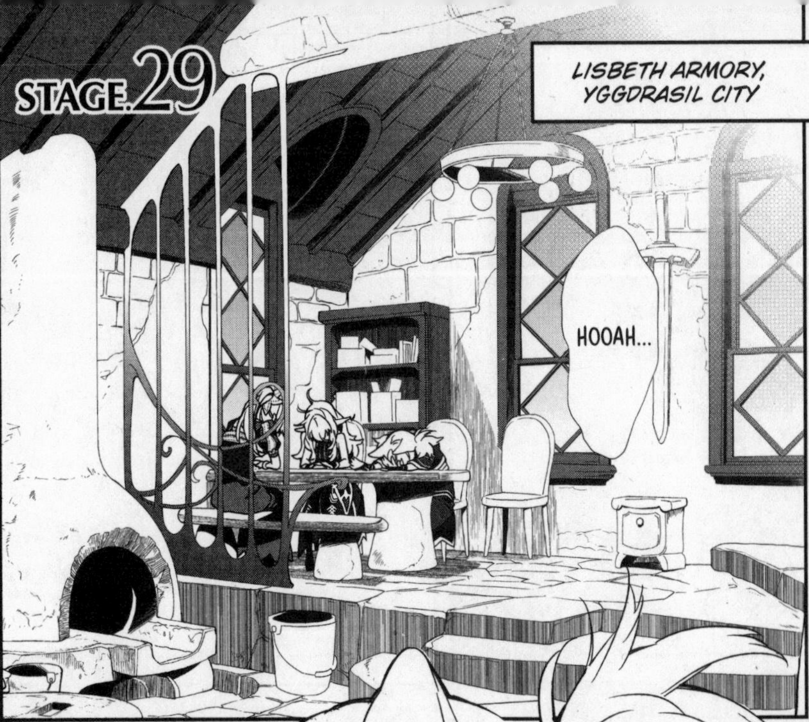
STAGE.29
LISBETH ARMORY, YGGDRASIL CITY
HOOAH...

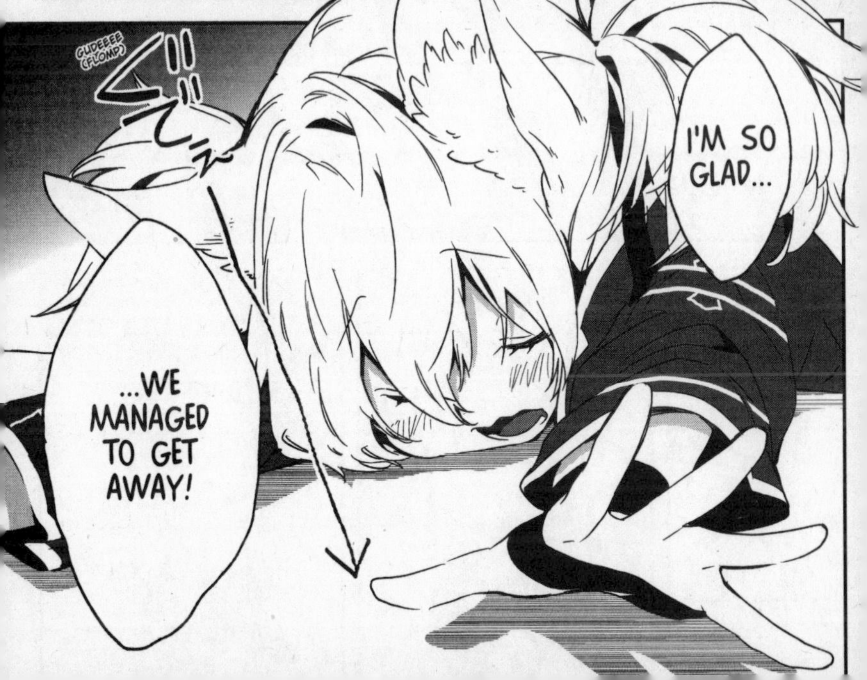
GUDEEEE (FLOMP)
I'M SO GLAD...
...WE MANAGED TO GET AWAY!

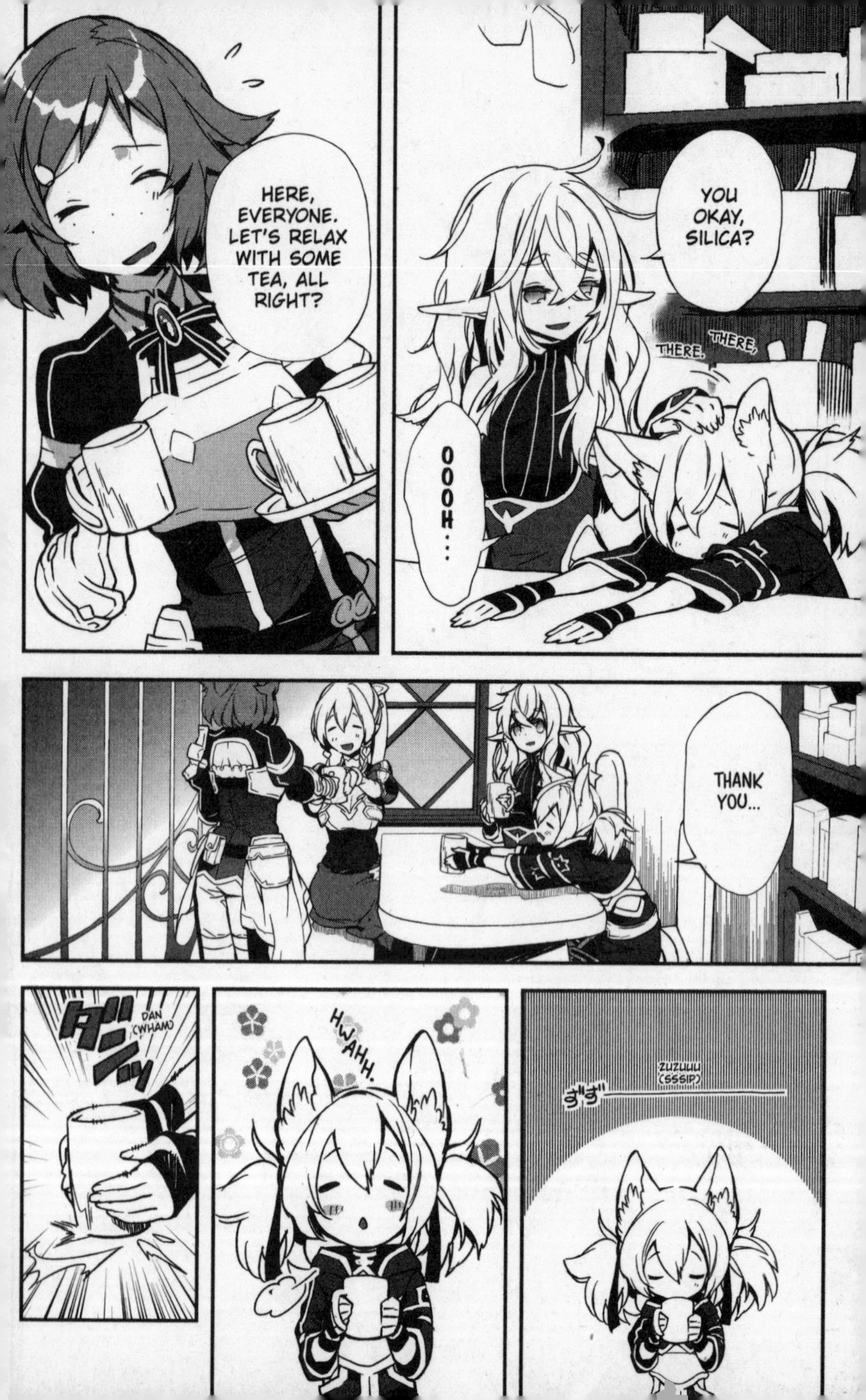
YOU OKAY, SILICA?
THERE, THERE.
OOOH...
HERE, EVERYONE. LET'S RELAX WITH SOME TEA, ALL RIGHT?
THANK YOU...
ZUZUUU (SSSIP)
HWAHH.
DAN (WHAM)

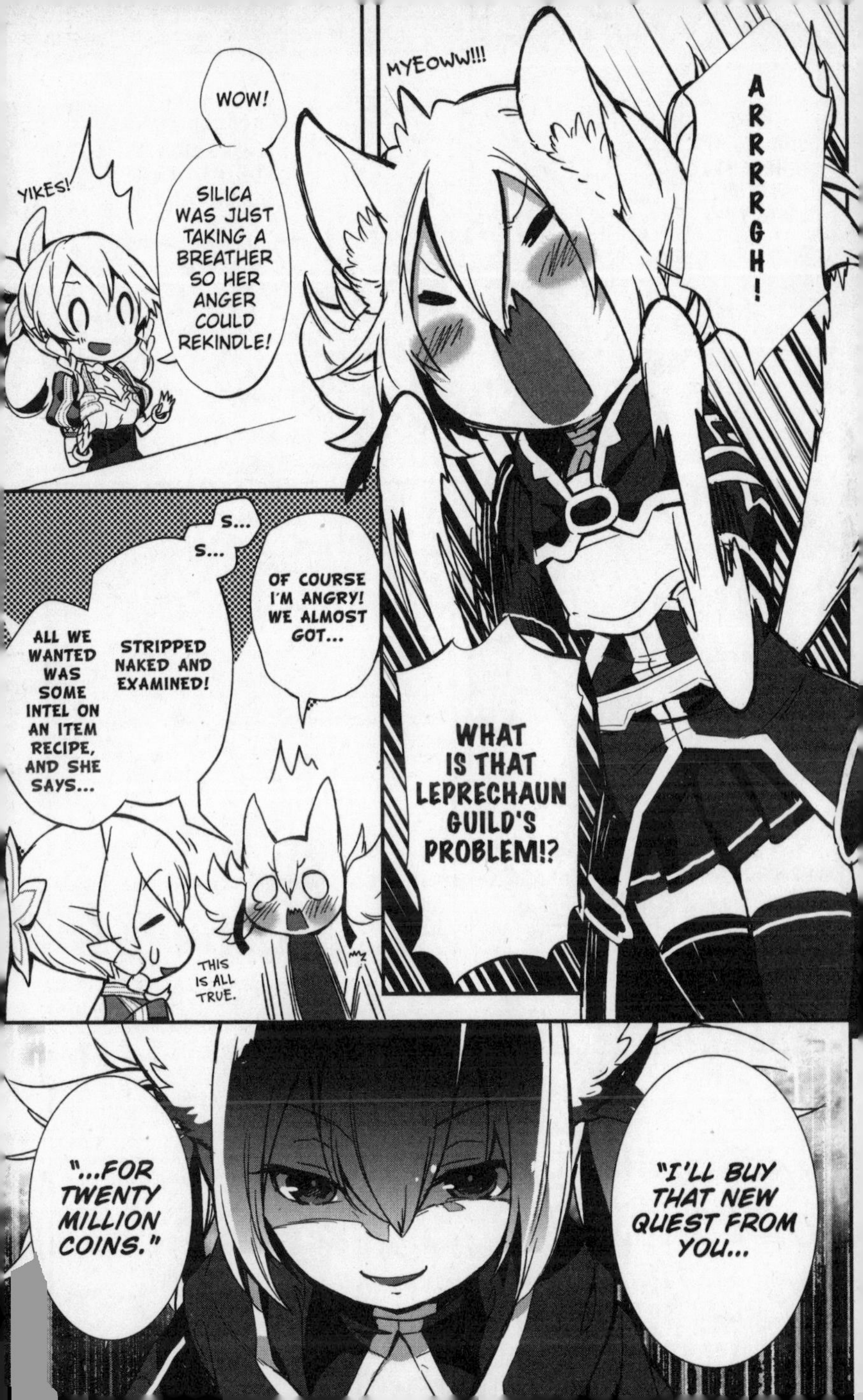
ARRRRGH!
MYEOWW!!!
WHAT IS THAT LEPRECHAUN GUILD'S PROBLEM!?
WOW!
SILICA WAS JUST TAKING A BREATHER SO HER ANGER COULD REKINDLE!
YIKES!
OF COURSE I'M ANGRY! WE ALMOST GOT...
S... S...
STRIPPED NAKED AND EXAMINED!
ALL WE WANTED WAS SOME INTEL ON AN ITEM RECIPE, AND SHE SAYS...
THIS IS ALL TRUE.
"I'LL BUY THAT NEW QUEST FROM YOU...
"...FOR TWENTY MILLION COINS."

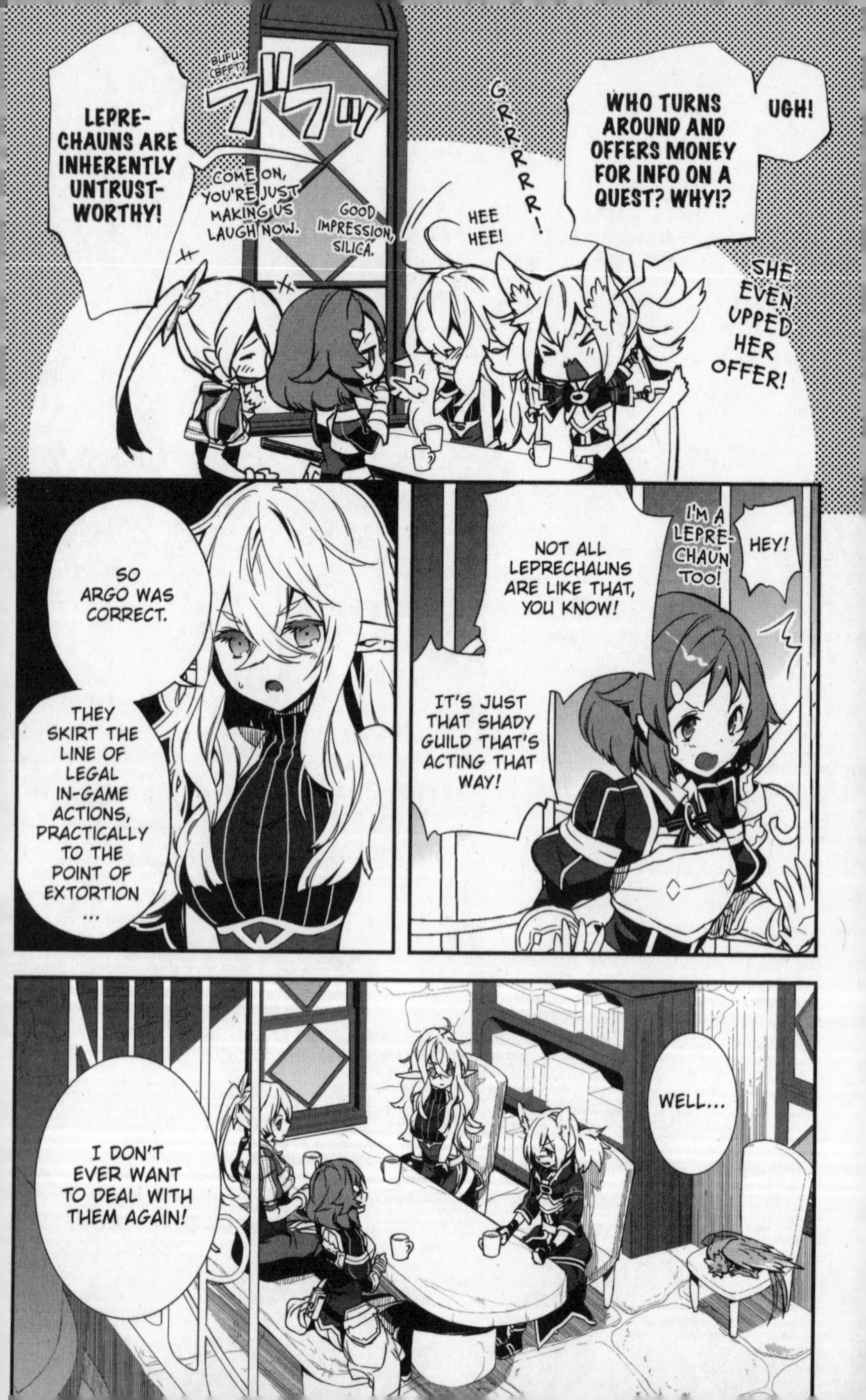
UGH!
WHO TURNS AROUND AND OFFERS MONEY FOR INFO ON A QUEST? WHY!?
GRRRRRR!
SHE EVEN UPPED HER OFFER!
HEE HEE!
GOOD IMPRESSION, SILICA.
COME ON, YOU'RE JUST MAKING US LAUGH NOW.
BUFU (BFFT)
ブフッ
LEPRECHAUNS ARE INHERENTLY UNTRUSTWORTHY!
HEY!
I'M A LEPRECHAUN TOO!
NOT ALL LEPRECHAUNS ARE LIKE THAT, YOU KNOW!
IT'S JUST THAT SHADY GUILD THAT'S ACTING THAT WAY!
SO ARGO WAS CORRECT.
THEY SKIRT THE LINE OF LEGAL IN-GAME ACTIONS, PRACTICALLY TO THE POINT OF EXTORTION...
WELL...
I DON'T EVER WANT TO DEAL WITH THEM AGAIN!

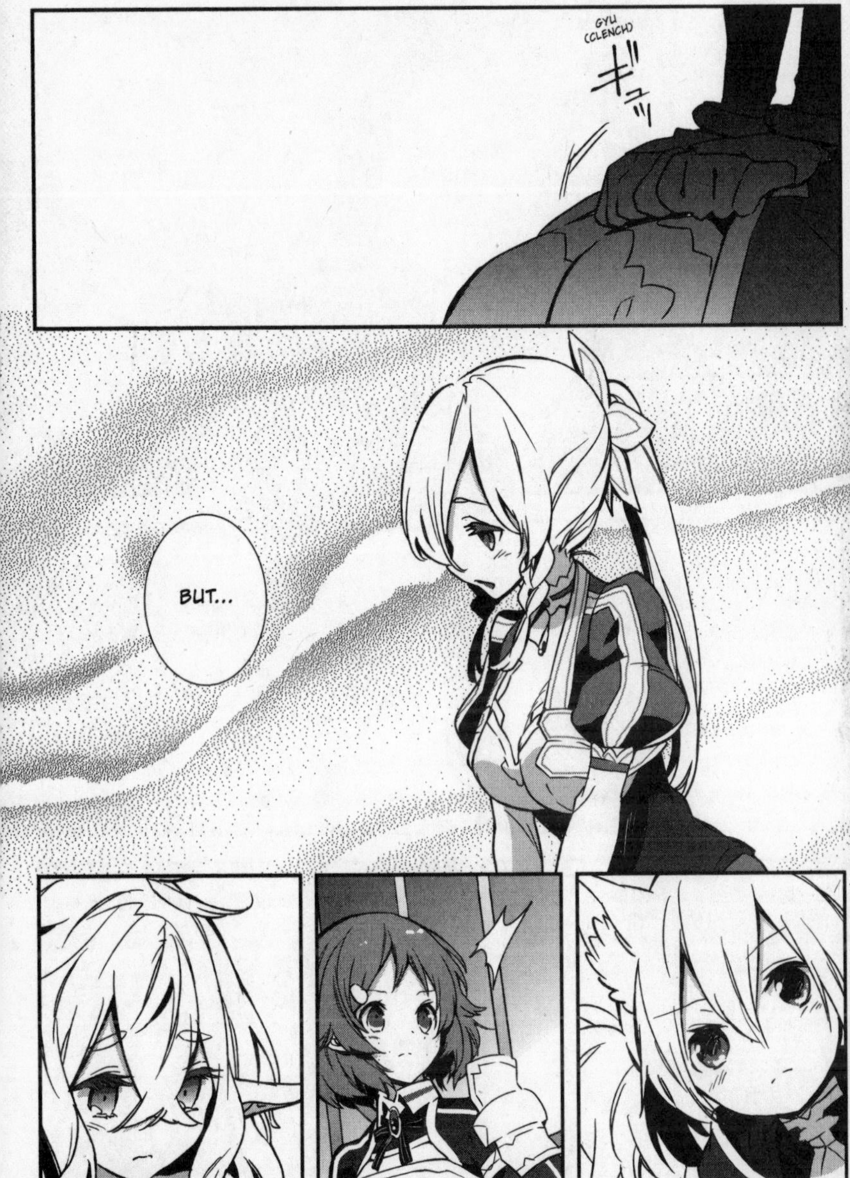
GYU (CLENCH)
ギュッ
BUT...

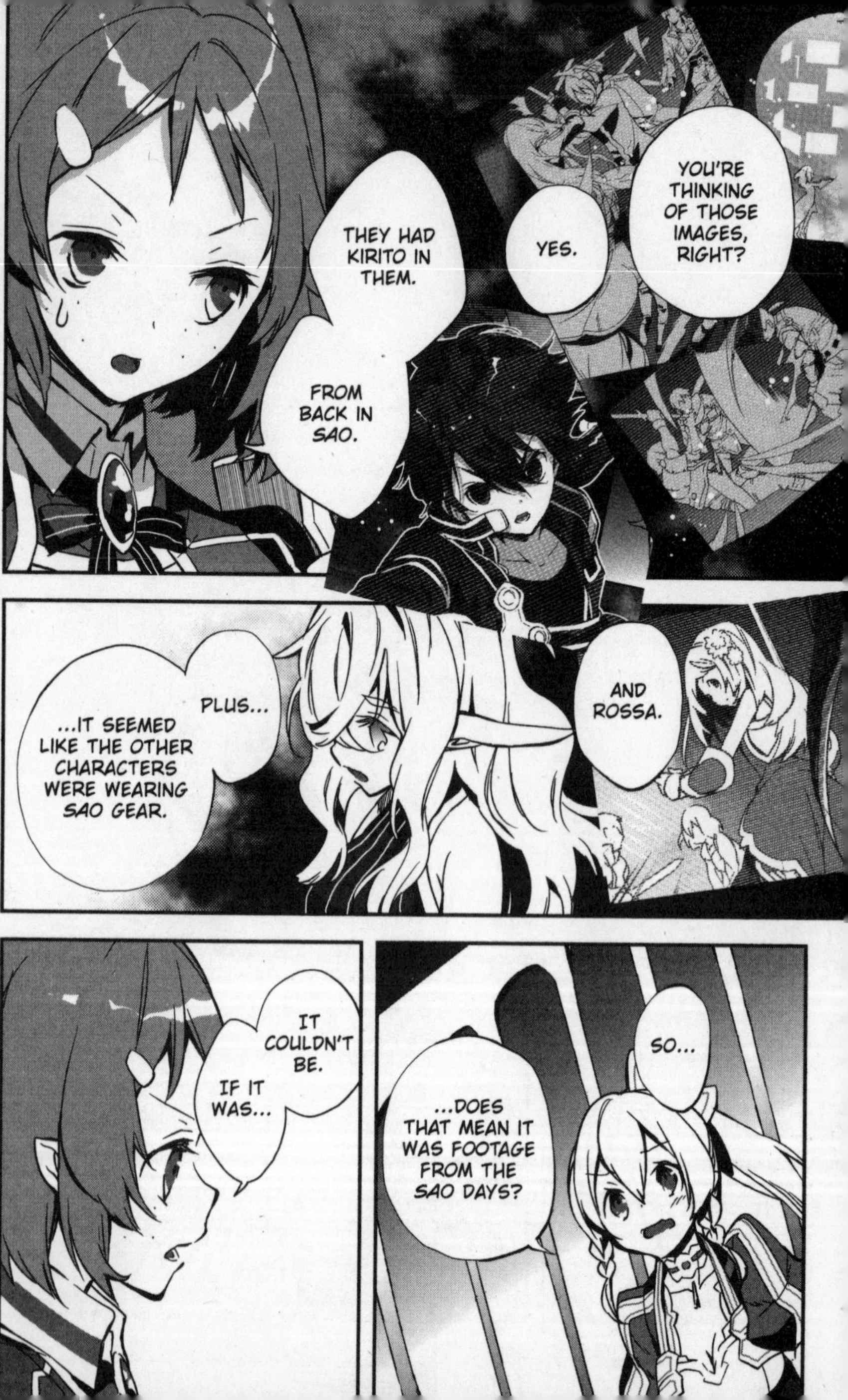
YOU'RE THINKING OF THOSE IMAGES, RIGHT?
YES.
THEY HAD KIRITO IN THEM.
FROM BACK IN SAO.
AND ROSSA.
PLUS...
...IT SEEMED LIKE THE OTHER CHARACTERS WERE WEARING SAO GEAR.
SO...
...DOES THAT MEAN IT WAS FOOTAGE FROM THE SAO DAYS?
IT COULDN'T BE.
IF IT WAS...

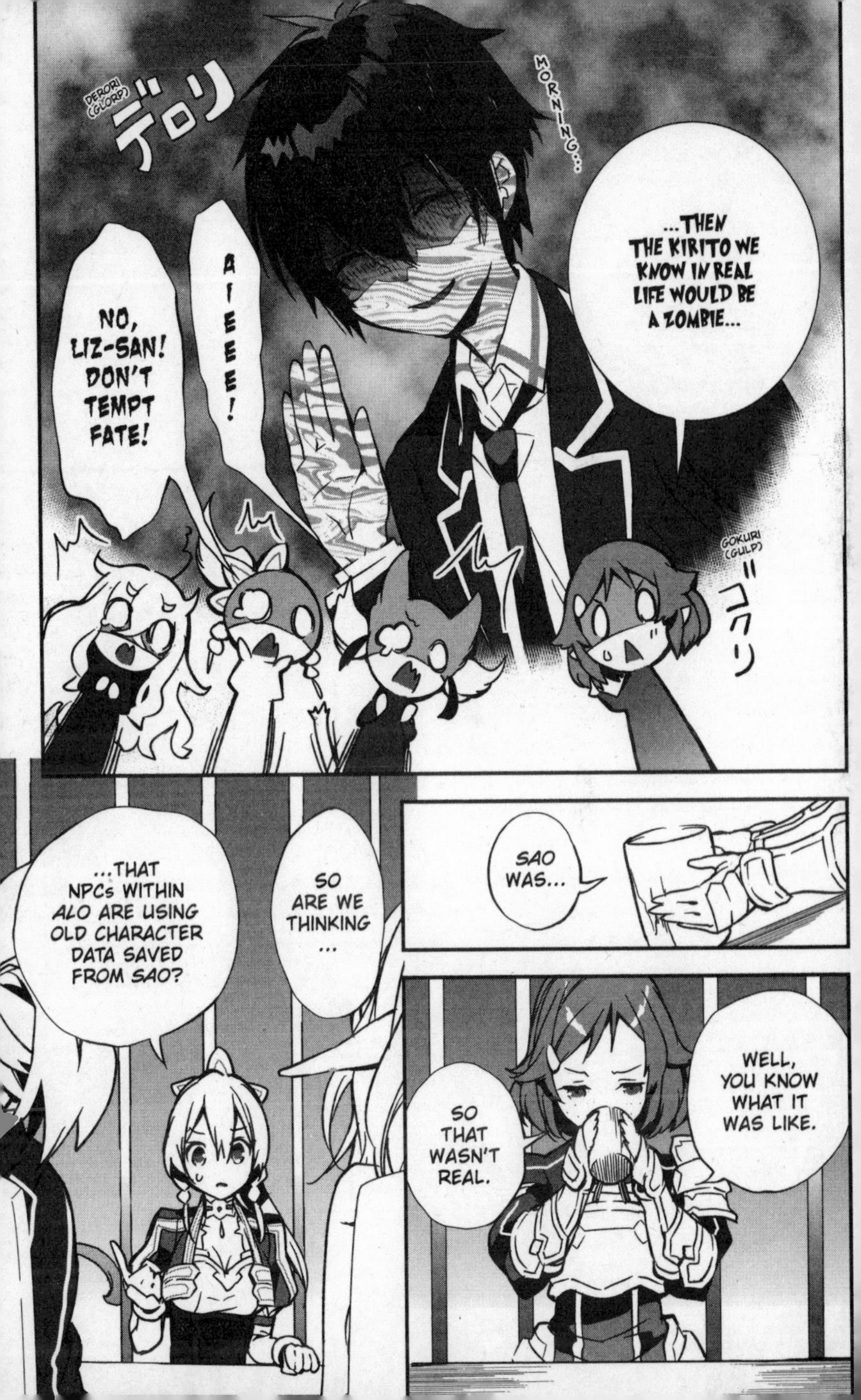
...THEN THE KIRITO WE KNOW IN REAL LIFE WOULD BE A ZOMBIE...
MORNING...
DERORI (GLORP)
デロリ
AIEEEE!
NO, LIZ-SAN! DON'T TEMPT FATE!
GOKURI (GULP)
ゴクリ
SAO WAS...
WELL, YOU KNOW WHAT IT WAS LIKE.
SO THAT WASN'T REAL.
SO ARE WE THINKING...
...THAT NPCs WITHIN ALO ARE USING OLD CHARACTER DATA SAVED FROM SAO?

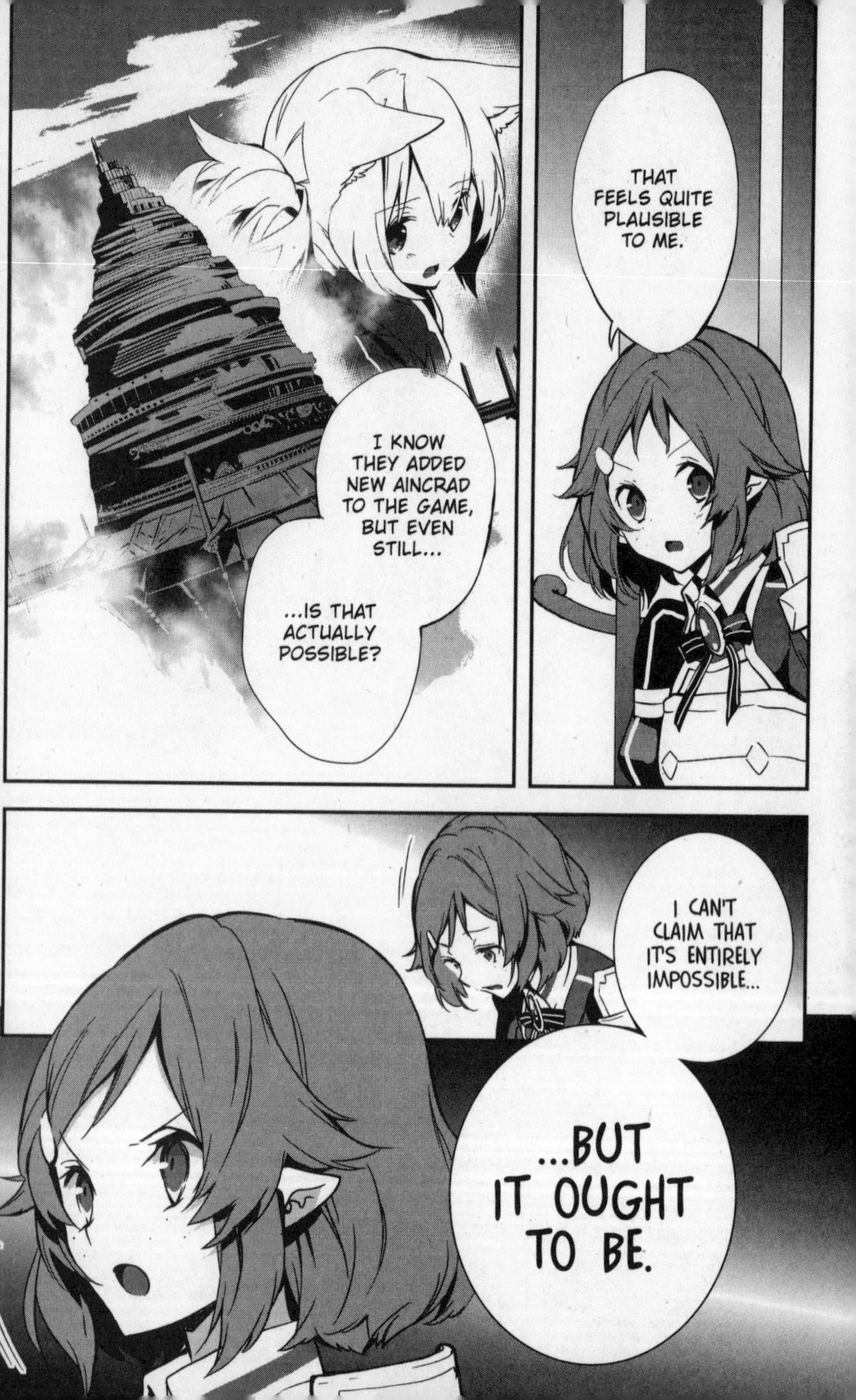
THAT FEELS QUITE PLAUSIBLE TO ME.
I KNOW THEY ADDED NEW AINCRAD TO THE GAME, BUT EVEN STILL...
...IS THAT ACTUALLY POSSIBLE?
I CAN'T CLAIM THAT IT'S ENTIRELY IMPOSSIBLE...
...BUT IT OUGHT TO BE.

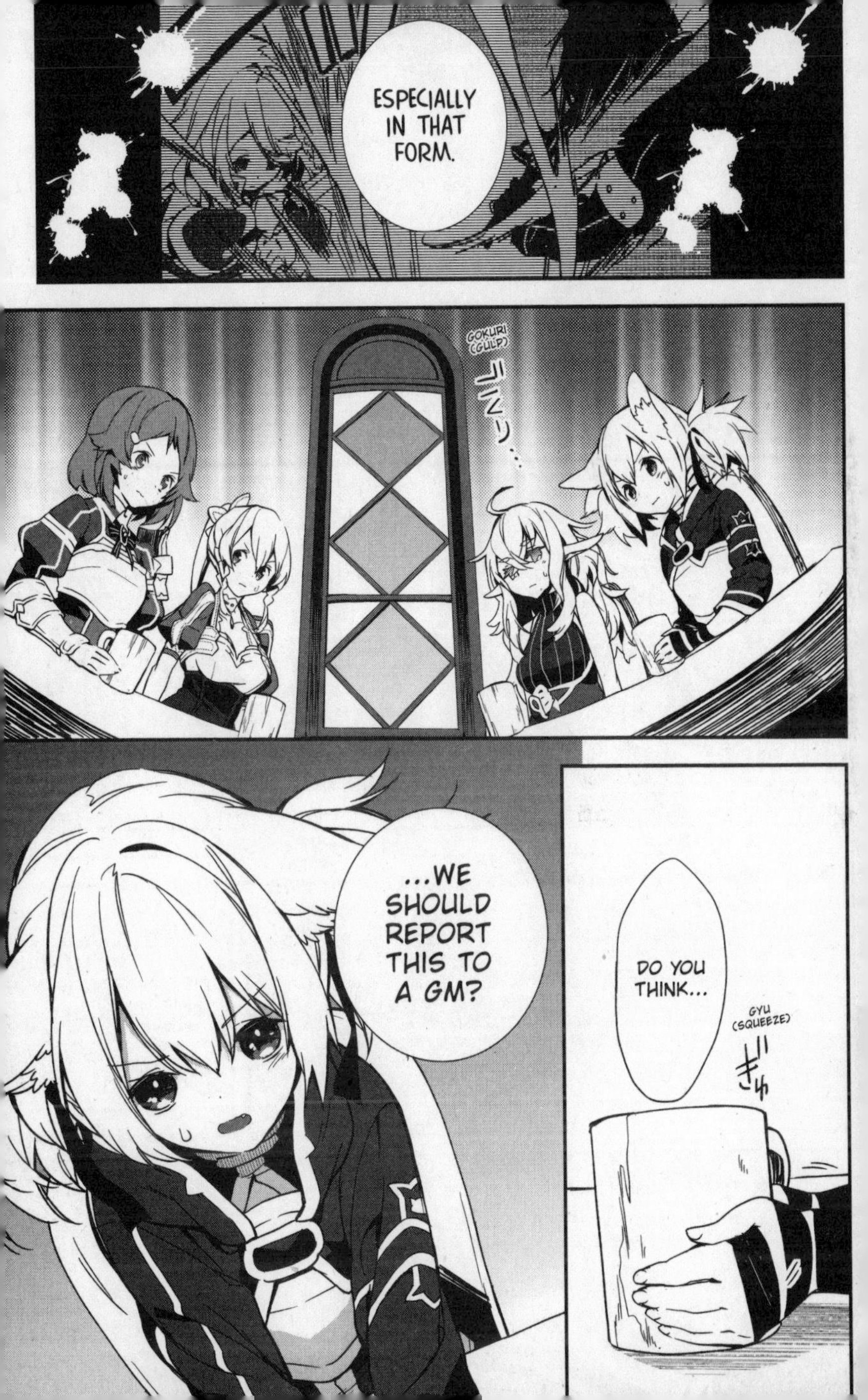
ESPECIALLY IN THAT FORM.
GOKURI (GULP)
ゴクリ…
DO YOU THINK...
GYU (SQUEEZE)
ぎゅ
...WE SHOULD REPORT THIS TO A GM?

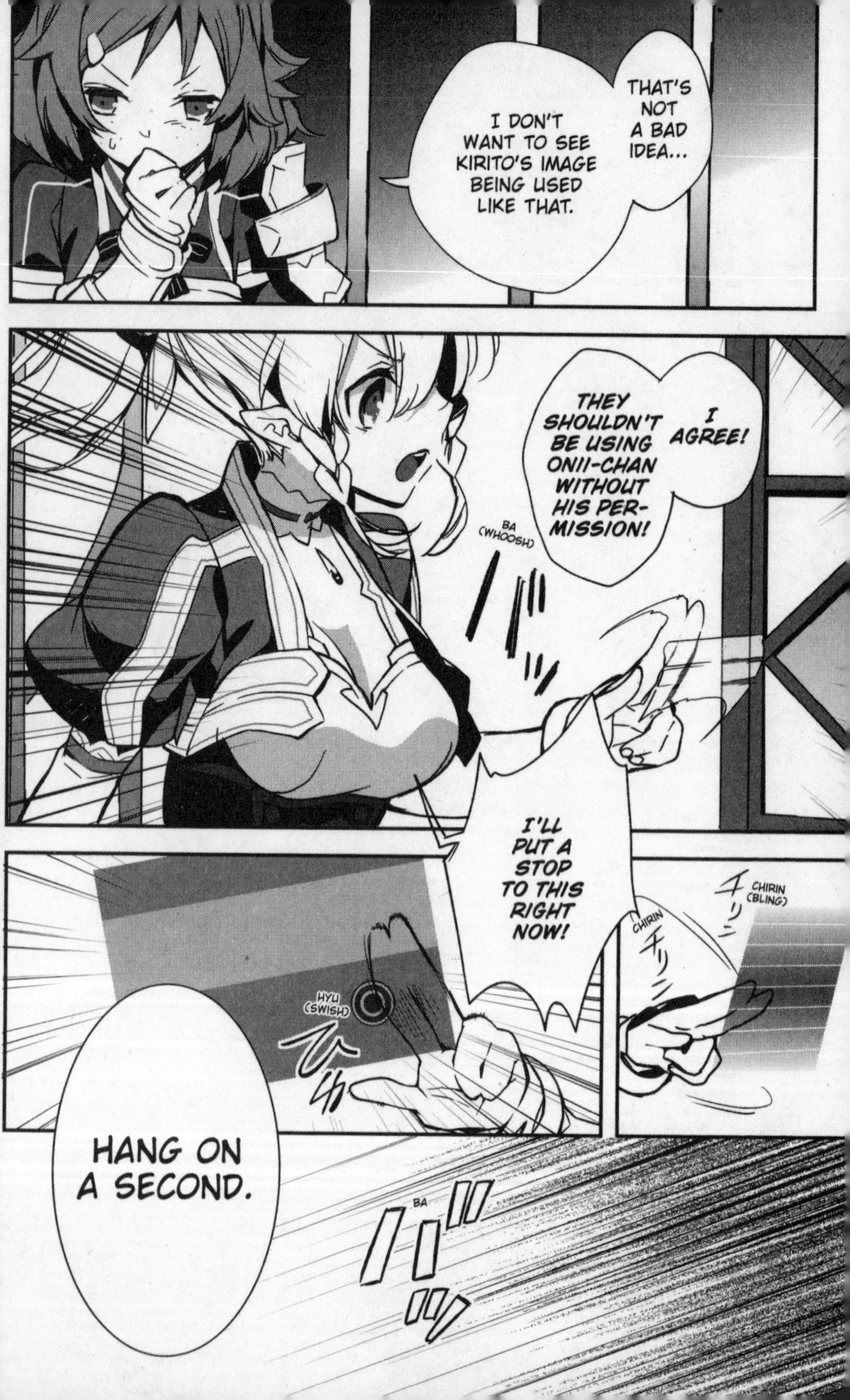
THAT'S NOT A BAD IDEA...
I DON'T WANT TO SEE KIRITO'S IMAGE BEING USED LIKE THAT.
I AGREE!
THEY SHOULDN'T BE USING ONII-CHAN WITHOUT HIS PER-MISSION!
BA (WHOOSH)
CHIRIN (BLING)
CHIRIN
I'LL PUT A STOP TO THIS RIGHT NOW!
HYU (SWISH)
HANG ON A SECOND.
BA

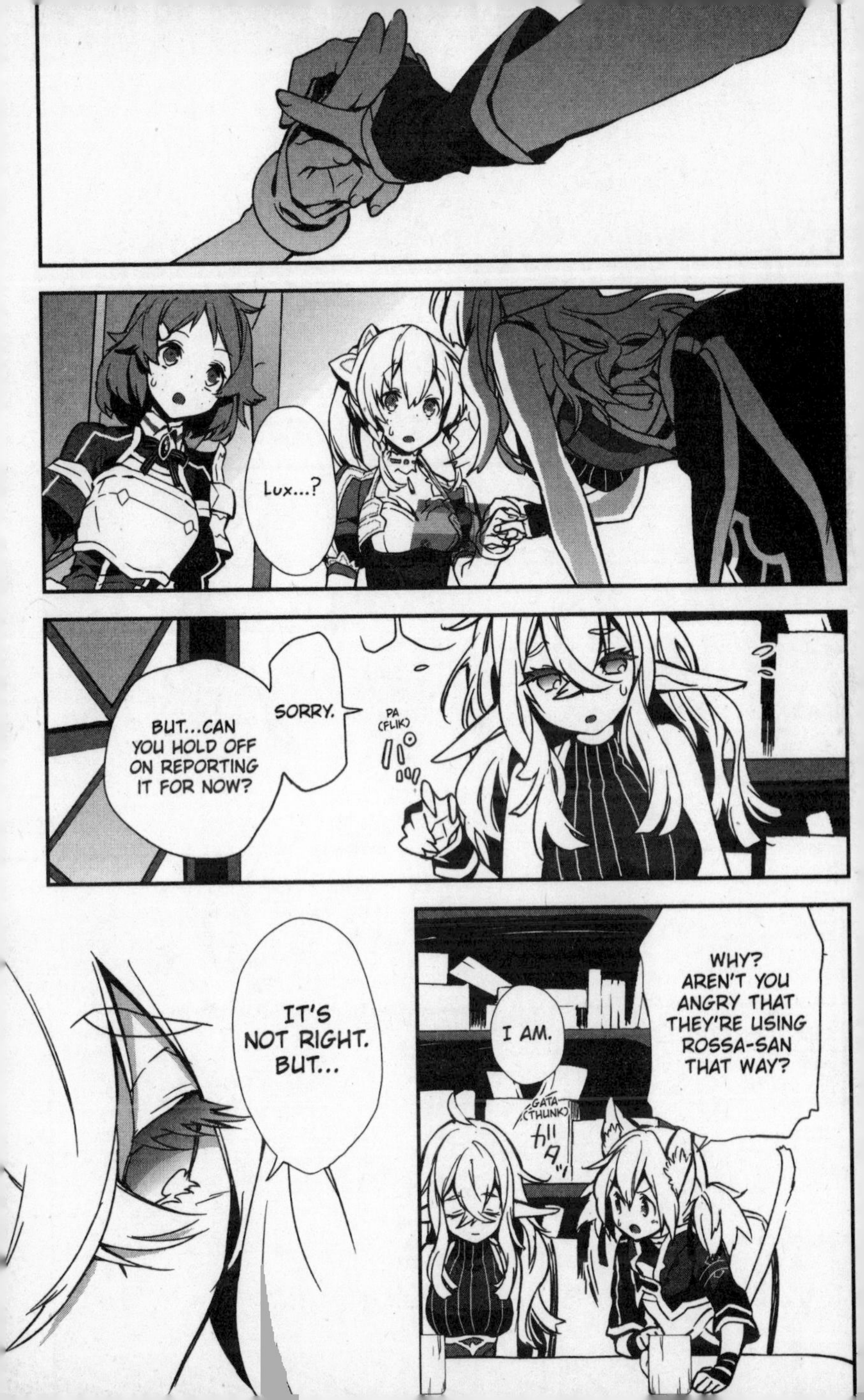
Lux...?
PA (FLIK)
SORRY.
BUT...CAN YOU HOLD OFF ON REPORTING IT FOR NOW?
WHY? AREN'T YOU ANGRY THAT THEY'RE USING ROSSA-SAN THAT WAY?
I AM.
GATA (THUNK)
IT'S NOT RIGHT. BUT...

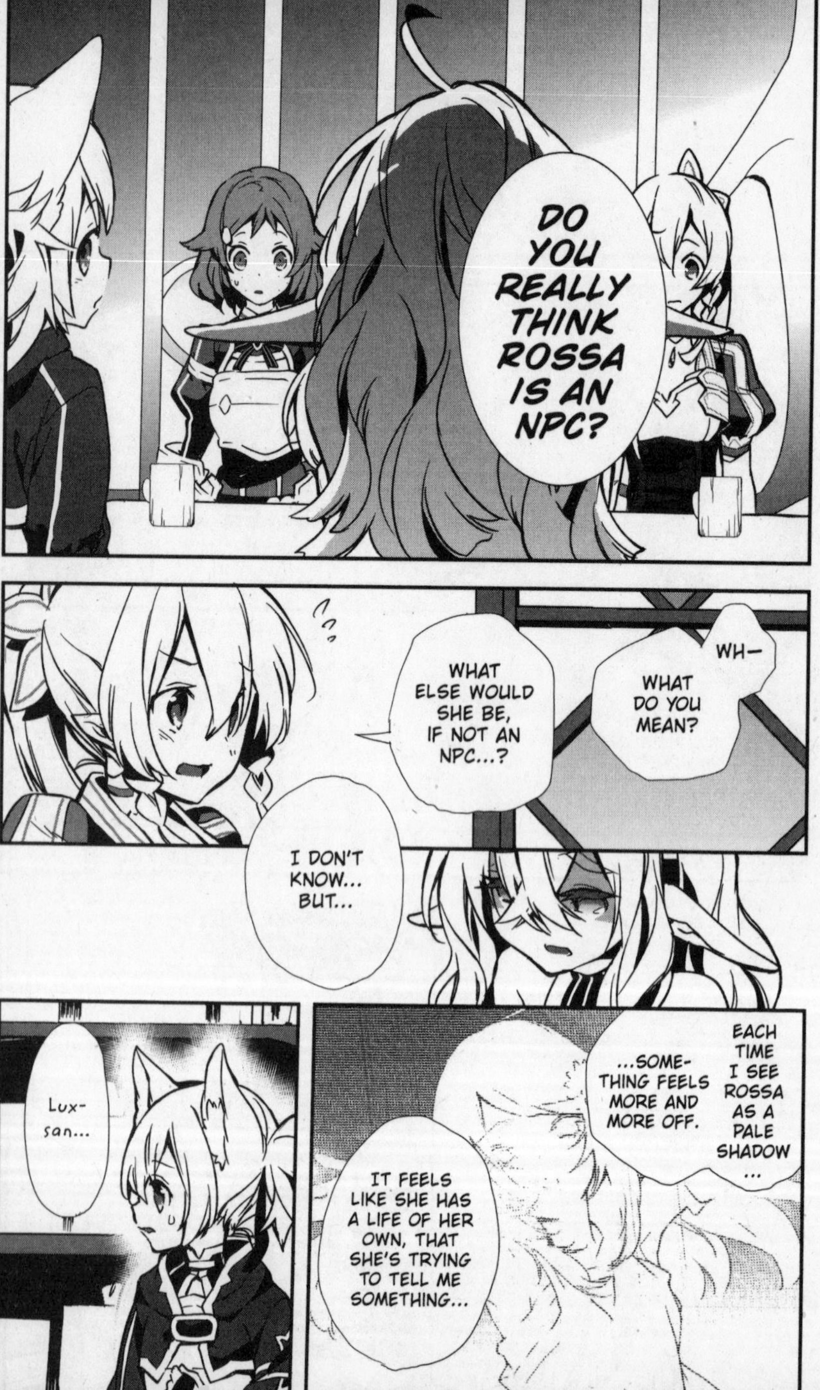
DO YOU REALLY THINK ROSSA IS AN NPC?
WH— WHAT DO YOU MEAN?
WHAT ELSE WOULD SHE BE, IF NOT AN NPC...?
I DON'T KNOW... BUT...
EACH TIME I SEE ROSSA AS A PALE SHADOW ...
...SOMETHING FEELS MORE AND MORE OFF.
IT FEELS LIKE SHE HAS A LIFE OF HER OWN, THAT SHE'S TRYING TO TELL ME SOMETHING...
Lux-san...

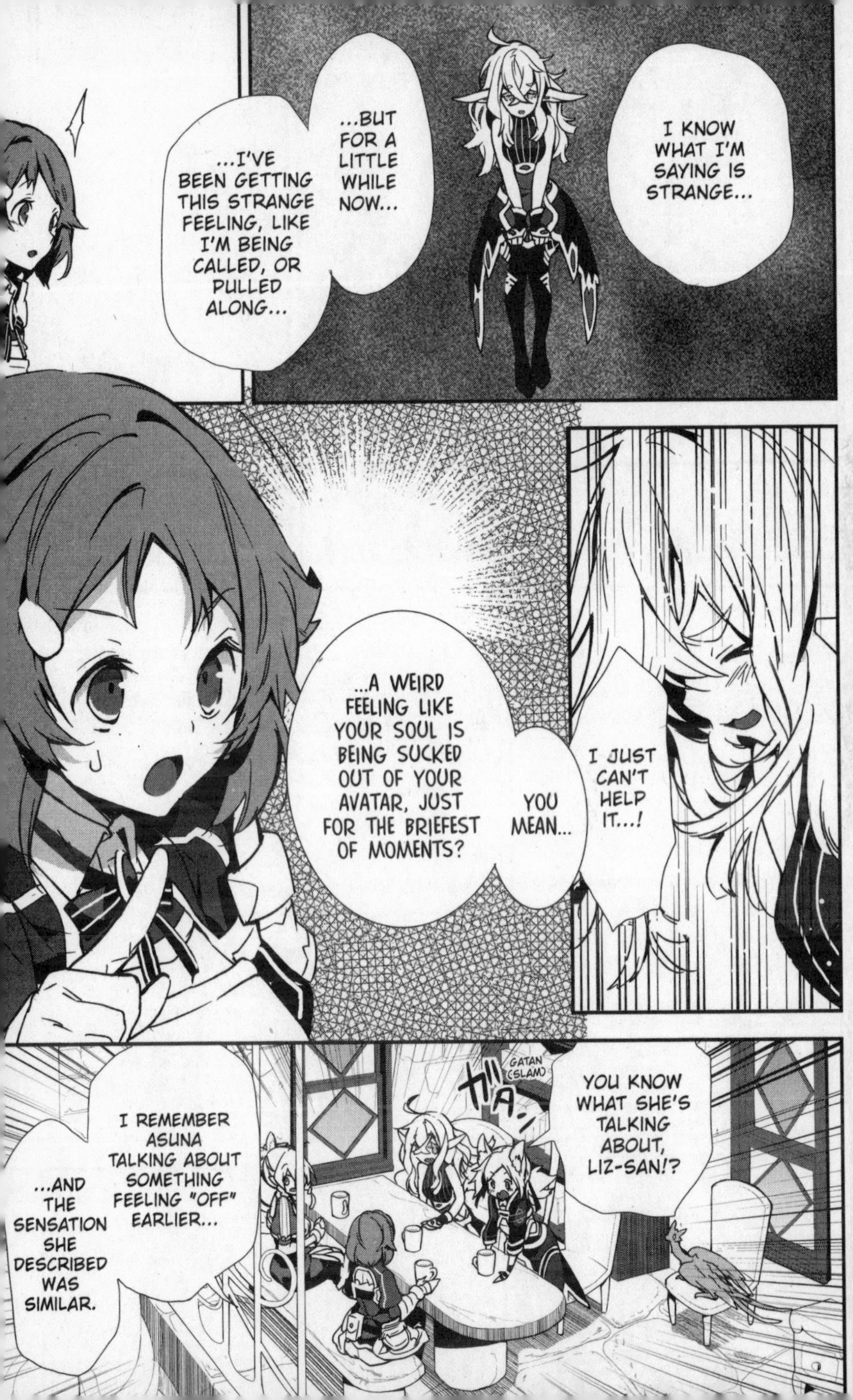
I KNOW WHAT I'M SAYING IS STRANGE...
...BUT FOR A LITTLE WHILE NOW...
...I'VE BEEN GETTING THIS STRANGE FEELING, LIKE I'M BEING CALLED, OR PULLED ALONG...
I JUST CAN'T HELP IT...!
YOU MEAN...
...A WEIRD FEELING LIKE YOUR SOUL IS BEING SUCKED OUT OF YOUR AVATAR, JUST FOR THE BRIEFEST OF MOMENTS?
GATAN (SLAM)
YOU KNOW WHAT SHE'S TALKING ABOUT, LIZ-SAN!?
I REMEMBER ASUNA TALKING ABOUT SOMETHING FEELING "OFF" EARLIER...
...AND THE SENSATION SHE DESCRIBED WAS SIMILAR.

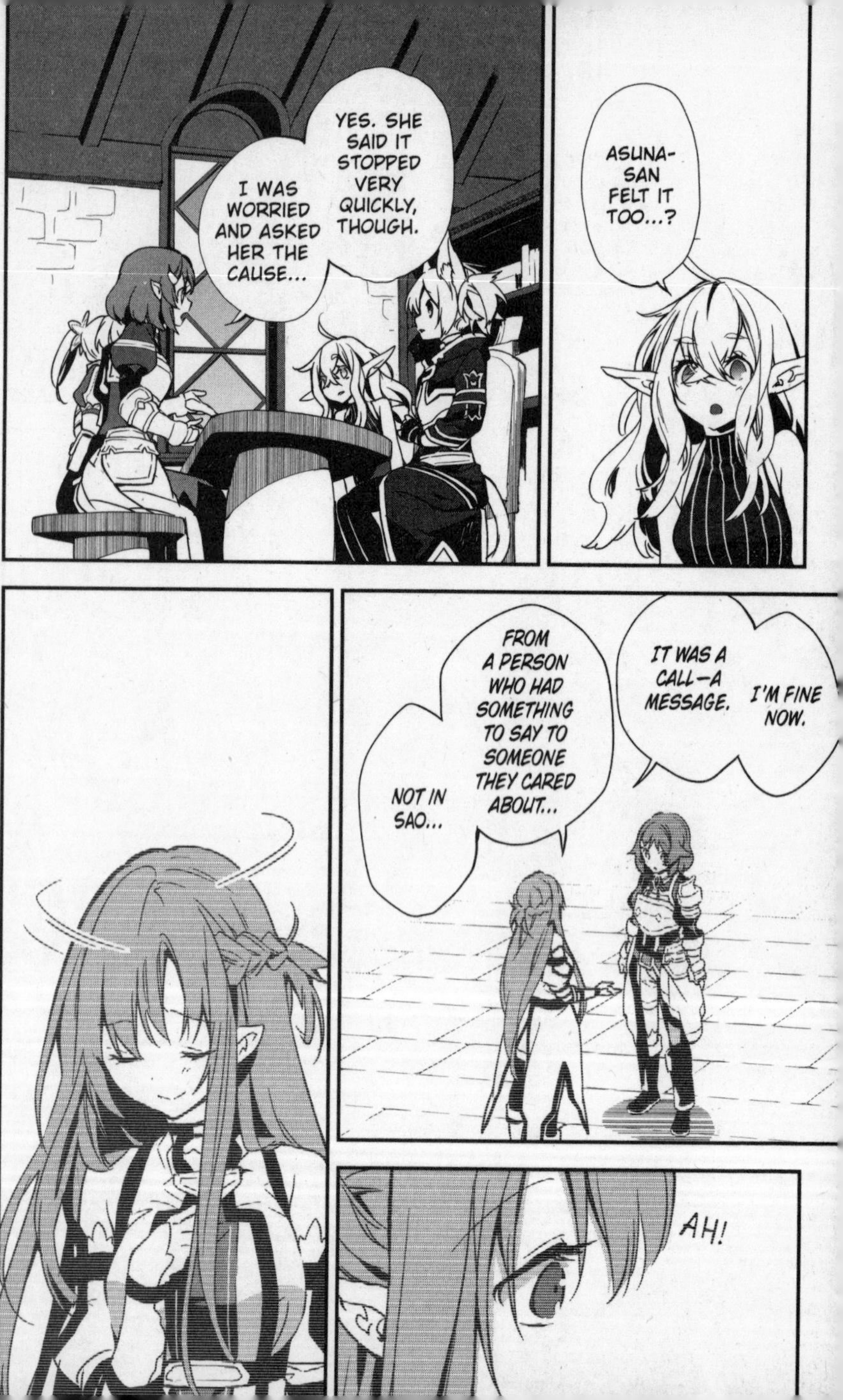
ASUNA-SAN FELT IT TOO...?
YES. SHE SAID IT STOPPED VERY QUICKLY, THOUGH.
I WAS WORRIED AND ASKED HER THE CAUSE...
I'M FINE NOW.
IT WAS A CALL—A MESSAGE.
FROM A PERSON WHO HAD SOMETHING TO SAY TO SOMEONE THEY CARED ABOUT...
NOT IN SAO...
AH!

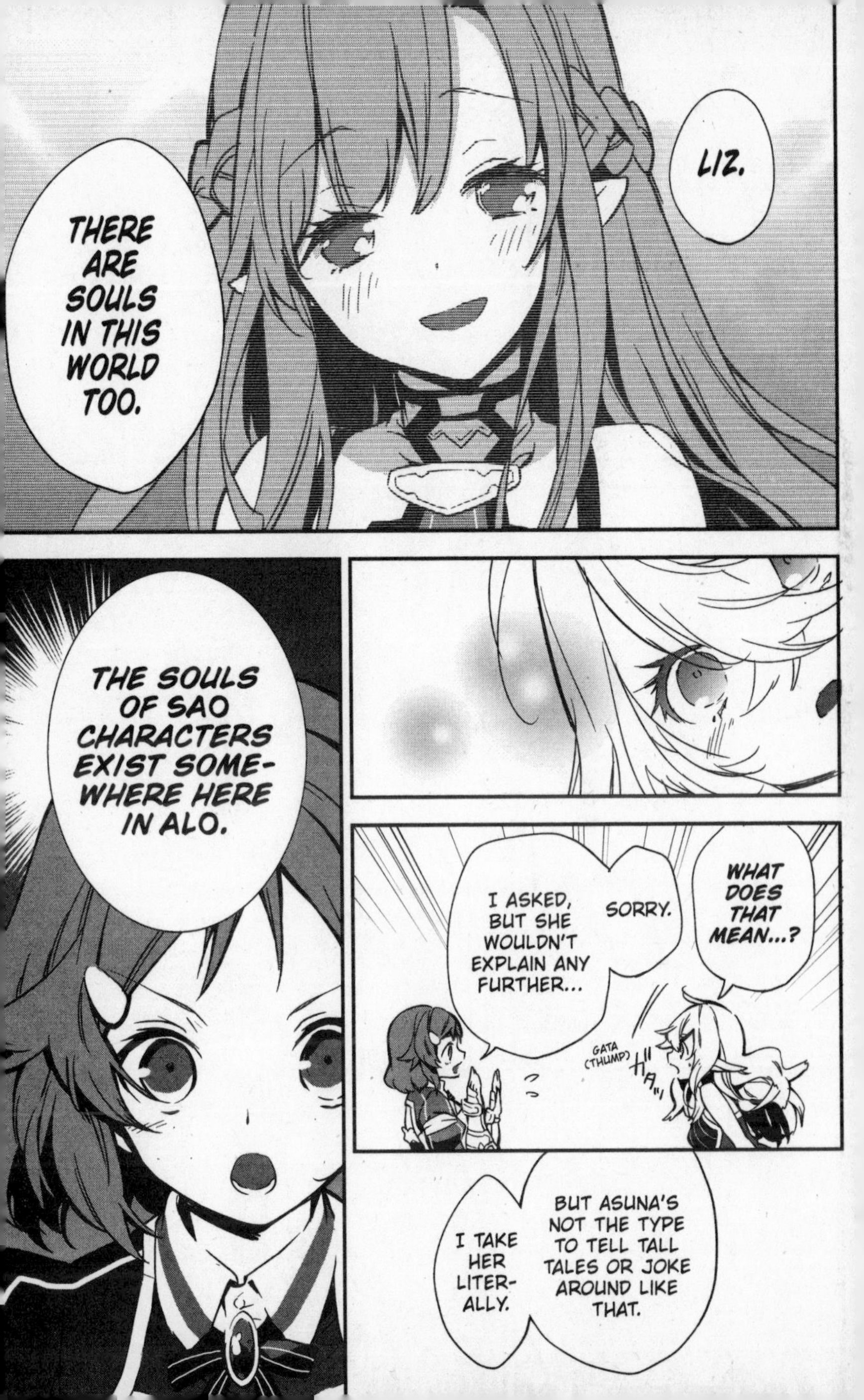
LIZ.
THERE ARE SOULS IN THIS WORLD TOO.
WHAT DOES THAT MEAN...?
SORRY.
I ASKED, BUT SHE WOULDN'T EXPLAIN ANY FURTHER...
GATA (THUMP)
THE SOULS OF SAO CHARACTERS EXIST SOMEWHERE HERE IN ALO.
BUT ASUNA'S NOT THE TYPE TO TELL TALL TALES OR JOKE AROUND LIKE THAT.
I TAKE HER LITERALLY.

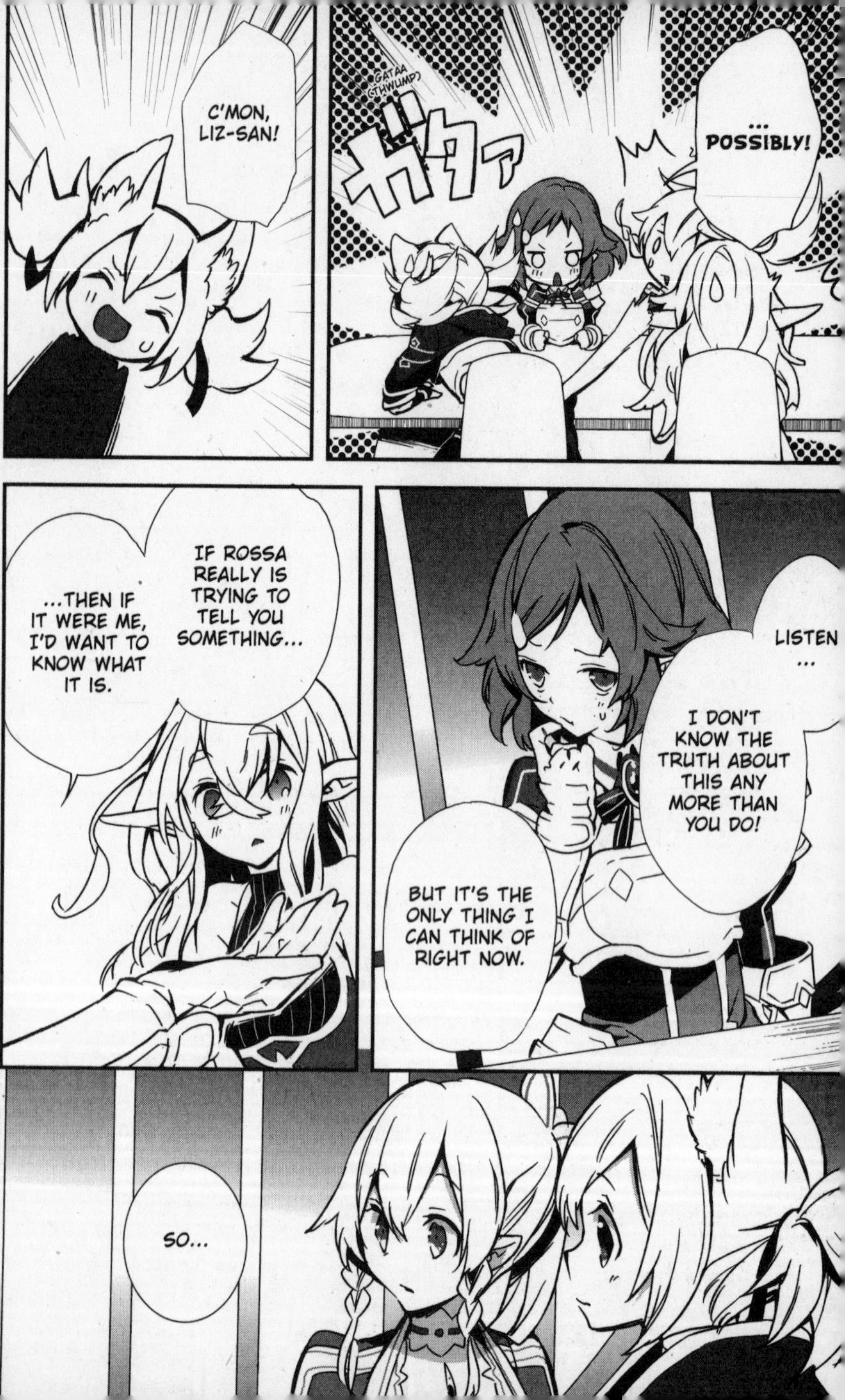
...POSSIBLY!
GATAA (THWUMP)
ガタァ
C'MON, LIZ-SAN!
LISTEN...
I DON'T KNOW THE TRUTH ABOUT THIS ANY MORE THAN YOU DO!
BUT IT'S THE ONLY THING I CAN THINK OF RIGHT NOW.
IF ROSSA REALLY IS TRYING TO TELL YOU SOMETHING...
...THEN IF IT WERE ME, I'D WANT TO KNOW WHAT IT IS.
SO...

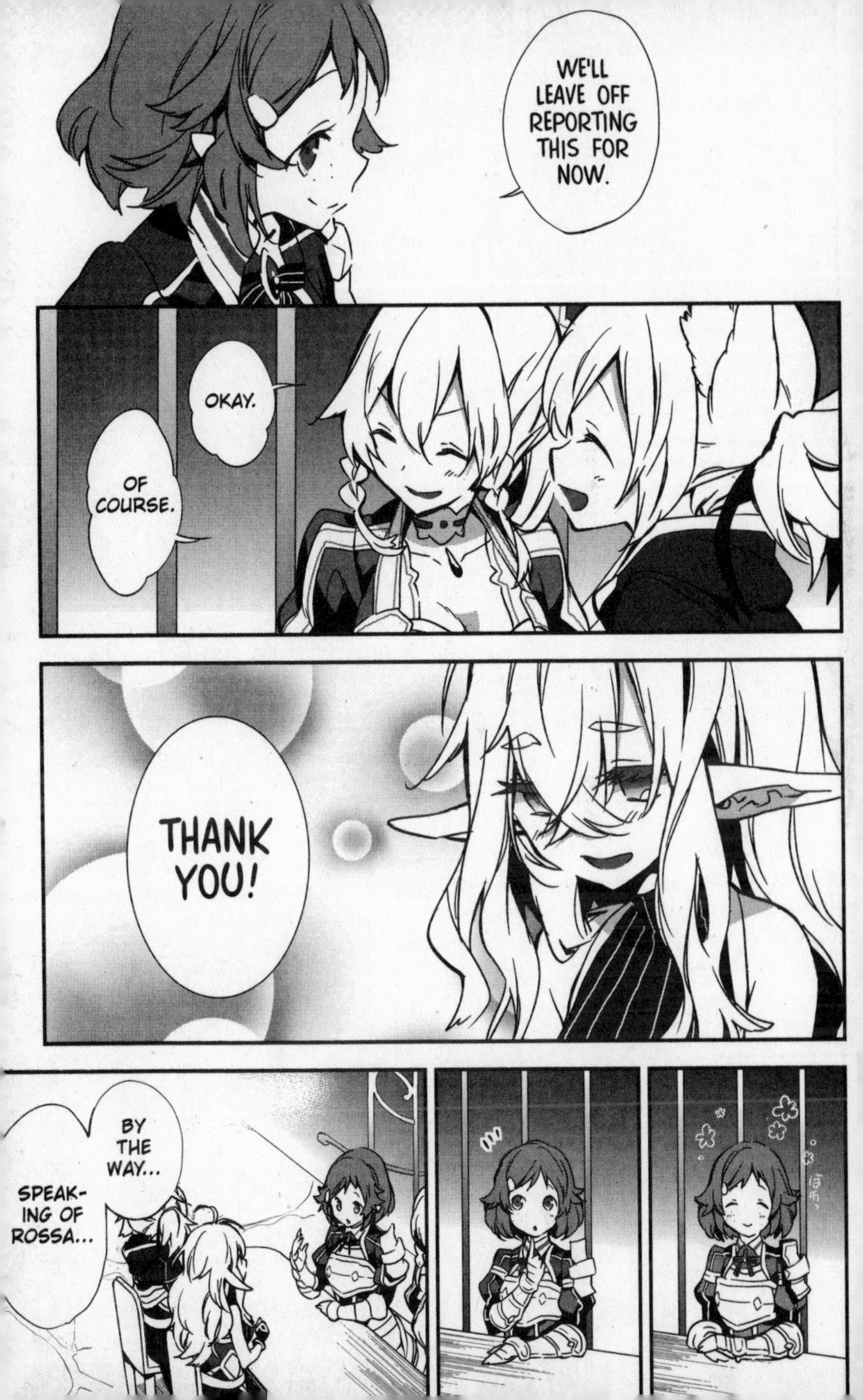
WE'LL LEAVE OFF REPORTING THIS FOR NOW.
OKAY.
OF COURSE.
THANK YOU!
BY THE WAY...
SPEAK-ING OF ROSSA...

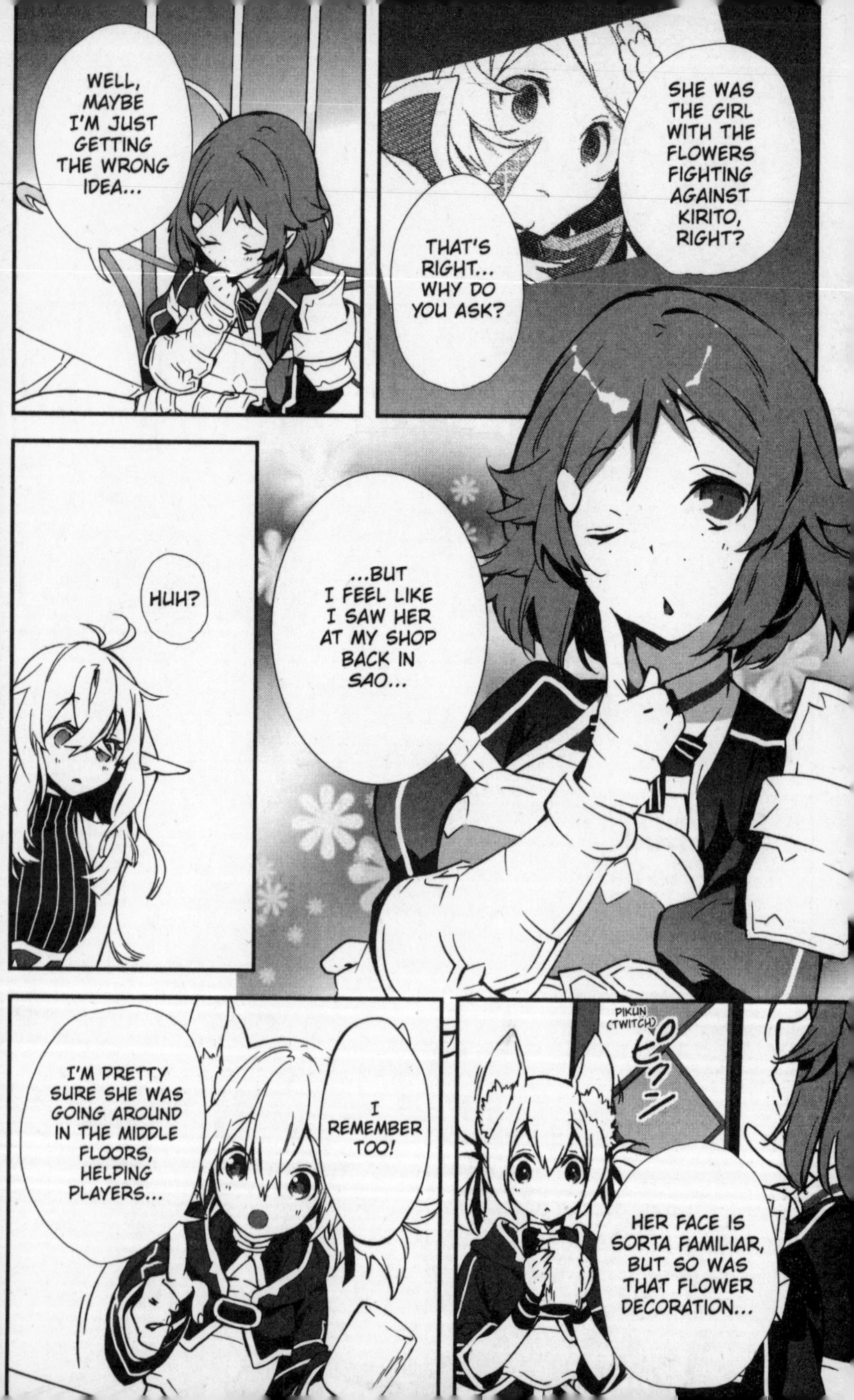
SHE WAS THE GIRL WITH THE FLOWERS FIGHTING AGAINST KIRITO, RIGHT?
THAT'S RIGHT... WHY DO YOU ASK?
WELL, MAYBE I'M JUST GETTING THE WRONG IDEA...
...BUT I FEEL LIKE I SAW HER AT MY SHOP BACK IN SAO...
HUH?
PIKUN (TWITCH)
HER FACE IS SORTA FAMILIAR, BUT SO WAS THAT FLOWER DECORATION...
I REMEMBER TOO!
I'M PRETTY SURE SHE WAS GOING AROUND IN THE MIDDLE FLOORS, HELPING PLAYERS...

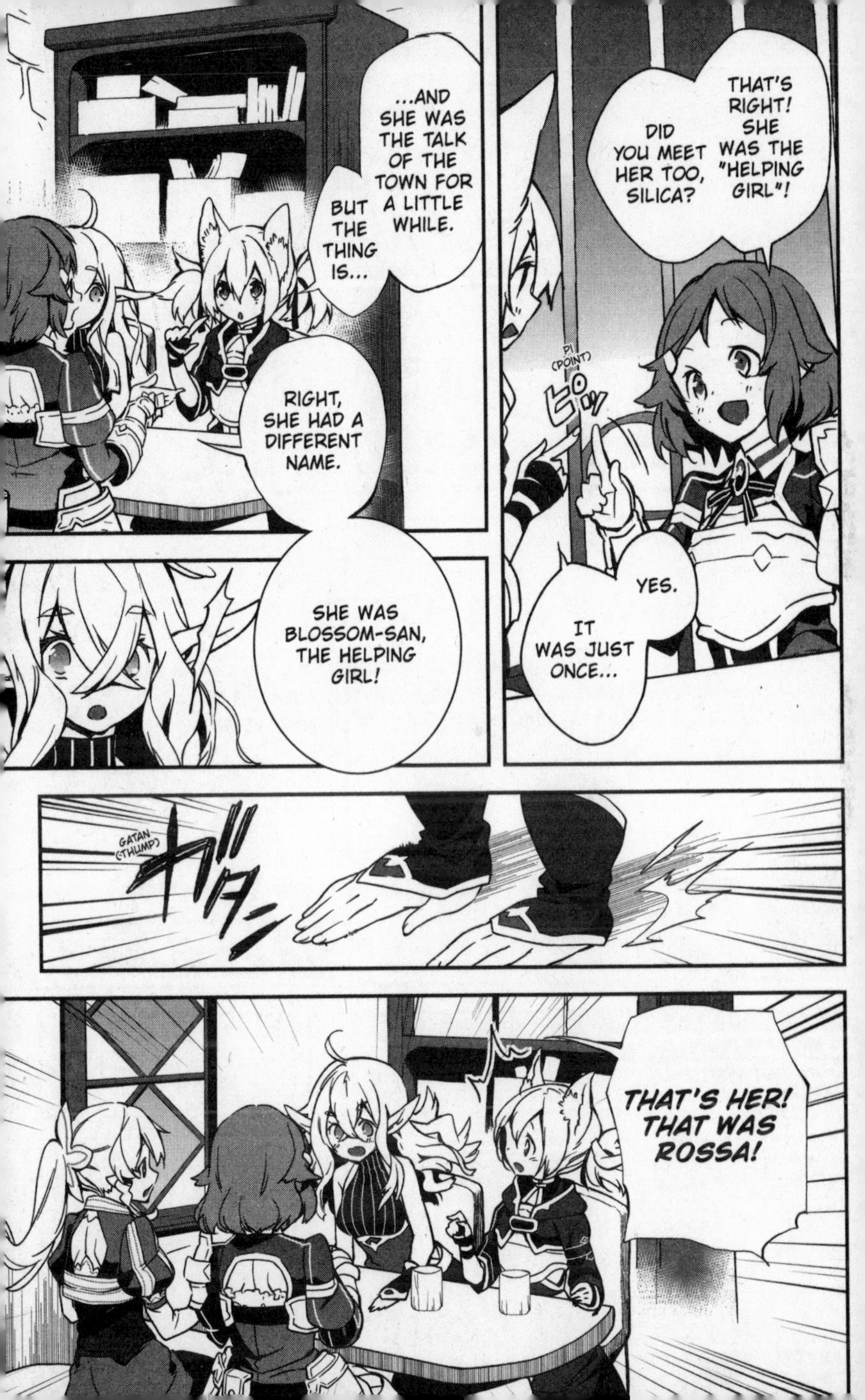
THAT'S RIGHT! SHE WAS THE "HELPING GIRL"!
DID YOU MEET HER TOO, SILICA?
PI (POINT)
YES.
IT WAS JUST ONCE...
...AND SHE WAS THE TALK OF THE TOWN FOR A LITTLE WHILE.
BUT THE THING IS...
RIGHT, SHE HAD A DIFFERENT NAME.
SHE WAS BLOSSOM-SAN, THE HELPING GIRL!
GATAN (THUMP)
THAT'S HER! THAT WAS ROSSA!

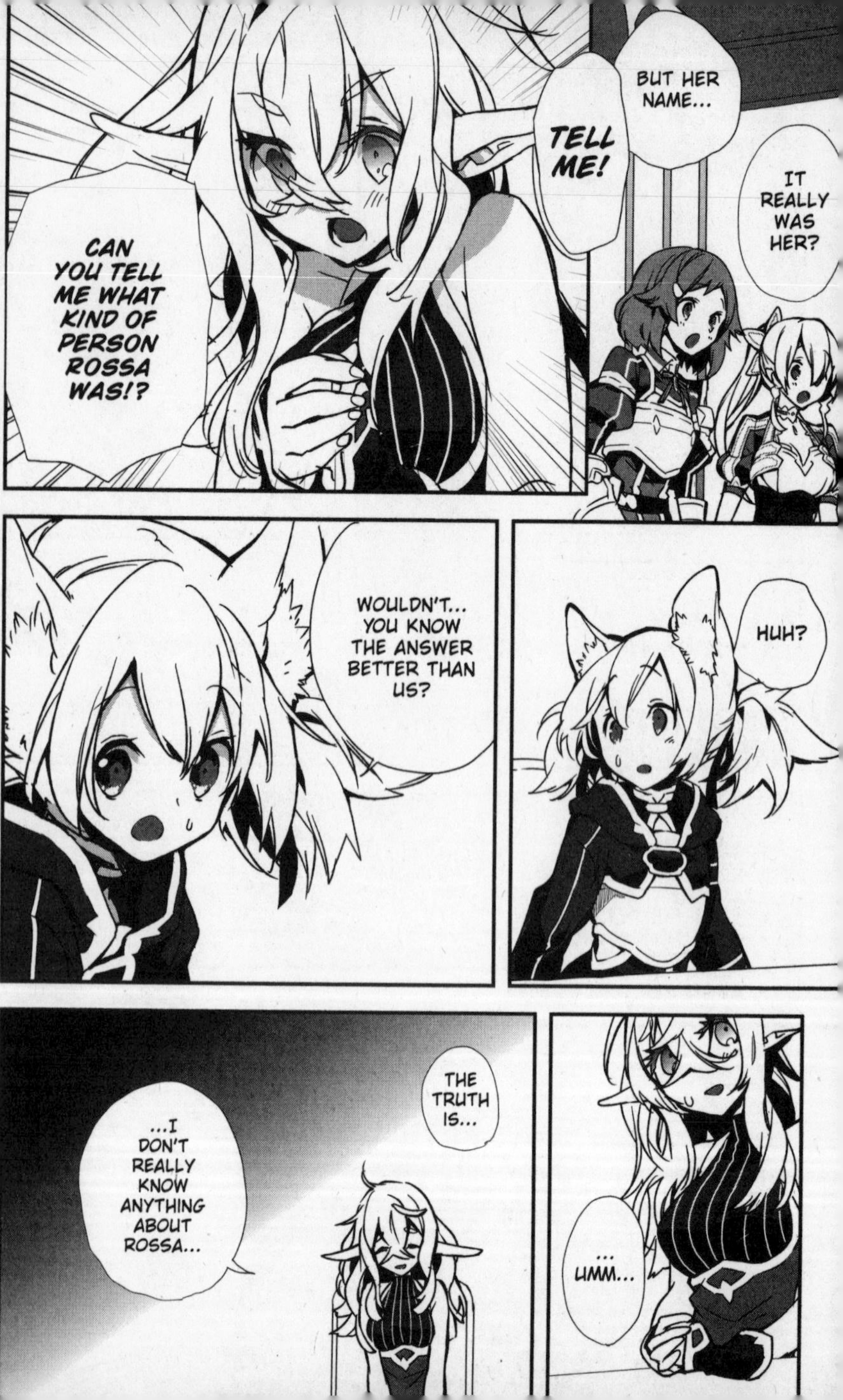
IT REALLY WAS HER?
BUT HER NAME...
TELL ME!
CAN YOU TELL ME WHAT KIND OF PERSON ROSSA WAS!?
HUH?
WOULDN'T... YOU KNOW THE ANSWER BETTER THAN US?
... UMM...
THE TRUTH IS...
...I DON'T REALLY KNOW ANYTHING ABOUT ROSSA...

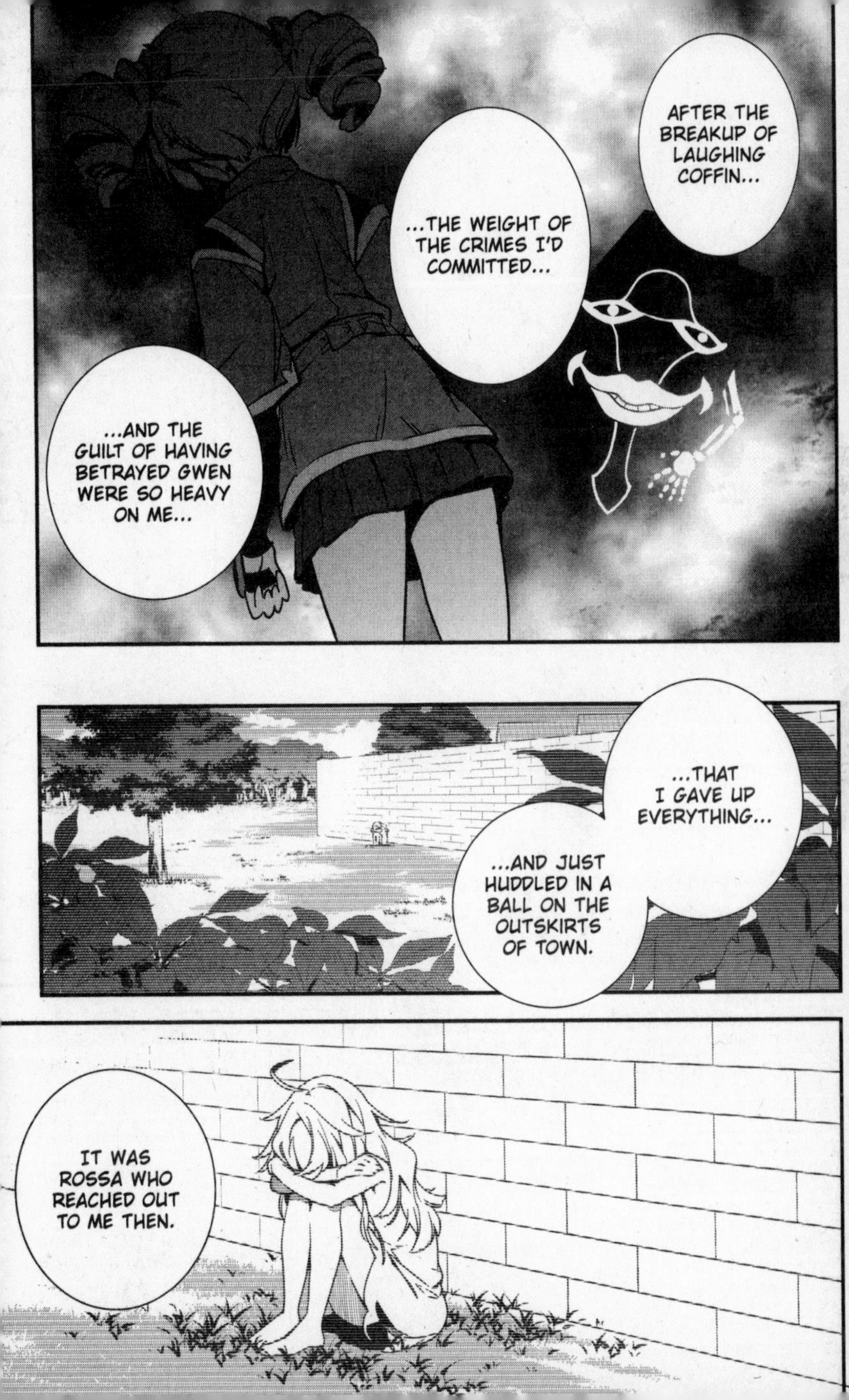
AFTER THE BREAKUP OF LAUGHING COFFIN...
...THE WEIGHT OF THE CRIMES I'D COMMITTED...
...AND THE GUILT OF HAVING BETRAYED GWEN WERE SO HEAVY ON ME...
...THAT I GAVE UP EVERYTHING...
...AND JUST HUDDLED IN A BALL ON THE OUTSKIRTS OF TOWN.
IT WAS ROSSA WHO REACHED OUT TO ME THEN.

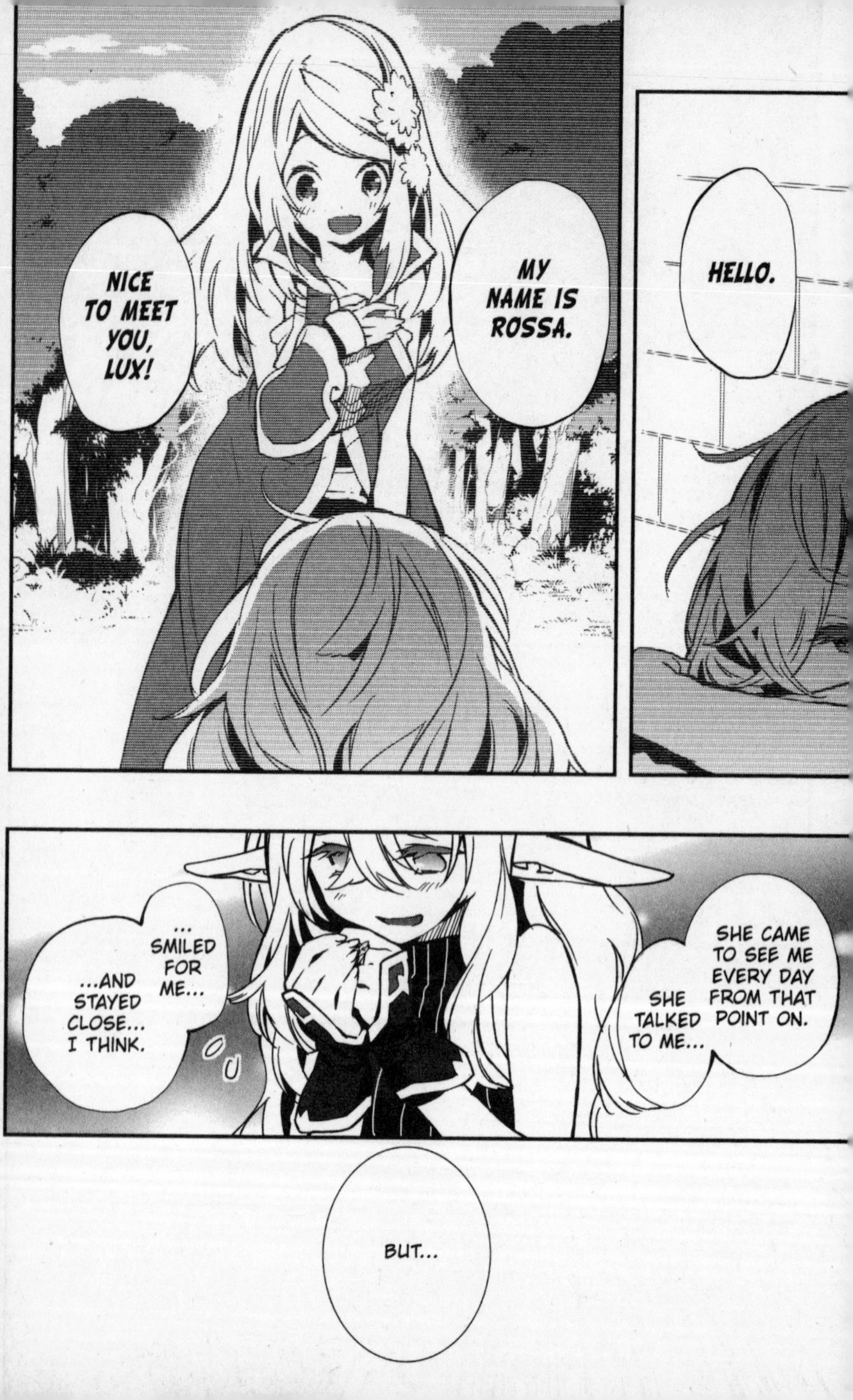
HELLO.
MY NAME IS ROSSA.
NICE TO MEET YOU, LUX!
SHE CAME TO SEE ME EVERY DAY FROM THAT POINT ON.
SHE TALKED TO ME...
...SMILED FOR ME...
...AND STAYED CLOSE... I THINK.
BUT...

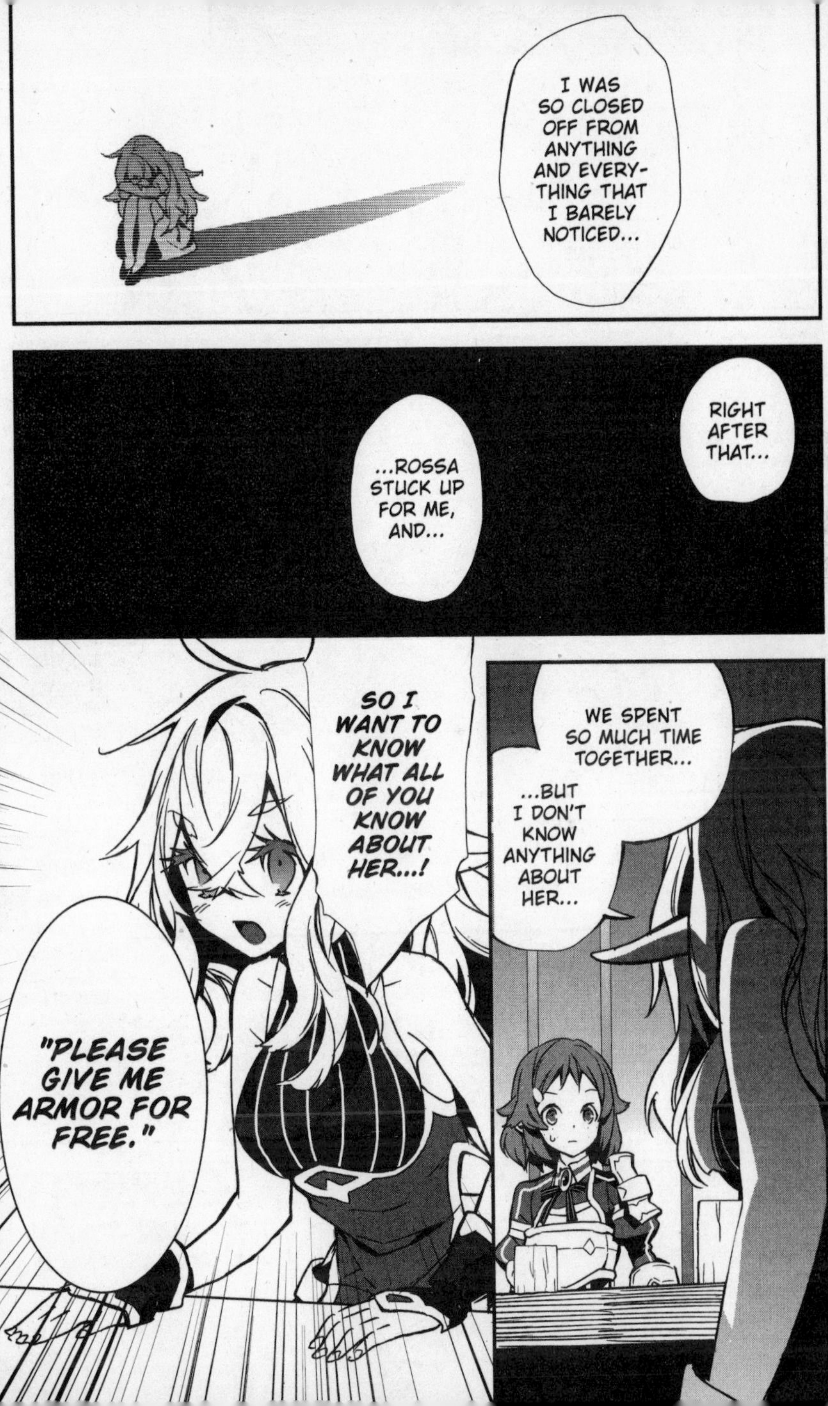
I WAS SO CLOSED OFF FROM ANYTHING AND EVERY-THING THAT I BARELY NOTICED...
RIGHT AFTER THAT...
...ROSSA STUCK UP FOR ME, AND...
WE SPENT SO MUCH TIME TOGETHER...
...BUT I DON'T KNOW ANYTHING ABOUT HER...
SO I WANT TO KNOW WHAT ALL OF YOU KNOW ABOUT HER...!
"PLEASE GIVE ME ARMOR FOR FREE."

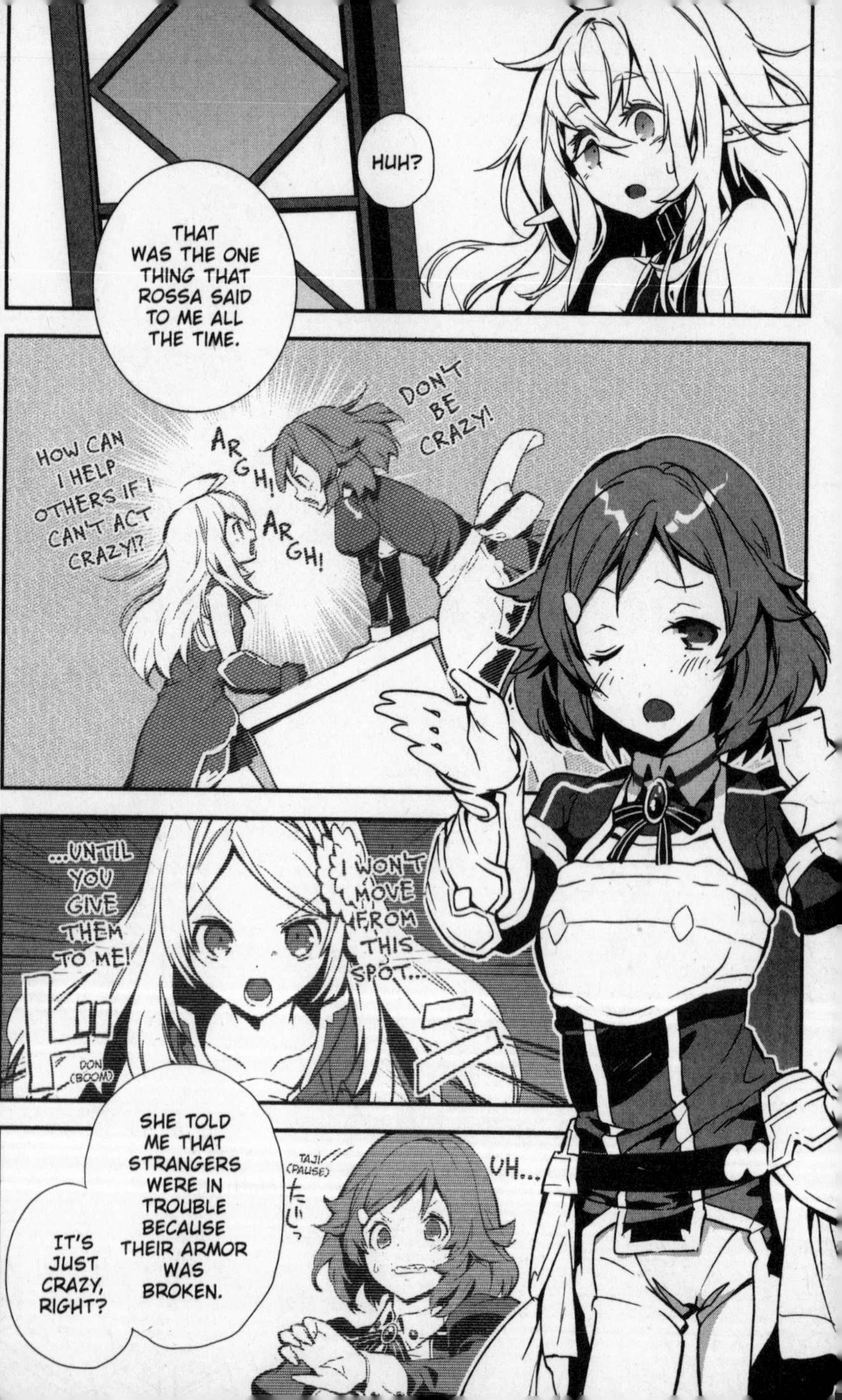
HUH?
THAT WAS THE ONE THING THAT ROSSA SAID TO ME ALL THE TIME.
DON'T BE CRAZY!
ARGH!
ARGH!
HOW CAN I HELP OTHERS IF I CAN'T ACT CRAZY!?
I WON'T MOVE FROM THIS SPOT...
...UNTIL YOU GIVE THEM TO ME!
DON (BOOM)
UH...
TAJI (PAUSE)
SHE TOLD ME THAT STRANGERS WERE IN TROUBLE BECAUSE THEIR ARMOR WAS BROKEN.
IT'S JUST CRAZY, RIGHT?

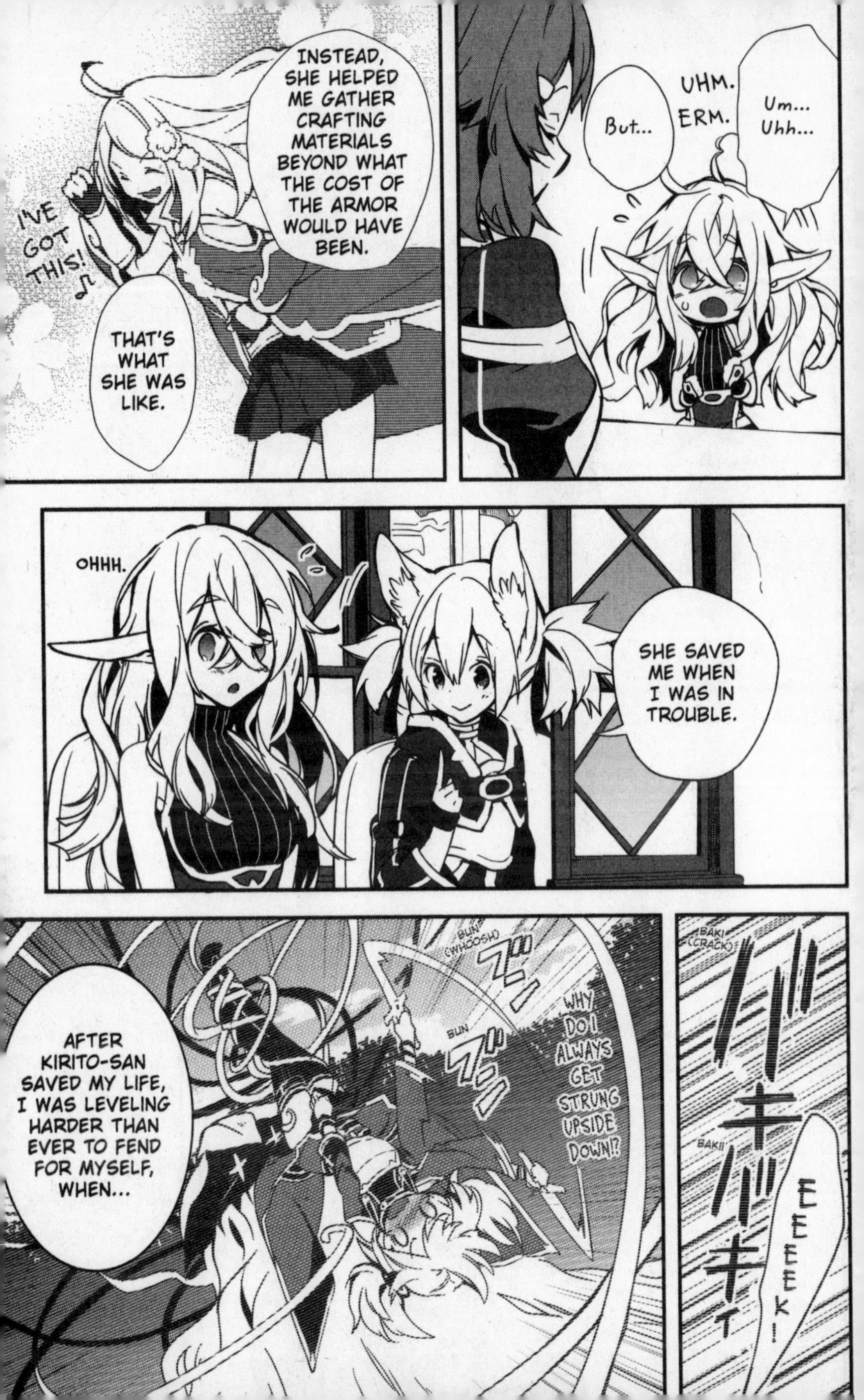
Um... Uhh...
UHM. ERM.
But...
INSTEAD, SHE HELPED ME GATHER CRAFTING MATERIALS BEYOND WHAT THE COST OF THE ARMOR WOULD HAVE BEEN.
I'VE GOT THIS! ♪
THAT'S WHAT SHE WAS LIKE.
SHE SAVED ME WHEN I WAS IN TROUBLE.
OHHH.
BAKI (CRACK)
BAKI
EEEEEK!
BUN (WHOOSH)
WHY DO I ALWAYS GET STRUNG UPSIDE DOWN!?
BUN
AFTER KIRITO-SAN SAVED MY LIFE, I WAS LEVELING HARDER THAN EVER TO FEND FOR MYSELF, WHEN...

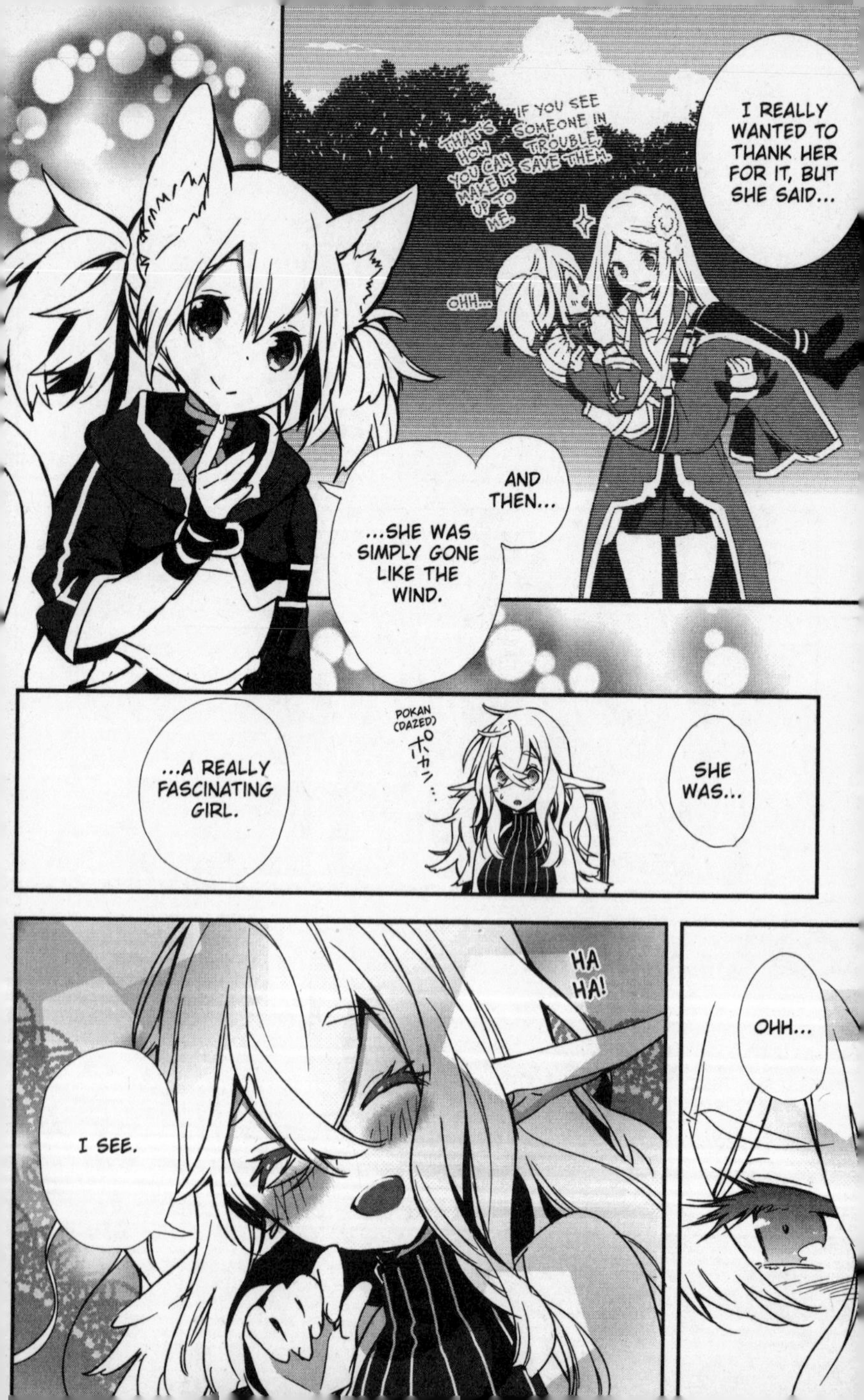
I REALLY WANTED TO THANK HER FOR IT, BUT SHE SAID...
IF YOU SEE SOMEONE IN TROUBLE, SAVE THEM.
THAT'S HOW YOU CAN MAKE IT UP TO ME.
OHH...
AND THEN...
...SHE WAS SIMPLY GONE LIKE THE WIND.
SHE WAS...
POKAN (DAZED)
ポカン…
...A REALLY FASCINATING GIRL.
OHH...
HA HA!
I SEE.

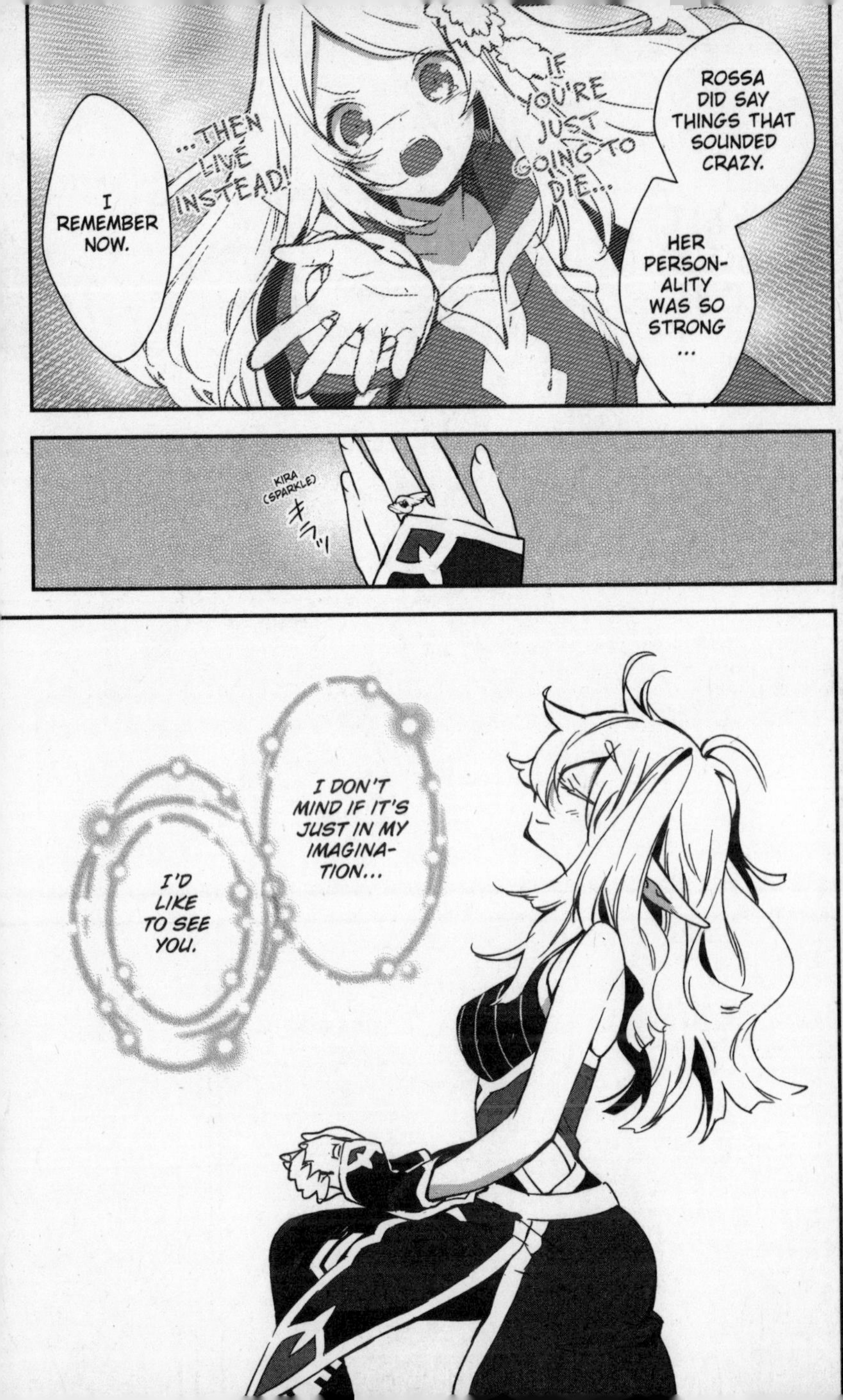
ROSSA DID SAY THINGS THAT SOUNDED CRAZY.
HER PERSON-ALITY WAS SO STRONG...
IF YOU'RE JUST GOING TO DIE...
...THEN LIVE INSTEAD!
I REMEMBER NOW.
KIRA (SPARKLE)
キラッ
I DON'T MIND IF IT'S JUST IN MY IMAGINA-TION...
I'D LIKE TO SEE YOU.

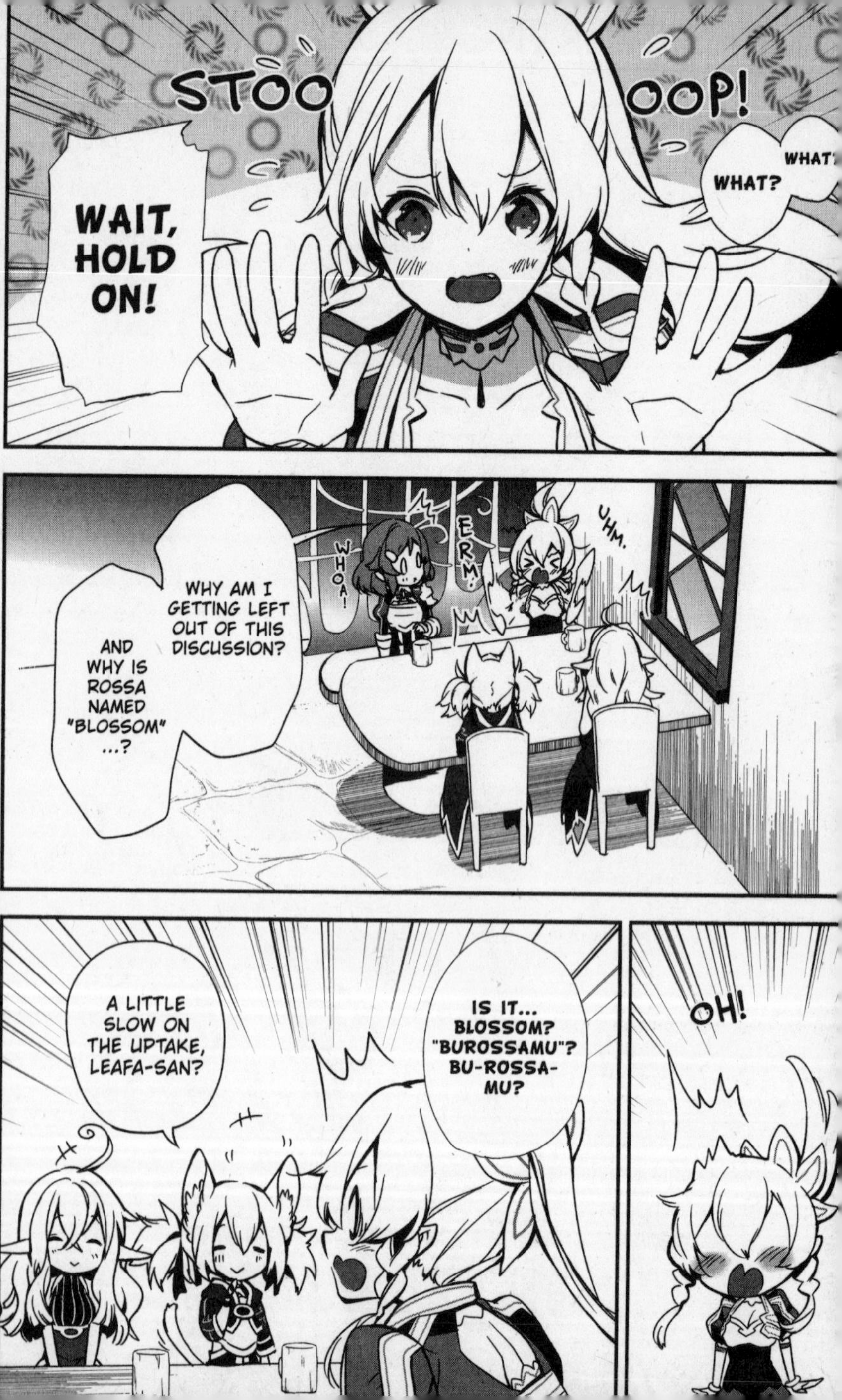
STOO
OOP!
WHAT?
WHAT?
WAIT, HOLD ON!
UHM.
ERM.
WHOA!
WHY AM I GETTING LEFT OUT OF THIS DISCUSSION?
AND WHY IS ROSSA NAMED "BLOSSOM"...?
OH!
IS IT... BLOSSOM? "BUROSSAMU"? BU-ROSSA-MU?
A LITTLE SLOW ON THE UPTAKE, LEAFA-SAN?

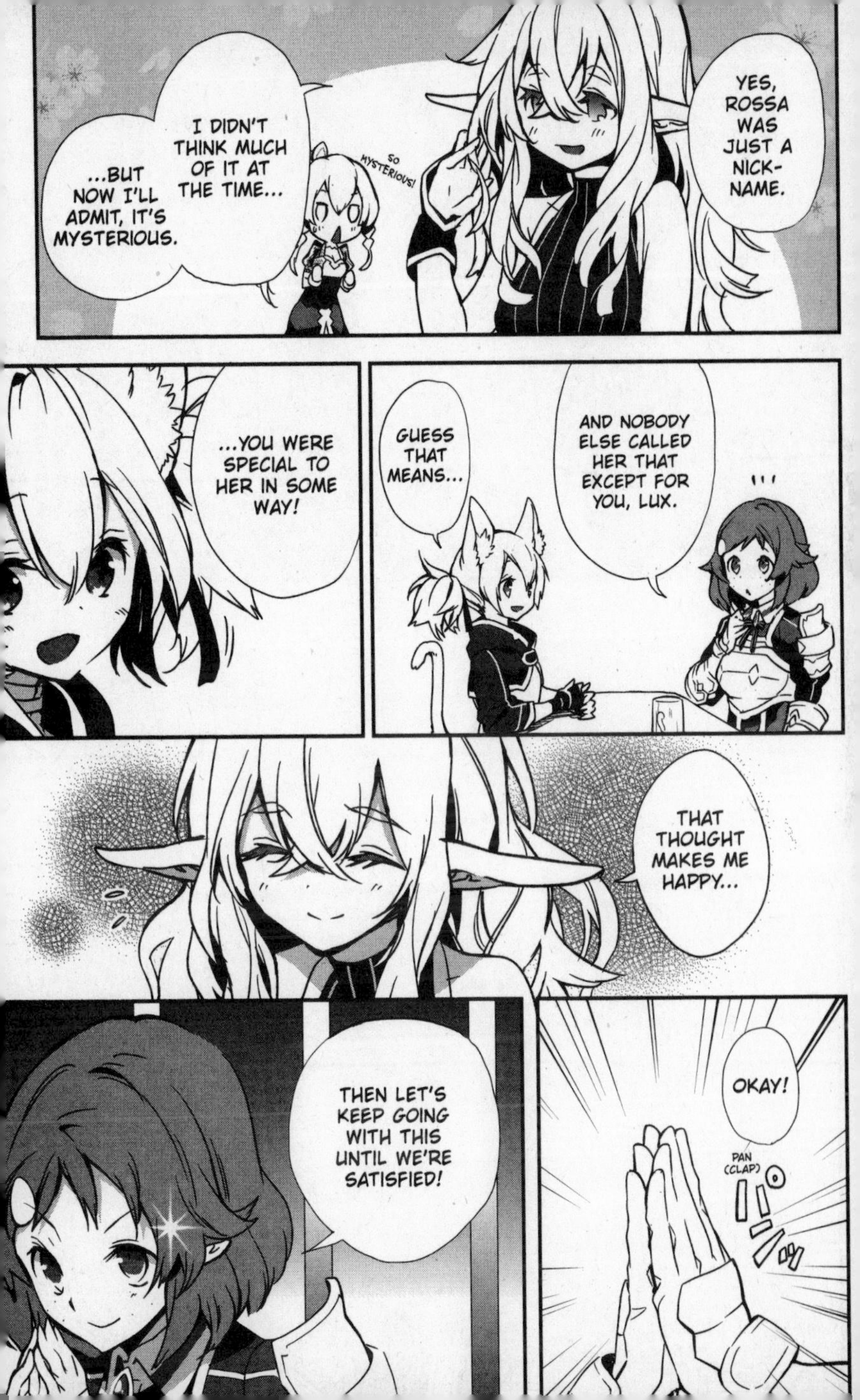
YES, ROSSA WAS JUST A NICK-NAME.
I DIDN'T THINK MUCH OF IT AT THE TIME...
SO MYSTERIOUS!
...BUT NOW I'LL ADMIT, IT'S MYSTERIOUS.
AND NOBODY ELSE CALLED HER THAT EXCEPT FOR YOU, LUX.
GUESS THAT MEANS...
...YOU WERE SPECIAL TO HER IN SOME WAY!
THAT THOUGHT MAKES ME HAPPY...
OKAY!
PAN (CLAP)
THEN LET'S KEEP GOING WITH THIS UNTIL WE'RE SATISFIED!

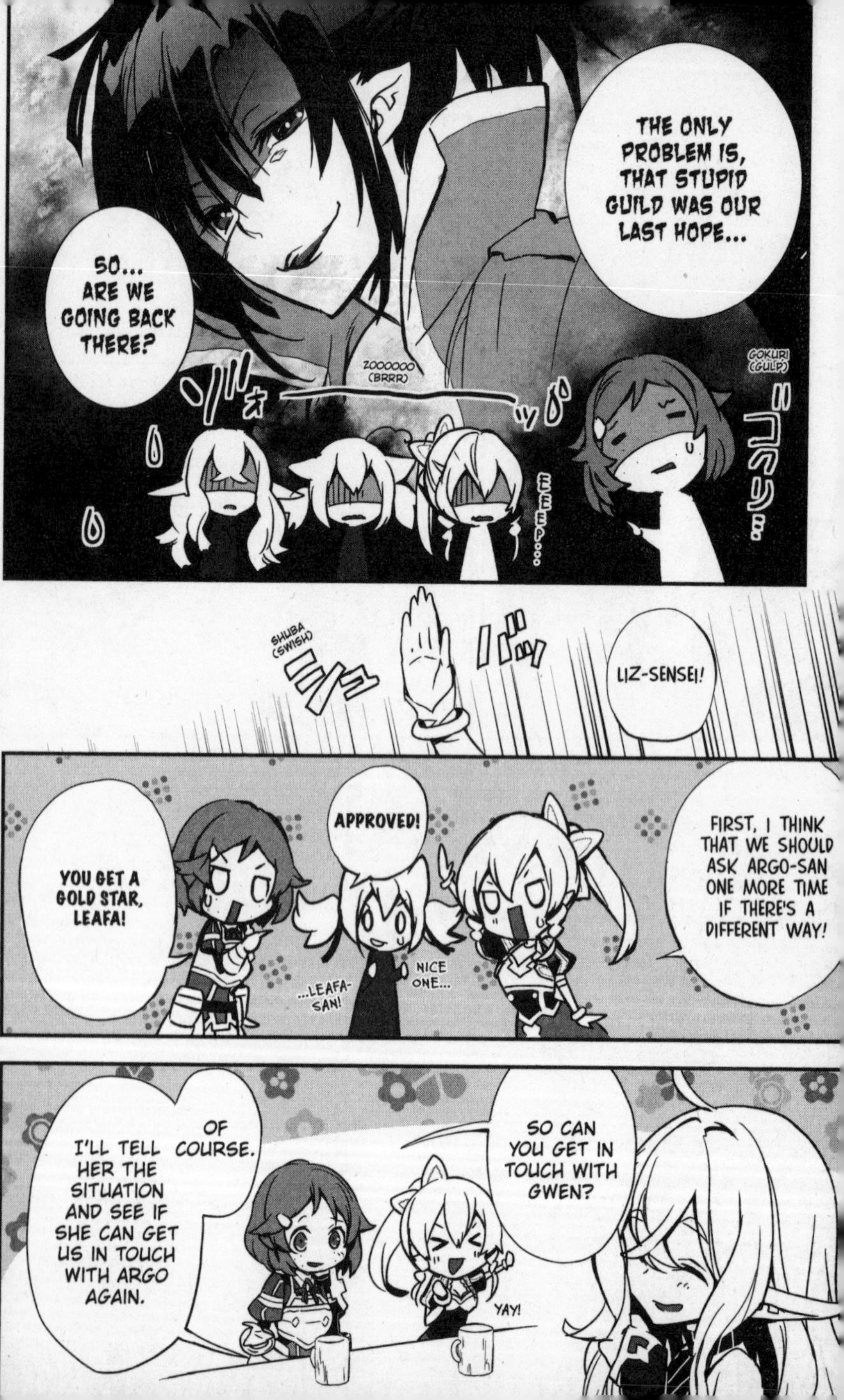
THE ONLY PROBLEM IS, THAT STUPID GUILD WAS OUR LAST HOPE...
SO... ARE WE GOING BACK THERE?
GOKURI (GULP)
ZOOOOOO (BRRR)
EEEEP...
LIZ-SENSEI!
SHUBA (SWISH)
FIRST, I THINK THAT WE SHOULD ASK ARGO-SAN ONE MORE TIME IF THERE'S A DIFFERENT WAY!
NICE ONE...
...LEAFA-SAN!
APPROVED!
YOU GET A GOLD STAR, LEAFA!
SO CAN YOU GET IN TOUCH WITH GWEN?
YAY!
OF COURSE.
I'LL TELL HER THE SITUATION AND SEE IF SHE CAN GET US IN TOUCH WITH ARGO AGAIN.

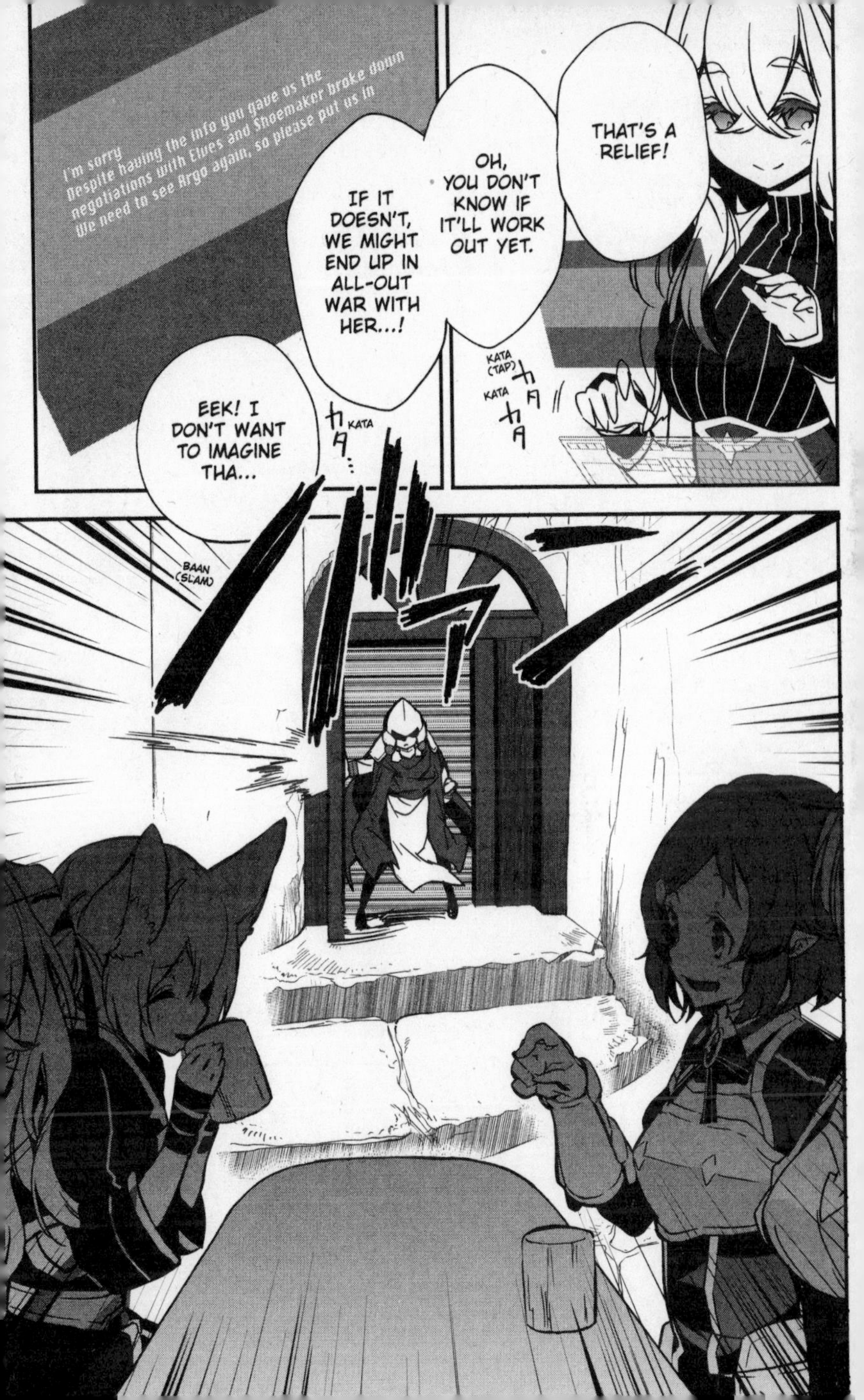
THAT'S A RELIEF!
OH, YOU DON'T KNOW IF IT'LL WORK OUT YET.
IF IT DOESN'T, WE MIGHT END UP IN ALL-OUT WAR WITH HER...!
KATA (TAP)
KATA
I'm sorry
Despite having the info you gave us the
negotiations with Elves and Shoemaker broke down
We need to see Argo again, so please put us in
EEK! I DON'T WANT TO IMAGINE THA...
KATA
BAAN (SLAM)

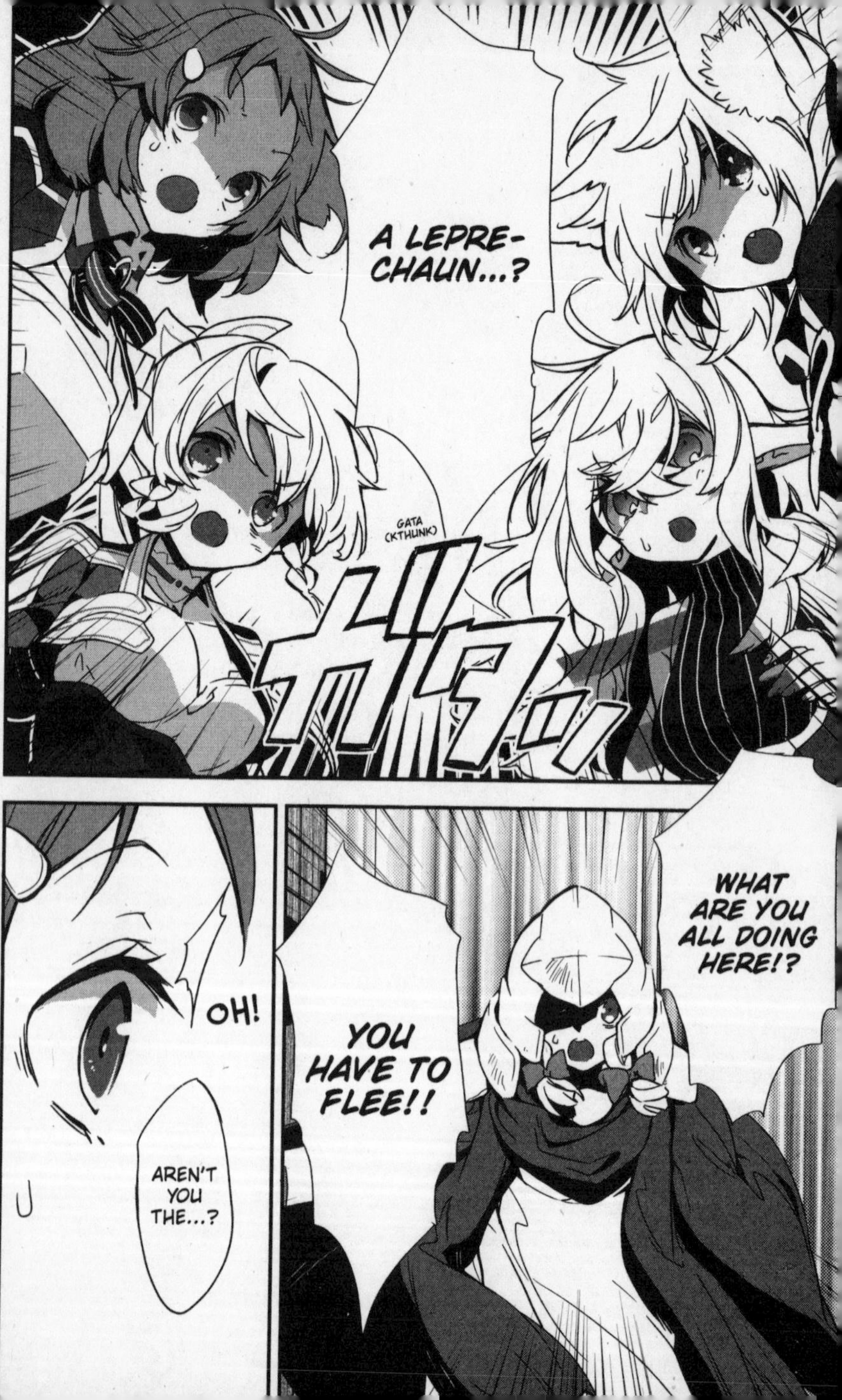
A LEPRE-CHAUN...?
GATA (KTHUNK)
WHAT ARE YOU ALL DOING HERE!?
YOU HAVE TO FLEE!!
OH!
AREN'T YOU THE...?

SWORD ART ONLINE
GIRLS' OPS

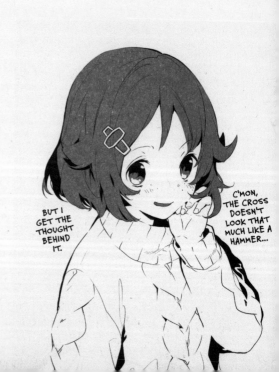

C'MON, THE CROSS DOESN'T LOOK THAT MUCH LIKE A HAMMER...
BUT I GET THE THOUGHT BEHIND IT.

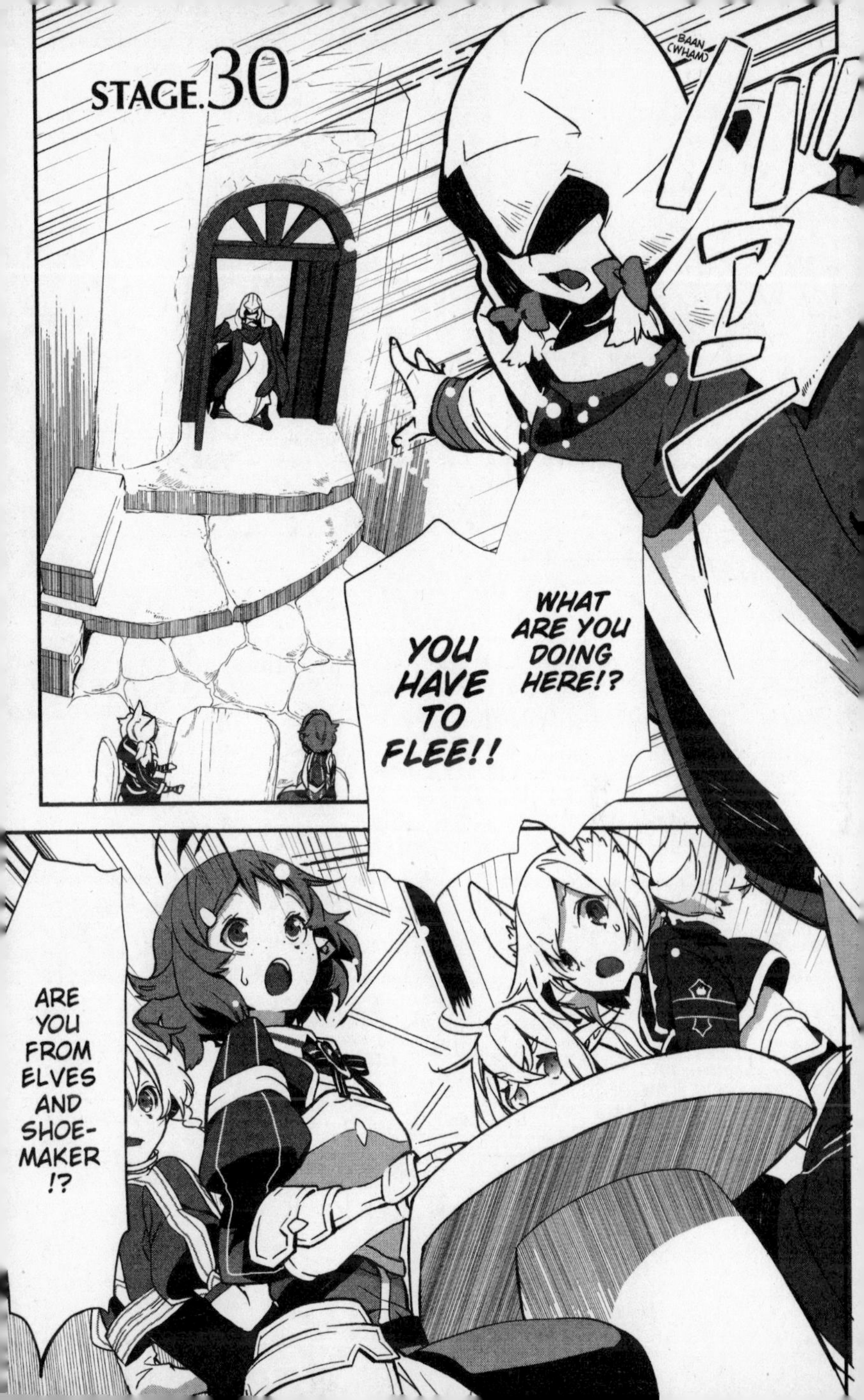
STAGE.30
BAAN (WHAM)
WHAT ARE YOU DOING HERE!? YOU HAVE TO FLEE!!
ARE YOU FROM ELVES AND SHOE-MAKER !?

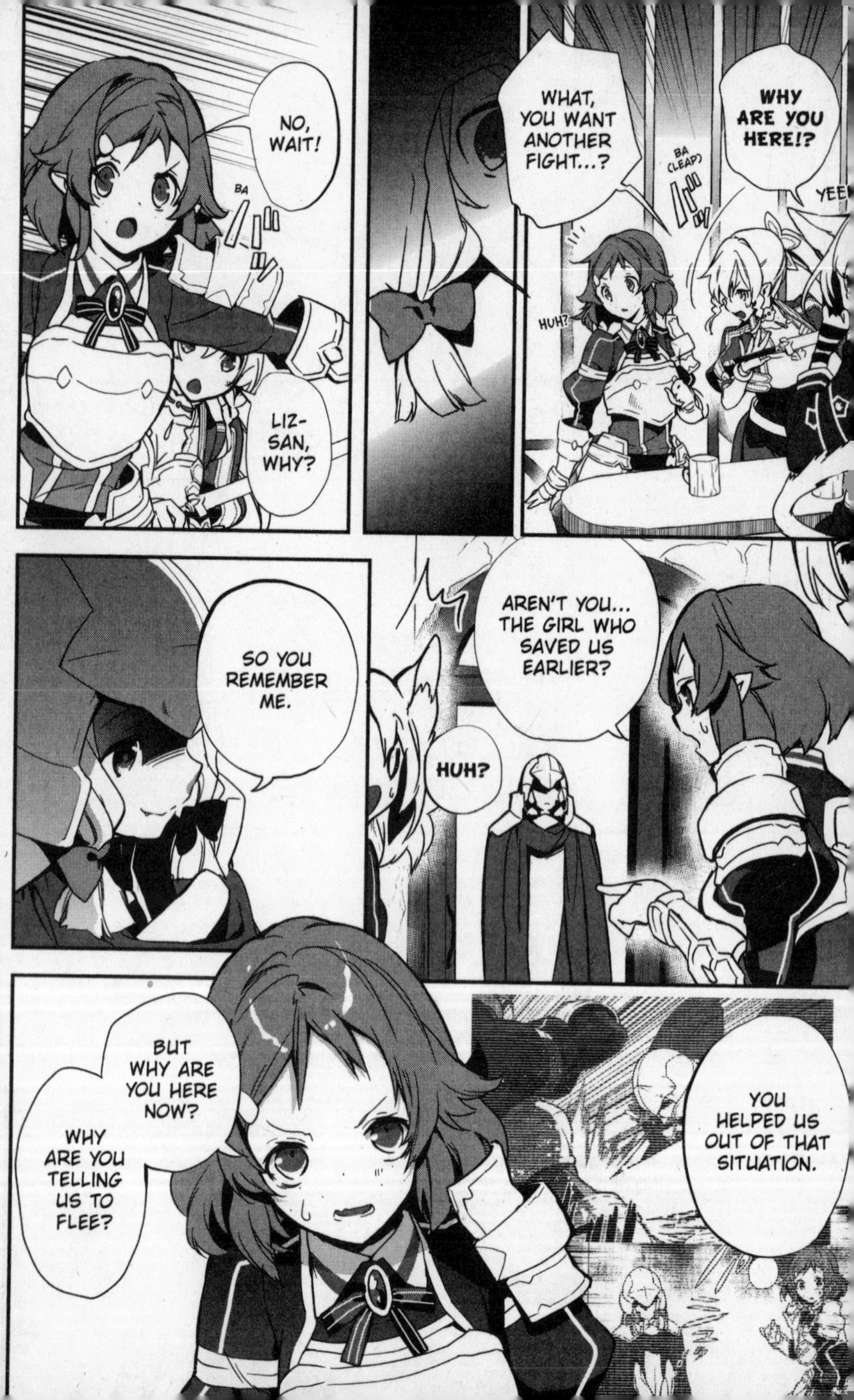
WHY ARE YOU HERE!?
YEE
BA (LEAP)
WHAT, YOU WANT ANOTHER FIGHT...?
HUH?
NO, WAIT!
BA
LIZ-SAN, WHY?
AREN'T YOU... THE GIRL WHO SAVED US EARLIER?
HUH?
SO YOU REMEMBER ME.
YOU HELPED US OUT OF THAT SITUATION.
BUT WHY ARE YOU HERE NOW?
WHY ARE YOU TELLING US TO FLEE?

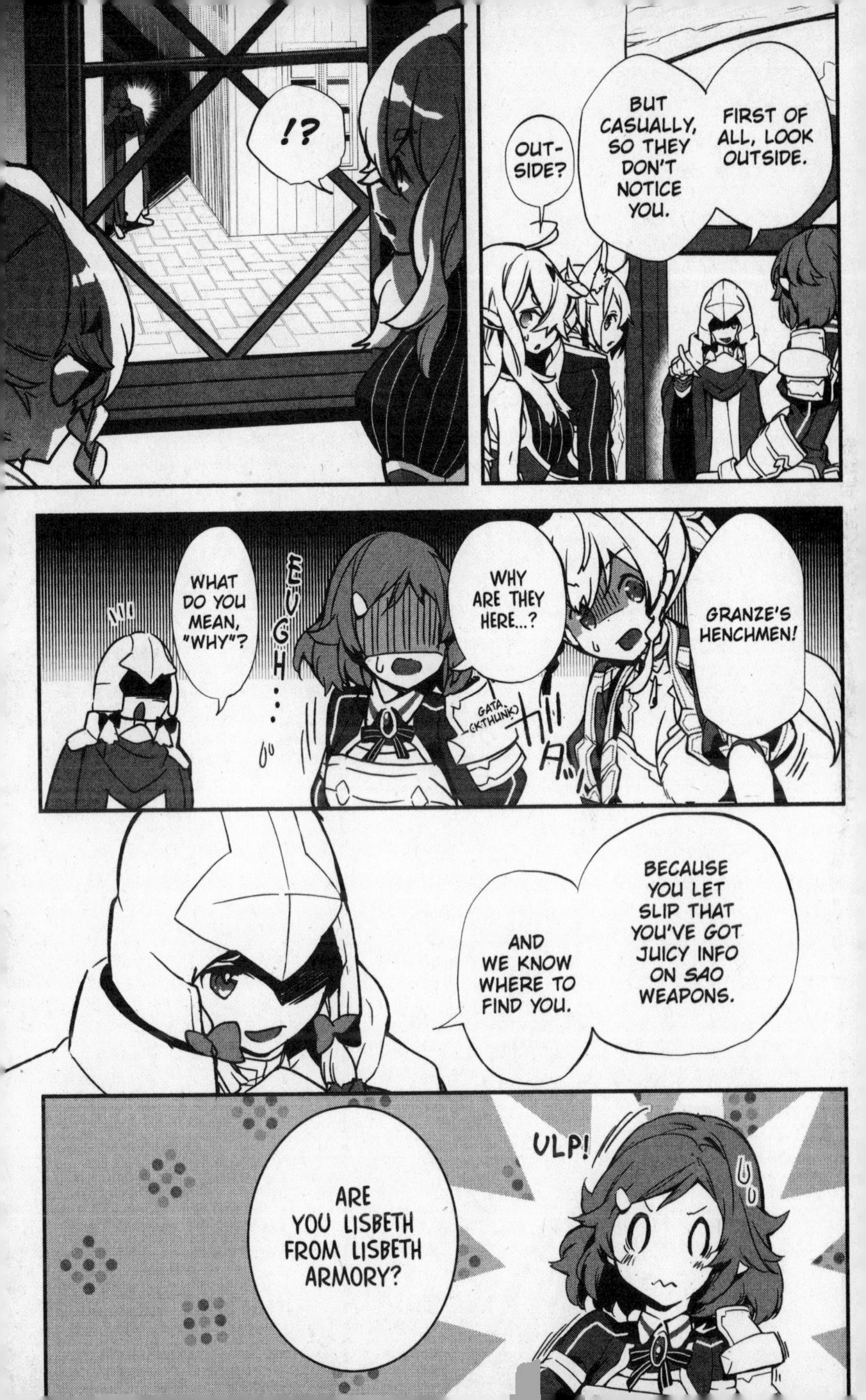
FIRST OF ALL, LOOK OUTSIDE.
BUT CASUALLY, SO THEY DON'T NOTICE YOU.
OUT-SIDE?
!?
GRANZE'S HENCHMEN!
WHY ARE THEY HERE...?
GATA (KTHUNK)
EUGH...
WHAT DO YOU MEAN, "WHY"?
BECAUSE YOU LET SLIP THAT YOU'VE GOT JUICY INFO ON SAO WEAPONS.
AND WE KNOW WHERE TO FIND YOU.
ULP!
ARE YOU LISBETH FROM LISBETH ARMORY?

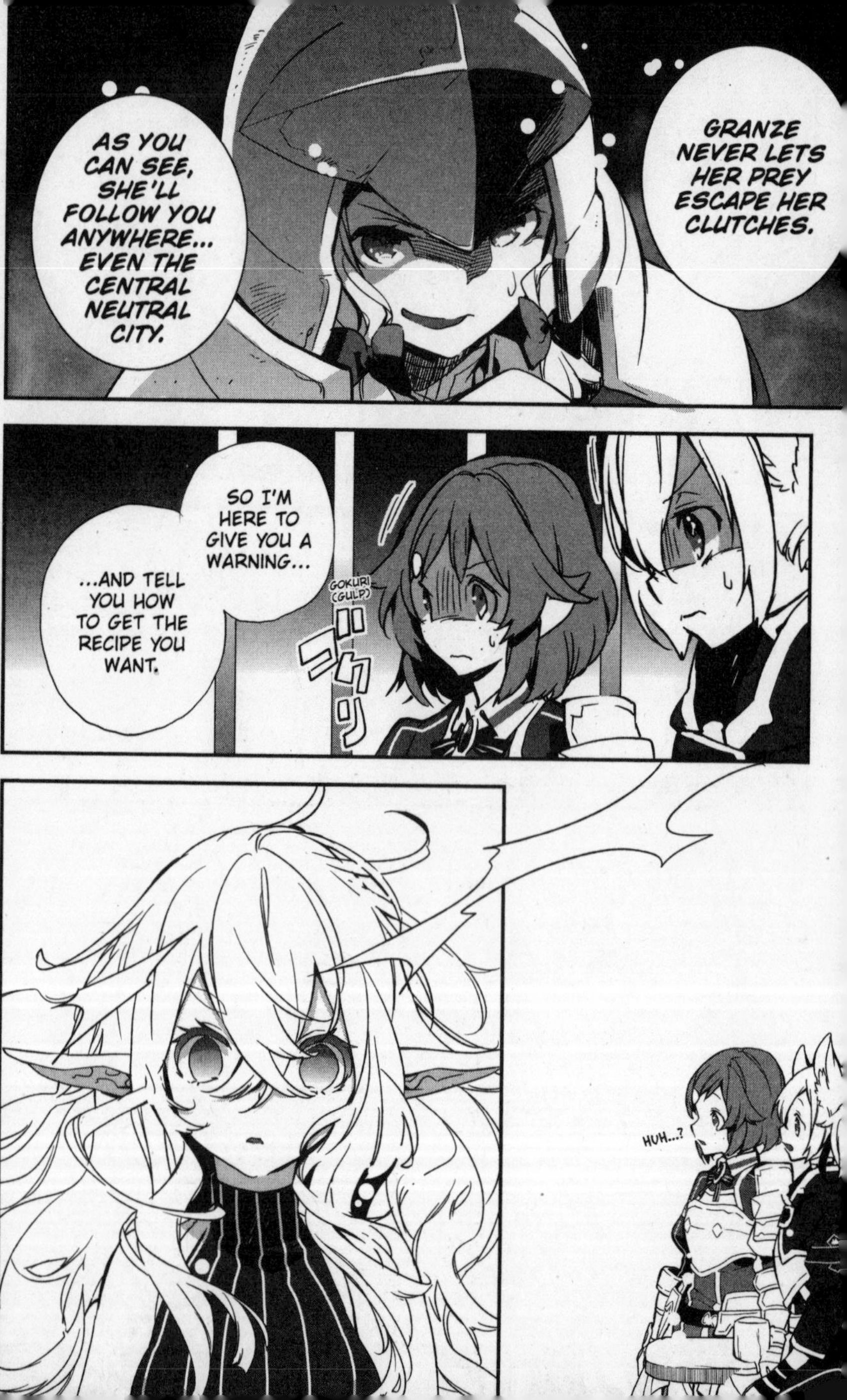
GRANZE NEVER LETS HER PREY ESCAPE HER CLUTCHES.
AS YOU CAN SEE, SHE'LL FOLLOW YOU ANYWHERE... EVEN THE CENTRAL NEUTRAL CITY.
GOKURI (GULP)
SO I'M HERE TO GIVE YOU A WARNING...
...AND TELL YOU HOW TO GET THE RECIPE YOU WANT.
HUH...?

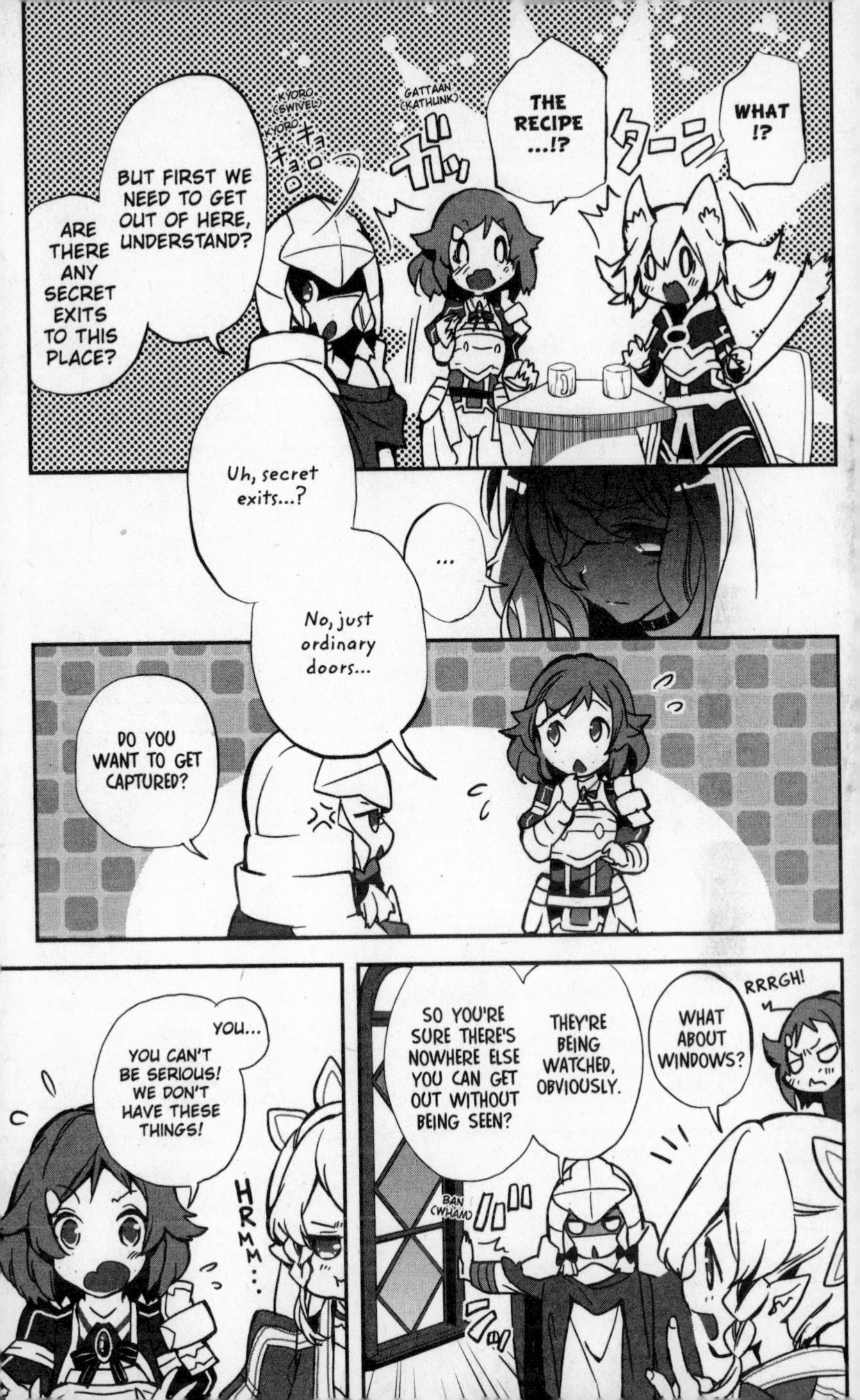
WHAT!?
THE RECIPE...!?
GATTAAN (KATHUNK)
KYORO KYORO (SWIVEL)
BUT FIRST WE NEED TO GET OUT OF HERE, UNDERSTAND?
ARE THERE ANY SECRET EXITS TO THIS PLACE?
...
Uh, secret exits...?
No, just ordinary doors...
DO YOU WANT TO GET CAPTURED?
RRRGH!
WHAT ABOUT WINDOWS?
THEY'RE BEING WATCHED, OBVIOUSLY.
SO YOU'RE SURE THERE'S NOWHERE ELSE YOU CAN GET OUT WITHOUT BEING SEEN?
BAN (WHAM)
YOU...
YOU CAN'T BE SERIOUS! WE DON'T HAVE THESE THINGS!
HRMM...

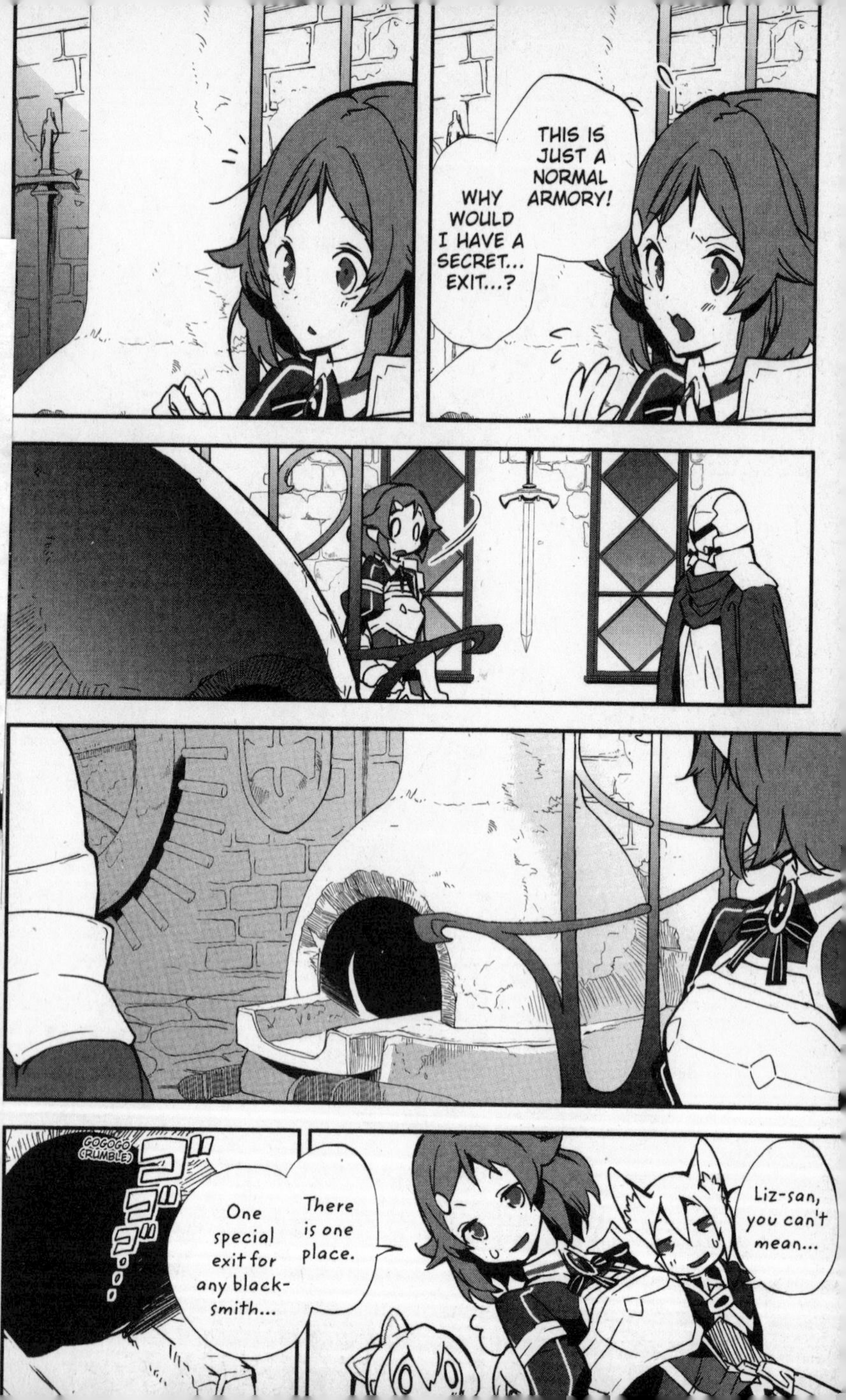
THIS IS JUST A NORMAL ARMORY!
WHY WOULD I HAVE A SECRET... EXIT...?
Liz-san, you can't mean...
There is one place.
One special exit for any black-smith...
GOGOGO (RUMBLE)
ゴゴゴ

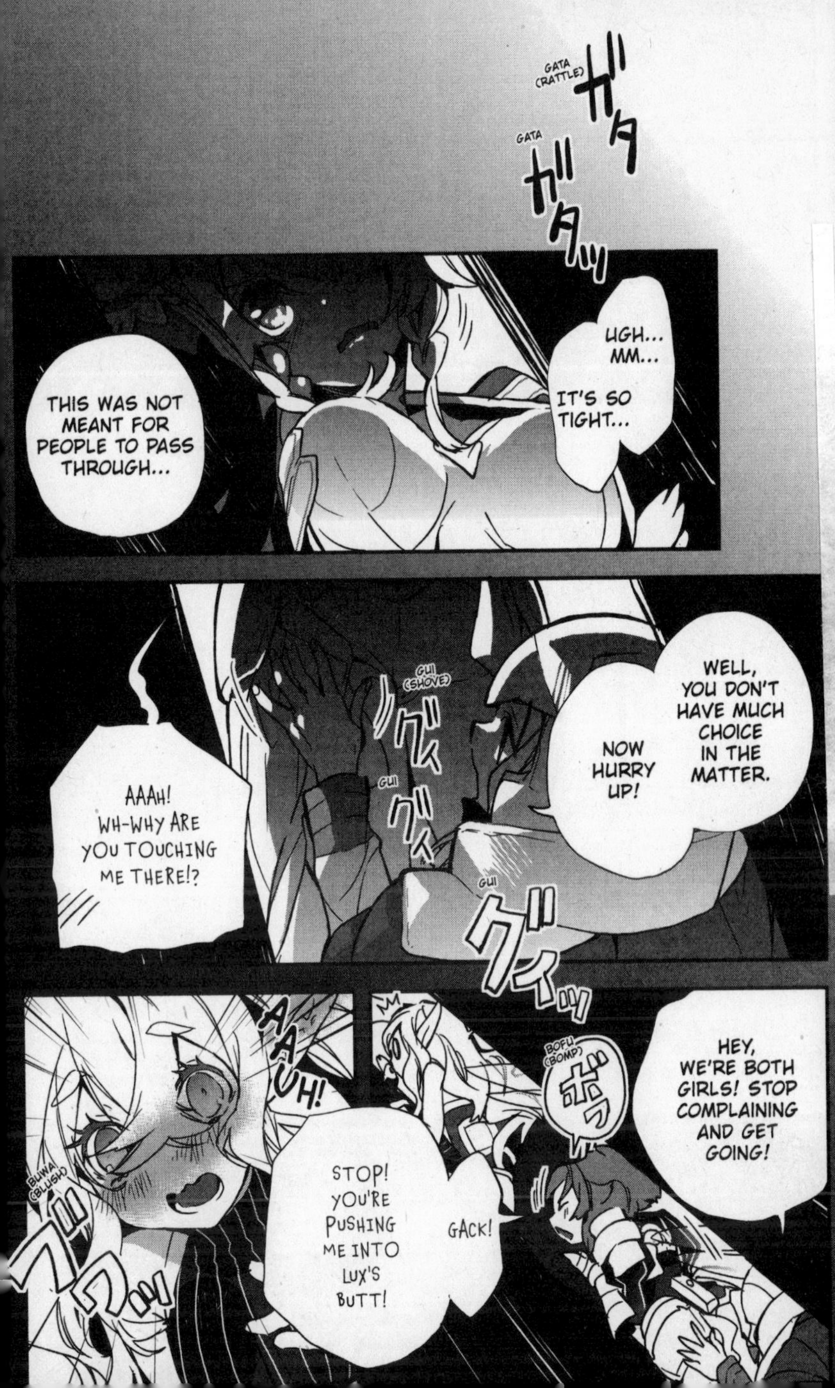
GATA (RATTLE)
GATA
UGH... MM...
IT'S SO TIGHT...
THIS WAS NOT MEANT FOR PEOPLE TO PASS THROUGH...
WELL, YOU DON'T HAVE MUCH CHOICE IN THE MATTER.
NOW HURRY UP!
GUI (SHOVE)
GUI
GUI
AAAH! WH-WHY ARE YOU TOUCHING ME THERE!?
HEY, WE'RE BOTH GIRLS! STOP COMPLAINING AND GET GOING!
BOFU (BOMP)
GACK!
AAAUH!
STOP! YOU'RE PUSHING ME INTO LUX'S BUTT!
BUWA (BLUSH)

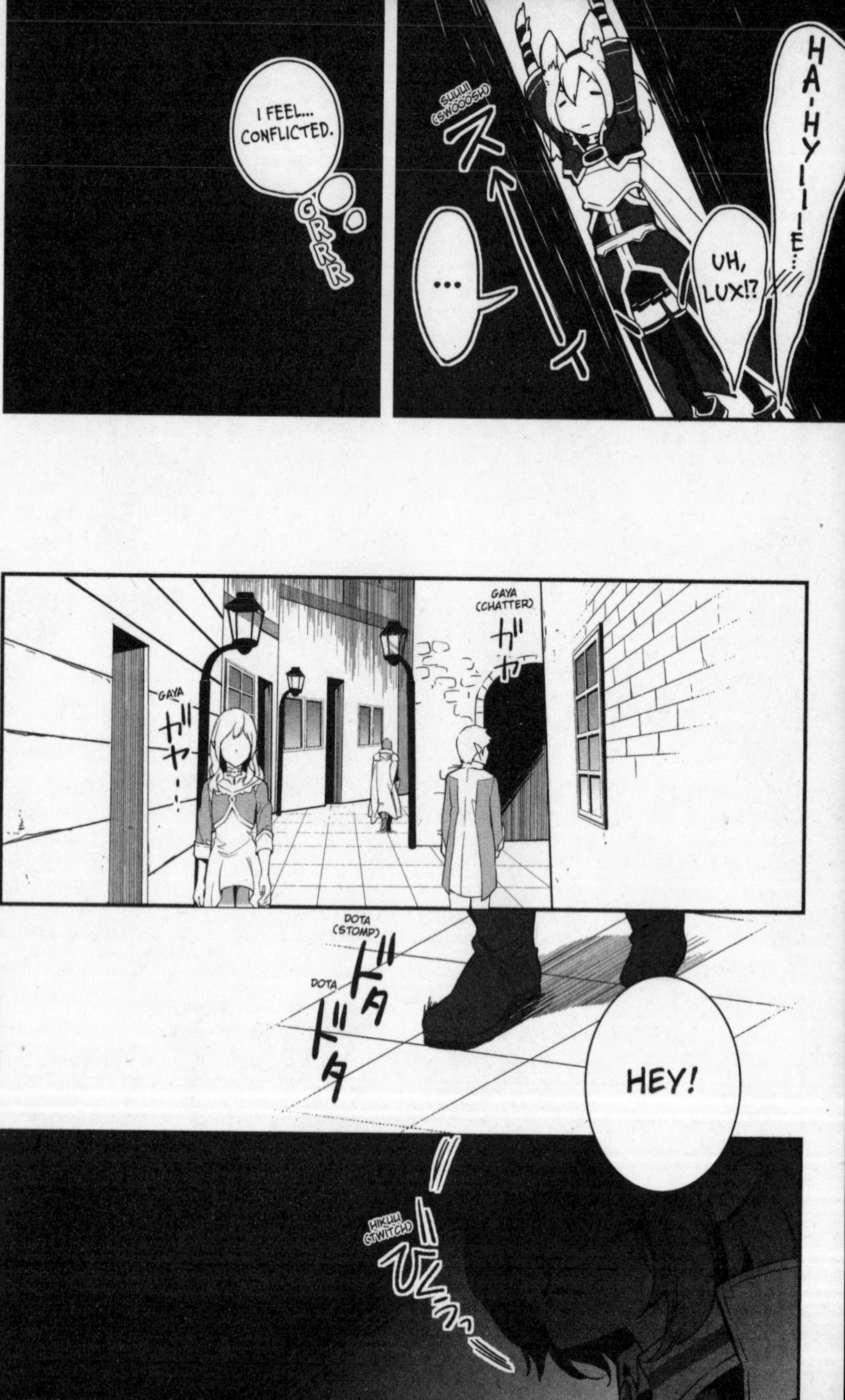
HA-HYIIIIE...
UH, LUX!?
SUUUU (SWOOOSH)
...
I FEEL... CONFLICTED.
GRRR
GAYA (CHATTER)
GAYA
DOTA (STOMP)
DOTA
HEY!
HIKUU (TWITCH)

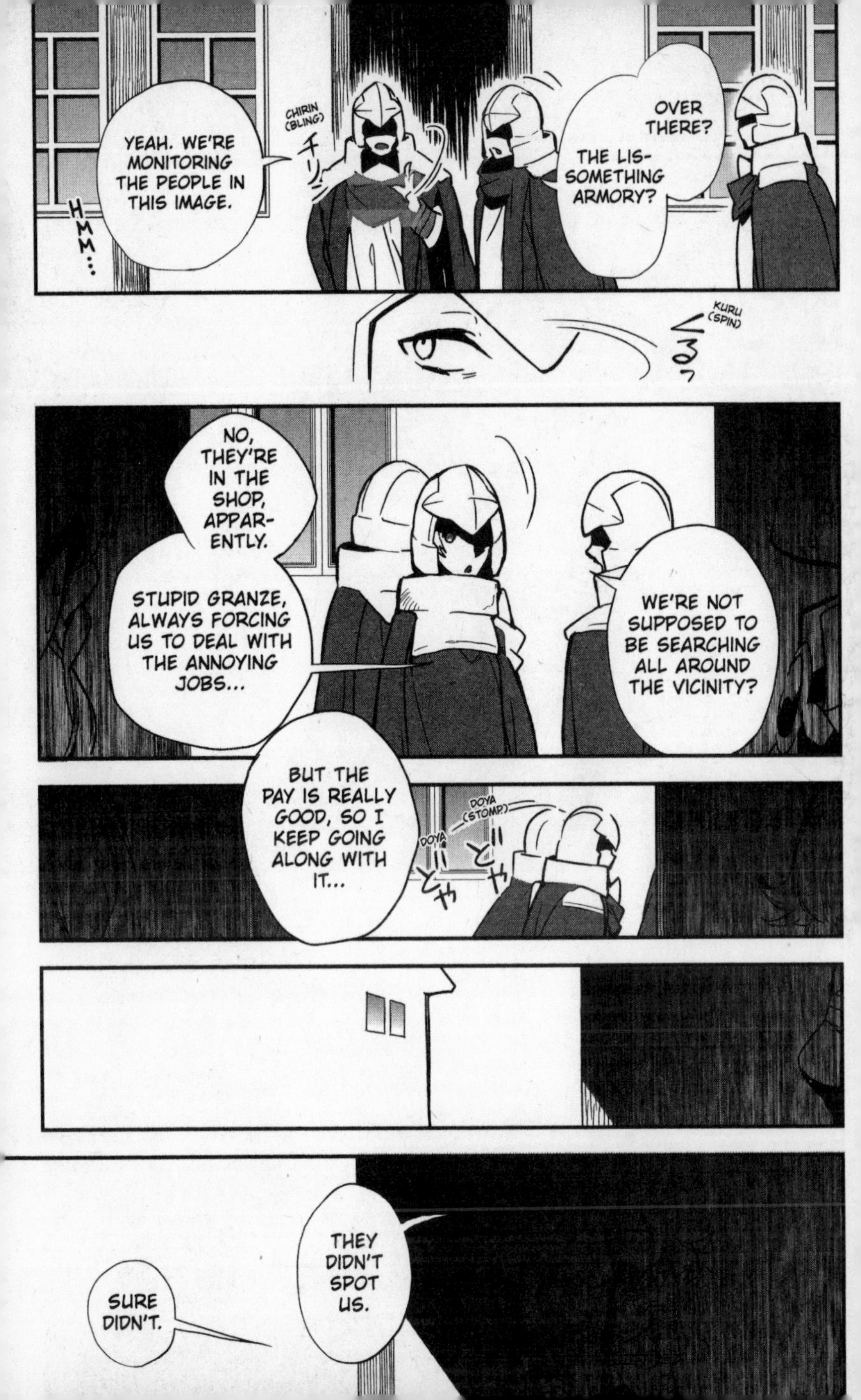
OVER THERE?
THE LIS-SOMETHING ARMORY?
CHIRIN (BLING)
YEAH. WE'RE MONITORING THE PEOPLE IN THIS IMAGE.
HMM...
KURU (SPIN)
WE'RE NOT SUPPOSED TO BE SEARCHING ALL AROUND THE VICINITY?
NO, THEY'RE IN THE SHOP, APPARENTLY.
STUPID GRANZE, ALWAYS FORCING US TO DEAL WITH THE ANNOYING JOBS...
DOYA (STOMP)
DOYA
BUT THE PAY IS REALLY GOOD, SO I KEEP GOING ALONG WITH IT...
THEY DIDN'T SPOT US.
SURE DIDN'T.

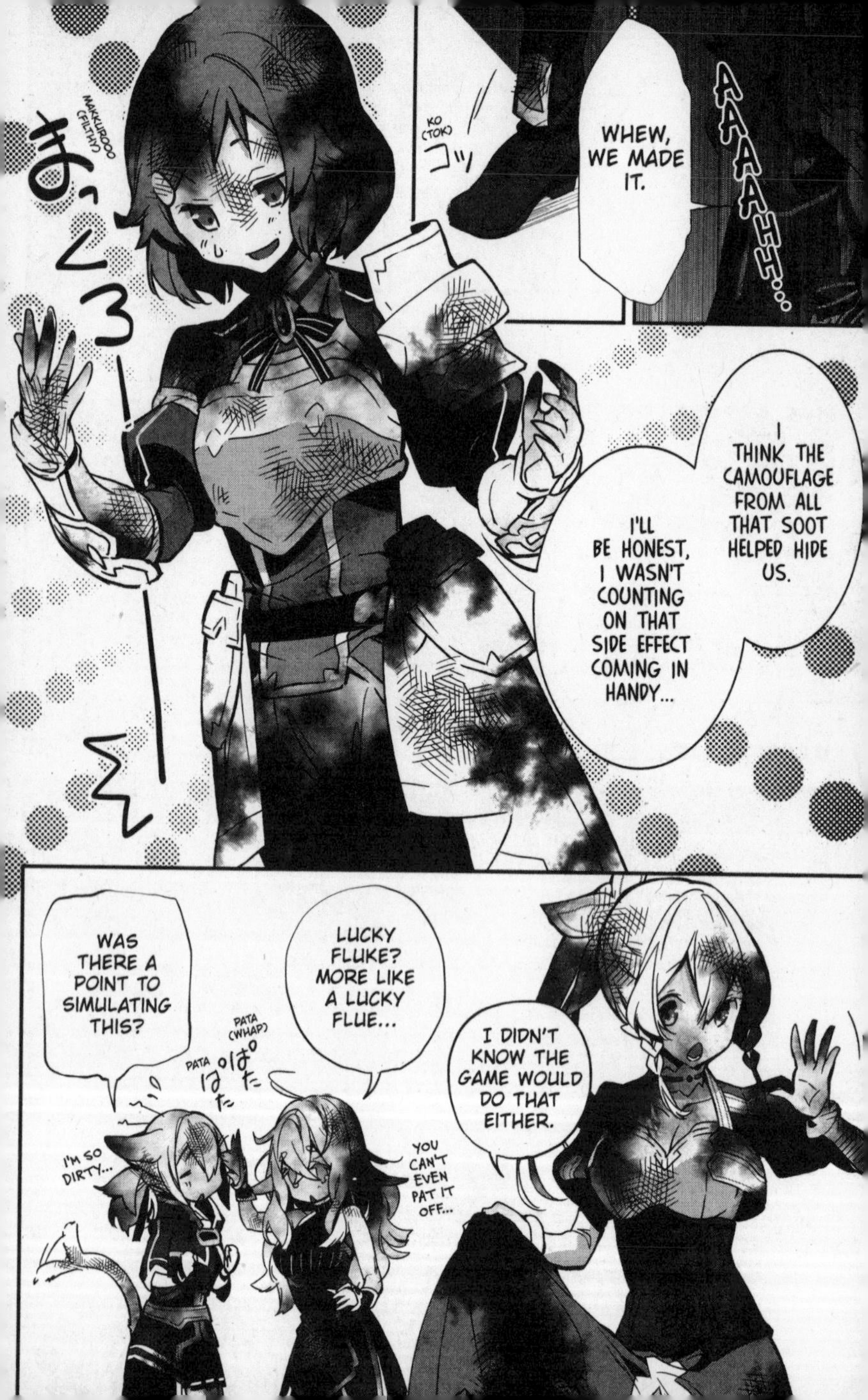
AAAAAHH...
WHEW, WE MADE IT.
KO (TOK)
コッ
I THINK THE CAMOUFLAGE FROM ALL THAT SOOT HELPED HIDE US.
I'LL BE HONEST, I WASN'T COUNTING ON THAT SIDE EFFECT COMING IN HANDY...
MAKKUROOO (FILTHY)
まっくろー
I DIDN'T KNOW THE GAME WOULD DO THAT EITHER.
LUCKY FLUKE? MORE LIKE A LUCKY FLUE...
YOU CAN'T EVEN PAT IT OFF...
PATA (WHAP)
PATA
ぱたぱた
WAS THERE A POINT TO SIMULATING THIS?
I'M SO DIRTY...

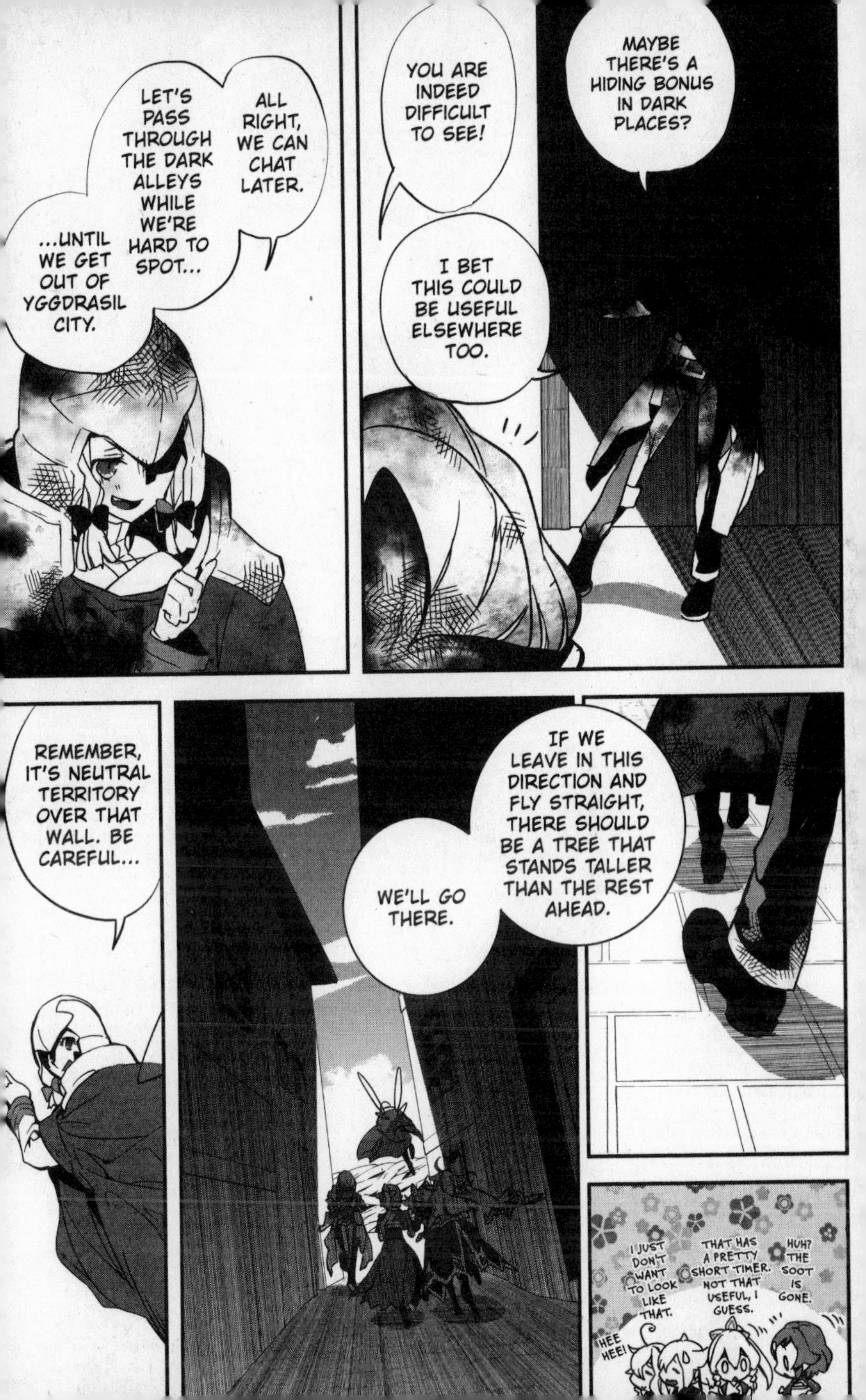
MAYBE THERE'S A HIDING BONUS IN DARK PLACES?
YOU ARE INDEED DIFFICULT TO SEE!
I BET THIS COULD BE USEFUL ELSEWHERE TOO.
ALL RIGHT, WE CAN CHAT LATER.
LET'S PASS THROUGH THE DARK ALLEYS WHILE WE'RE HARD TO SPOT...
...UNTIL WE GET OUT OF YGGDRASIL CITY.
IF WE LEAVE IN THIS DIRECTION AND FLY STRAIGHT, THERE SHOULD BE A TREE THAT STANDS TALLER THAN THE REST AHEAD.
HUH? THE SOOT IS GONE.
THAT HAS A PRETTY SHORT TIMER. NOT THAT USEFUL, I GUESS.
I JUST DON'T WANT TO LOOK LIKE THAT.
HEE HEE!
WE'LL GO THERE.
REMEMBER, IT'S NEUTRAL TERRITORY OVER THAT WALL. BE CAREFUL...

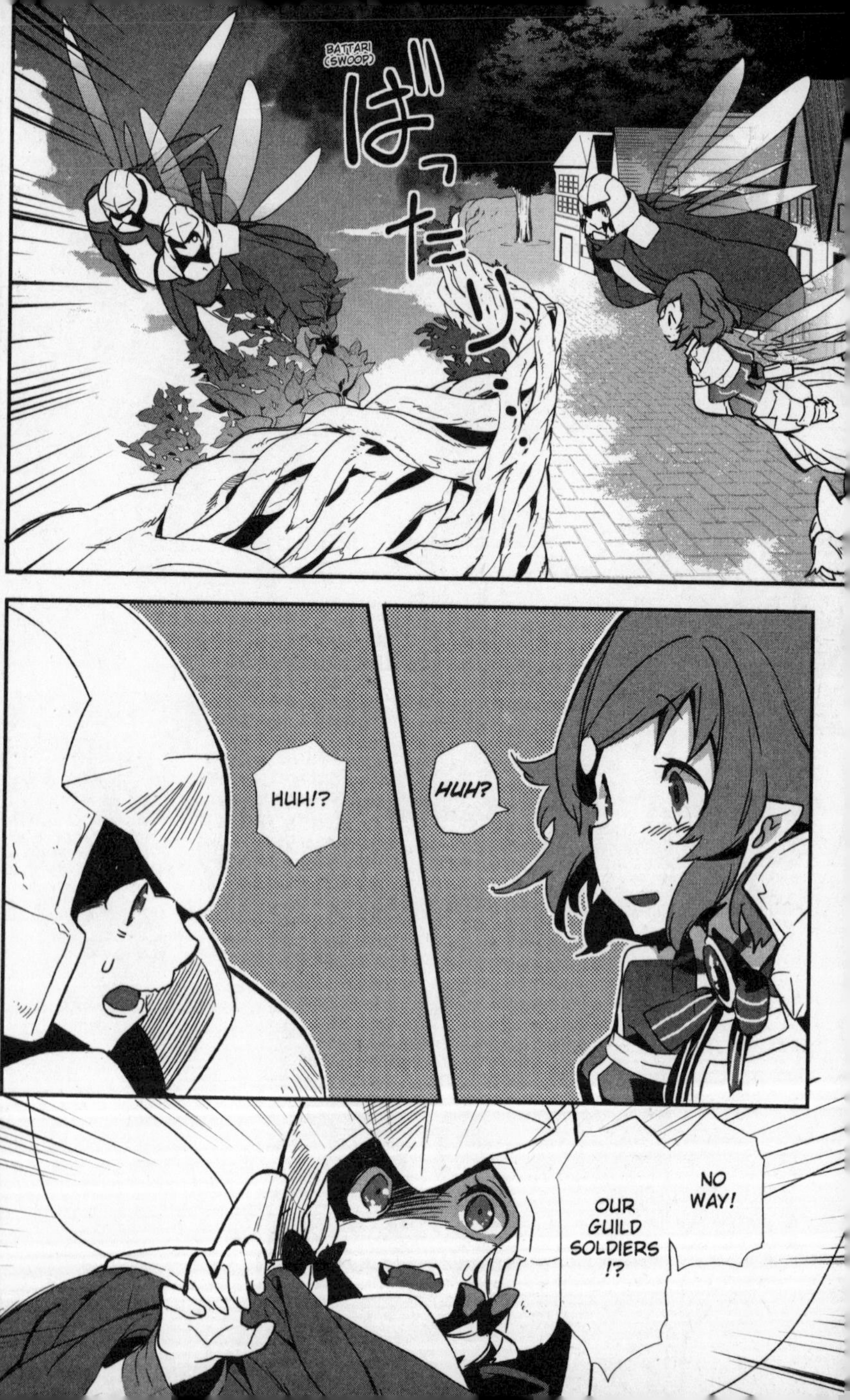
BATTARI (SWOOP)
ばったり
HUH?
HUH!?
NO WAY!
OUR GUILD SOLDIERS !?

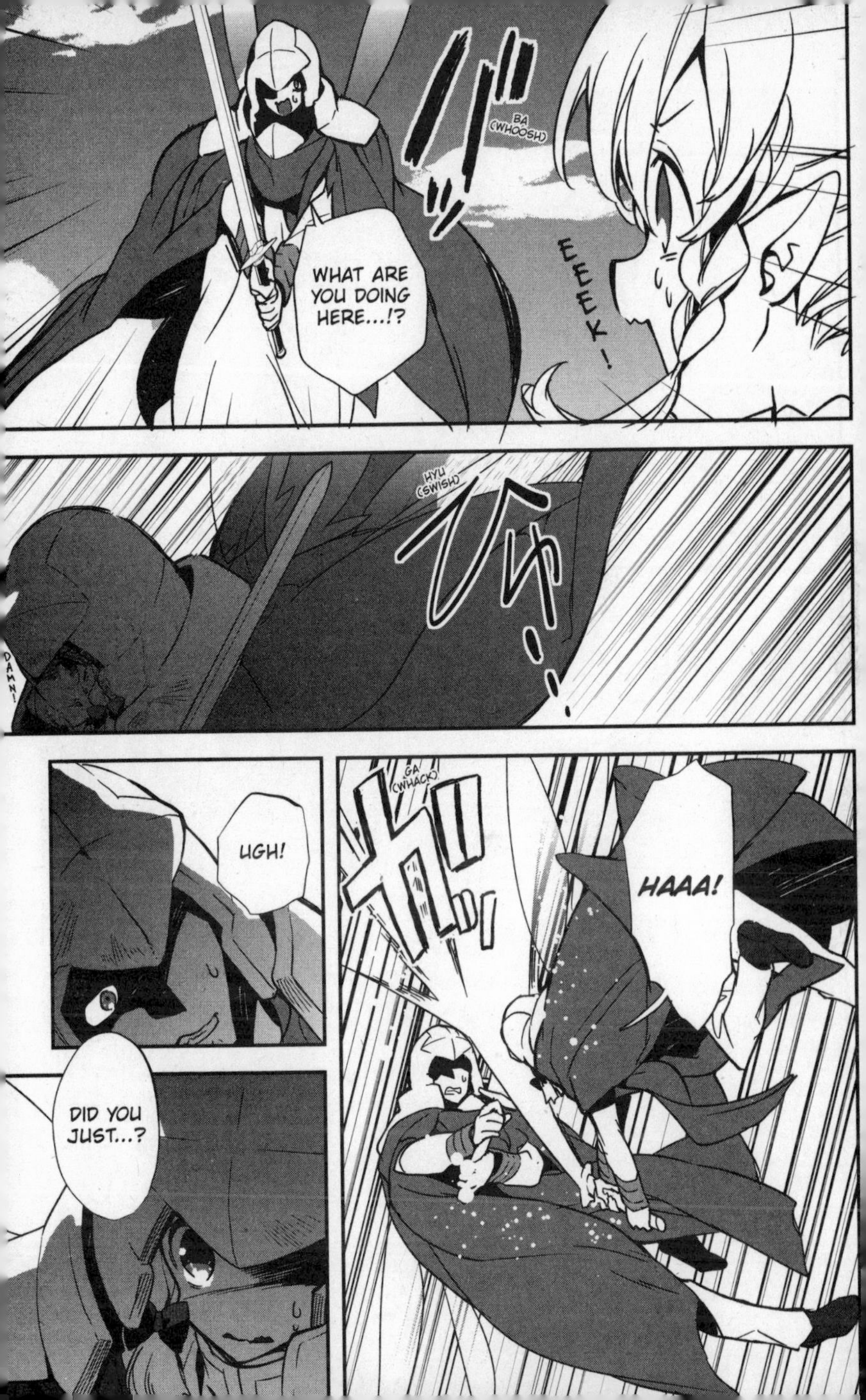
BA (WHOOSH)
EEEEK!
WHAT ARE YOU DOING HERE...!?
HYU (SWISH)
DAMN!
GA (WHACK)
HAAA!
UGH!
DID YOU JUST...?

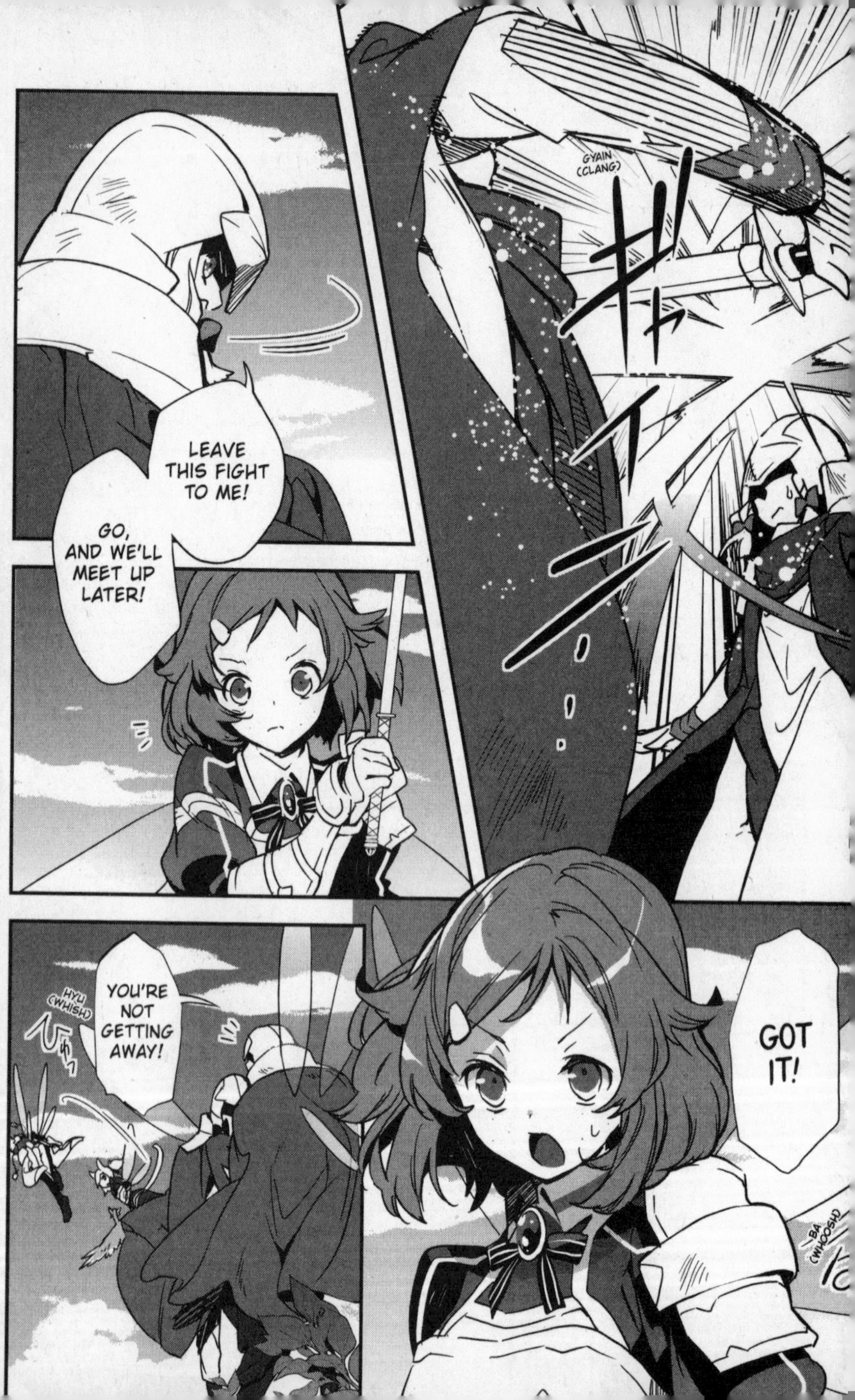

GYAIN (CLANG)
LEAVE THIS FIGHT TO ME!
GO, AND WE'LL MEET UP LATER!
GOT IT!
BA (WHOOSH)
YOU'RE NOT GETTING AWAY!
HYU (WHISH)

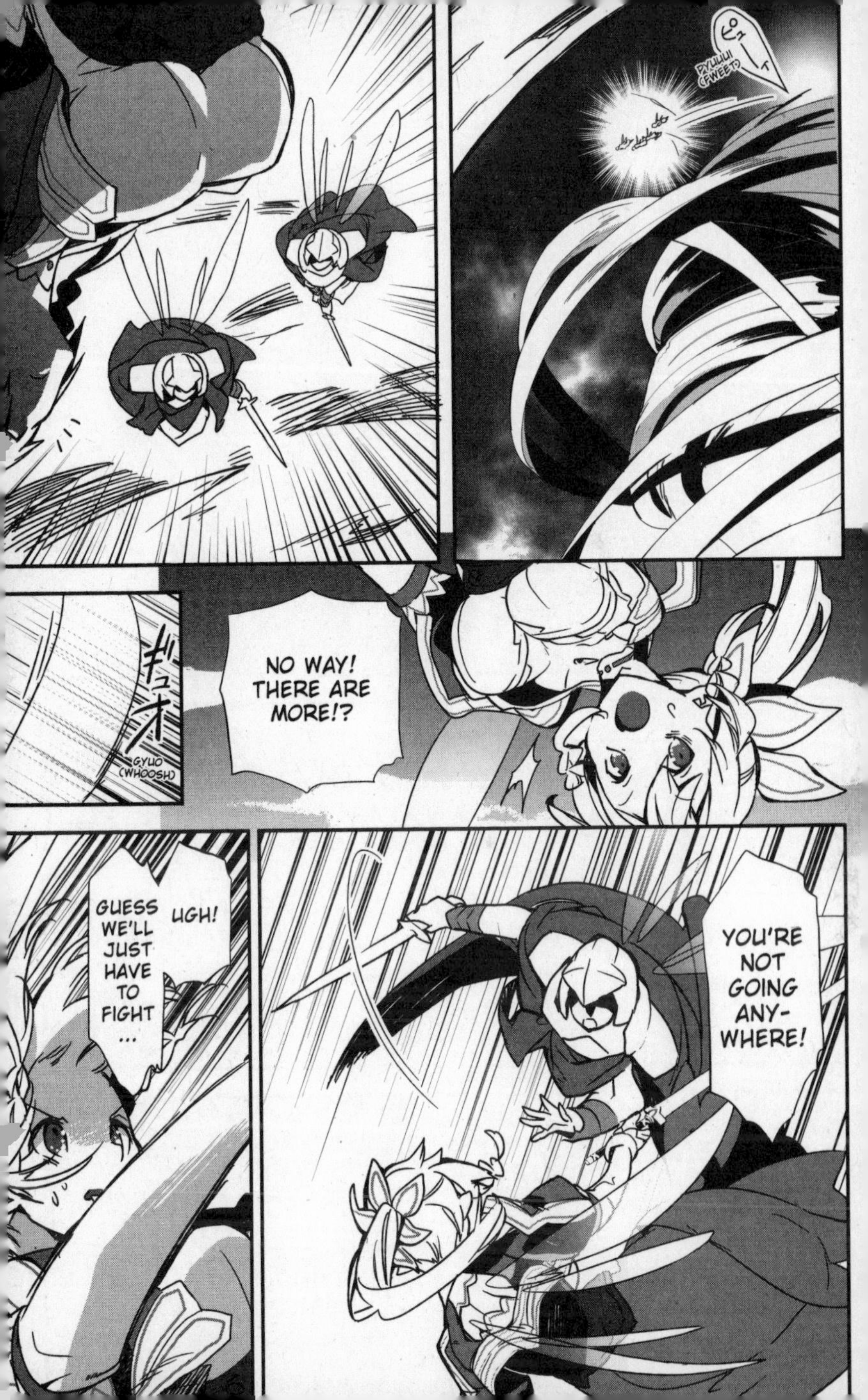
PYUHUI (FWEET)
NO WAY! THERE ARE MORE!?
GYUO (WHOOSH)
YOU'RE NOT GOING ANY-WHERE!
UGH!
GUESS WE'LL JUST HAVE TO FIGHT...

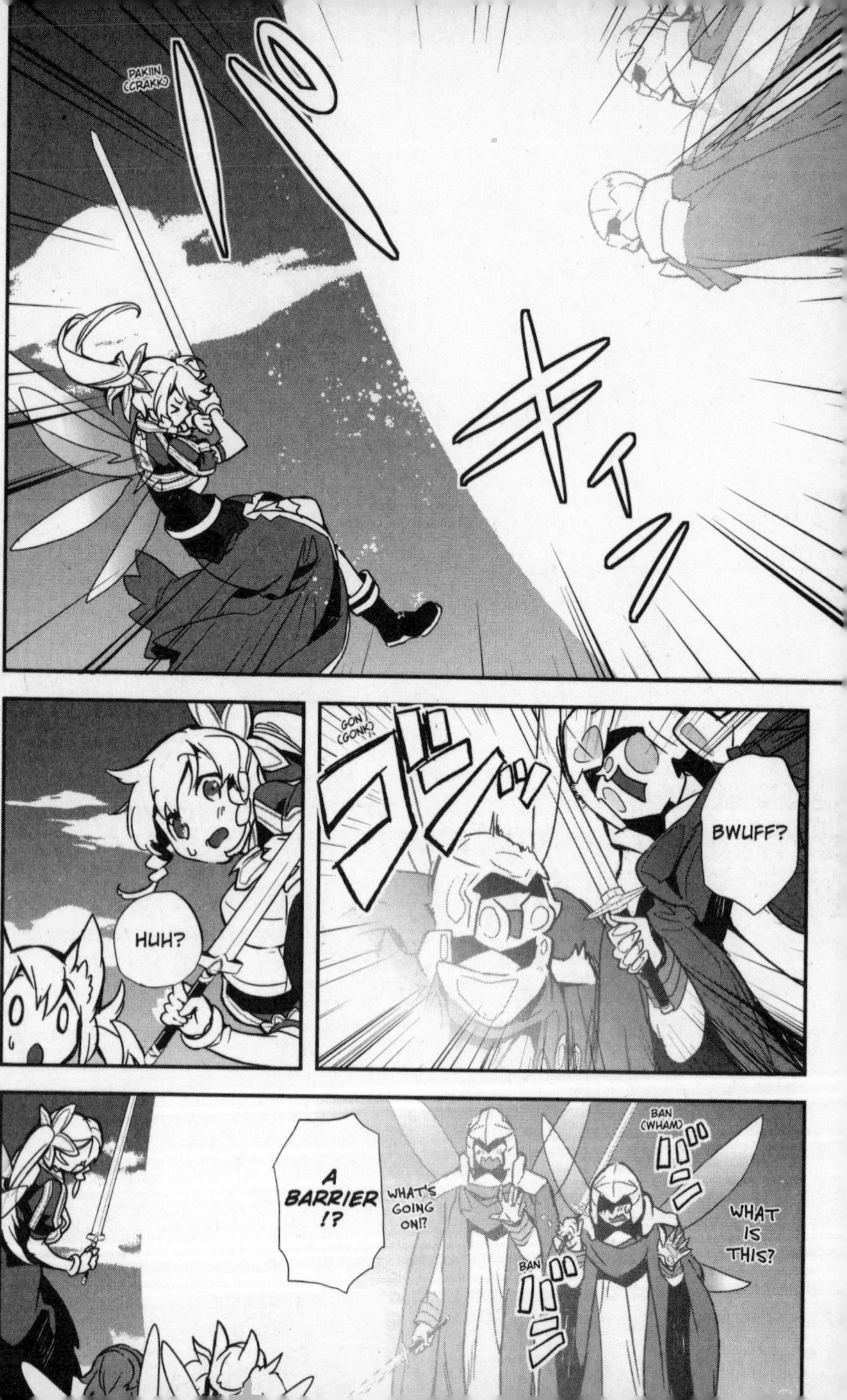
PAKIIN (CRAKK)
GON (GONK)
BWUFF?
HUH?
BAN (WHAM)
WHAT IS THIS?
BAN
WHAT'S GOING ON!?
A BARRIER!?

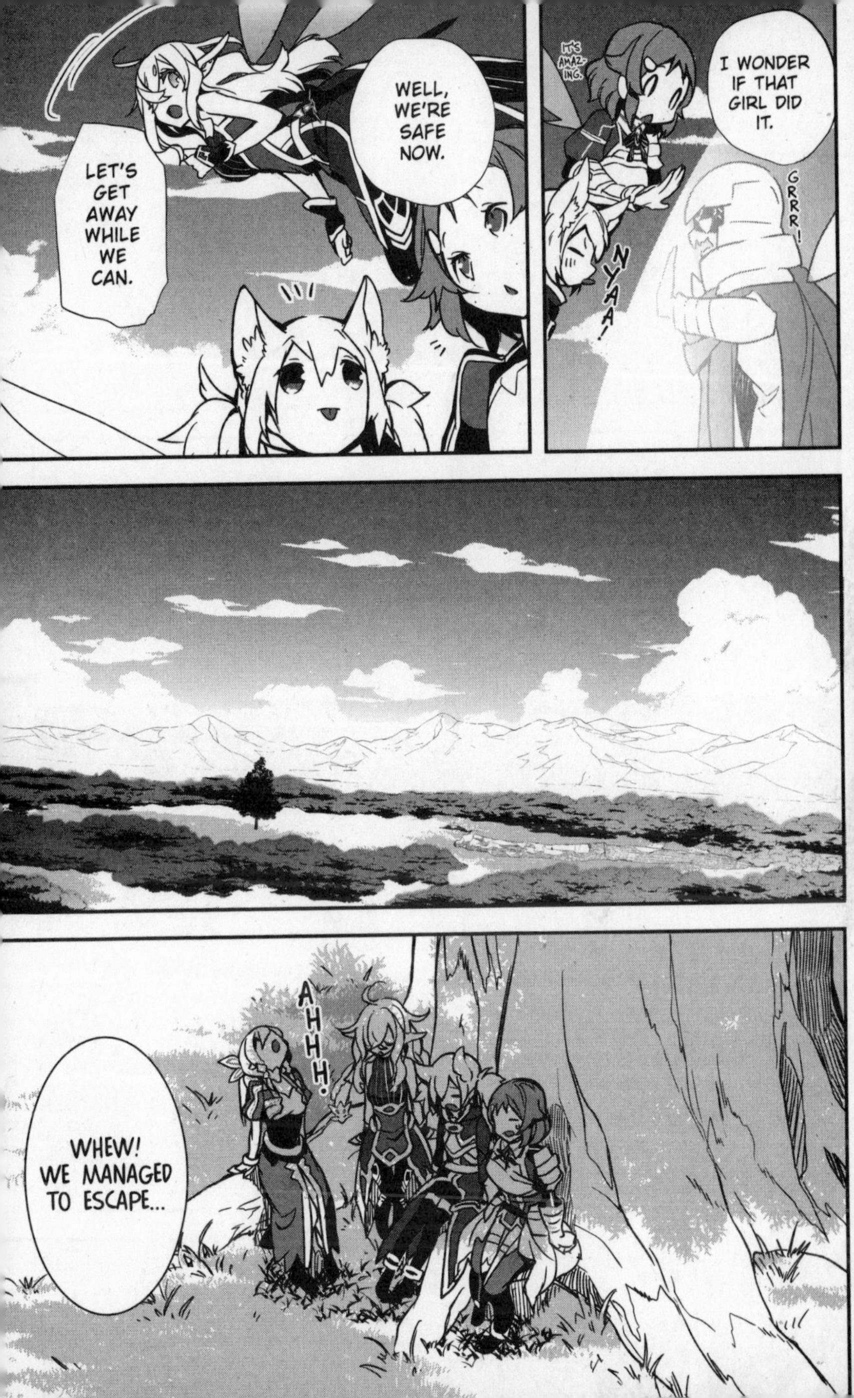
I WONDER IF THAT GIRL DID IT.
IT'S AMAZ-ING.
GRRR!
NYAA!
WELL, WE'RE SAFE NOW.
LET'S GET AWAY WHILE WE CAN.
AHHH.
WHEW! WE MANAGED TO ESCAPE...

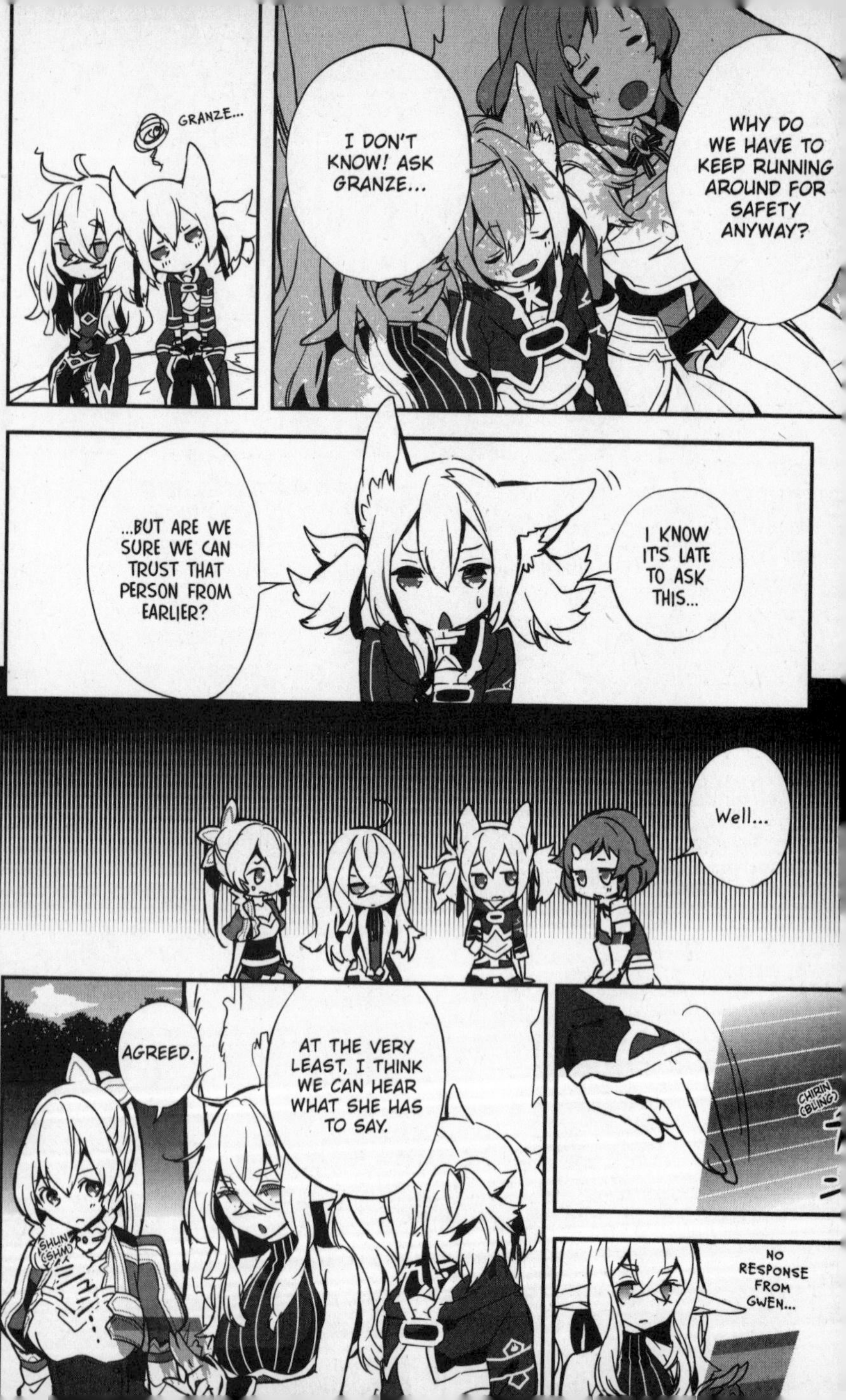
WHY DO WE HAVE TO KEEP RUNNING AROUND FOR SAFETY ANYWAY?
I DON'T KNOW! ASK GRANZE...
GRANZE...
I KNOW IT'S LATE TO ASK THIS...
...BUT ARE WE SURE WE CAN TRUST THAT PERSON FROM EARLIER?
Well...
CHIRIN (BLING)
NO RESPONSE FROM GWEN...
AT THE VERY LEAST, I THINK WE CAN HEAR WHAT SHE HAS TO SAY.
AGREED.
SHUN (SHM)

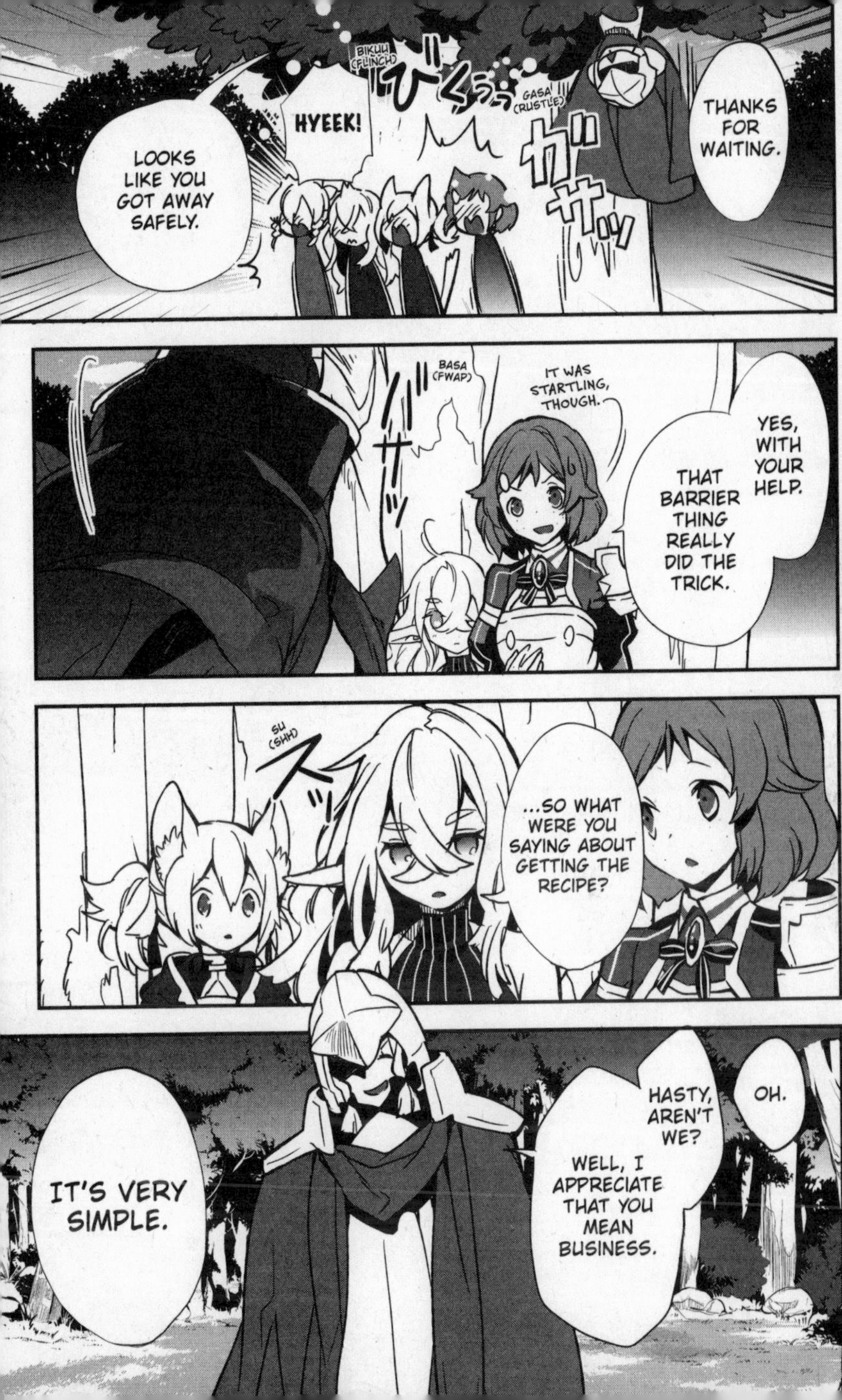
THANKS FOR WAITING.
GASA (RUSTLE)
BIKUU (FLINCH)
HYEEK!
LOOKS LIKE YOU GOT AWAY SAFELY.
YES, WITH YOUR HELP.
THAT BARRIER THING REALLY DID THE TRICK.
IT WAS STARTLING, THOUGH.
BASA (FWAP)
...SO WHAT WERE YOU SAYING ABOUT GETTING THE RECIPE?
SU (SHH)
OH.
HASTY, AREN'T WE?
WELL, I APPRECIATE THAT YOU MEAN BUSINESS.
IT'S VERY SIMPLE.

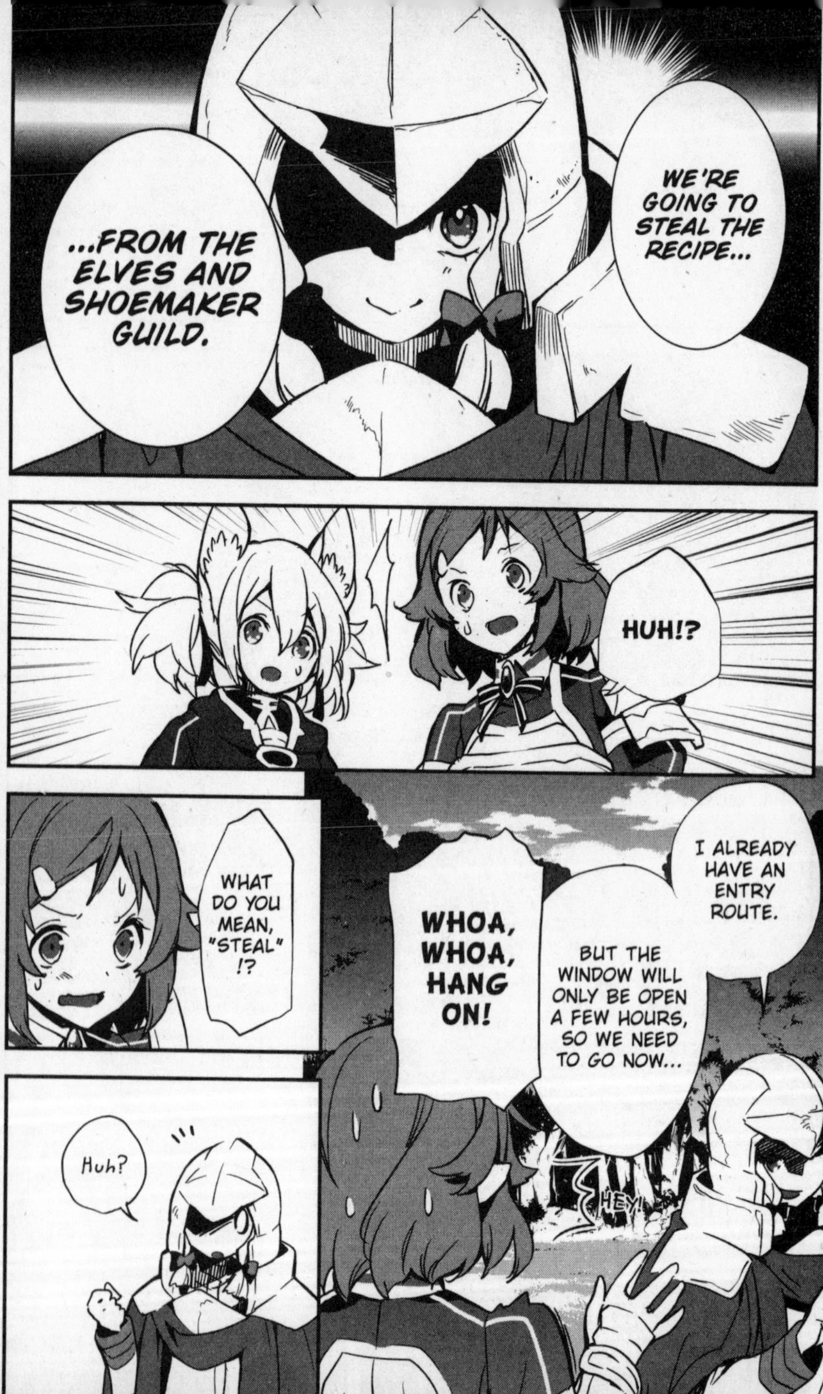
WE'RE GOING TO STEAL THE RECIPE...
...FROM THE ELVES AND SHOEMAKER GUILD.
HUH!?
I ALREADY HAVE AN ENTRY ROUTE.
BUT THE WINDOW WILL ONLY BE OPEN A FEW HOURS, SO WE NEED TO GO NOW...
WHOA, WHOA, HANG ON!
HEY!
WHAT DO YOU MEAN, "STEAL"!?
Huh?

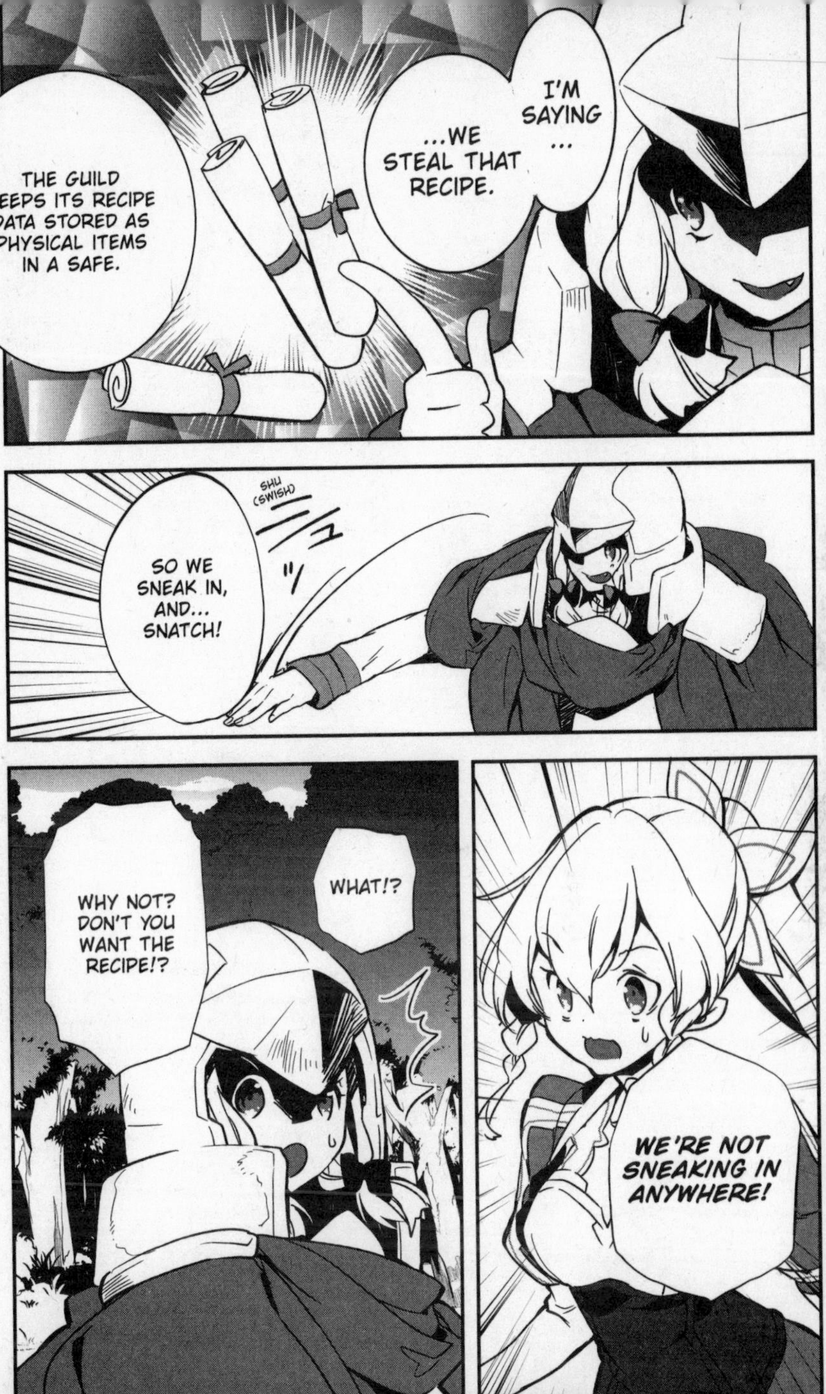
I'M SAYING ...
...WE STEAL THAT RECIPE.
THE GUILD KEEPS ITS RECIPE DATA STORED AS PHYSICAL ITEMS IN A SAFE.
SHU (SWISH)
SO WE SNEAK IN, AND... SNATCH!
WE'RE NOT SNEAKING IN ANYWHERE!
WHAT!?
WHY NOT? DON'T YOU WANT THE RECIPE!?

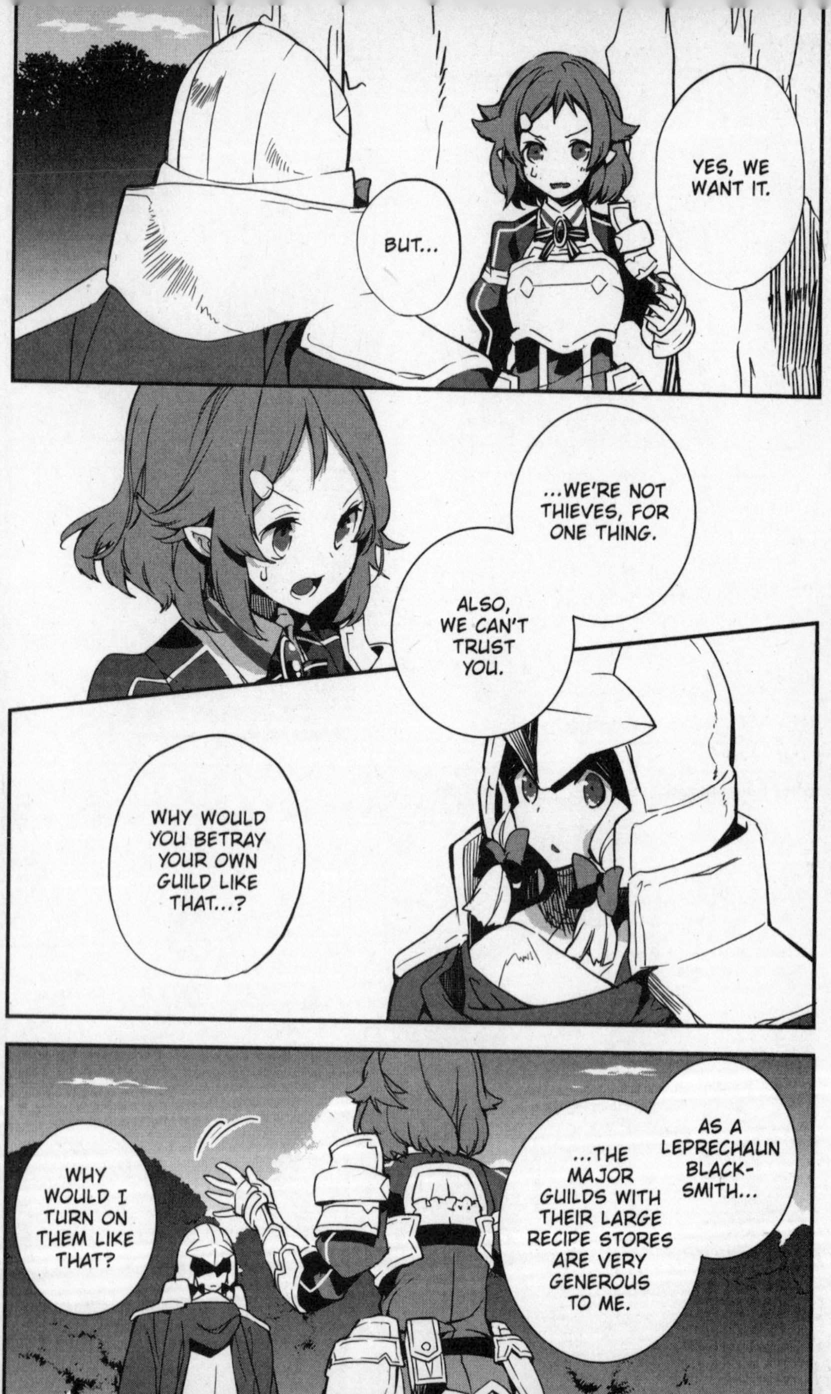
YES, WE WANT IT.
BUT...
...WE'RE NOT THIEVES, FOR ONE THING.
ALSO, WE CAN'T TRUST YOU.
WHY WOULD YOU BETRAY YOUR OWN GUILD LIKE THAT...?
AS A LEPRECHAUN BLACK-SMITH...
...THE MAJOR GUILDS WITH THEIR LARGE RECIPE STORES ARE VERY GENEROUS TO ME.
WHY WOULD I TURN ON THEM LIKE THAT?

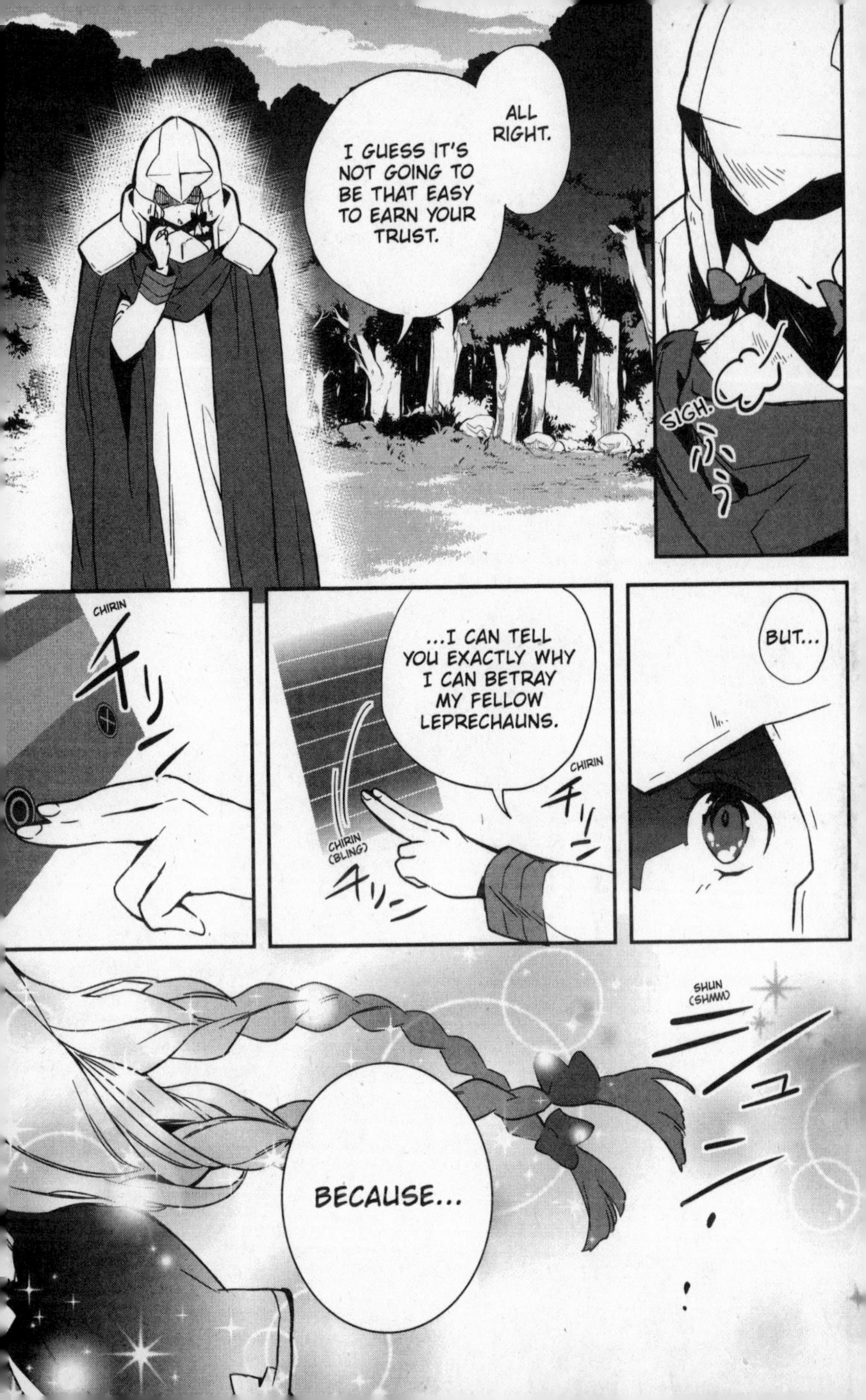
SIGH.
ALL RIGHT.
I GUESS IT'S NOT GOING TO BE THAT EASY TO EARN YOUR TRUST.
BUT...
...I CAN TELL YOU EXACTLY WHY I CAN BETRAY MY FELLOW LEPRECHAUNS.
CHIRIN
CHIRIN (BLING)
CHIRIN
SHUN (SHMM)
BECAUSE...

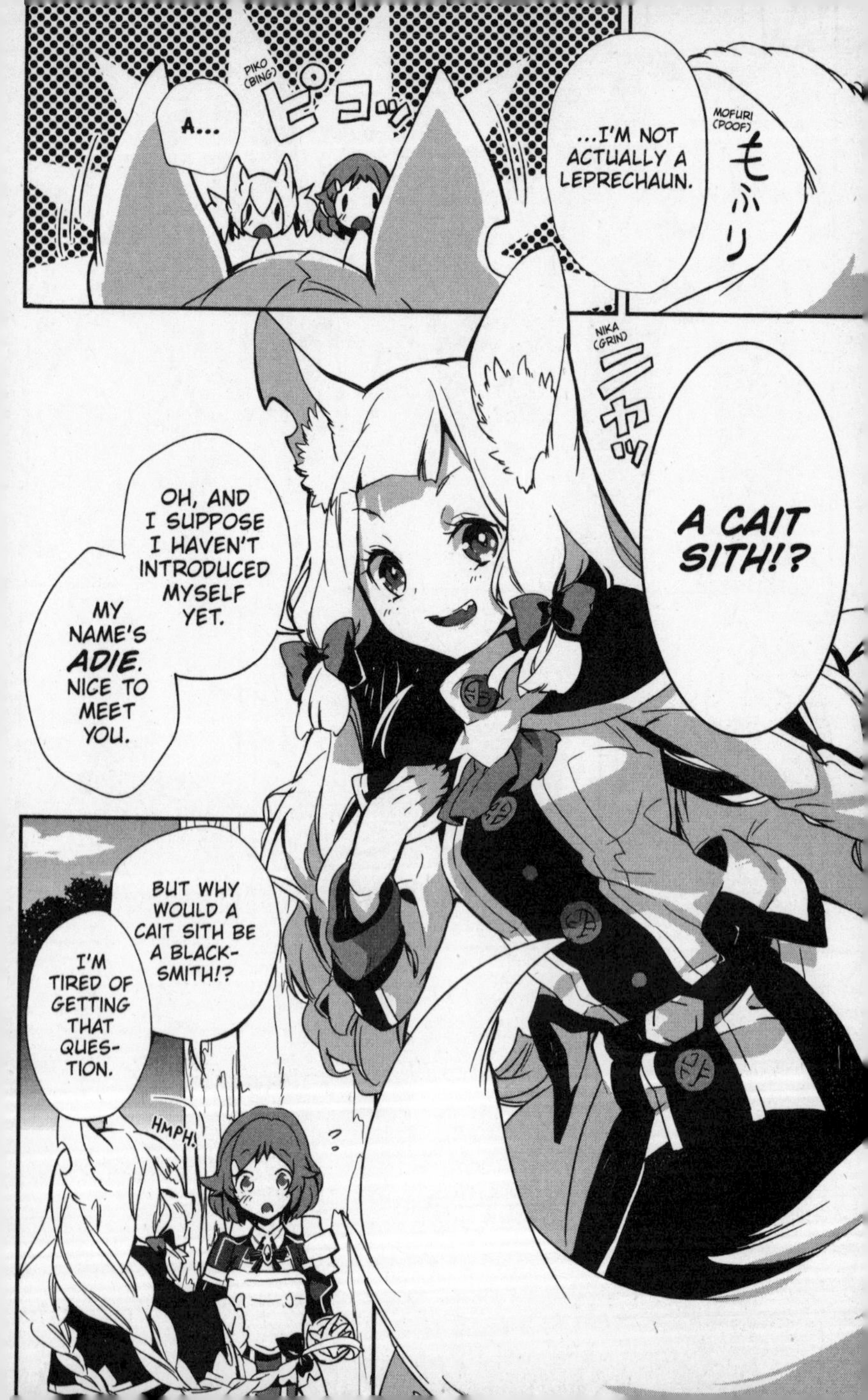
...I'M NOT ACTUALLY A LEPRECHAUN.
MOFURI (POOF)
もふり
PIKO (BING)
ピコッ
A...
NIKA (GRIN)
ニカッ
A CAIT SITH!?
OH, AND I SUPPOSE I HAVEN'T INTRODUCED MYSELF YET.
MY NAME'S ADIE. NICE TO MEET YOU.
BUT WHY WOULD A CAIT SITH BE A BLACK-SMITH!?
I'M TIRED OF GETTING THAT QUES-TION.
HMPH!

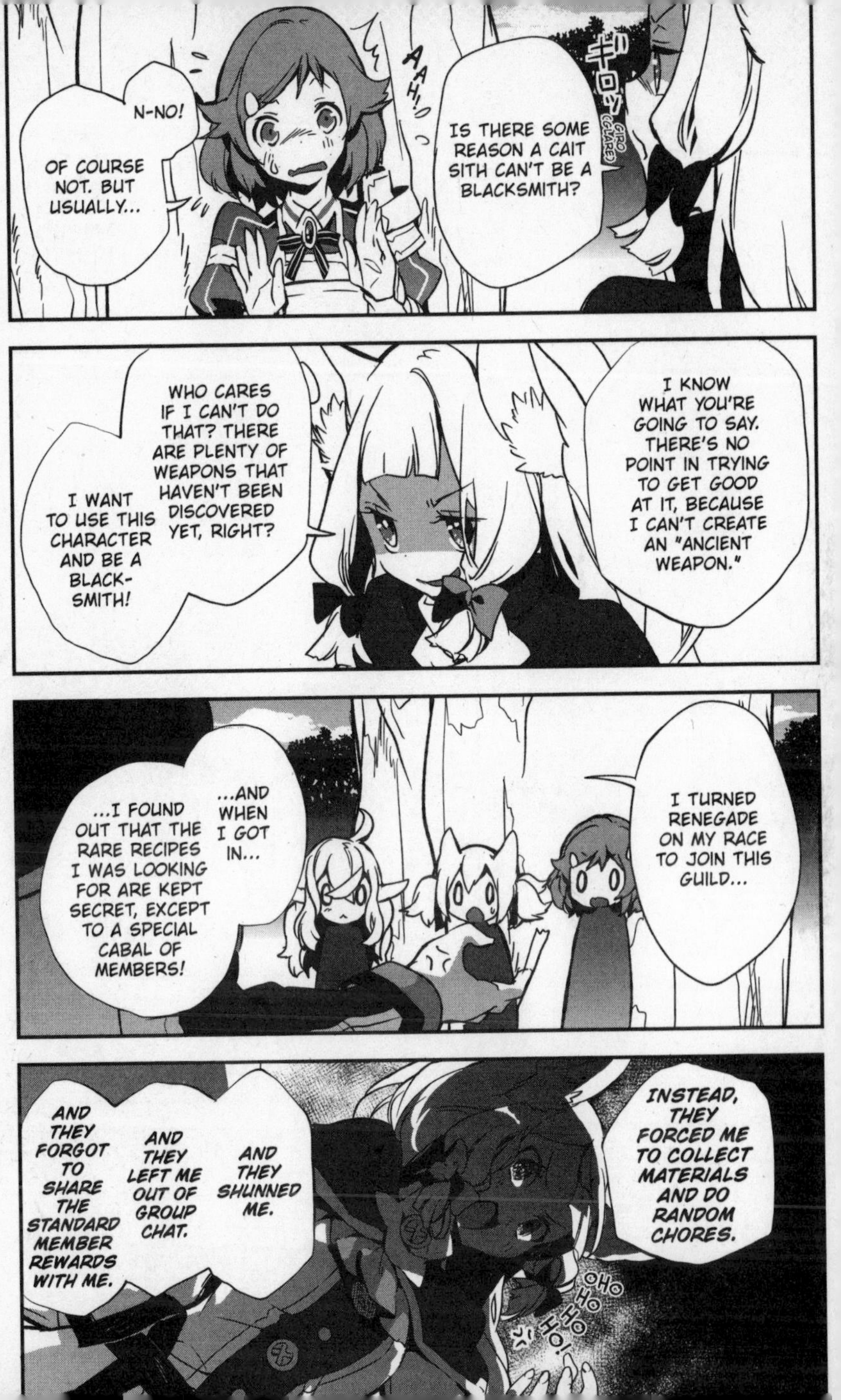
ギロッ GIRO (GLARE)
IS THERE SOME REASON A CAIT SITH CAN'T BE A BLACKSMITH?
AAH!
N-NO!
OF COURSE NOT. BUT USUALLY...
I KNOW WHAT YOU'RE GOING TO SAY. THERE'S NO POINT IN TRYING TO GET GOOD AT IT, BECAUSE I CAN'T CREATE AN "ANCIENT WEAPON."
WHO CARES IF I CAN'T DO THAT? THERE ARE PLENTY OF WEAPONS THAT HAVEN'T BEEN DISCOVERED YET, RIGHT?
I WANT TO USE THIS CHARACTER AND BE A BLACK-SMITH!
I TURNED RENEGADE ON MY RACE TO JOIN THIS GUILD...
...AND WHEN I GOT IN...
...I FOUND OUT THAT THE RARE RECIPES I WAS LOOKING FOR ARE KEPT SECRET, EXCEPT TO A SPECIAL CABAL OF MEMBERS!
INSTEAD, THEY FORCED ME TO COLLECT MATERIALS AND DO RANDOM CHORES.
OHO HO HO HO!
AND THEY SHUNNED ME.
AND THEY LEFT ME OUT OF GROUP CHAT.
AND THEY FORGOT TO SHARE THE STANDARD MEMBER REWARDS WITH ME.

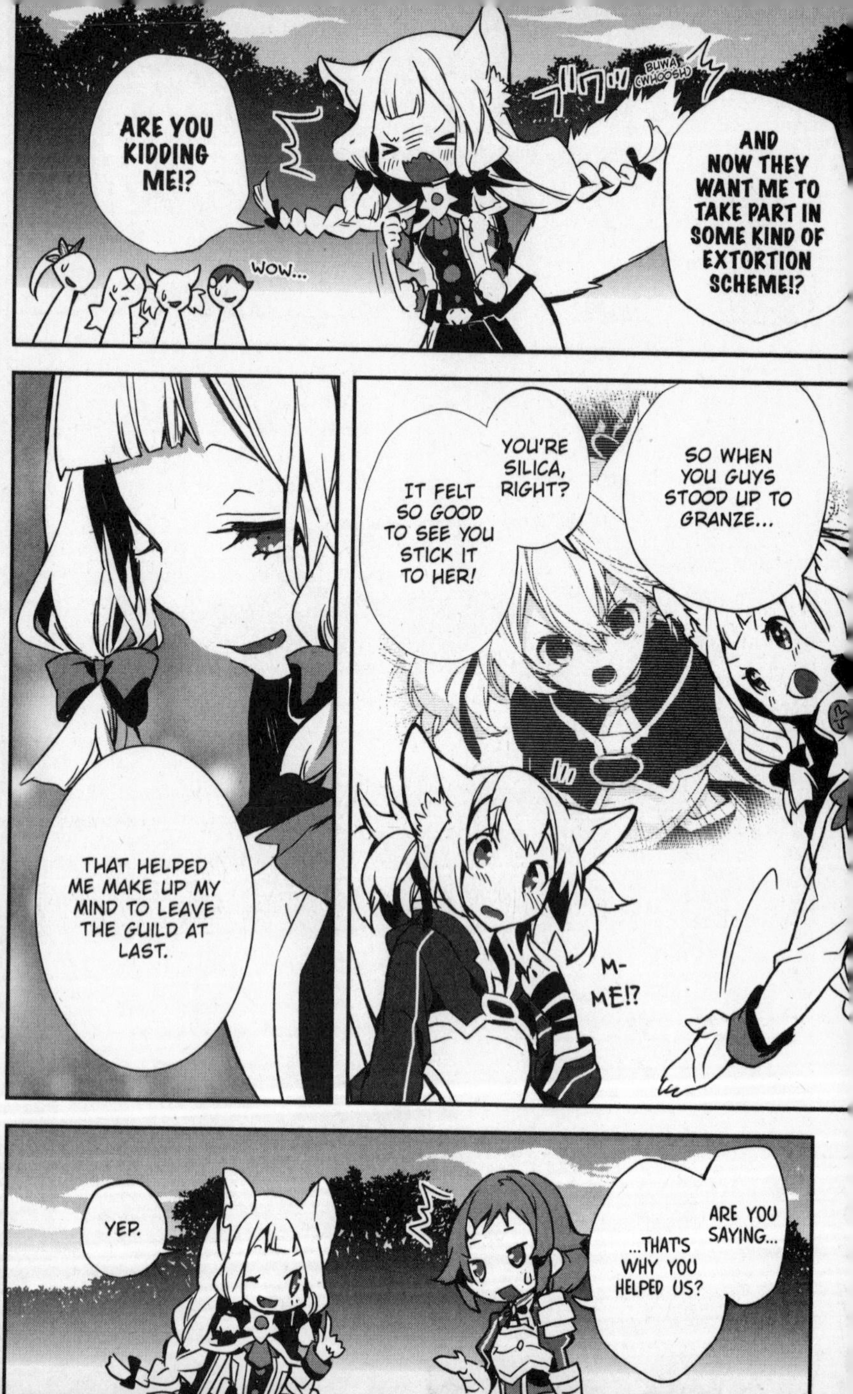

BUWA (WHOOSH)
AND NOW THEY WANT ME TO TAKE PART IN SOME KIND OF EXTORTION SCHEME!?
ARE YOU KIDDING ME!?
WOW...
SO WHEN YOU GUYS STOOD UP TO GRANZE...
YOU'RE SILICA, RIGHT?
IT FELT SO GOOD TO SEE YOU STICK IT TO HER!
M- ME!?
THAT HELPED ME MAKE UP MY MIND TO LEAVE THE GUILD AT LAST.
ARE YOU SAYING...
...THAT'S WHY YOU HELPED US?
YEP.

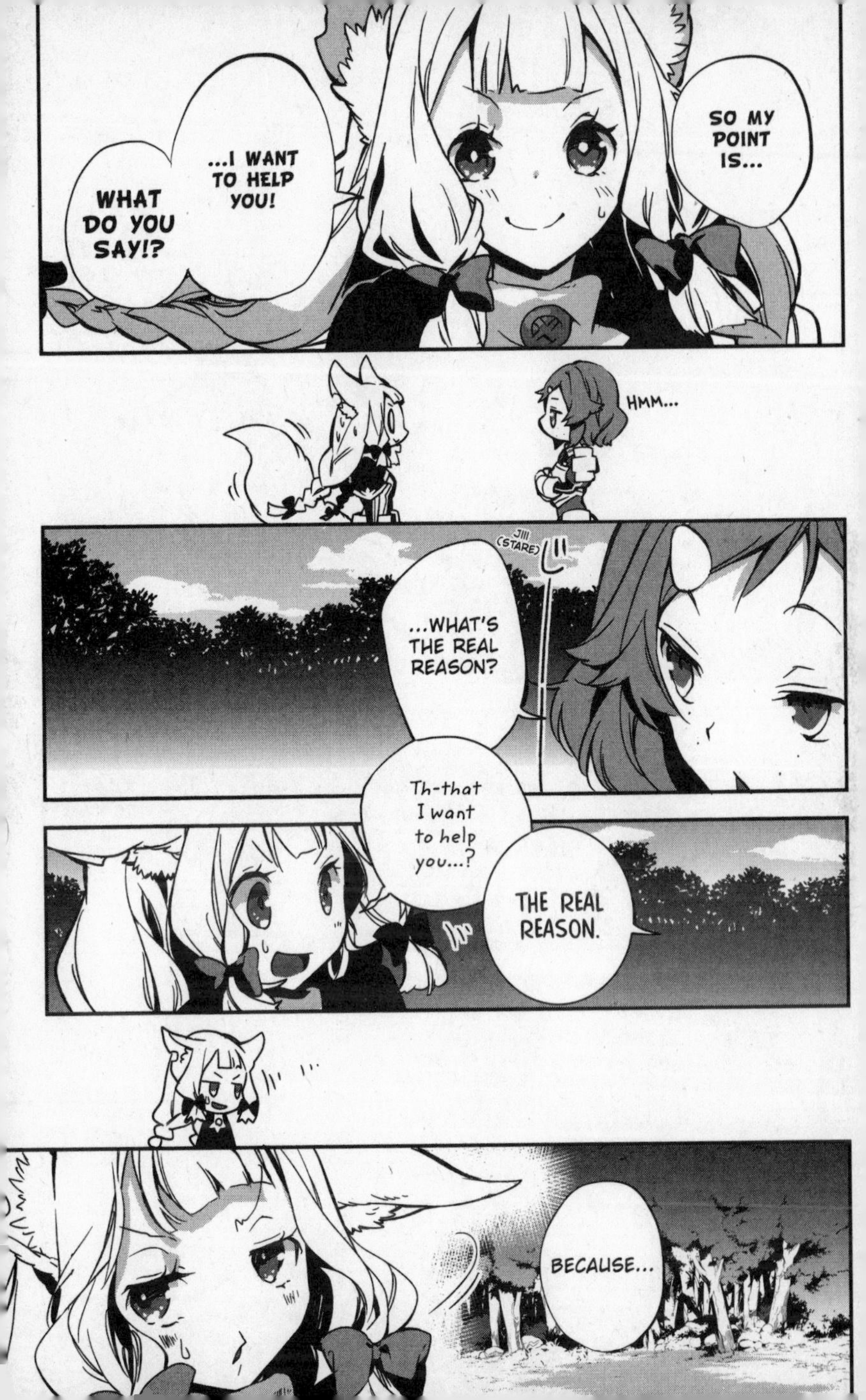
SO MY POINT IS...
...I WANT TO HELP YOU!
WHAT DO YOU SAY!?
HMM...
JIII (STARE)
...WHAT'S THE REAL REASON?
Th-that I want to help you...?
THE REAL REASON.
BECAUSE...

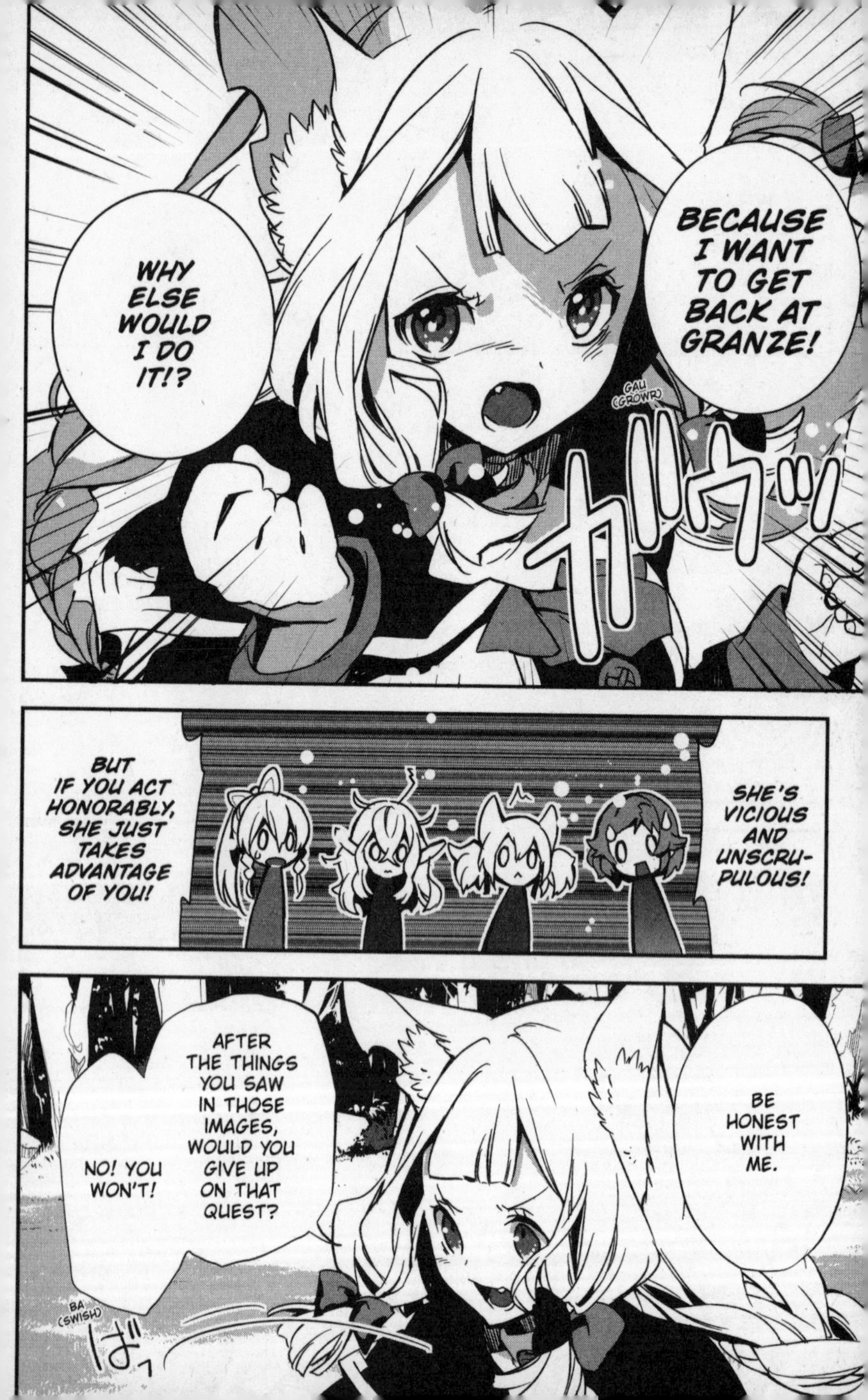
BECAUSE I WANT TO GET BACK AT GRANZE!
WHY ELSE WOULD I DO IT!?
GAU (GROWR)
SHE'S VICIOUS AND UNSCRU-PULOUS!
BUT IF YOU ACT HONORABLY, SHE JUST TAKES ADVANTAGE OF YOU!
BE HONEST WITH ME.
AFTER THE THINGS YOU SAW IN THOSE IMAGES, WOULD YOU GIVE UP ON THAT QUEST?
NO! YOU WON'T!
BA (SWISH)

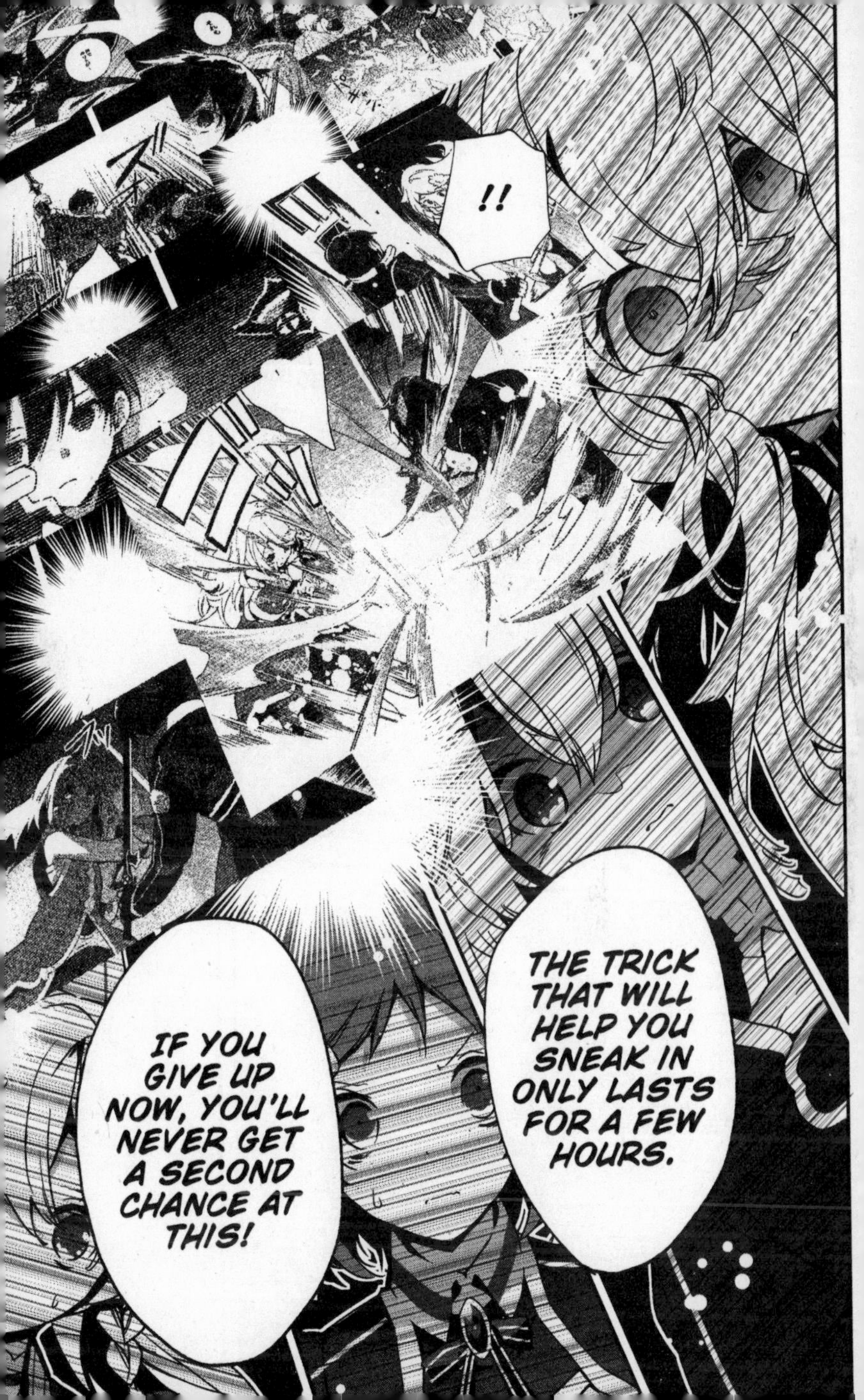
!!
THE TRICK THAT WILL HELP YOU SNEAK IN ONLY LASTS FOR A FEW HOURS.
IF YOU GIVE UP NOW, YOU'LL NEVER GET A SECOND CHANCE AT THIS!

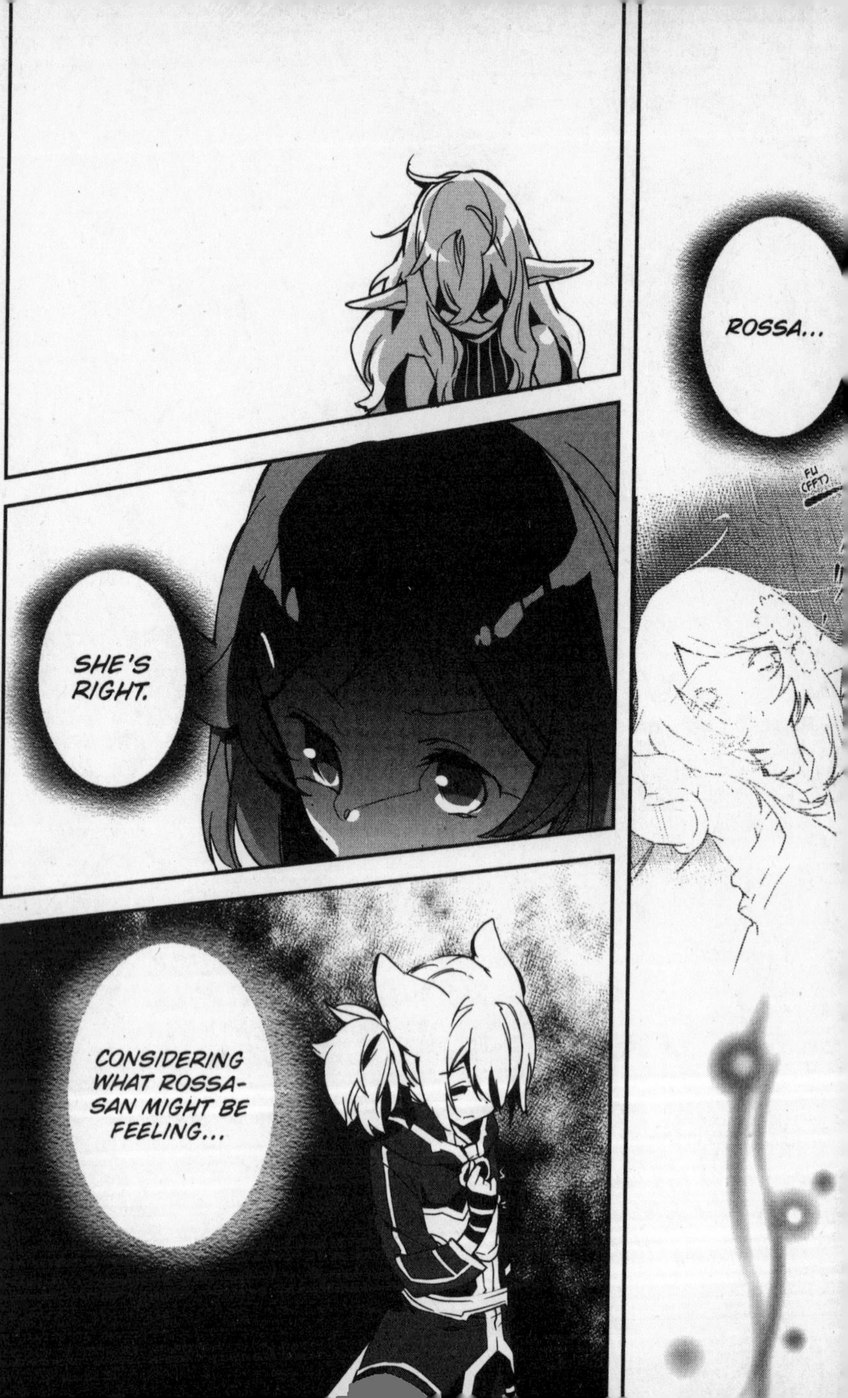
ROSSA...
FU (FFT)
SHE'S RIGHT.
CONSIDERING WHAT ROSSA-SAN MIGHT BE FEELING...

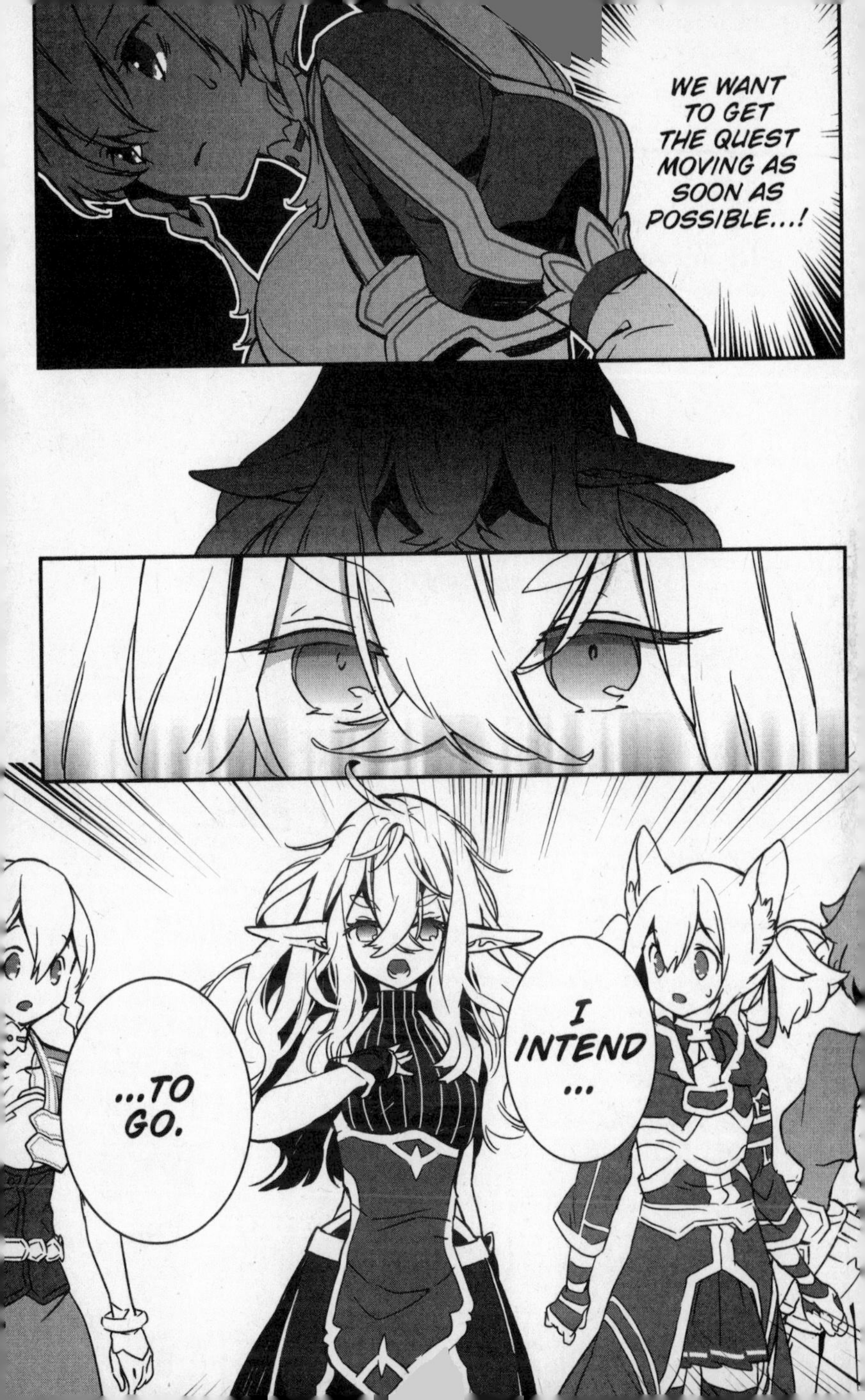
WE WANT TO GET THE QUEST MOVING AS SOON AS POSSIBLE...!
I INTEND ...
...TO GO.

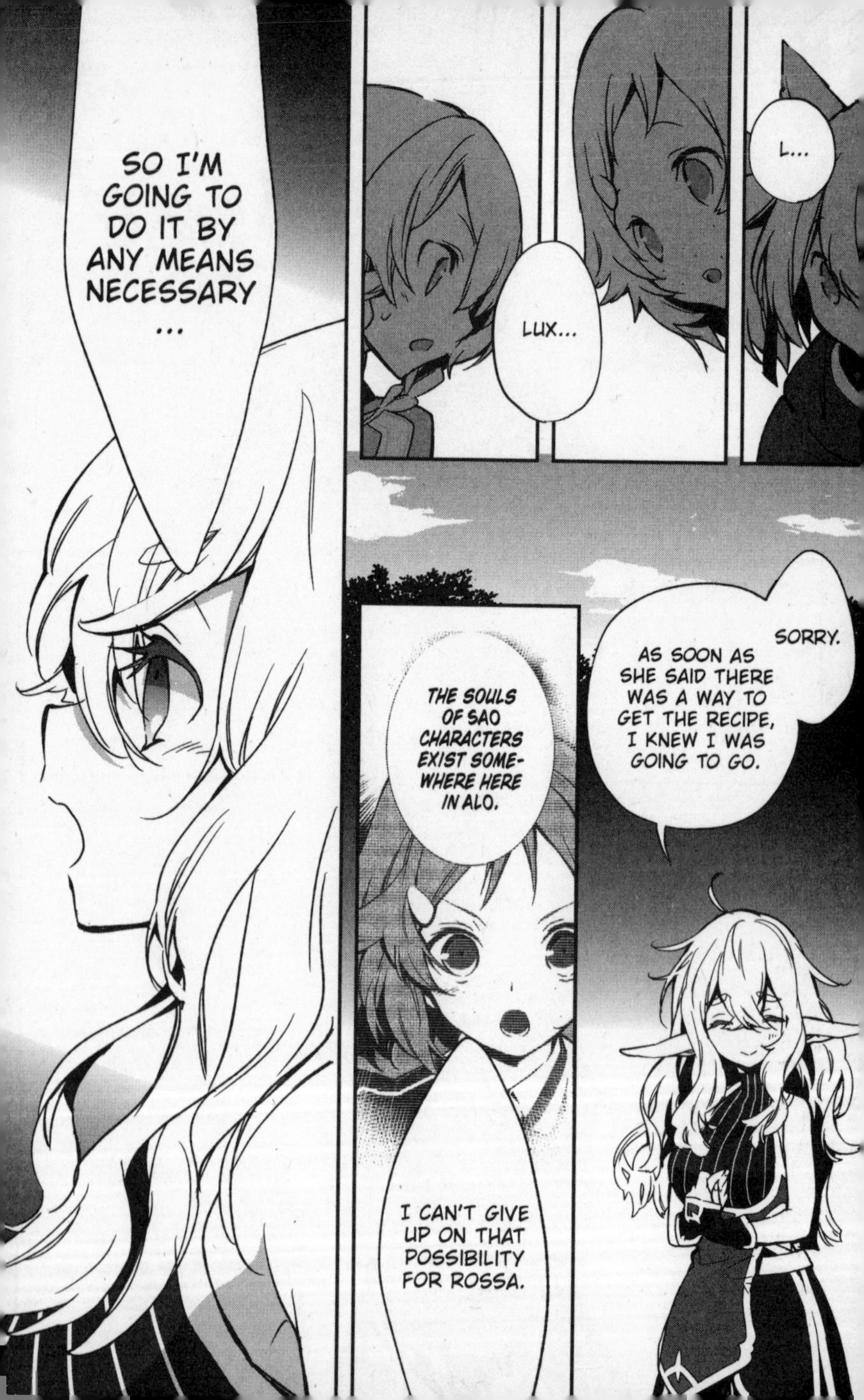
L...
LUX...
SORRY.
AS SOON AS SHE SAID THERE WAS A WAY TO GET THE RECIPE, I KNEW I WAS GOING TO GO.
THE SOULS OF SAO CHARACTERS EXIST SOME-WHERE HERE IN ALO.
I CAN'T GIVE UP ON THAT POSSIBILITY FOR ROSSA.
SO I'M GOING TO DO IT BY ANY MEANS NECESSARY...

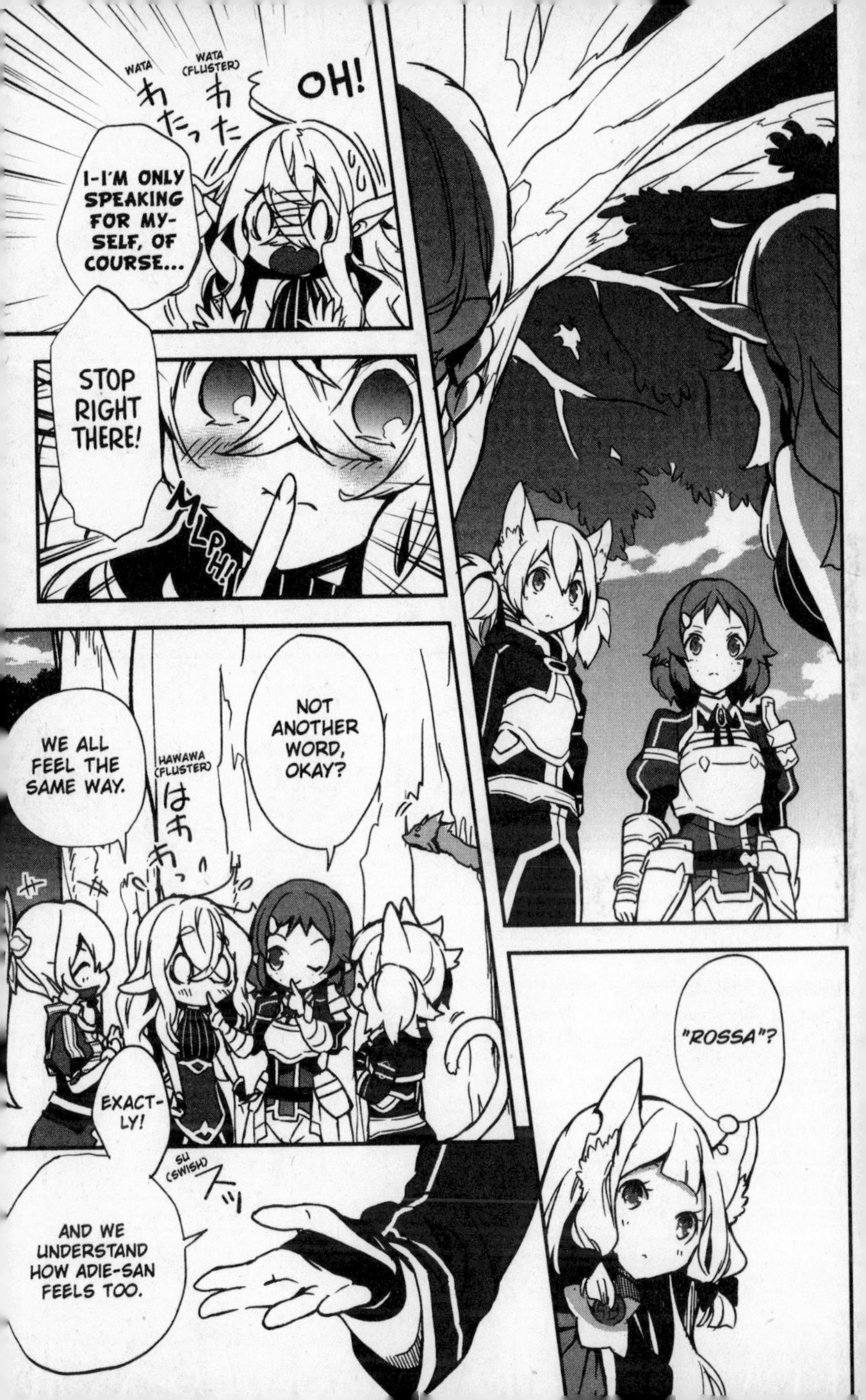
OH!
WATA WATA (FLUSTER)
わたわたっ
I-I'M ONLY SPEAKING FOR MY-SELF, OF COURSE...
STOP RIGHT THERE!
MLPH!
NOT ANOTHER WORD, OKAY?
WE ALL FEEL THE SAME WAY.
HAWAWA (FLUSTER)
はわわっ
EXACT-LY!
"ROSSA"?
SU (SWISH)
スッ
AND WE UNDERSTAND HOW ADIE-SAN FEELS TOO.

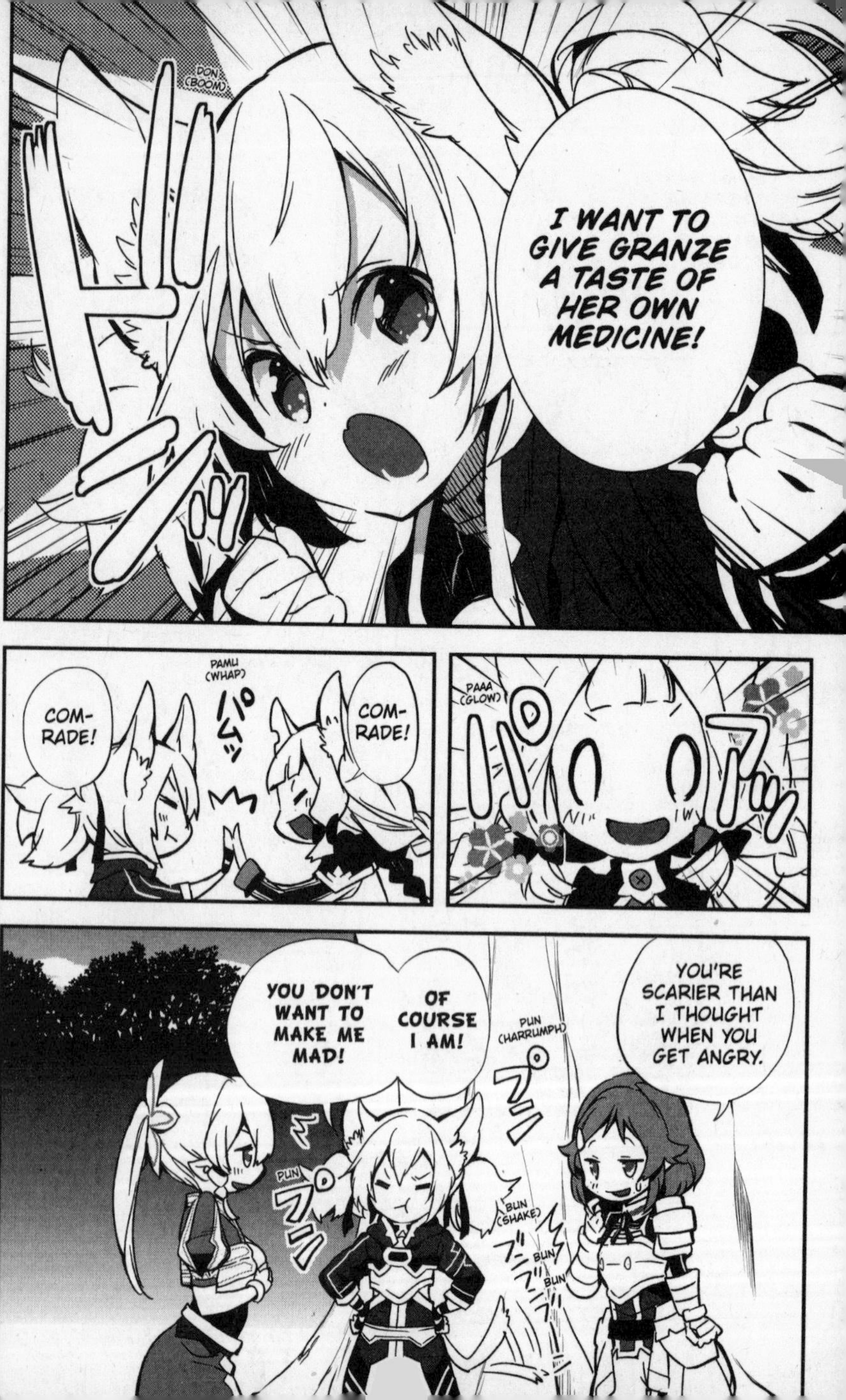
DON (BOOM)
I WANT TO GIVE GRANZE A TASTE OF HER OWN MEDICINE!
PAAA (GLOW)
COM-RADE!
PAMU (WHAP)
COM-RADE!
YOU'RE SCARIER THAN I THOUGHT WHEN YOU GET ANGRY.
PUN (HARRUMPH)
OF COURSE I AM!
YOU DON'T WANT TO MAKE ME MAD!
PUN
BUN (SHAKE)
BUN
BUN

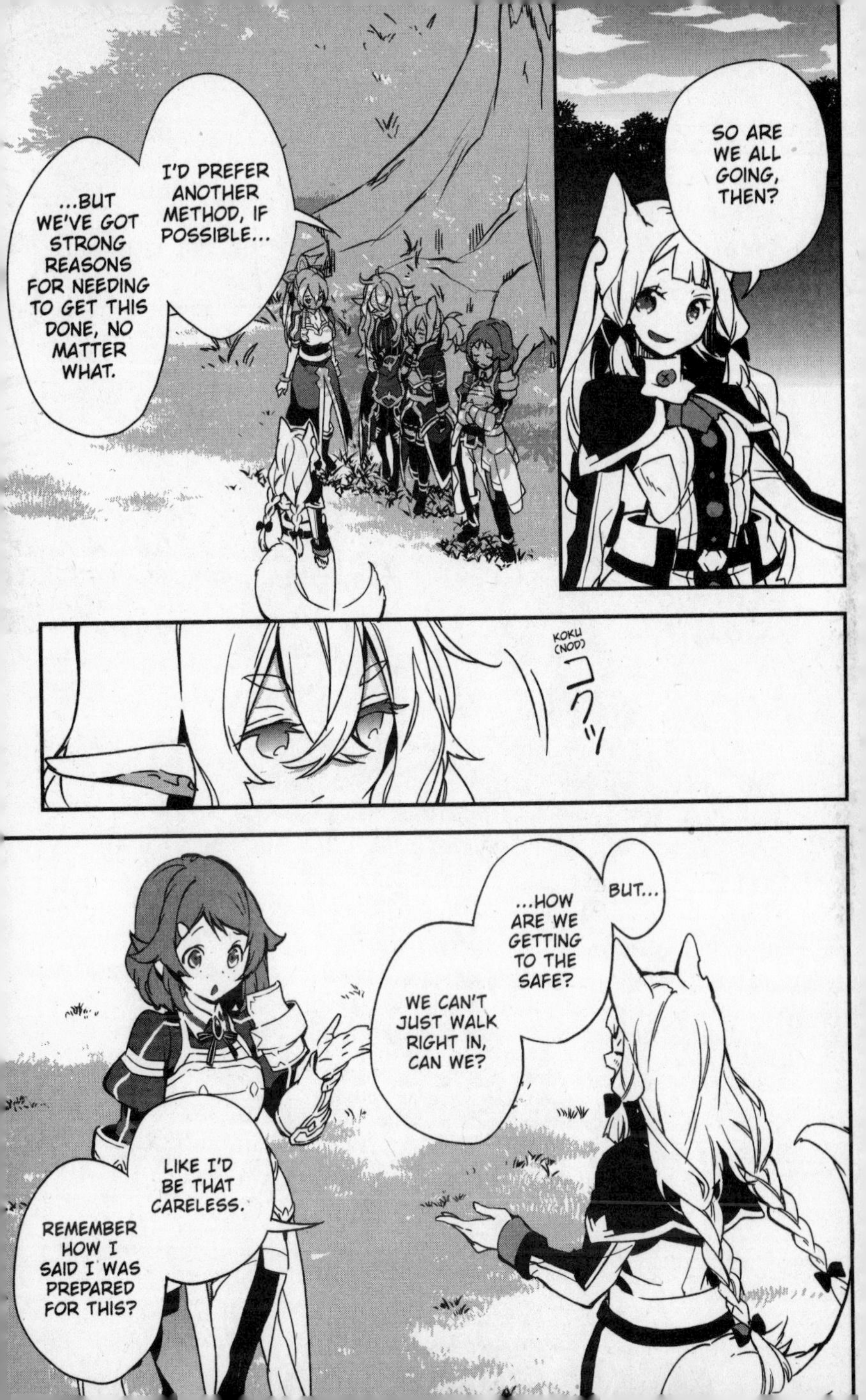
SO ARE WE ALL GOING, THEN?
I'D PREFER ANOTHER METHOD, IF POSSIBLE...
...BUT WE'VE GOT STRONG REASONS FOR NEEDING TO GET THIS DONE, NO MATTER WHAT.
KOKU (NOD)
コクッ
BUT...
...HOW ARE WE GETTING TO THE SAFE?
WE CAN'T JUST WALK RIGHT IN, CAN WE?
LIKE I'D BE THAT CARELESS.
REMEMBER HOW I SAID I WAS PREPARED FOR THIS?

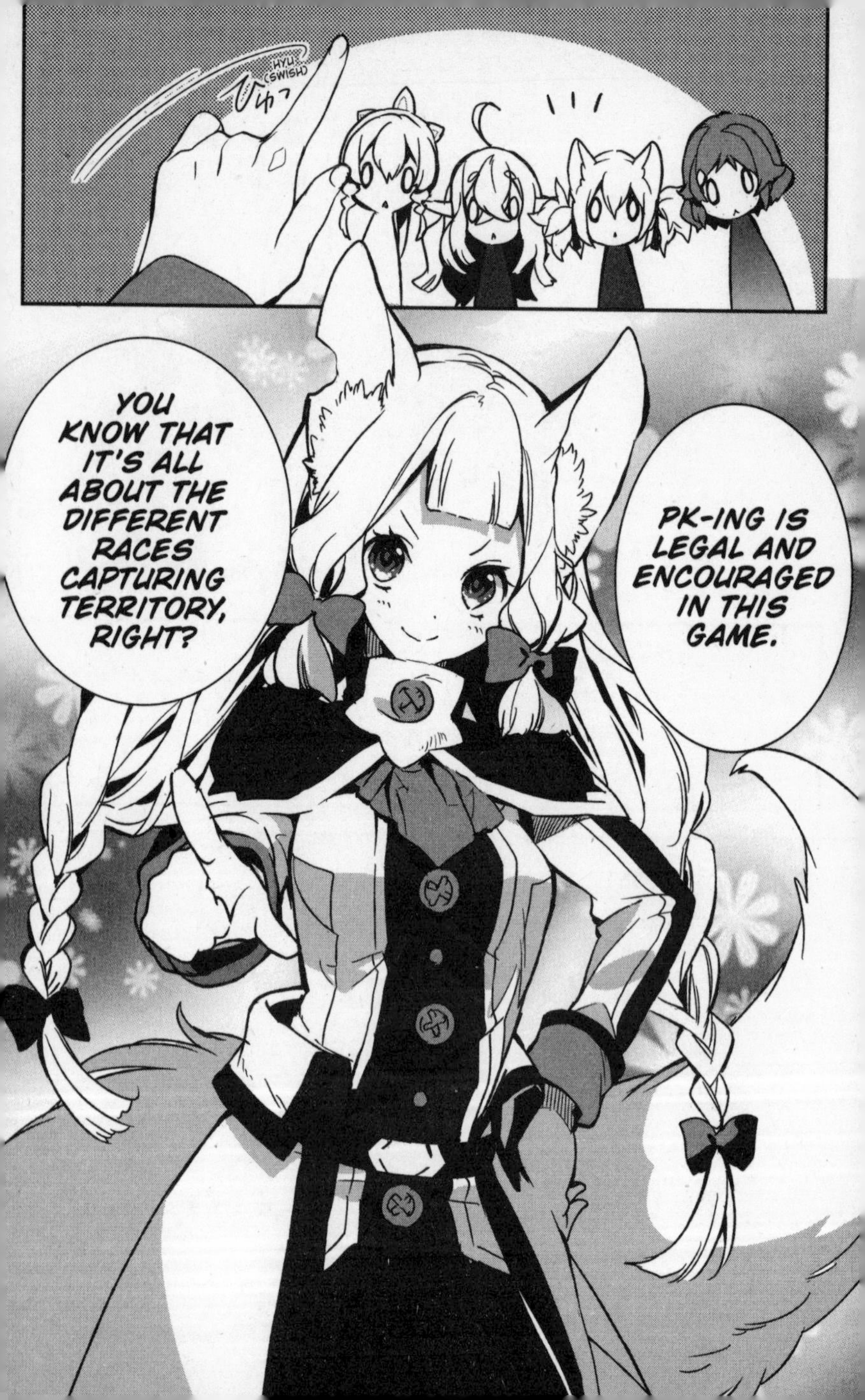
HYU (SWISH)
ひゅっ
PK-ING IS LEGAL AND ENCOURAGED IN THIS GAME.
YOU KNOW THAT IT'S ALL ABOUT THE DIFFERENT RACES CAPTURING TERRITORY, RIGHT?

SWORD ART ONLINE
GIRLS' OPS

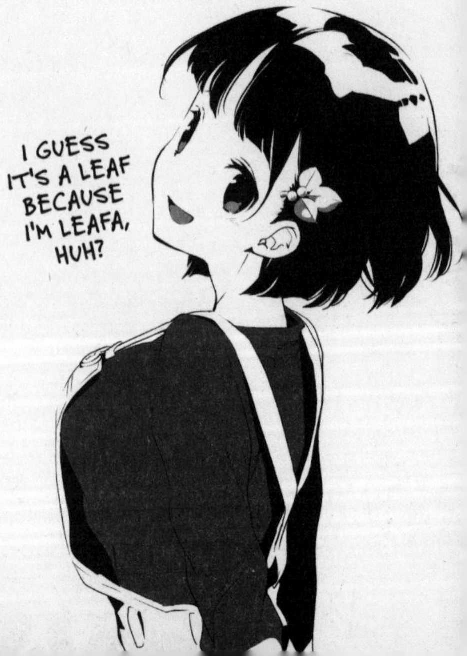
I GUESS IT'S A LEAF BECAUSE I'M LEAFA, HUH?

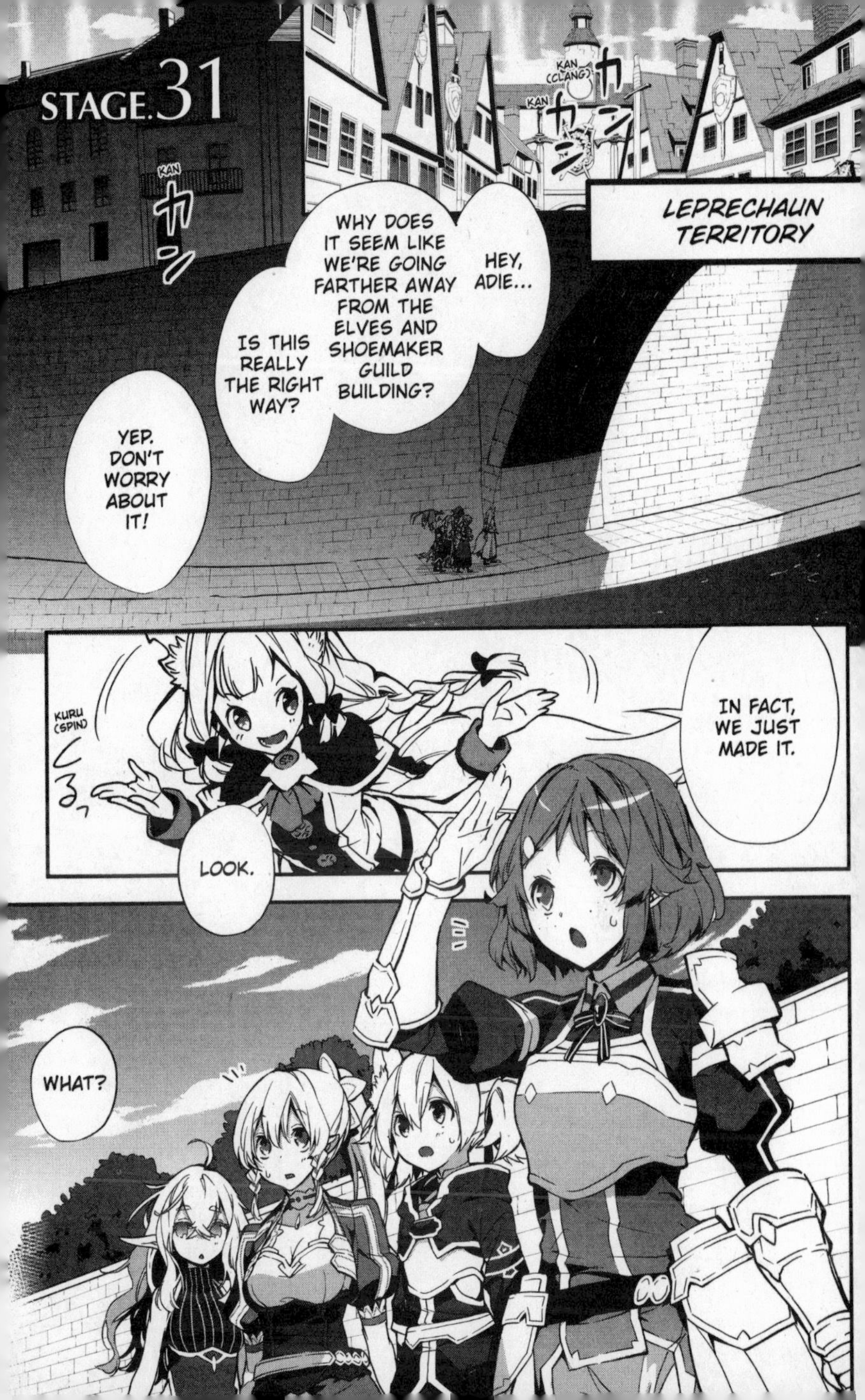
STAGE.31
KAN (CLANG) カン
KAN カン
LEPRECHAUN TERRITORY
HEY, ADIE...
WHY DOES IT SEEM LIKE WE'RE GOING FARTHER AWAY FROM THE ELVES AND SHOEMAKER GUILD BUILDING?
IS THIS REALLY THE RIGHT WAY?
KAN カン
YEP. DON'T WORRY ABOUT IT!
IN FACT, WE JUST MADE IT.
KURU (SPIN) くるっ
LOOK.
WHAT?

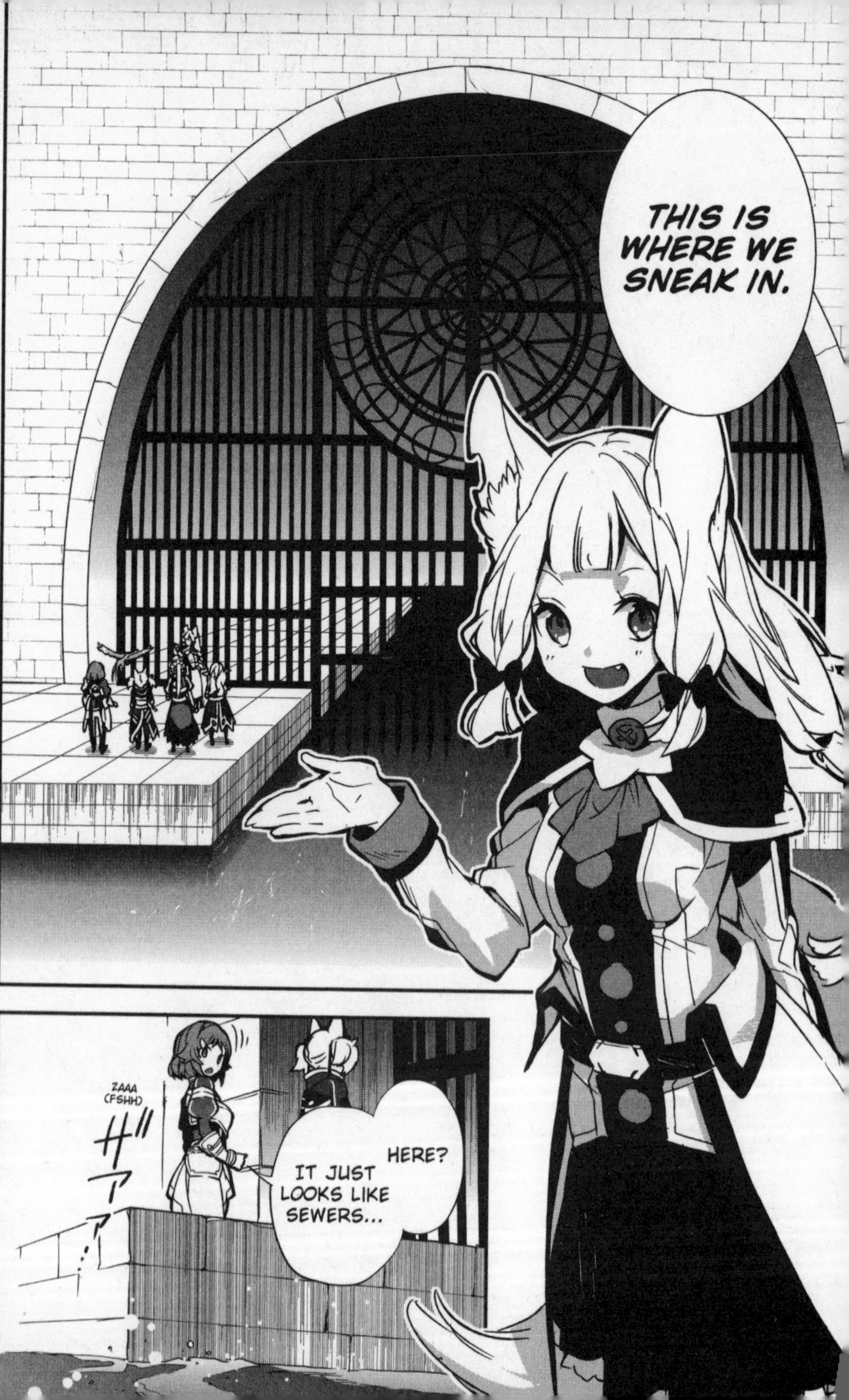
THIS IS WHERE WE SNEAK IN.
HERE? IT JUST LOOKS LIKE SEWERS...
ZAAA (FSHH)
ザァァ…

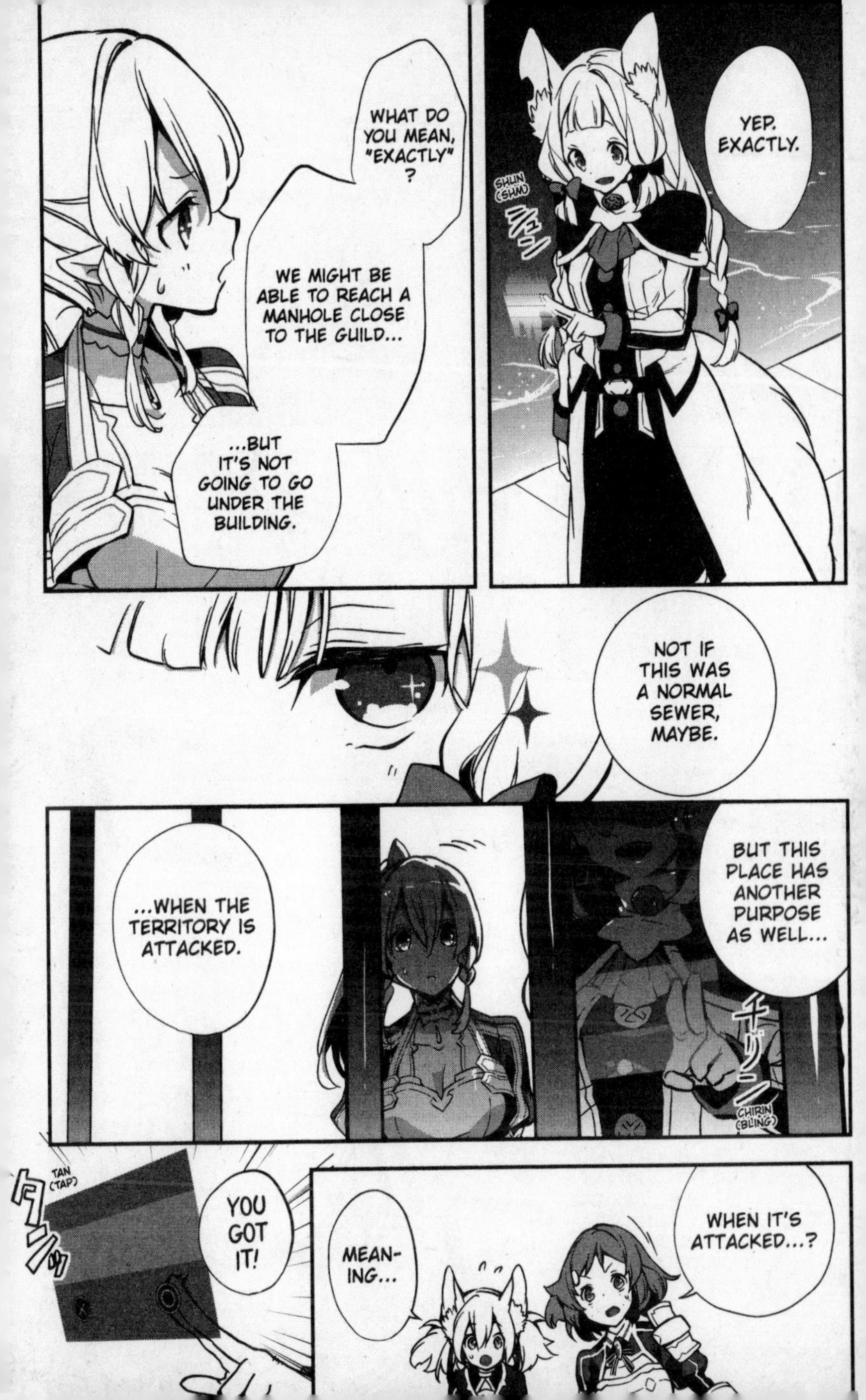
YEP. EXACTLY.
SHUN (SHUN)
WHAT DO YOU MEAN, "EXACTLY"?
WE MIGHT BE ABLE TO REACH A MANHOLE CLOSE TO THE GUILD...
...BUT IT'S NOT GOING TO GO UNDER THE BUILDING.
NOT IF THIS WAS A NORMAL SEWER, MAYBE.
BUT THIS PLACE HAS ANOTHER PURPOSE AS WELL...
CHIRIN (BLING)
...WHEN THE TERRITORY IS ATTACKED.
WHEN IT'S ATTACKED...?
MEAN-ING...
YOU GOT IT!
TAN (TAP)

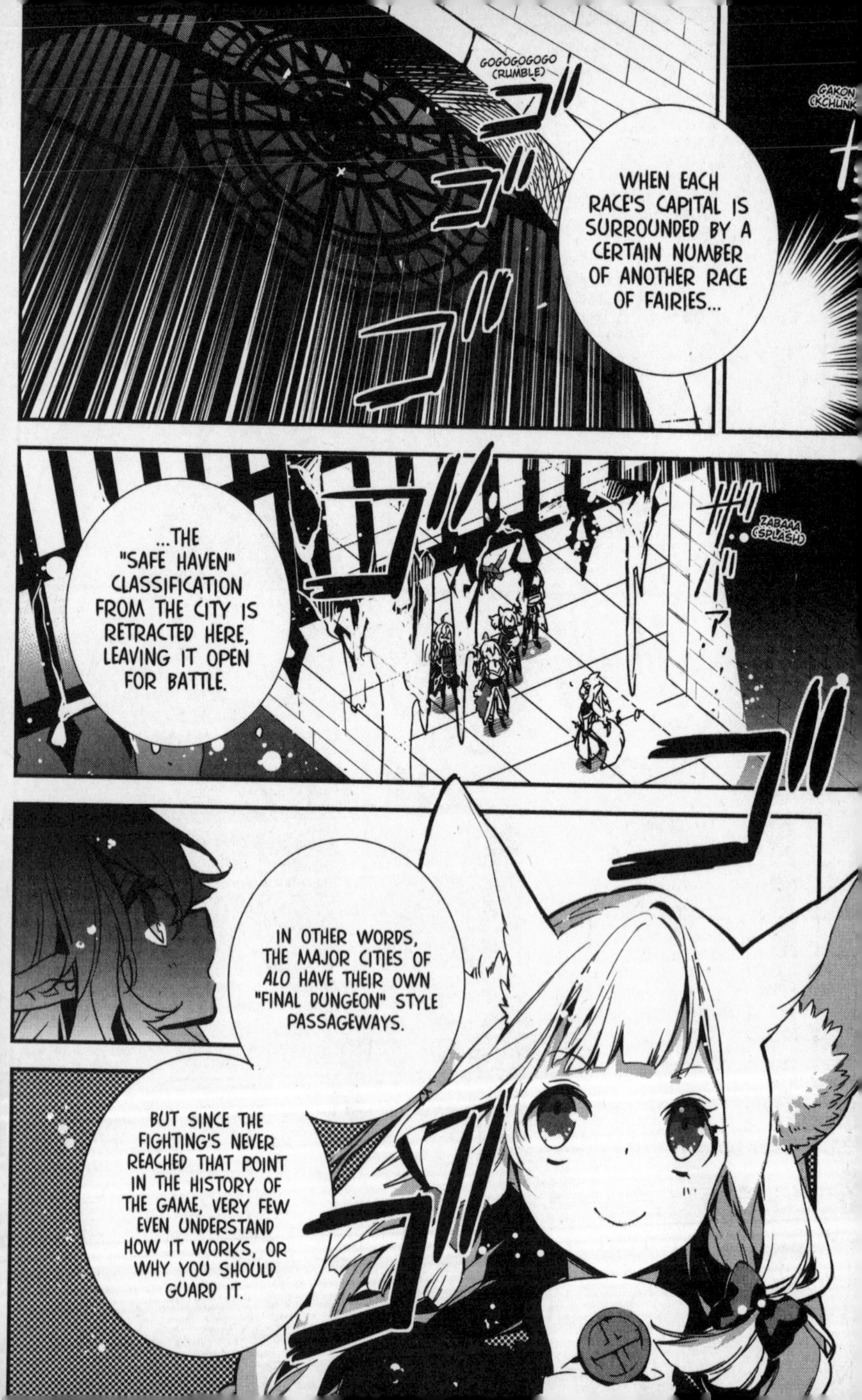
GAKON (KCHUNK)
GOGOGOGOGO (RUMBLE)
WHEN EACH RACE'S CAPITAL IS SURROUNDED BY A CERTAIN NUMBER OF ANOTHER RACE OF FAIRIES...
ZABAAA (SPLASH)
..."SAFE HAVEN" CLASSIFICATION FROM THE CITY IS RETRACTED HERE, LEAVING IT OPEN FOR BATTLE.
IN OTHER WORDS, THE MAJOR CITIES OF ALO HAVE THEIR OWN "FINAL DUNGEON" STYLE PASSAGEWAYS.
BUT SINCE THE FIGHTING'S NEVER REACHED THAT POINT IN THE HISTORY OF THE GAME, VERY FEW EVEN UNDERSTAND HOW IT WORKS, OR WHY YOU SHOULD GUARD IT.

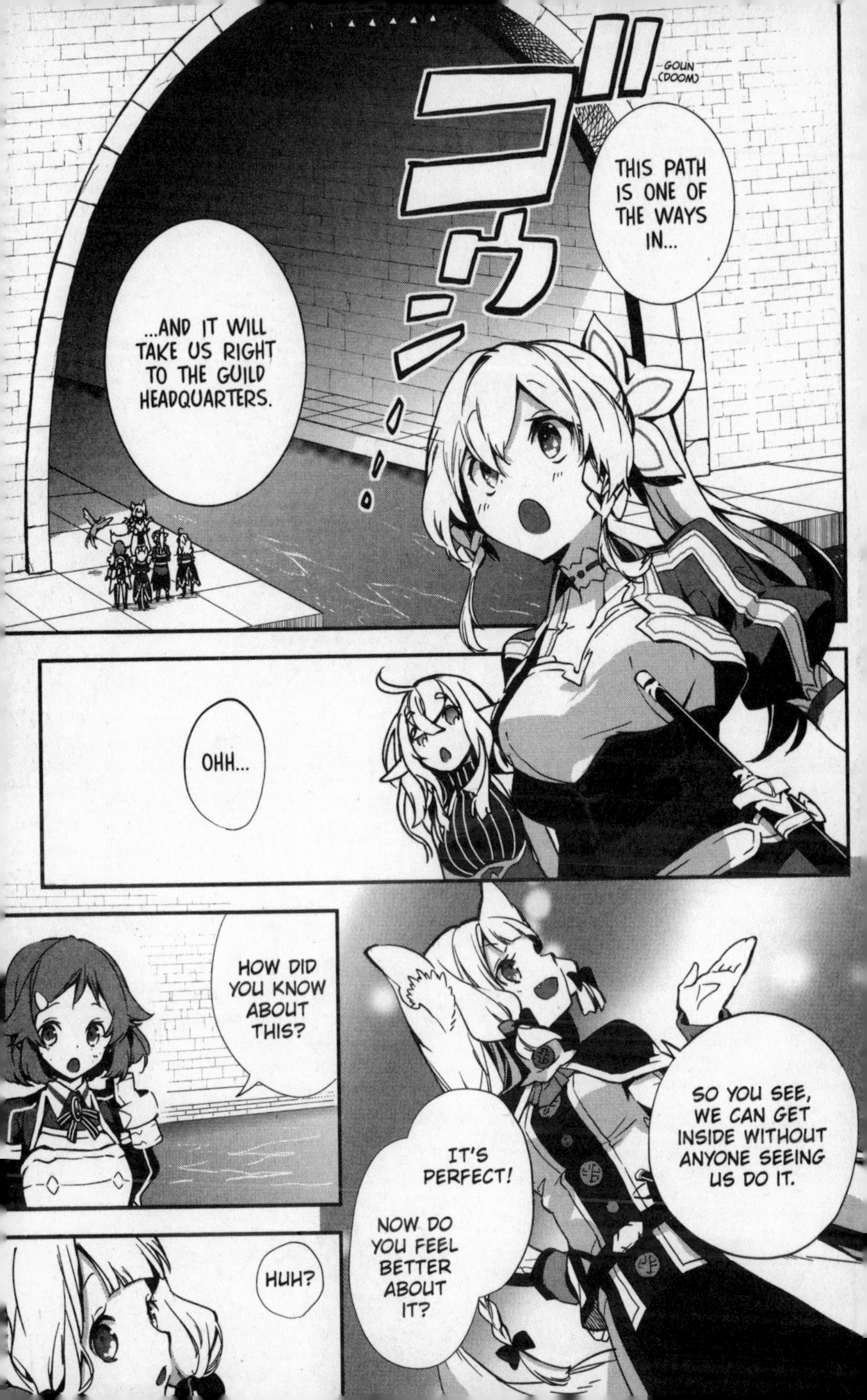
ゴウン
GOUN (DOOM)
THIS PATH IS ONE OF THE WAYS IN...
...AND IT WILL TAKE US RIGHT TO THE GUILD HEADQUARTERS.
OHH...
SO YOU SEE, WE CAN GET INSIDE WITHOUT ANYONE SEEING US DO IT.
IT'S PERFECT!
NOW DO YOU FEEL BETTER ABOUT IT?
HOW DID YOU KNOW ABOUT THIS?
HUH?

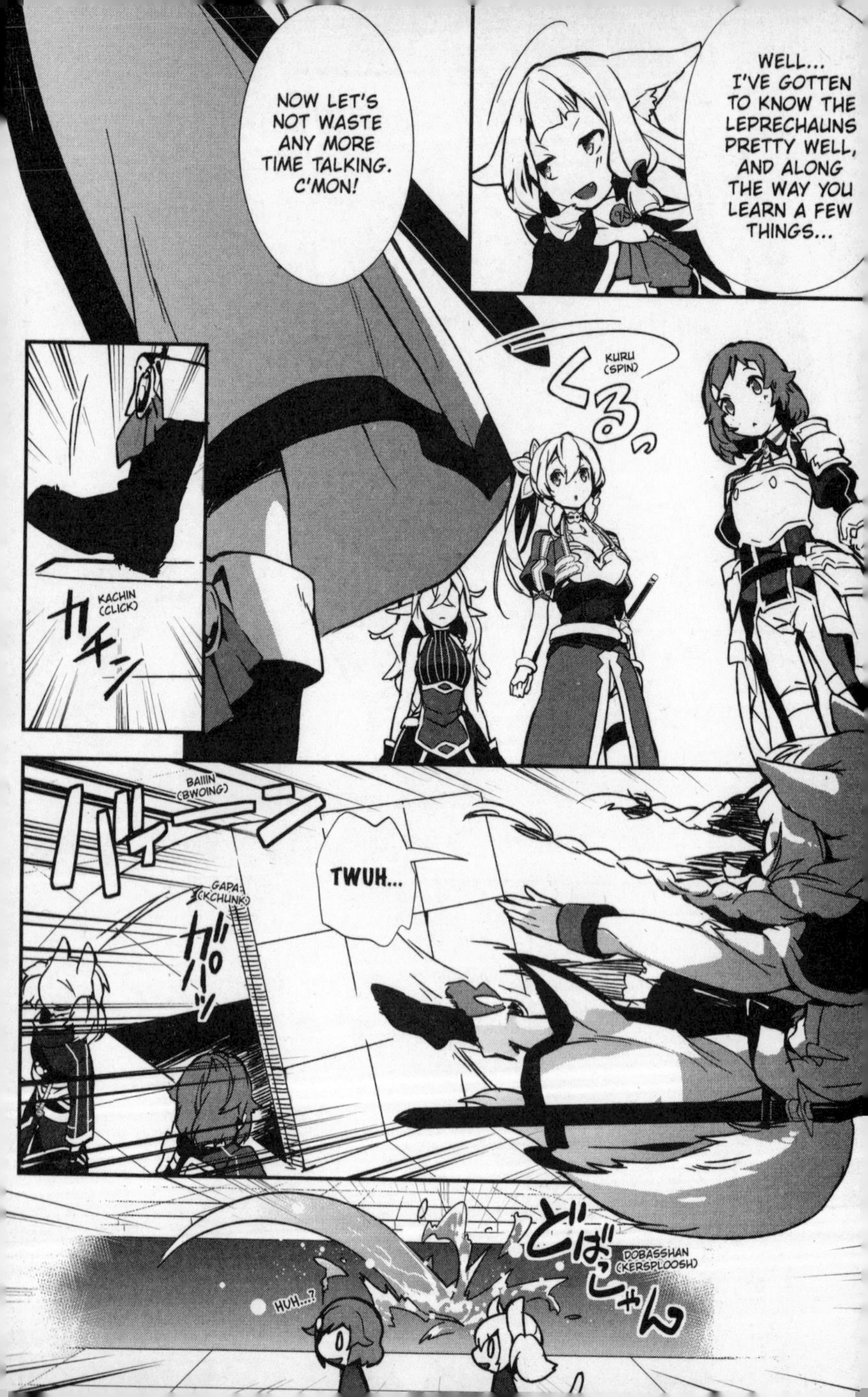
WELL... I'VE GOTTEN TO KNOW THE LEPRECHAUNS PRETTY WELL, AND ALONG THE WAY YOU LEARN A FEW THINGS...
NOW LET'S NOT WASTE ANY MORE TIME TALKING. C'MON!
くるっ
KURU (SPIN)
カチン
KACHIN (CLICK)
バィイーン
BAIIIN (BWOING)
TWUH...
ガパッ
GAPA (KCHUNK)
どばっしゃん
DOBASSHAN (KERSPLOOSH)
HUH...?

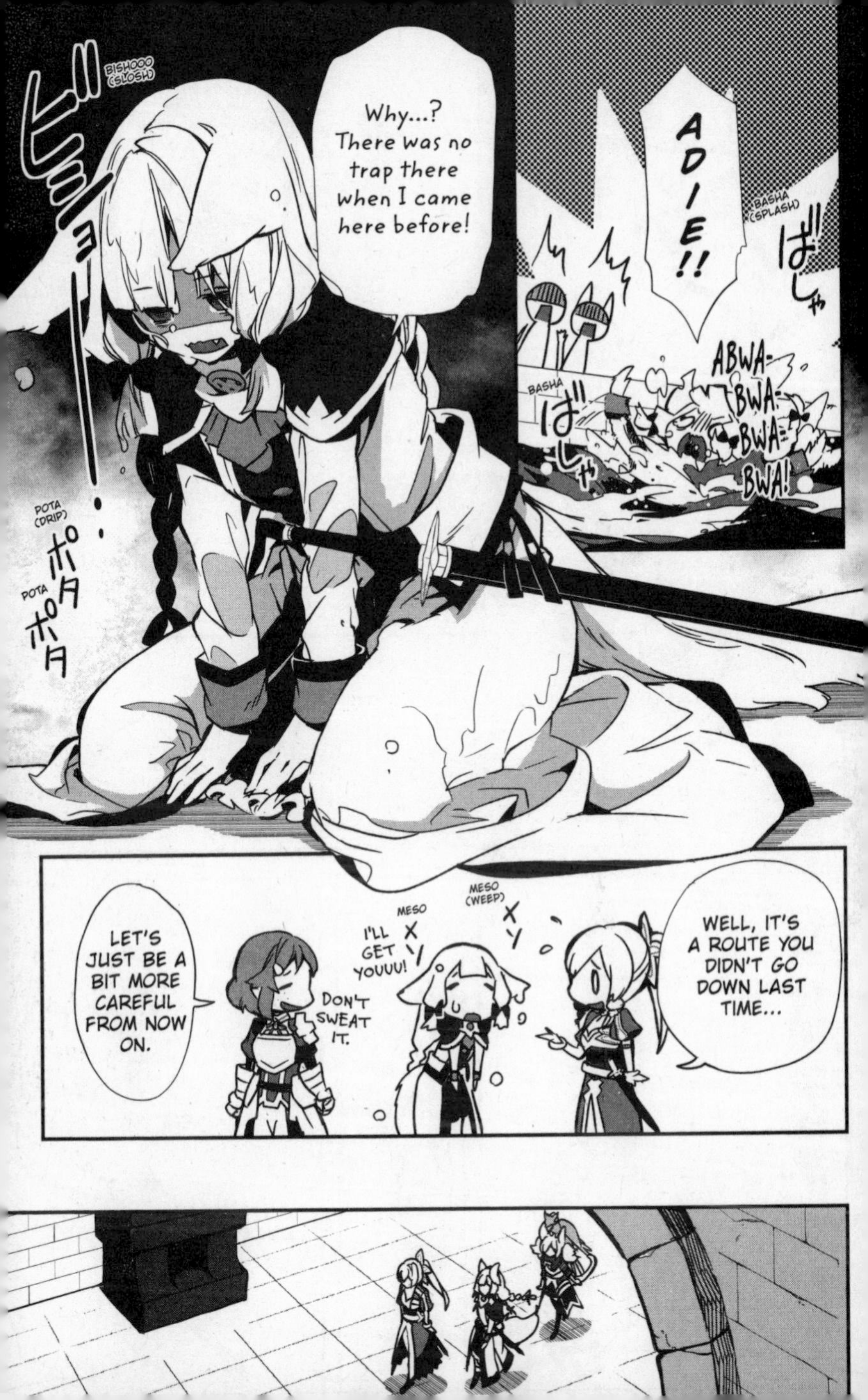
ADIE!!
BASHA (SPLASH)
ばしゃ
ABWA-BWA-BWA-BWA!
BASHA
ばしゃ
BISHOOO (SLOSH)
ビショーー…
Why...? There was no trap there when I came here before!
POTA (DRIP)
POTA
ポタポタ
WELL, IT'S A ROUTE YOU DIDN'T GO DOWN LAST TIME...
MESO (WEEP)
メソ
I'LL GET YOUUU!
MESO
メソ
DON'T SWEAT IT.
LET'S JUST BE A BIT MORE CAREFUL FROM NOW ON.

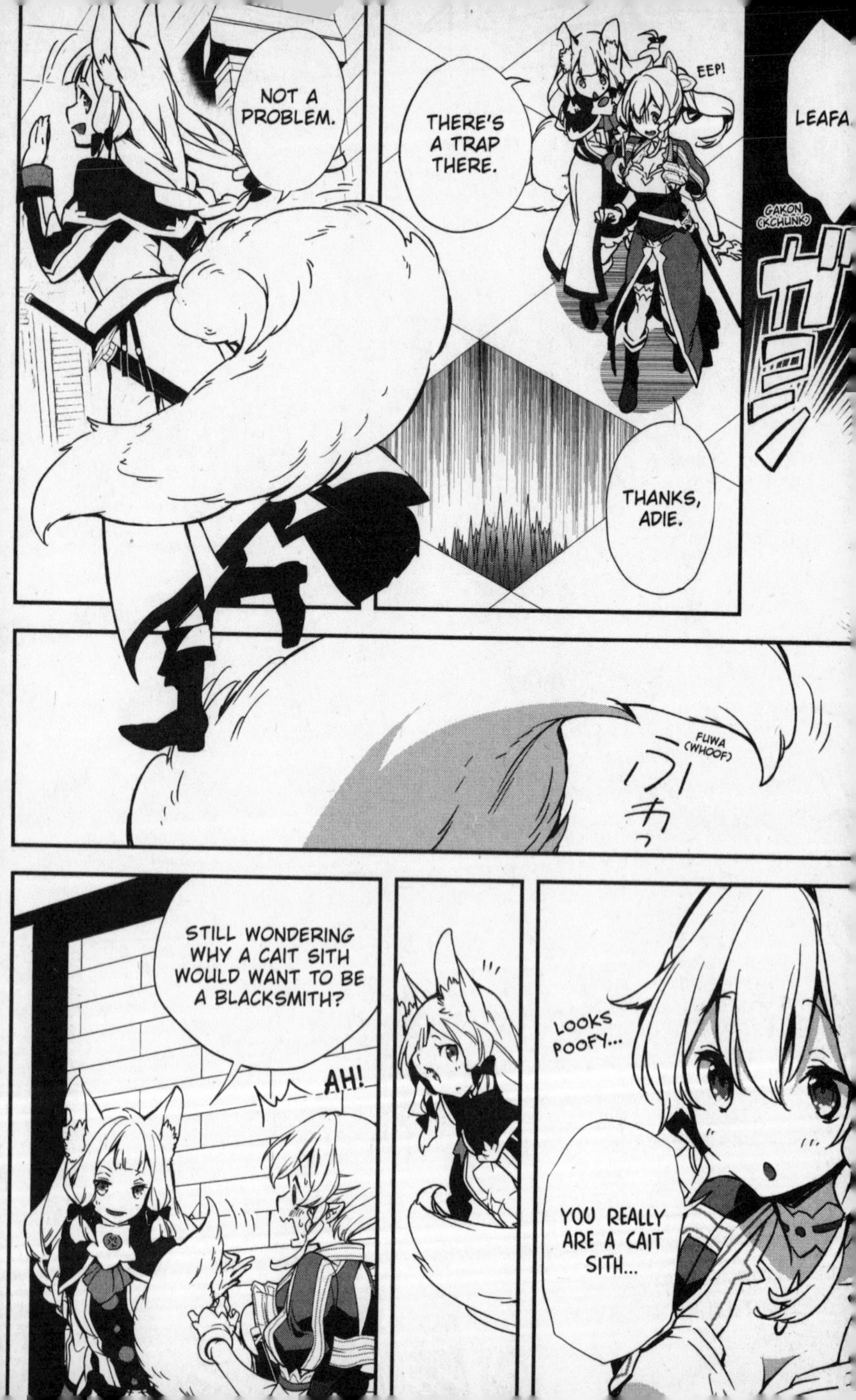
LEAFA.
GAKON (KCHUNK)
EEP!
THERE'S A TRAP THERE.
THANKS, ADIE.
NOT A PROBLEM.
FUWA (WHOOF)
LOOKS POOFY...
YOU REALLY ARE A CAIT SITH...
STILL WONDERING WHY A CAIT SITH WOULD WANT TO BE A BLACKSMITH?
AH!

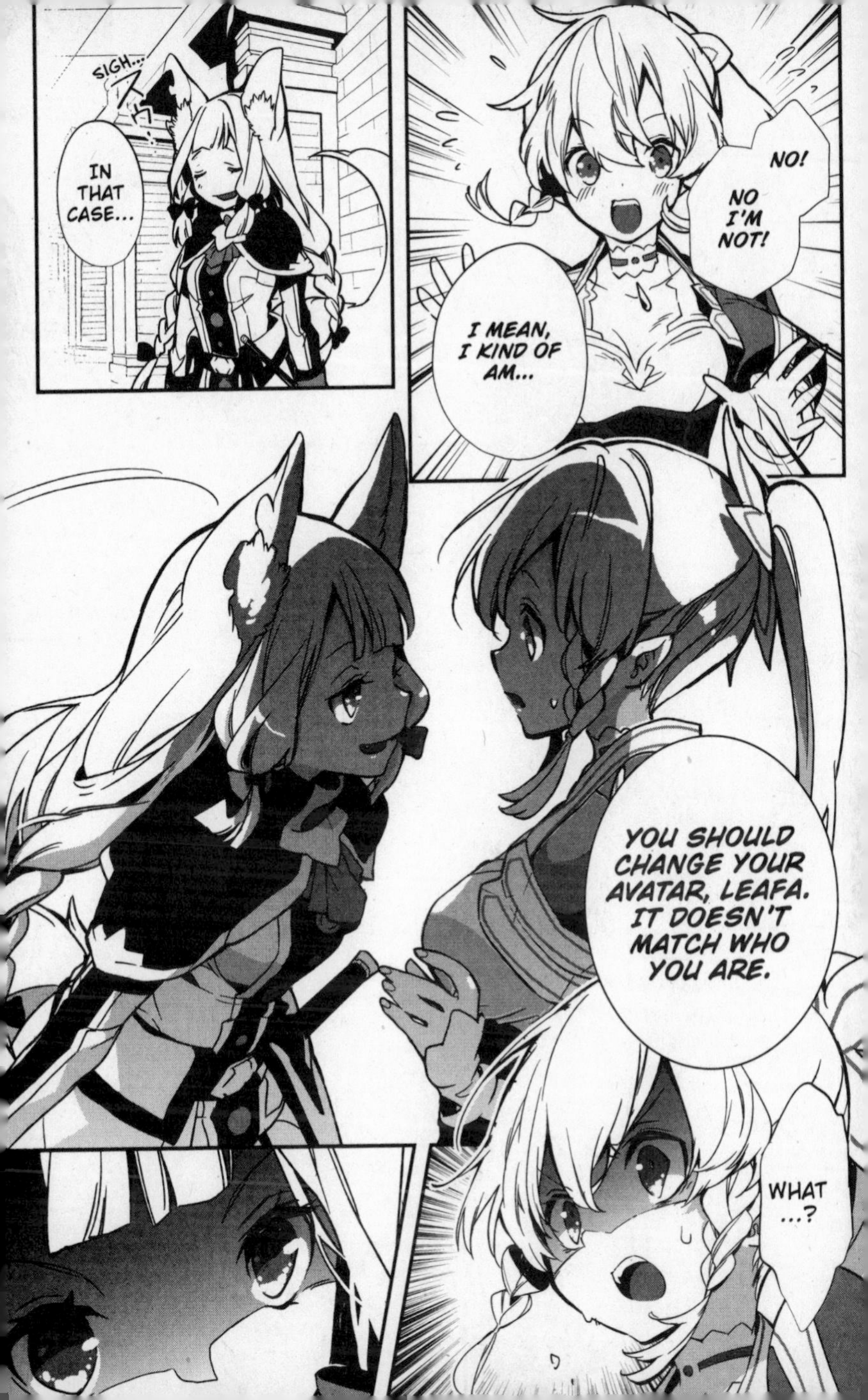
NO!
NO I'M NOT!
I MEAN, I KIND OF AM...
SIGH...
IN THAT CASE...
YOU SHOULD CHANGE YOUR AVATAR, LEAFA. IT DOESN'T MATCH WHO YOU ARE.
WHAT ...?

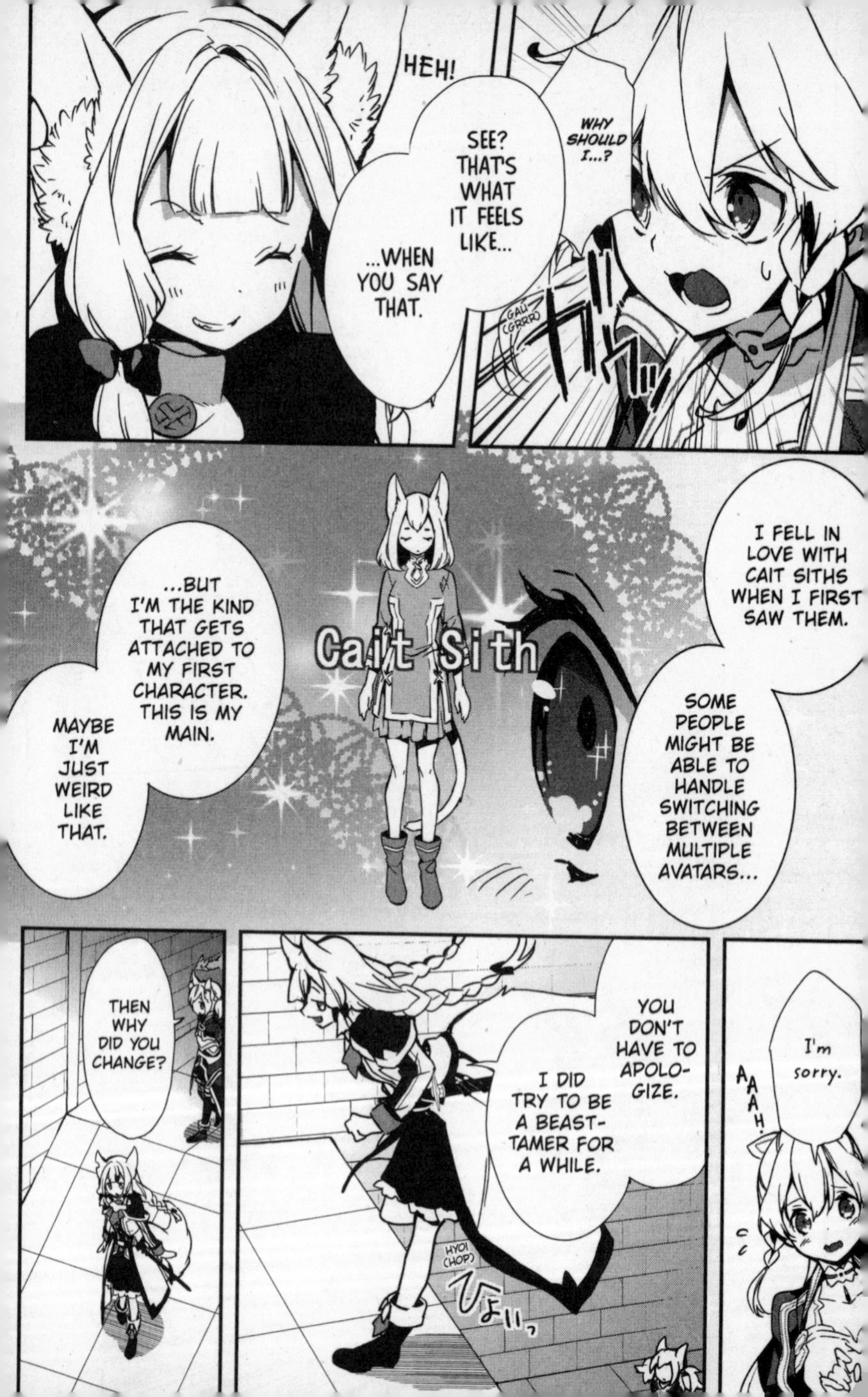
WHY SHOULD I...?
GAU (GRRR)
HEH!
SEE? THAT'S WHAT IT FEELS LIKE...
...WHEN YOU SAY THAT.
I FELL IN LOVE WITH CAIT SITHS WHEN I FIRST SAW THEM.
SOME PEOPLE MIGHT BE ABLE TO HANDLE SWITCHING BETWEEN MULTIPLE AVATARS...
Cait Sith
...BUT I'M THE KIND THAT GETS ATTACHED TO MY FIRST CHARACTER. THIS IS MY MAIN.
MAYBE I'M JUST WEIRD LIKE THAT.
AAAH!
I'm sorry.
YOU DON'T HAVE TO APOLOGIZE.
I DID TRY TO BE A BEAST-TAMER FOR A WHILE.
HYOI (HOP)
THEN WHY DID YOU CHANGE?

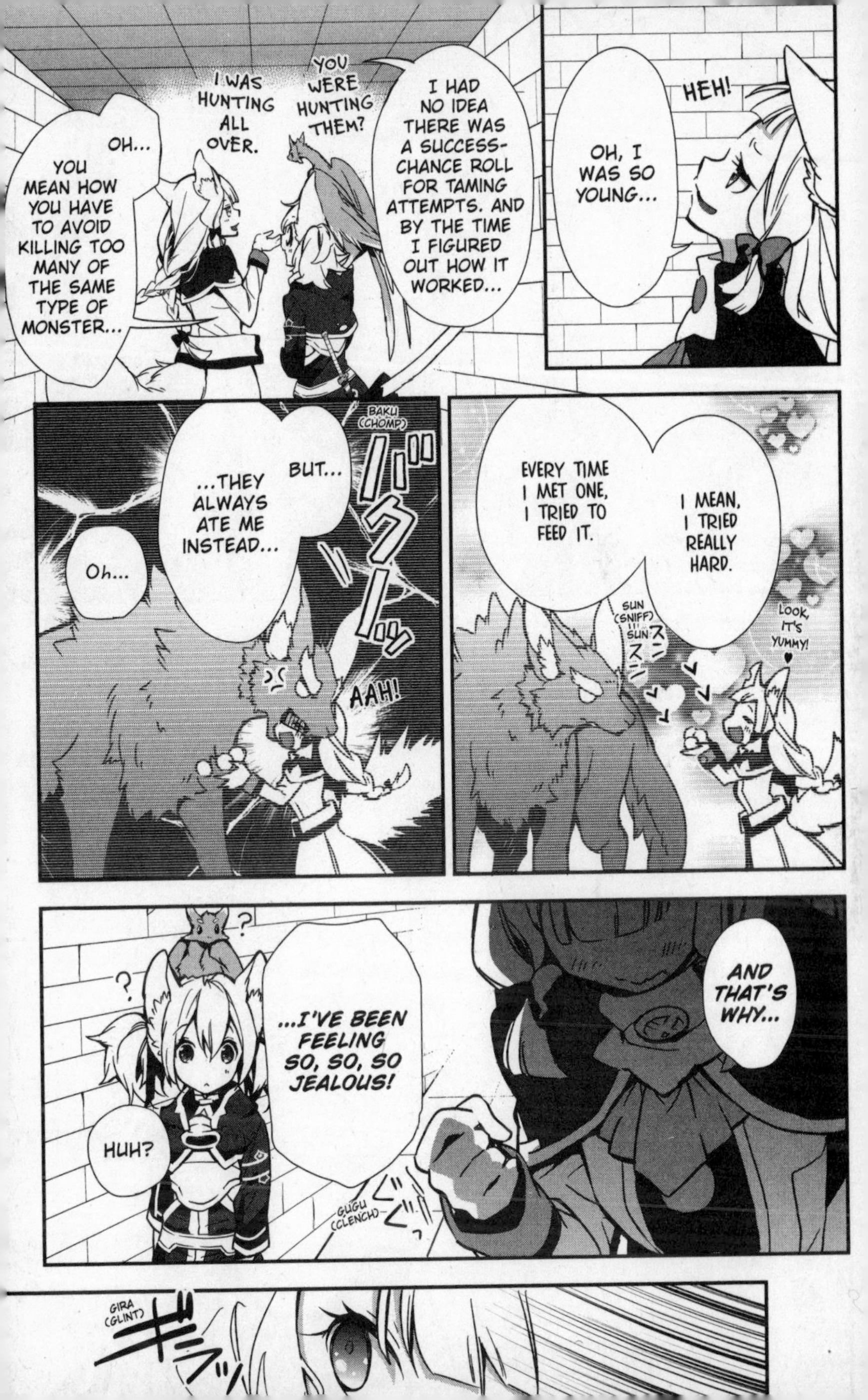
HEH!
OH, I WAS SO YOUNG...
I HAD NO IDEA THERE WAS A SUCCESS-CHANCE ROLL FOR TAMING ATTEMPTS. AND BY THE TIME I FIGURED OUT HOW IT WORKED...
YOU WERE HUNTING THEM?
I WAS HUNTING ALL OVER.
OH... YOU MEAN HOW YOU HAVE TO AVOID KILLING TOO MANY OF THE SAME TYPE OF MONSTER...
I MEAN, I TRIED REALLY HARD.
EVERY TIME I MET ONE, I TRIED TO FEED IT.
LOOK, IT'S YUMMY!
SUN (SNIFF) SUN
BAKU (CHOMP)
BUT...
...THEY ALWAYS ATE ME INSTEAD...
AAH!
Oh...
AND THAT'S WHY...
...I'VE BEEN FEELING SO, SO, SO JEALOUS!
GUGU (CLENCH)
HUH?
GIRA (GLINT)

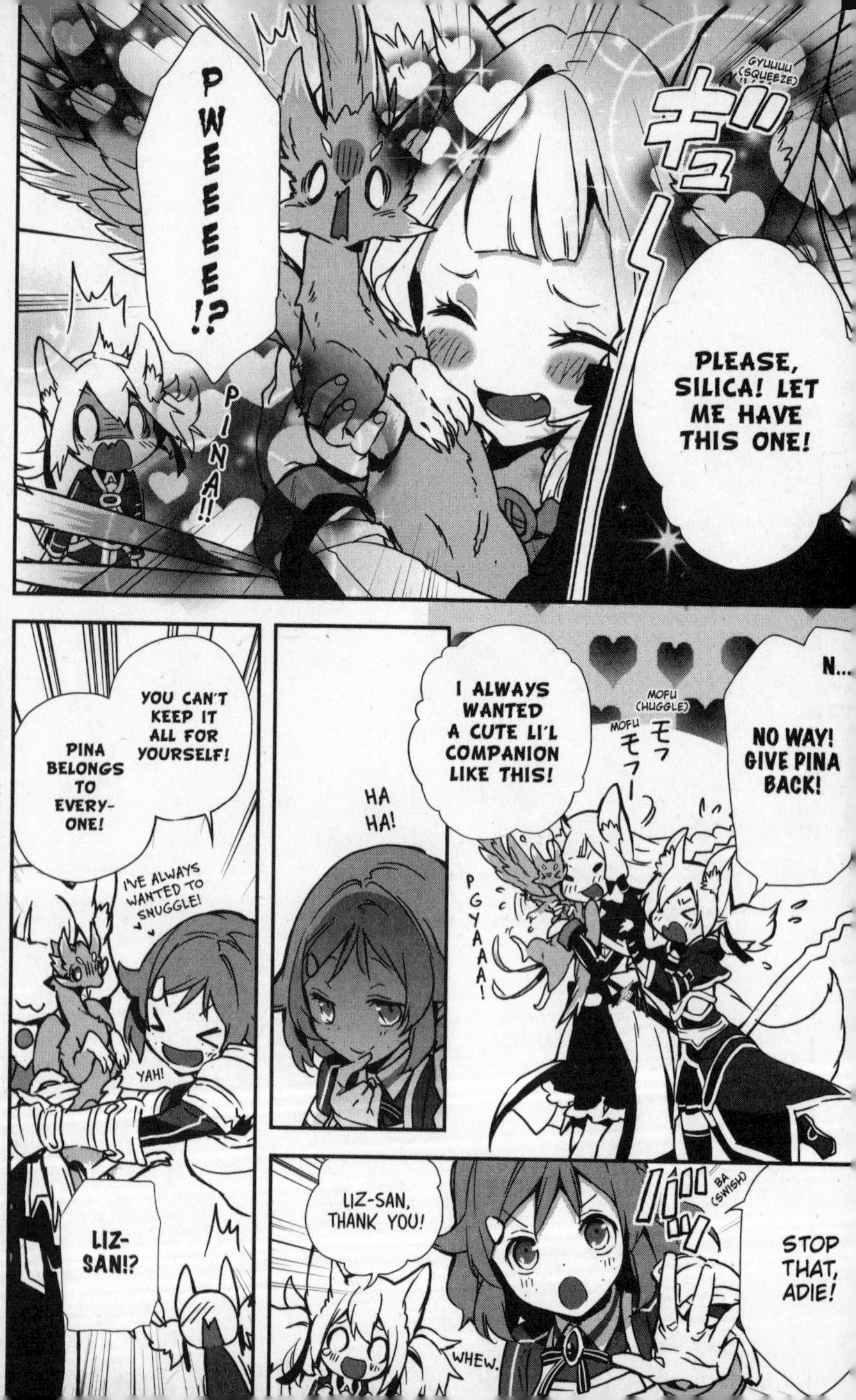
GYUUUU (SQUEEZE)
ギュ
PLEASE, SILICA! LET ME HAVE THIS ONE!
PWEEEEE!?
PINA!!
N...
NO WAY! GIVE PINA BACK!
MOFU (HUGGLE) MOFU
モフ モフー
I ALWAYS WANTED A CUTE LI'L COMPANION LIKE THIS!
PGYAAA!
HA HA!
YOU CAN'T KEEP IT ALL FOR YOURSELF!
PINA BELONGS TO EVERY-ONE!
I'VE ALWAYS WANTED TO SNUGGLE!
YAH!
BA (SWISH)
STOP THAT, ADIE!
LIZ-SAN, THANK YOU!
WHEW.
LIZ-SAN!?

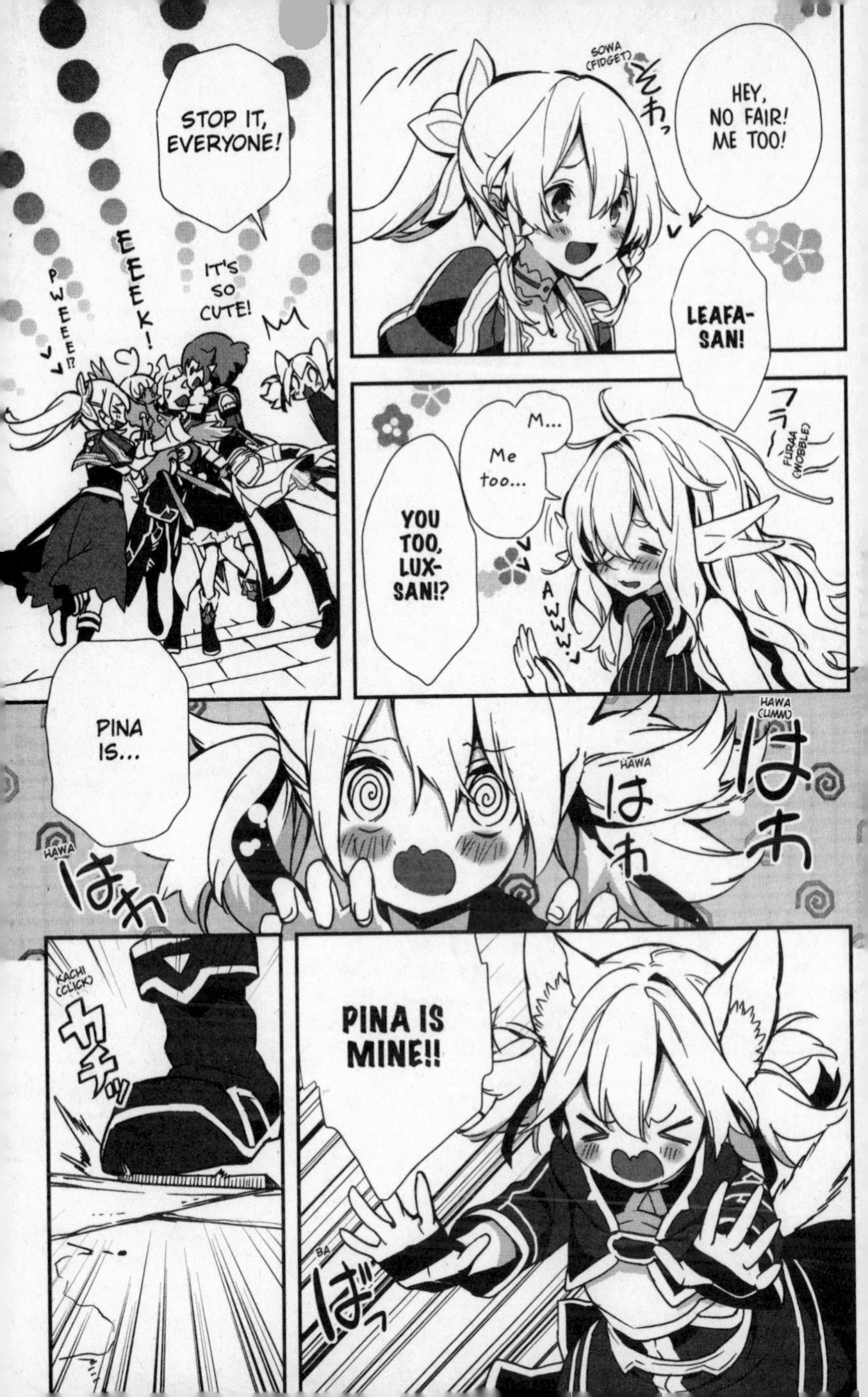
SOWA (FIDGET)
そわっ
HEY, NO FAIR! ME TOO!
LEAFA-SAN!
FURAA (WOBBLE)
フラ~
M...
Me too...
AWWW...
YOU TOO, LUX-SAN!?
STOP IT, EVERYONE!
EEEEK!
IT'S SO CUTE!
PWEEEE!?
HAWA (UMM)
はわ
HAWA
はわ
HAWA
はわ
PINA IS...
PINA IS MINE!!
BA
ばっ
KACHI (CLICK)
カチッ
...

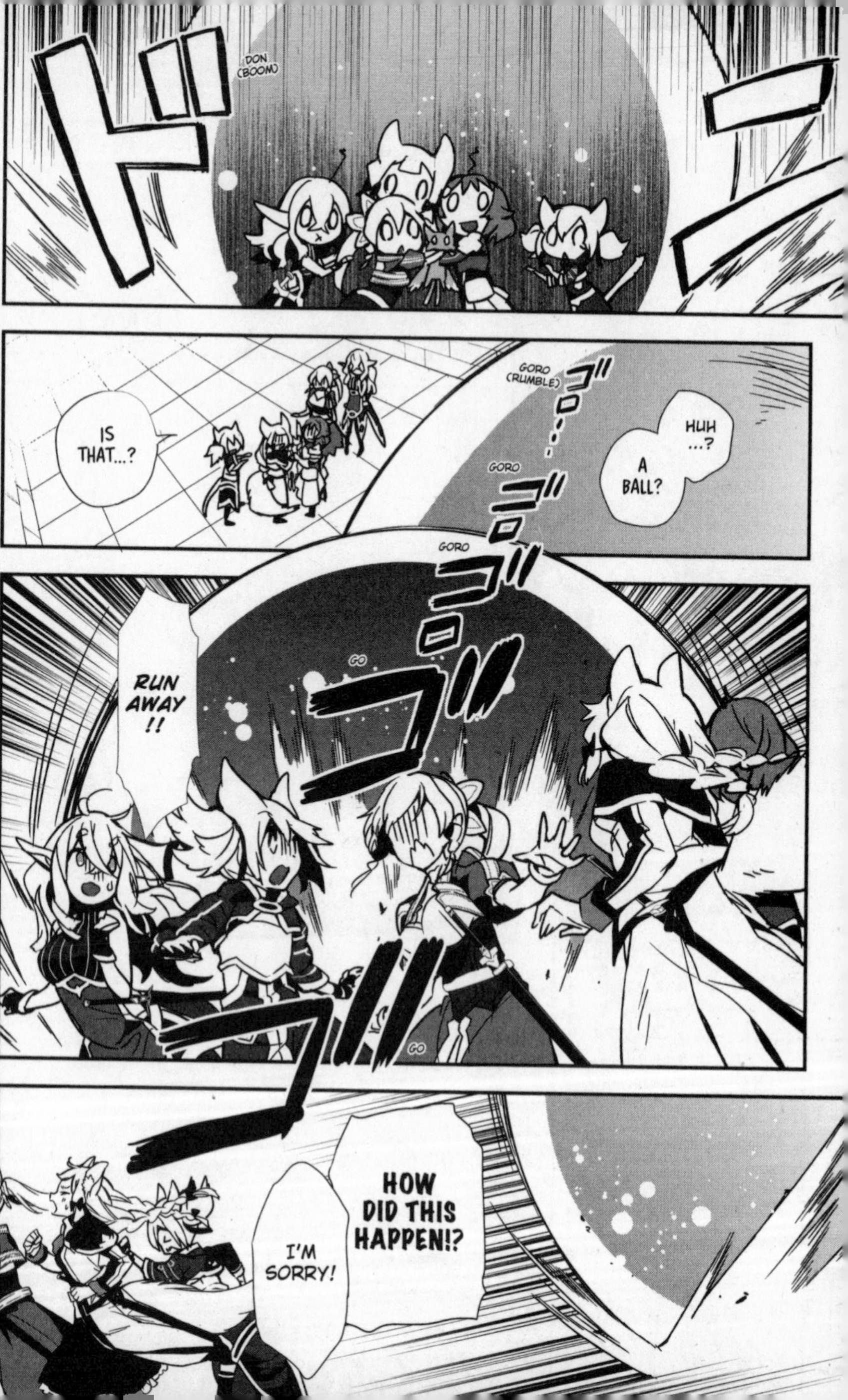
DON (BOOM)
GORO (RUMBLE)
HUH ...?
A BALL?
GORO
IS THAT...?
GORO
GO
RUN AWAY!!
GO
HOW DID THIS HAPPEN!?
I'M SORRY!

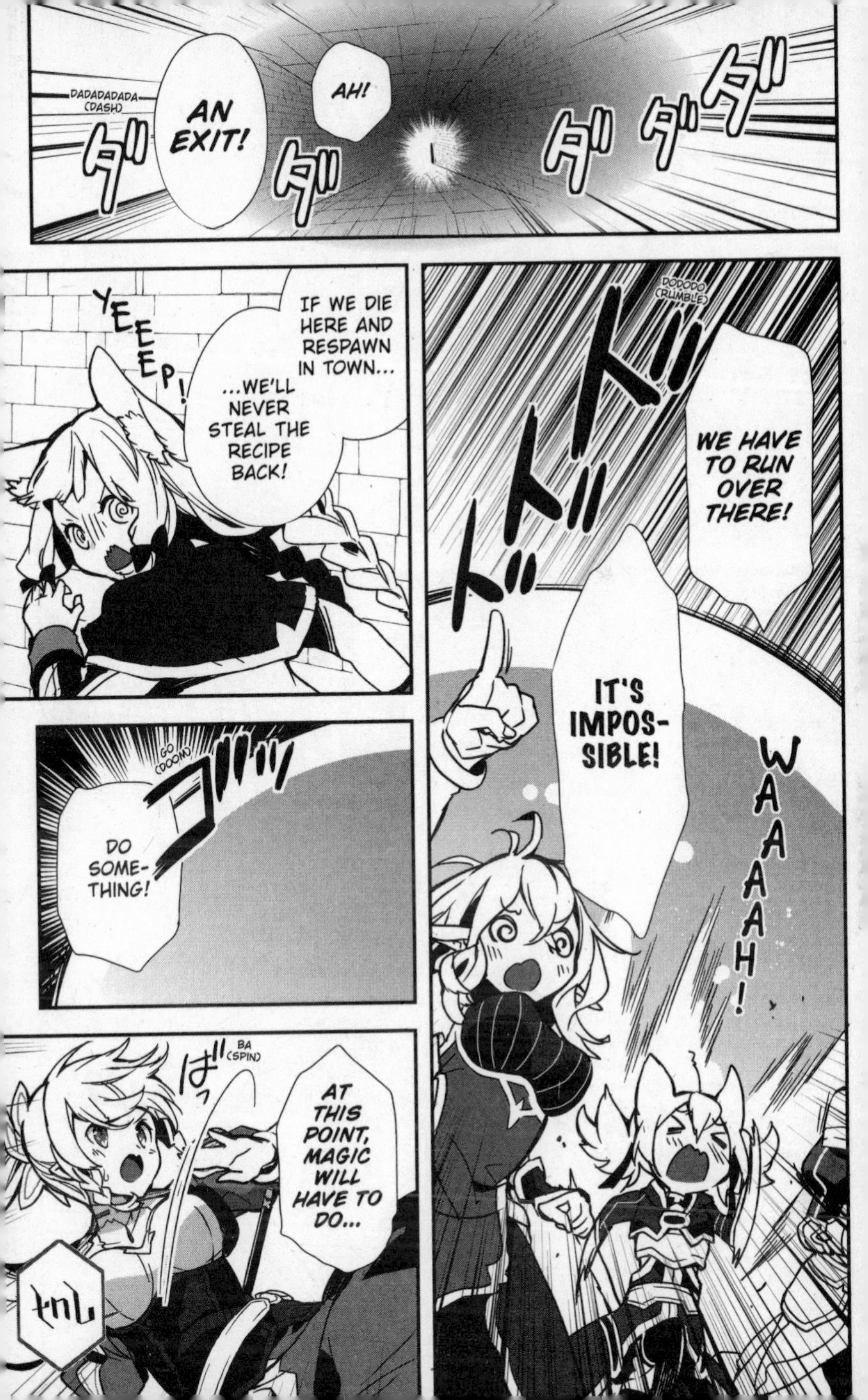
AH!
AN EXIT!
DADADADADA (DASH)
DODODO (RUMBLE)
WE HAVE TO RUN OVER THERE!
IT'S IMPOSSIBLE!
WAAAAAAH!
YEEEEP!
IF WE DIE HERE AND RESPAWN IN TOWN...
...WE'LL NEVER STEAL THE RECIPE BACK!
GO (DOOM)
DO SOMETHING!
BA (SPIN)
AT THIS POINT, MAGIC WILL HAVE TO DO...

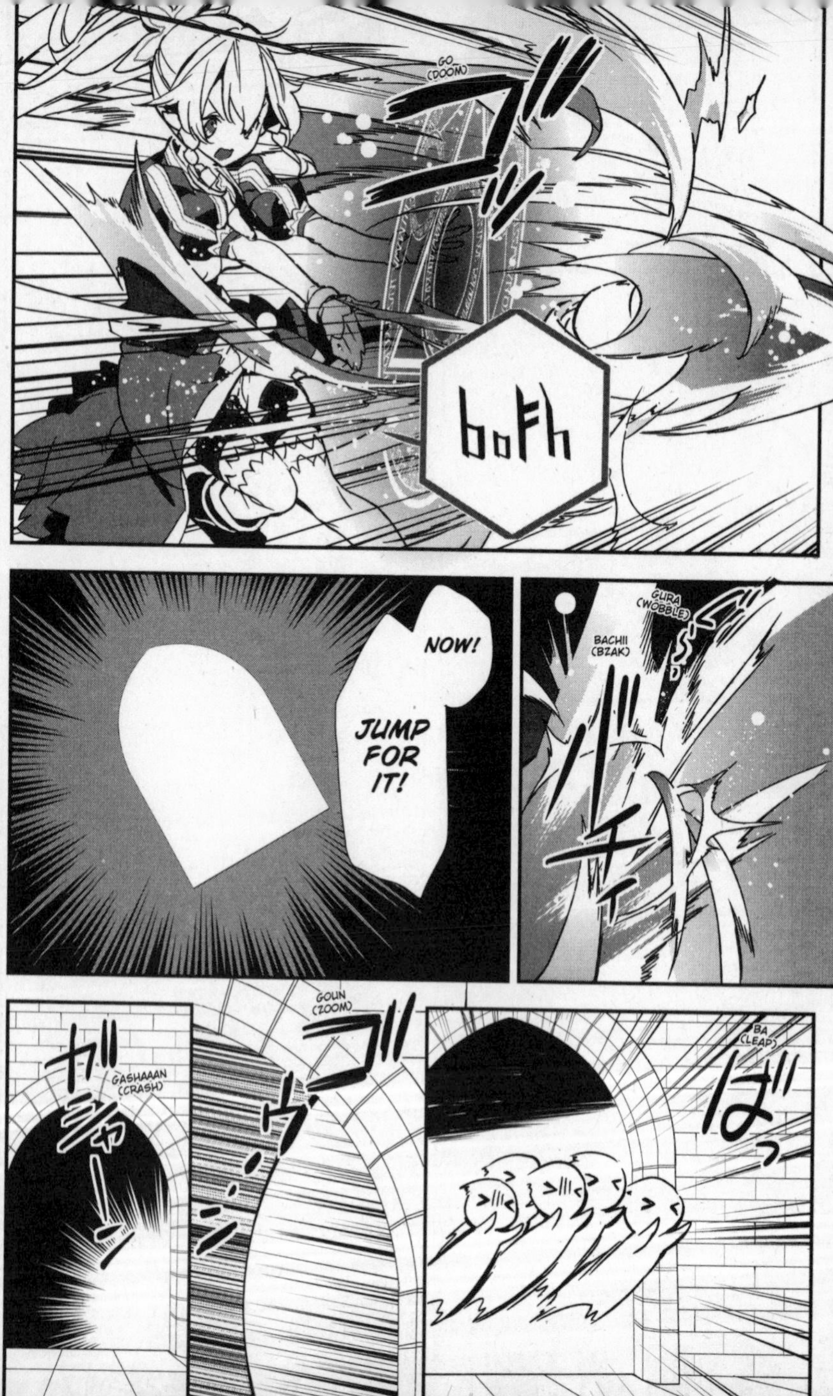
GO (DOOM)
GURA (WOBBLE)
BACHII (BZAK)
NOW!
JUMP FOR IT!
BA (LEAP)
GOUN (ZOOM)
GASHAAAN (CRASH)

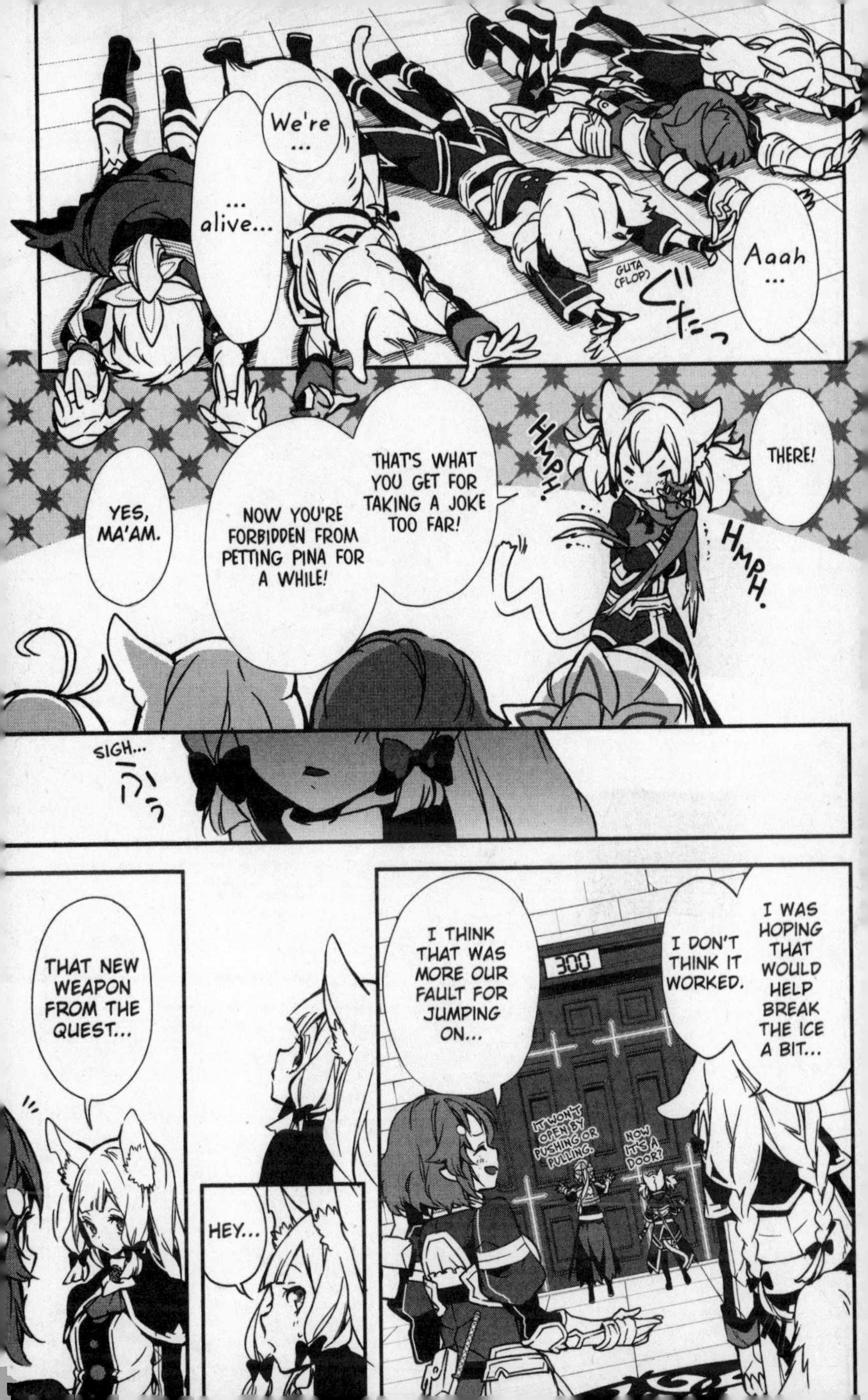

Aaah ...
GUTA (FLOP)
We're ...
... alive...
THERE!
HMPH.
HMPH.
THAT'S WHAT YOU GET FOR TAKING A JOKE TOO FAR!
NOW YOU'RE FORBIDDEN FROM PETTING PINA FOR A WHILE!
YES, MA'AM.
SIGH...
I WAS HOPING THAT WOULD HELP BREAK THE ICE A BIT...
I DON'T THINK IT WORKED.
I THINK THAT WAS MORE OUR FAULT FOR JUMPING ON...
300
NOW IT'S A DOOR?
IT WON'T OPEN BY PUSHING OR PULLING.
THAT NEW WEAPON FROM THE QUEST...
HEY...

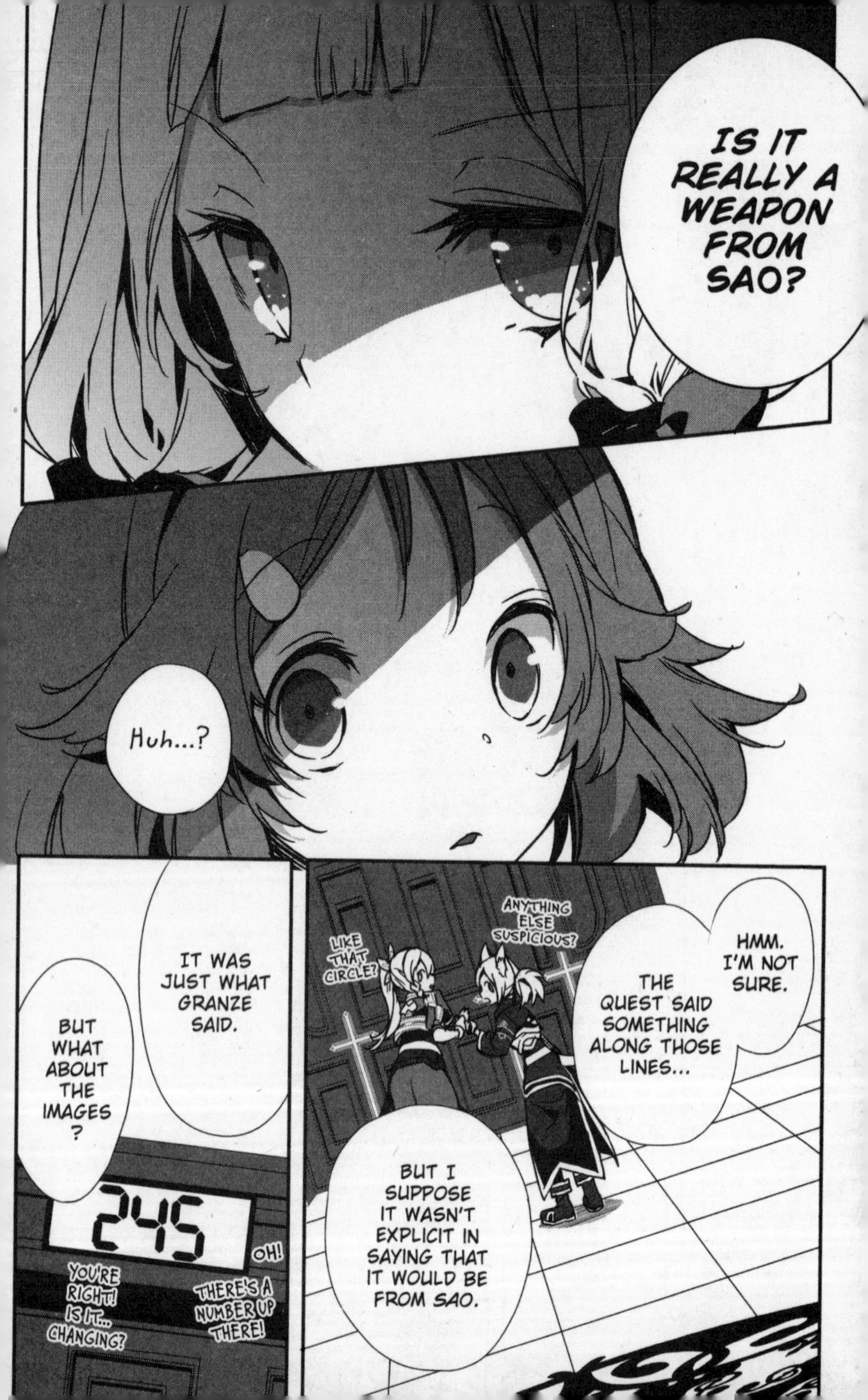
IS IT REALLY A WEAPON FROM SAO?
Huh...?
HMM. I'M NOT SURE.
THE QUEST SAID SOMETHING ALONG THOSE LINES...
ANYTHING ELSE SUSPICIOUS?
LIKE THAT CIRCLE?
BUT I SUPPOSE IT WASN'T EXPLICIT IN SAYING THAT IT WOULD BE FROM SAO.
IT WAS JUST WHAT GRANZE SAID.
BUT WHAT ABOUT THE IMAGES?
245
OH!
THERE'S A NUMBER UP THERE!
YOU'RE RIGHT! IS IT... CHANGING?

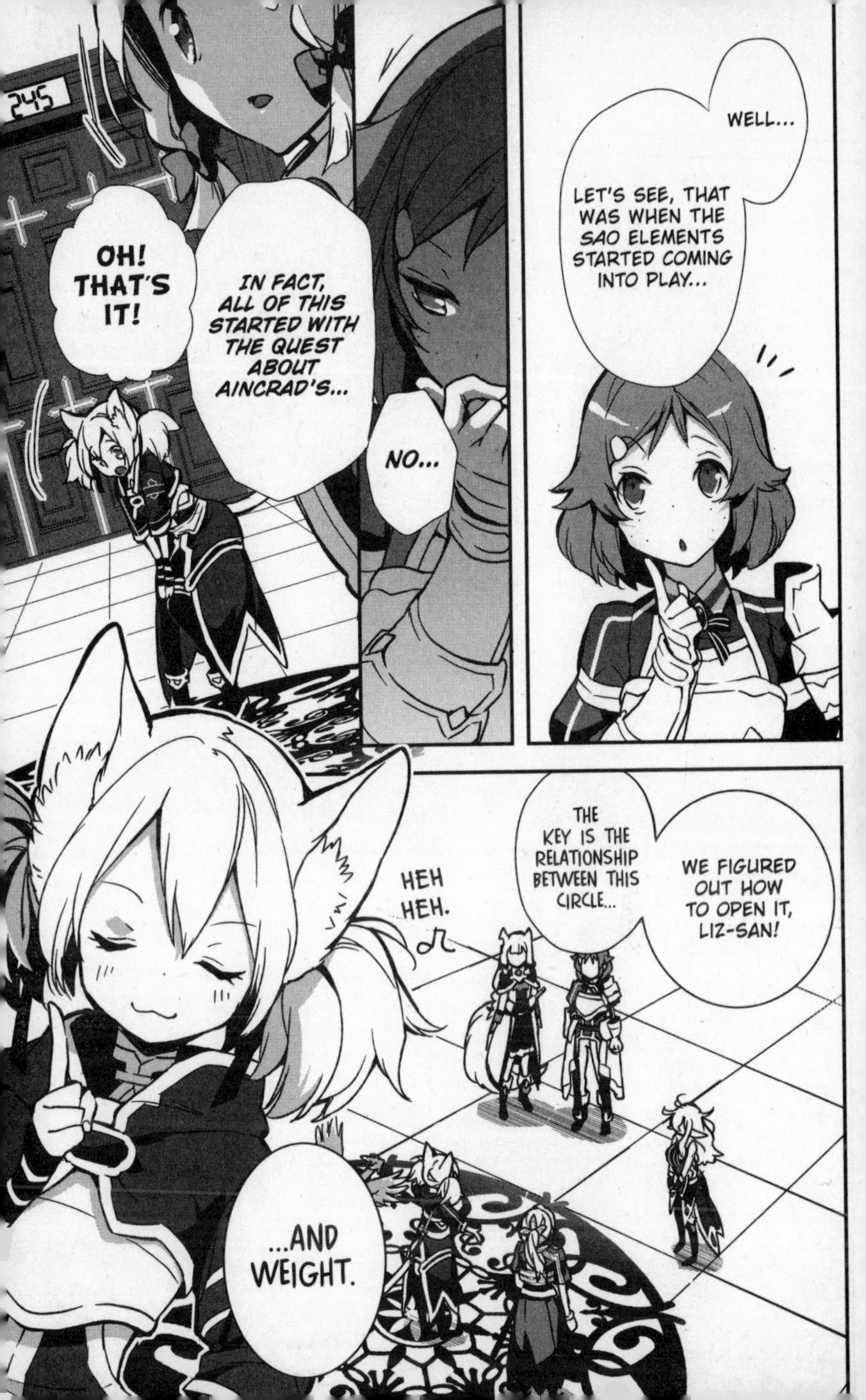
WELL...
LET'S SEE, THAT WAS WHEN THE SAO ELEMENTS STARTED COMING INTO PLAY...
IN FACT, ALL OF THIS STARTED WITH THE QUEST ABOUT AINCRAD'S...
NO...
245
OH! THAT'S IT!
WE FIGURED OUT HOW TO OPEN IT, LIZ-SAN!
THE KEY IS THE RELATIONSHIP BETWEEN THIS CIRCLE...
HEH HEH.
...AND WEIGHT.

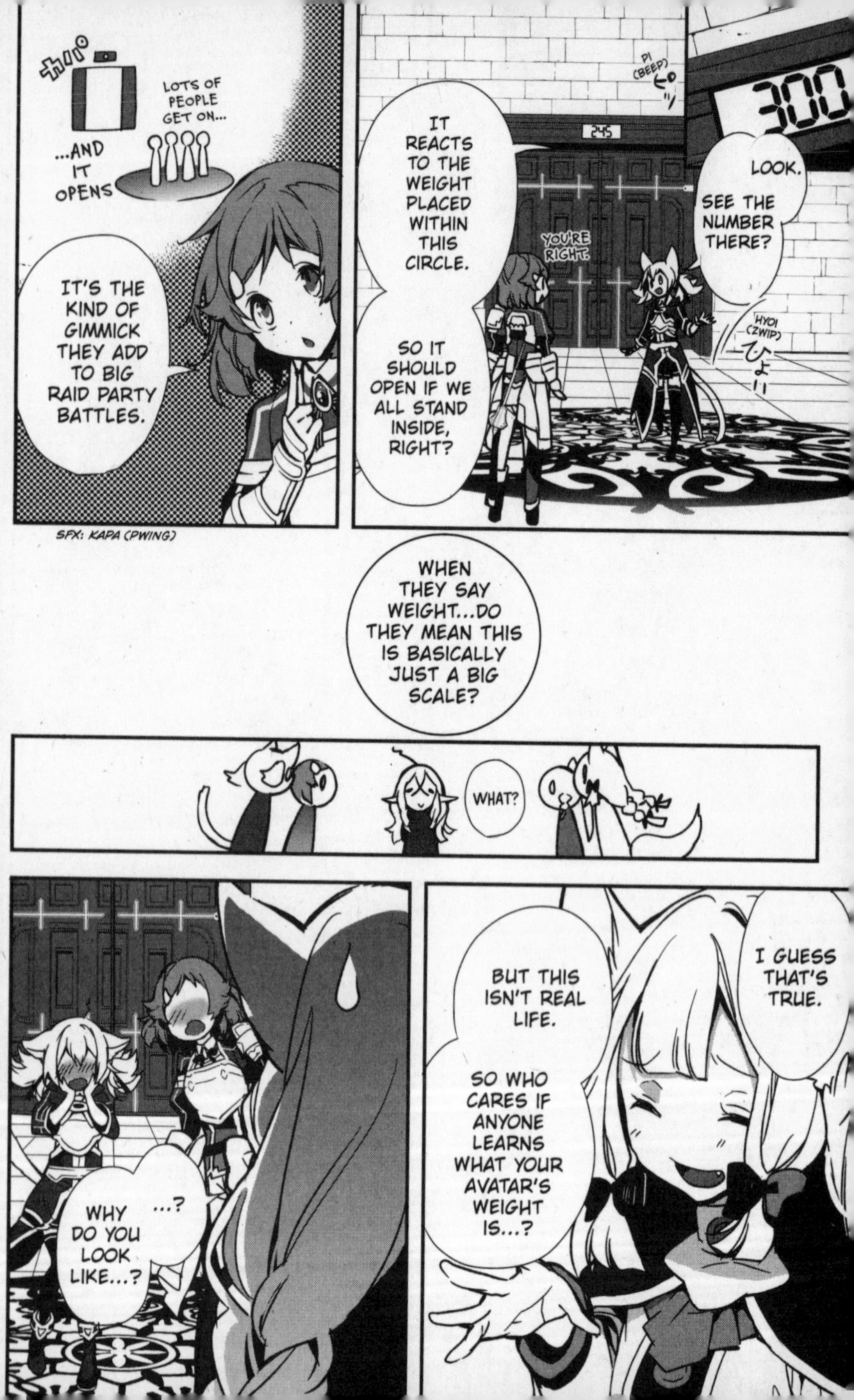
300
PI (BEEP)
LOOK.
SEE THE NUMBER THERE?
HYOI (ZWIP)
YOU'RE RIGHT.
245
IT REACTS TO THE WEIGHT PLACED WITHIN THIS CIRCLE.
SO IT SHOULD OPEN IF WE ALL STAND INSIDE, RIGHT?
LOTS OF PEOPLE GET ON...
...AND IT OPENS
IT'S THE KIND OF GIMMICK THEY ADD TO BIG RAID PARTY BATTLES.
SFX: KAPA (PWING)
WHEN THEY SAY WEIGHT...DO THEY MEAN THIS IS BASICALLY JUST A BIG SCALE?
WHAT?
I GUESS THAT'S TRUE.
BUT THIS ISN'T REAL LIFE.
SO WHO CARES IF ANYONE LEARNS WHAT YOUR AVATAR'S WEIGHT IS...?
...?
WHY DO YOU LOOK LIKE...?

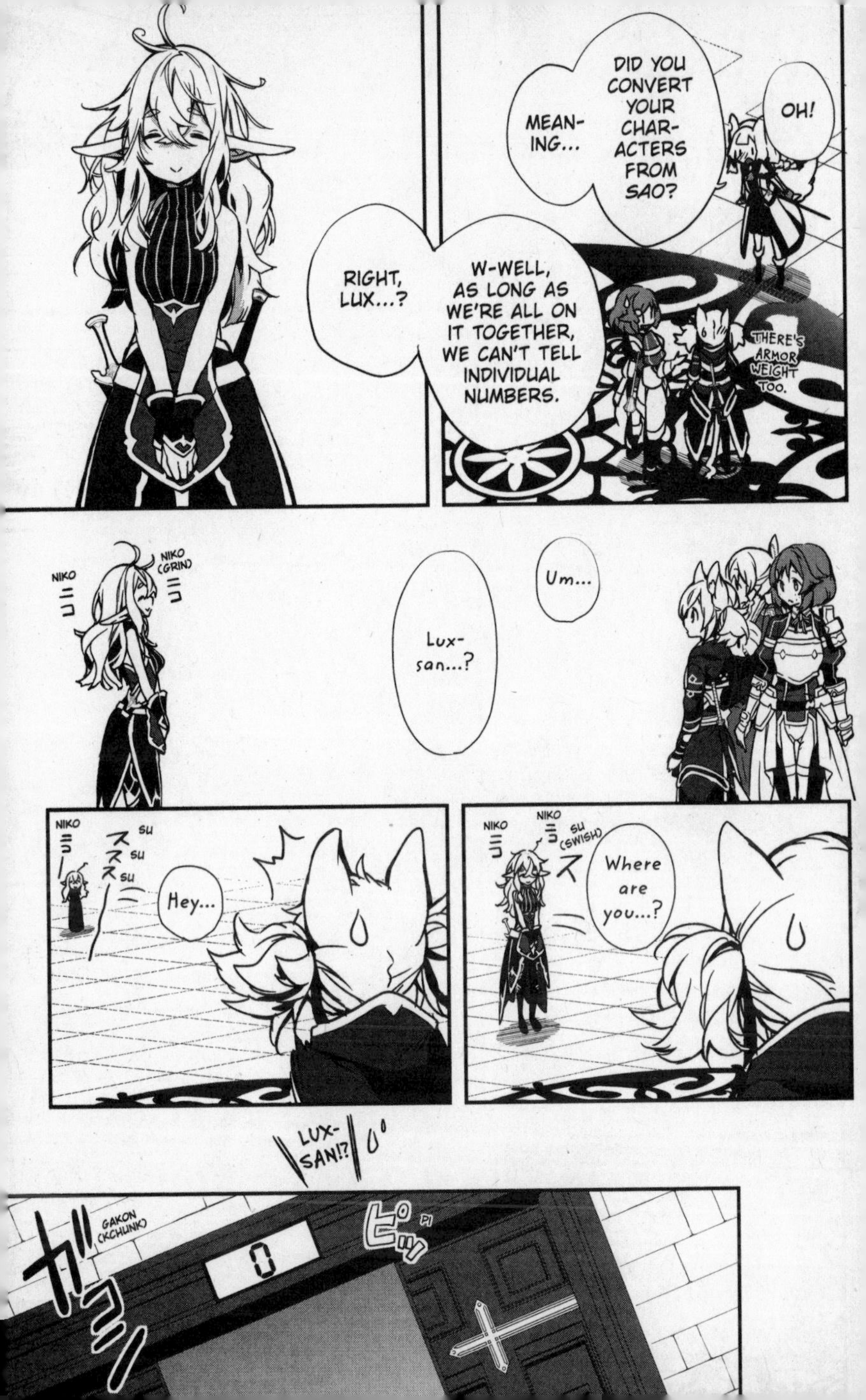
OH!
MEANING...
DID YOU CONVERT YOUR CHARACTERS FROM SAO?
W-WELL, AS LONG AS WE'RE ALL ON IT TOGETHER, WE CAN'T TELL INDIVIDUAL NUMBERS.
RIGHT, LUX...?
THERE'S ARMOR WEIGHT TOO.
Um...
Lux-san...?
NIKO (GRIN)
NIKO
Where are you...?
SU (SWISH)
NIKO
NIKO
Hey...
SU SU SU
NIKO
LUX-SAN!?
PI
GAKON (KCHUNK)
0

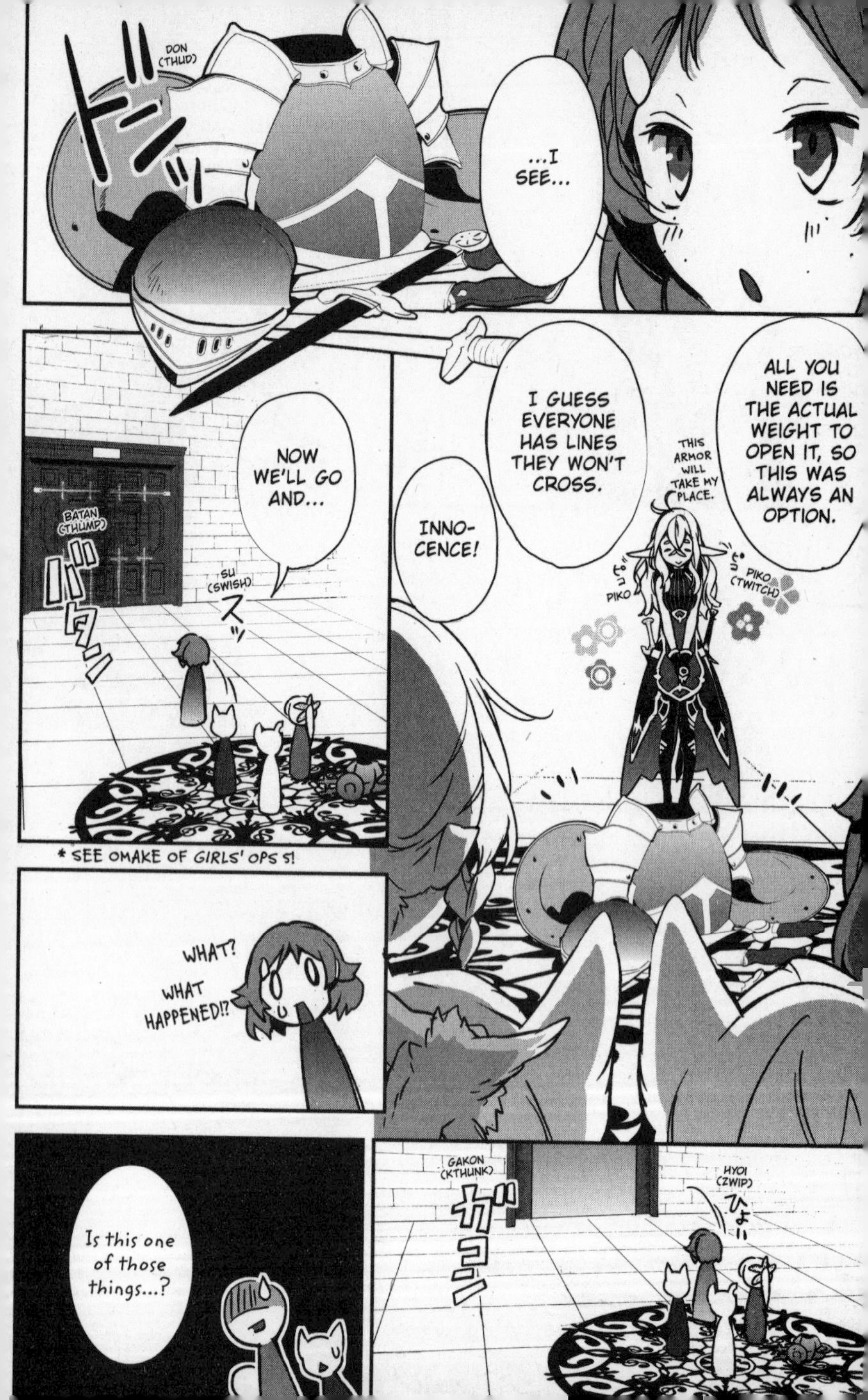
...I SEE...
DON (THUD)
ALL YOU NEED IS THE ACTUAL WEIGHT TO OPEN IT, SO THIS WAS ALWAYS AN OPTION.
THIS ARMOR WILL TAKE MY PLACE.
I GUESS EVERYONE HAS LINES THEY WON'T CROSS.
PIKO (TWITCH)
PIKO
INNO-CENCE!
NOW WE'LL GO AND...
SU (SWISH)
BATAN (THUMP)
* SEE OMAKE OF GIRLS' OPS 5!
WHAT?
WHAT HAPPENED!?
GAKON (KTHUNK)
HYOI (ZWIP)
Is this one of those things...?

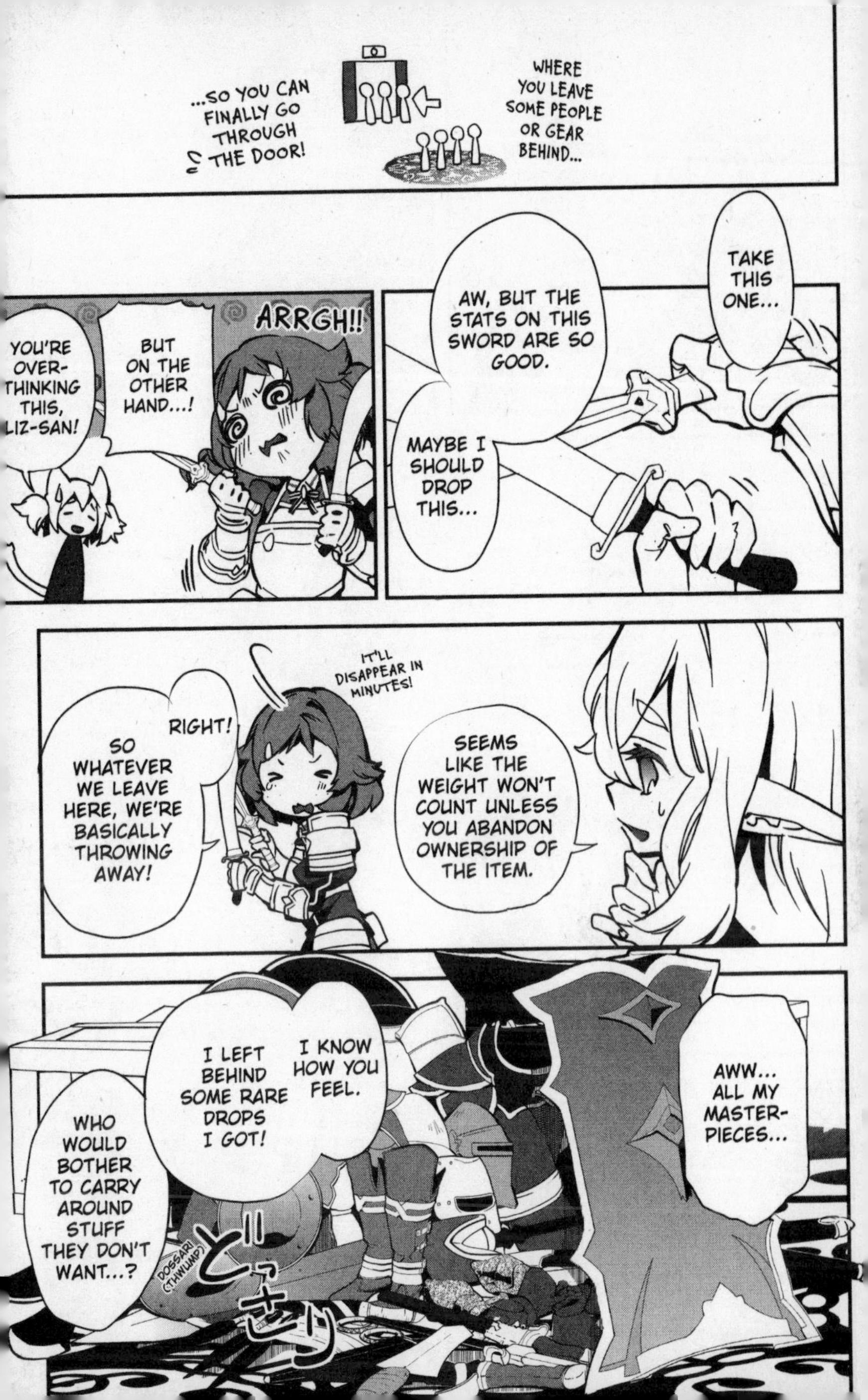
WHERE YOU LEAVE SOME PEOPLE OR GEAR BEHIND...
...SO YOU CAN FINALLY GO THROUGH THE DOOR!
TAKE THIS ONE...
AW, BUT THE STATS ON THIS SWORD ARE SO GOOD.
MAYBE I SHOULD DROP THIS...
ARRGH!!
BUT ON THE OTHER HAND...!
YOU'RE OVER-THINKING THIS, LIZ-SAN!
SEEMS LIKE THE WEIGHT WON'T COUNT UNLESS YOU ABANDON OWNERSHIP OF THE ITEM.
IT'LL DISAPPEAR IN MINUTES!
RIGHT!
SO WHATEVER WE LEAVE HERE, WE'RE BASICALLY THROWING AWAY!
AWW... ALL MY MASTER-PIECES...
I KNOW HOW YOU FEEL.
I LEFT BEHIND SOME RARE DROPS I GOT!
WHO WOULD BOTHER TO CARRY AROUND STUFF THEY DON'T WANT...?
どっさり
DOSSARI (THWUMP)

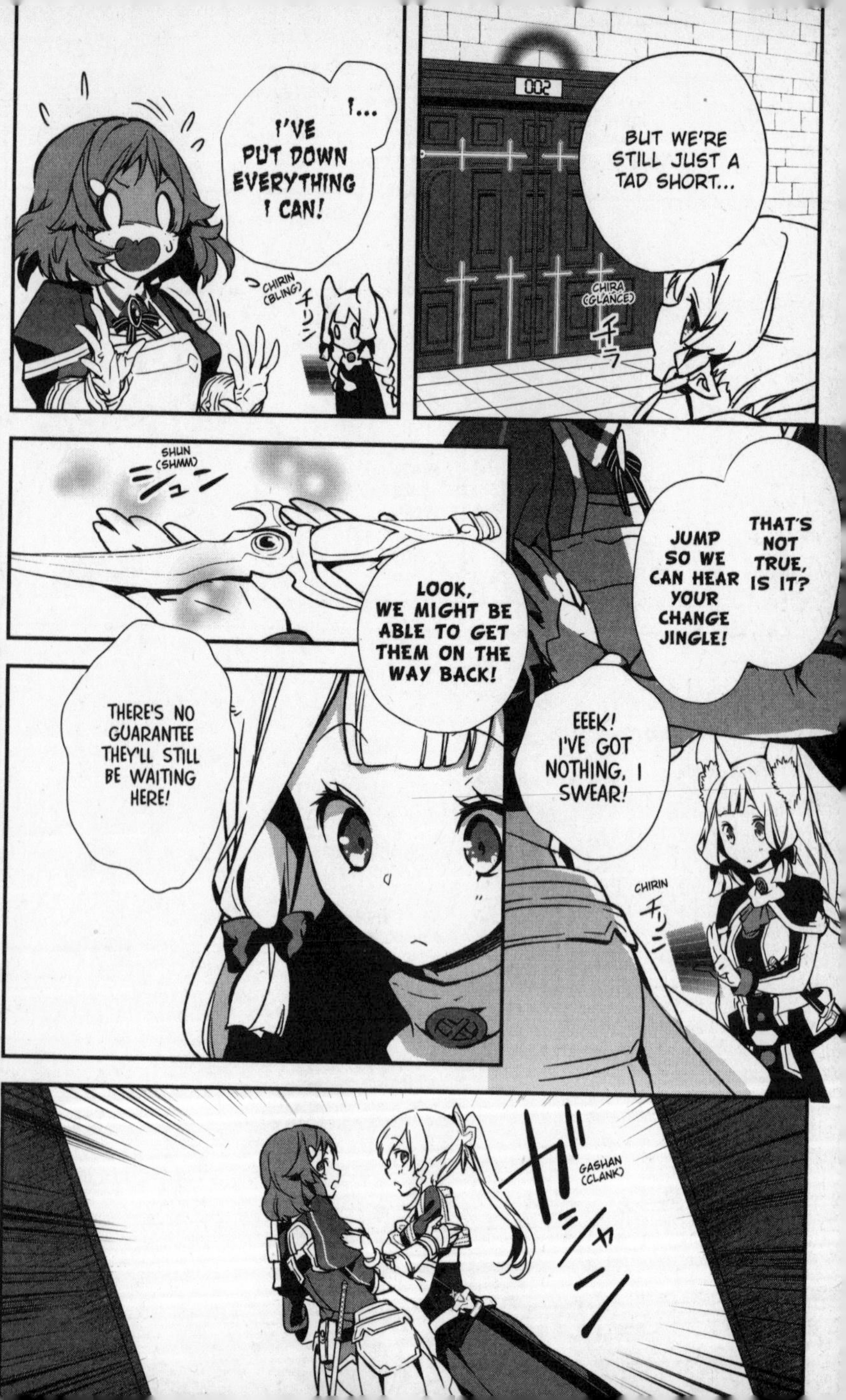
BUT WE'RE STILL JUST A TAD SHORT...
CHIRA (GLANCE)
チラ
I... I'VE PUT DOWN EVERYTHING I CAN!
CHIRIN (BLING)
チリン
THAT'S NOT TRUE, IS IT?
JUMP SO WE CAN HEAR YOUR CHANGE JINGLE!
EEEK! I'VE GOT NOTHING, I SWEAR!
CHIRIN
チリン
SHUN (SHMM)
シュン
LOOK, WE MIGHT BE ABLE TO GET THEM ON THE WAY BACK!
THERE'S NO GUARANTEE THEY'LL STILL BE WAITING HERE!
GASHAN (CLANK)
ガシャン

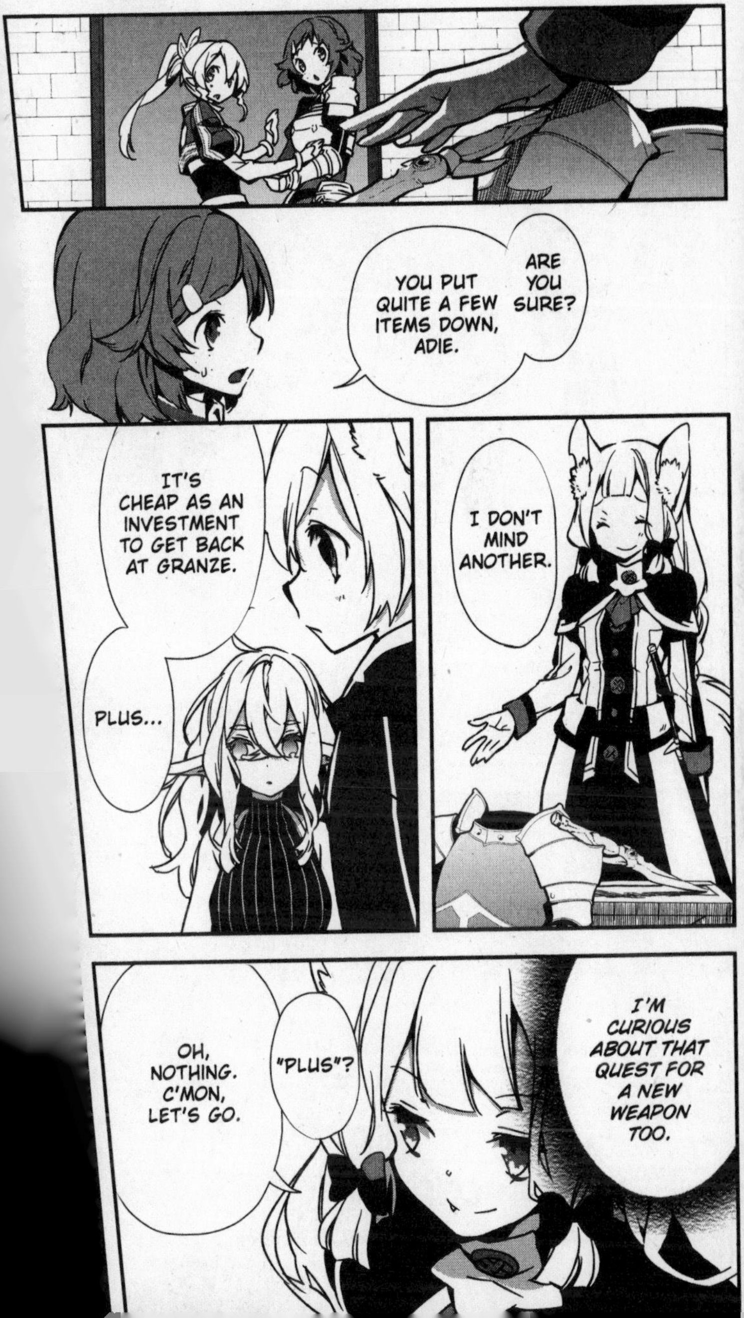
ARE YOU SURE?
YOU PUT QUITE A FEW ITEMS DOWN, ADIE.
I DON'T MIND ANOTHER.
IT'S CHEAP AS AN INVESTMENT TO GET BACK AT GRANZE.
PLUS...
I'M CURIOUS ABOUT THAT QUEST FOR A NEW WEAPON TOO.
"PLUS"?
OH, NOTHING. C'MON, LET'S GO.

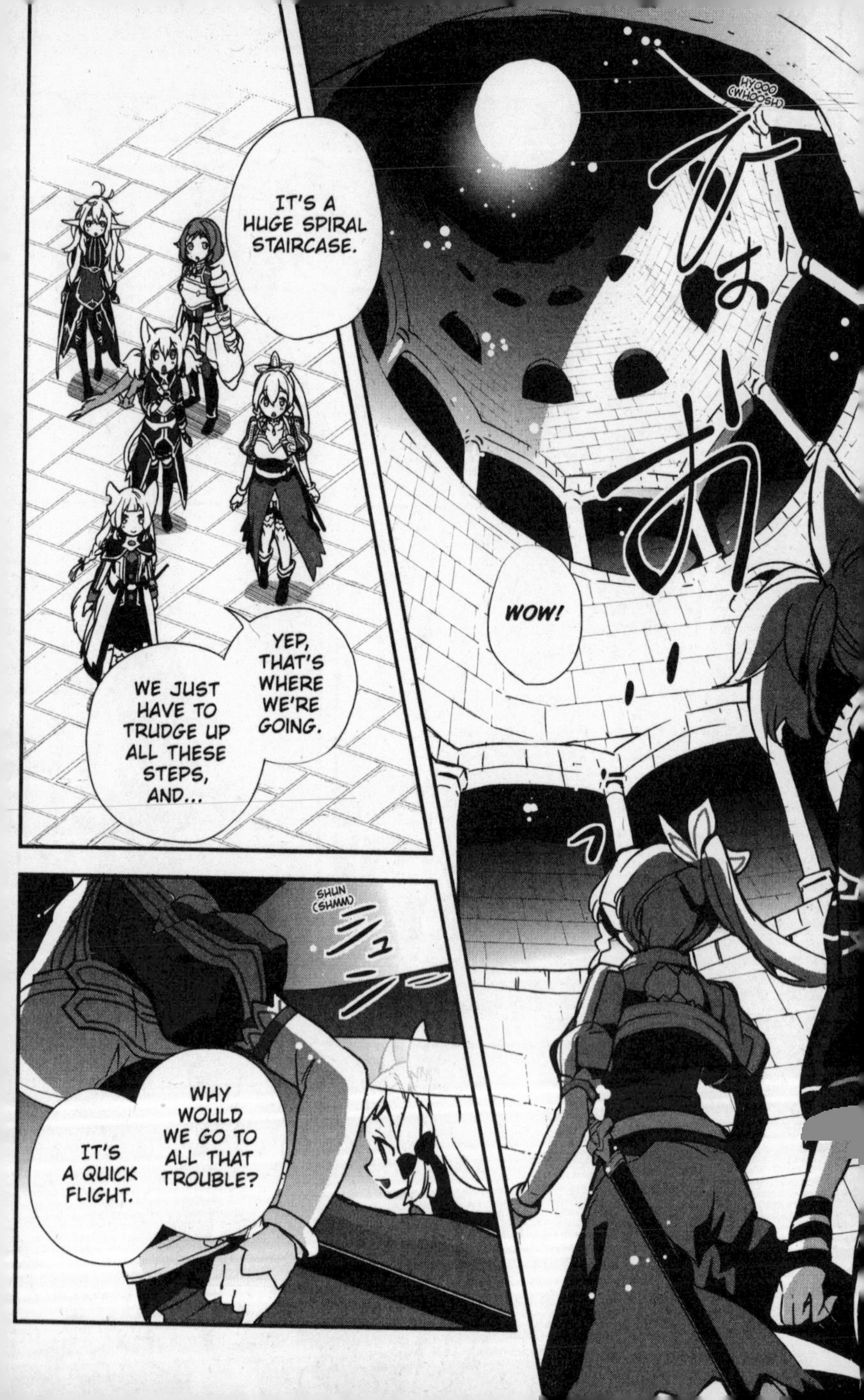
HYOOO (WHOOSH)
WOW!
IT'S A HUGE SPIRAL STAIRCASE.
YEP, THAT'S WHERE WE'RE GOING.
WE JUST HAVE TO TRUDGE UP ALL THESE STEPS, AND...
SHUN (SHMM)
WHY WOULD WE GO TO ALL THAT TROUBLE?
IT'S A QUICK FLIGHT.

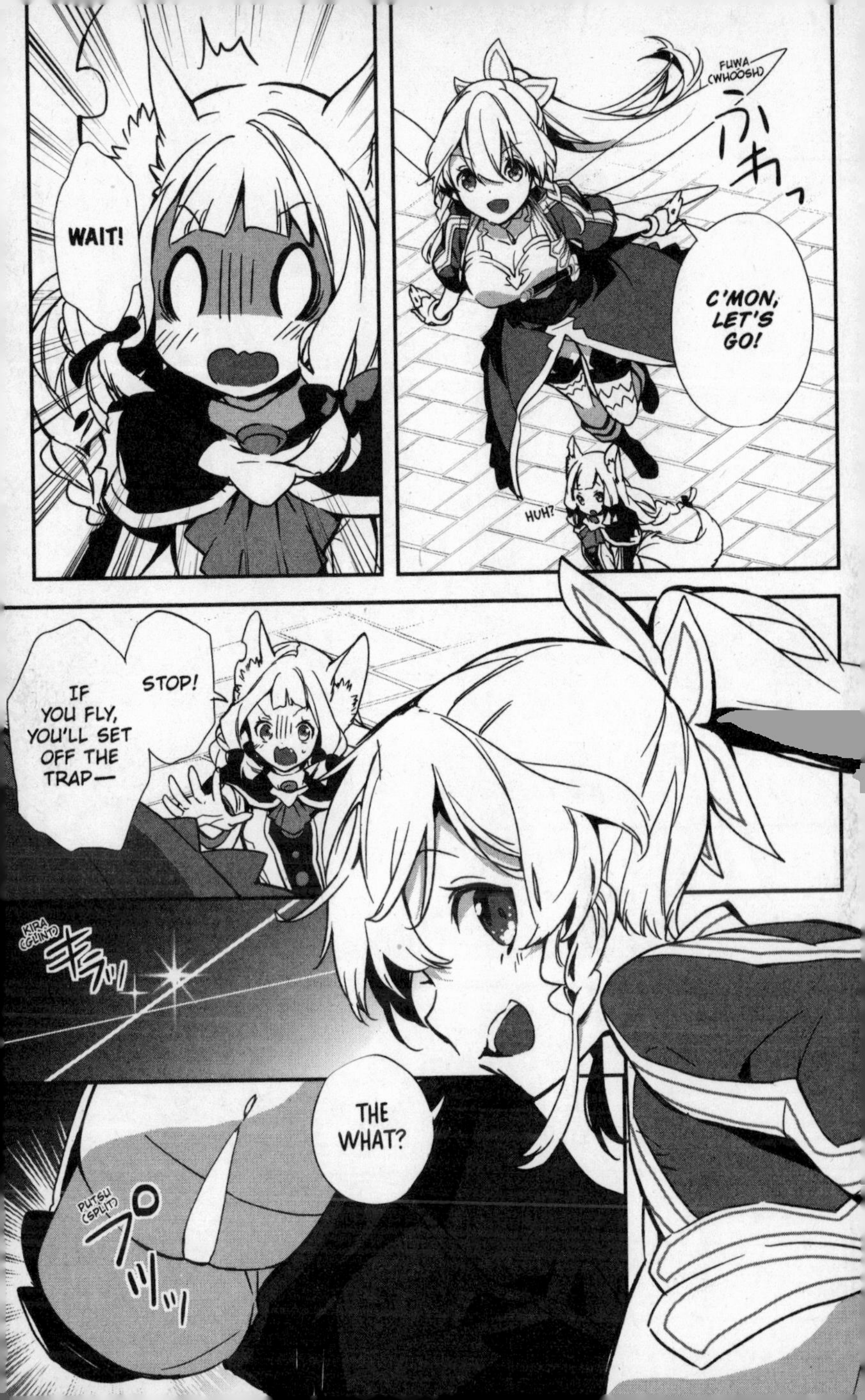
FUWA (WHOOSH)
C'MON, LET'S GO!
HUH?
WAIT!
STOP!
IF YOU FLY, YOU'LL SET OFF THE TRAP—
KIRA (GLINT)
THE WHAT?
PUTSU (SPLIT)

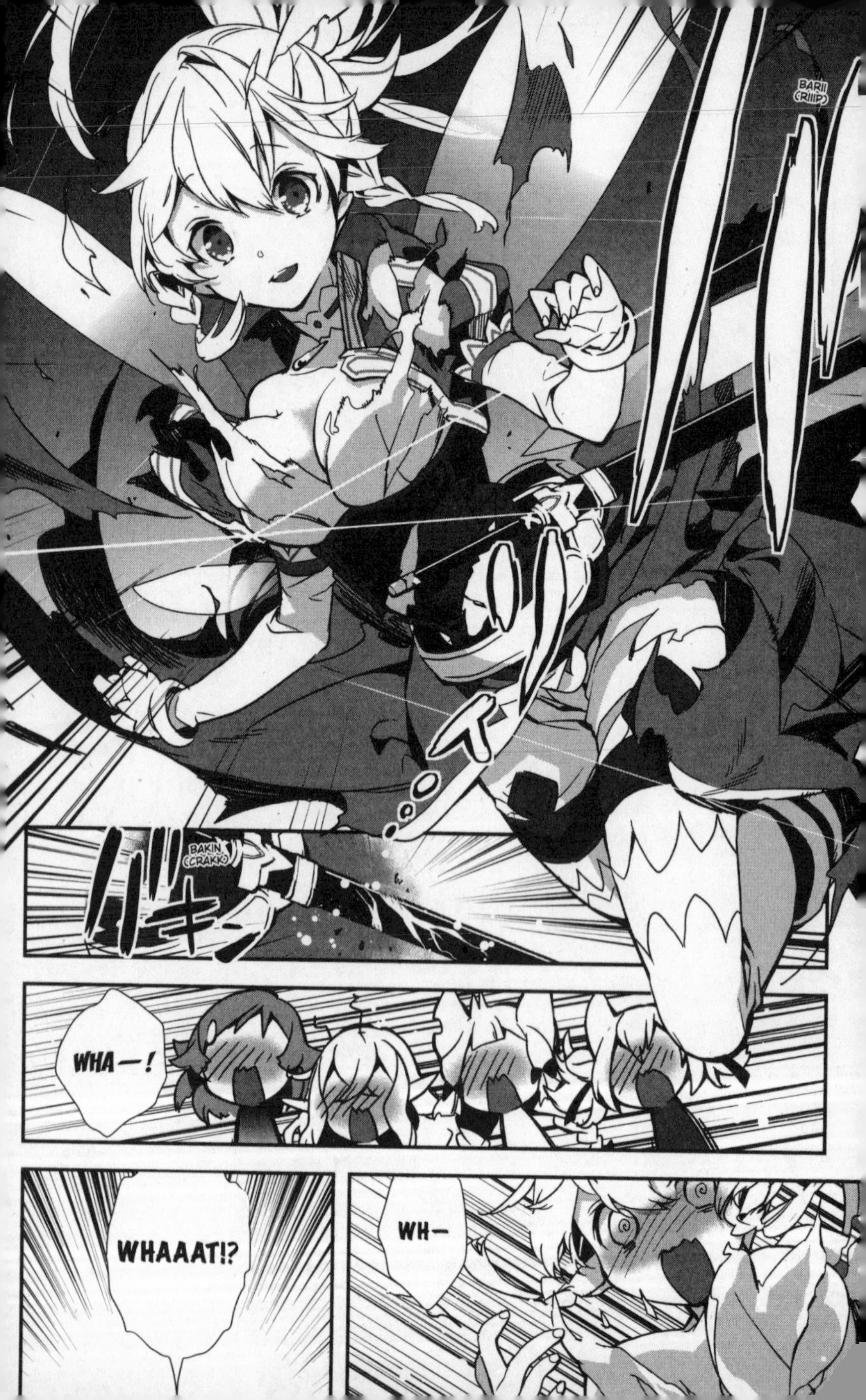
BARII (RIIIP)
BAKIN (CRAKK)
WHA—!
WH—
WHAAAT!?

SWORD ART ONLINE
GIRLS' OPS

I DIDN'T DO ANYTHING, AND I DON'T DRESS JAPANESE STYLE IN REAL LIFE...

...BUT IT'S NICE... I GUESS...

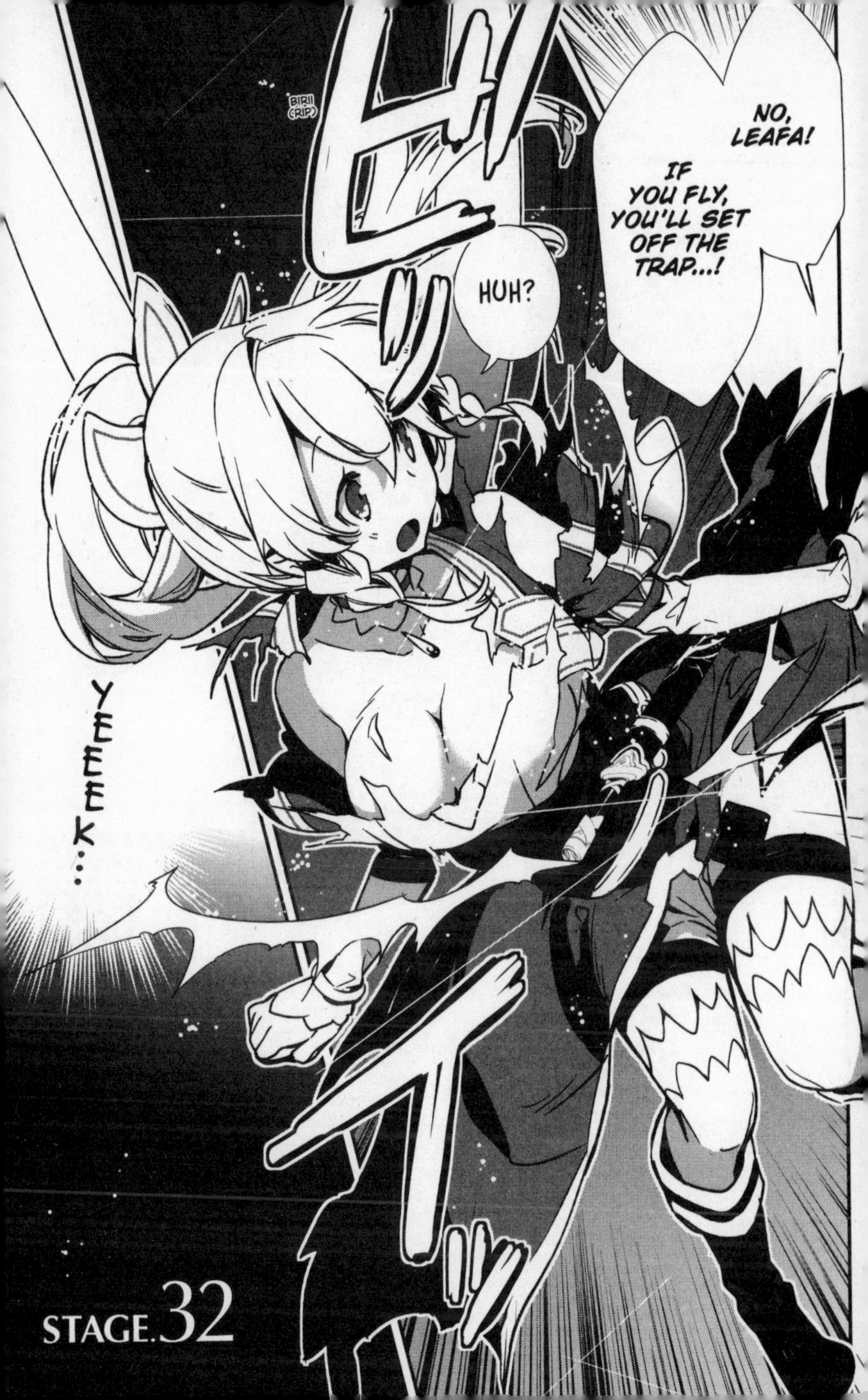
NO, LEAFA!
IF YOU FLY, YOU'LL SET OFF THE TRAP...!
HUH?
BIRII (RIP)
YEEEEK...

STAGE.32

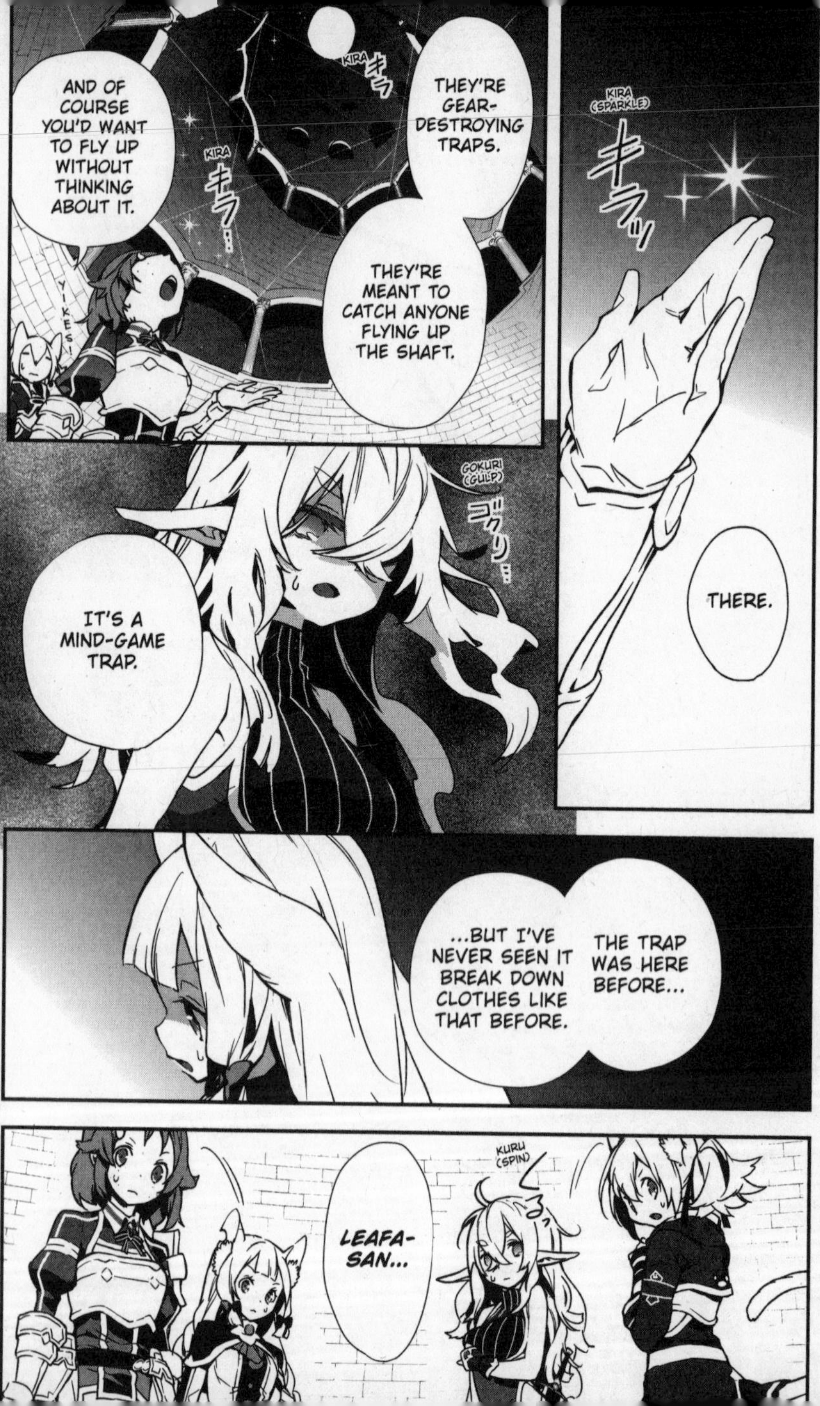
KIRA (SPARKLE)
THERE.
THEY'RE GEAR-DESTROYING TRAPS.
KIRA
THEY'RE MEANT TO CATCH ANYONE FLYING UP THE SHAFT.
AND OF COURSE YOU'D WANT TO FLY UP WITHOUT THINKING ABOUT IT.
KIRA
YIKES!
GOKURI (GULP)
IT'S A MIND-GAME TRAP.
THE TRAP WAS HERE BEFORE...
...BUT I'VE NEVER SEEN IT BREAK DOWN CLOTHES LIKE THAT BEFORE.
KURU (SPIN)
LEAFA-SAN...

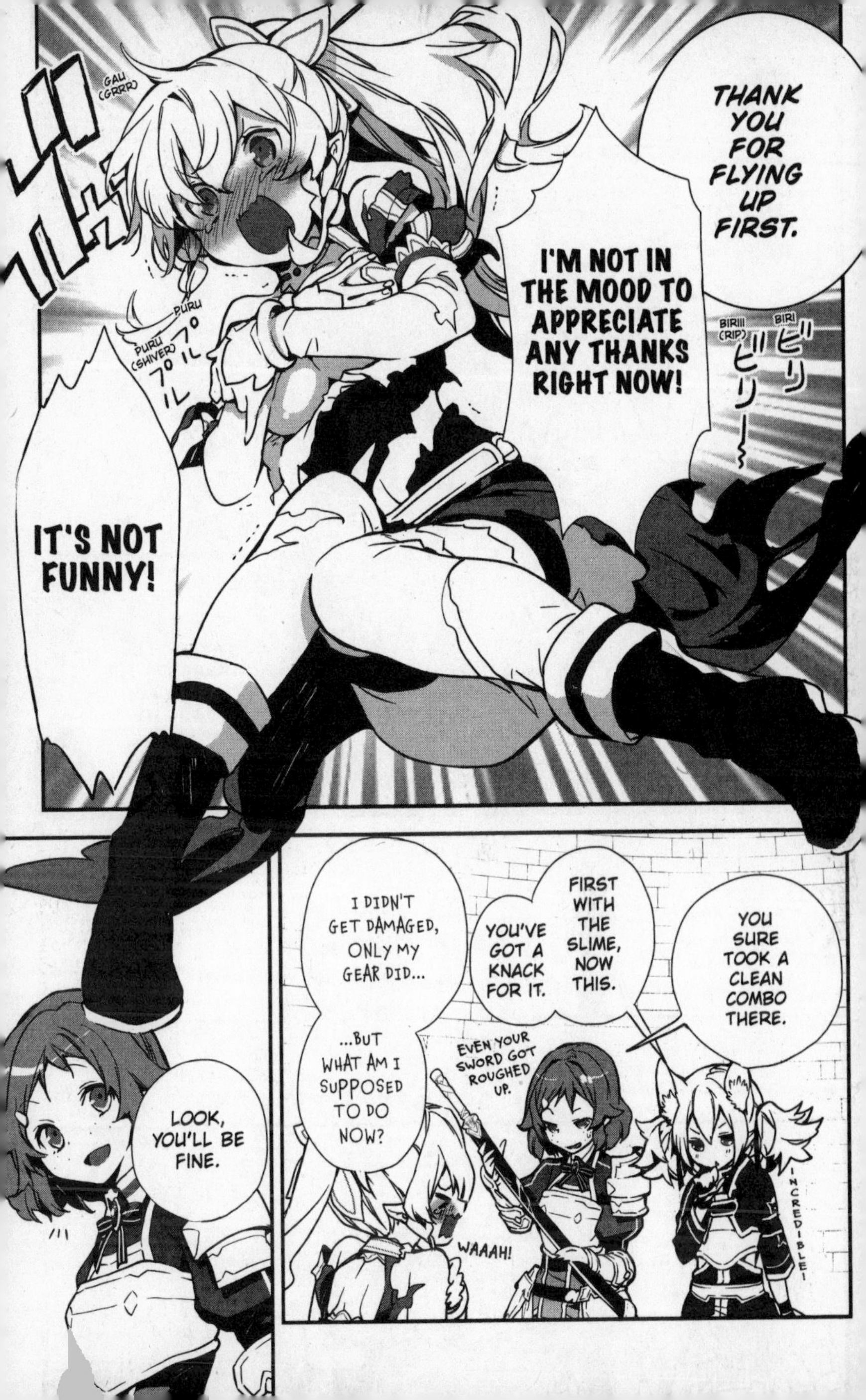
THANK YOU FOR FLYING UP FIRST.
BIRI BIRIII (RIP) ビリビリ～
I'M NOT IN THE MOOD TO APPRECIATE ANY THANKS RIGHT NOW!
GAU (GRRR)
PURU PURU (SHIVER) プルプル
IT'S NOT FUNNY!
YOU SURE TOOK A CLEAN COMBO THERE.
INCREDIBLE!
FIRST WITH THE SLIME, NOW THIS.
YOU'VE GOT A KNACK FOR IT.
EVEN YOUR SWORD GOT ROUGHED UP.
I DIDN'T GET DAMAGED, ONLY MY GEAR DID...
...BUT WHAT AM I SUPPOSED TO DO NOW?
WAAAH!
LOOK, YOU'LL BE FINE.

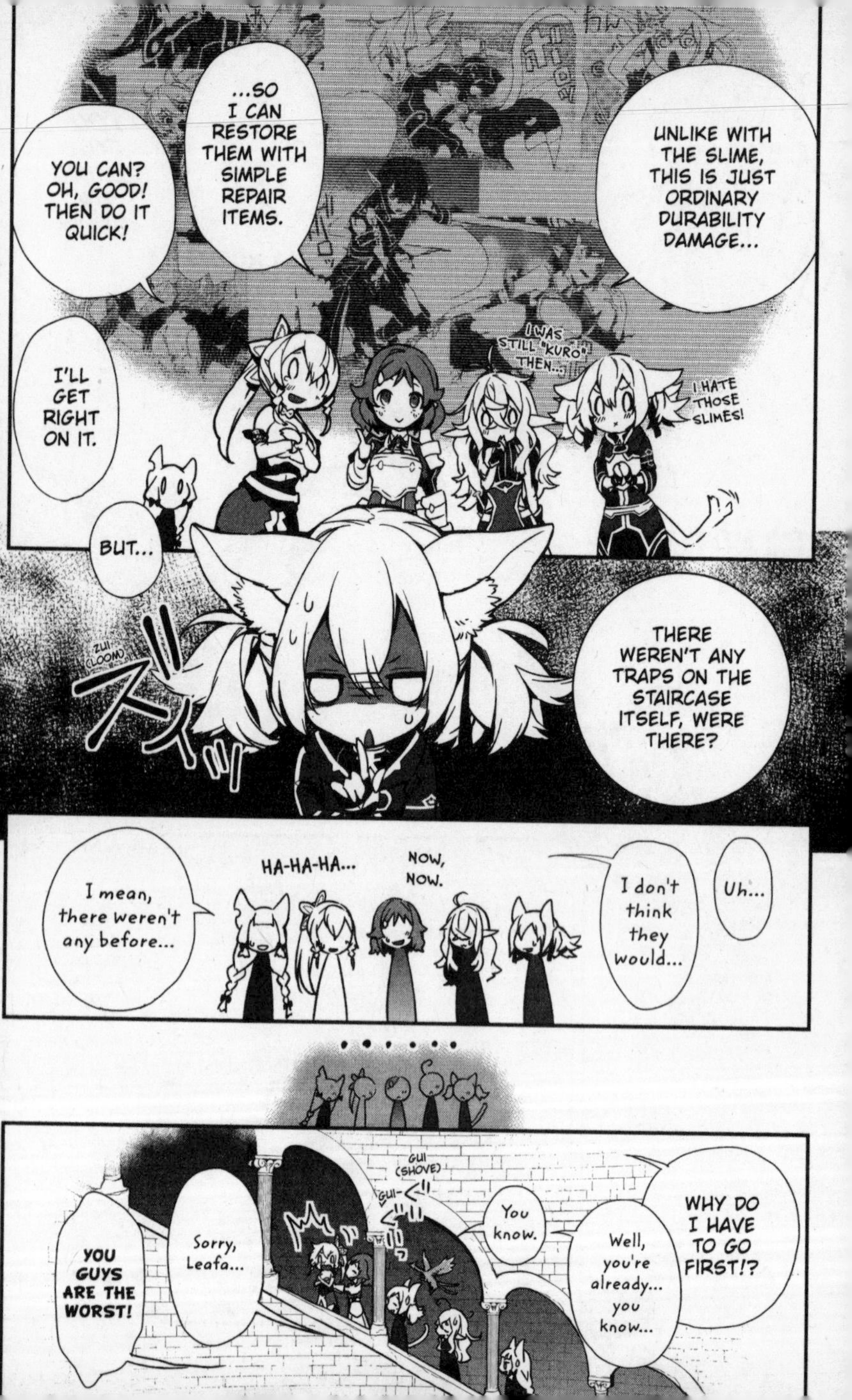
UNLIKE WITH THE SLIME, THIS IS JUST ORDINARY DURABILITY DAMAGE...
...SO I CAN RESTORE THEM WITH SIMPLE REPAIR ITEMS.
YOU CAN? OH, GOOD! THEN DO IT QUICK!
I HATE THOSE SLIMES!
I WAS STILL "KURO" THEN...
I'LL GET RIGHT ON IT.
BUT...
THERE WEREN'T ANY TRAPS ON THE STAIRCASE ITSELF, WERE THERE?
ZUI (LOOM)
Uh...
I don't think they would...
NOW, NOW.
HA-HA-HA...
I mean, there weren't any before...
......
WHY DO I HAVE TO GO FIRST!?
Well, you're already... you know...
You know.
GUI (SHOVE)
GUI-
Sorry, Leafa...
YOU GUYS ARE THE WORST!

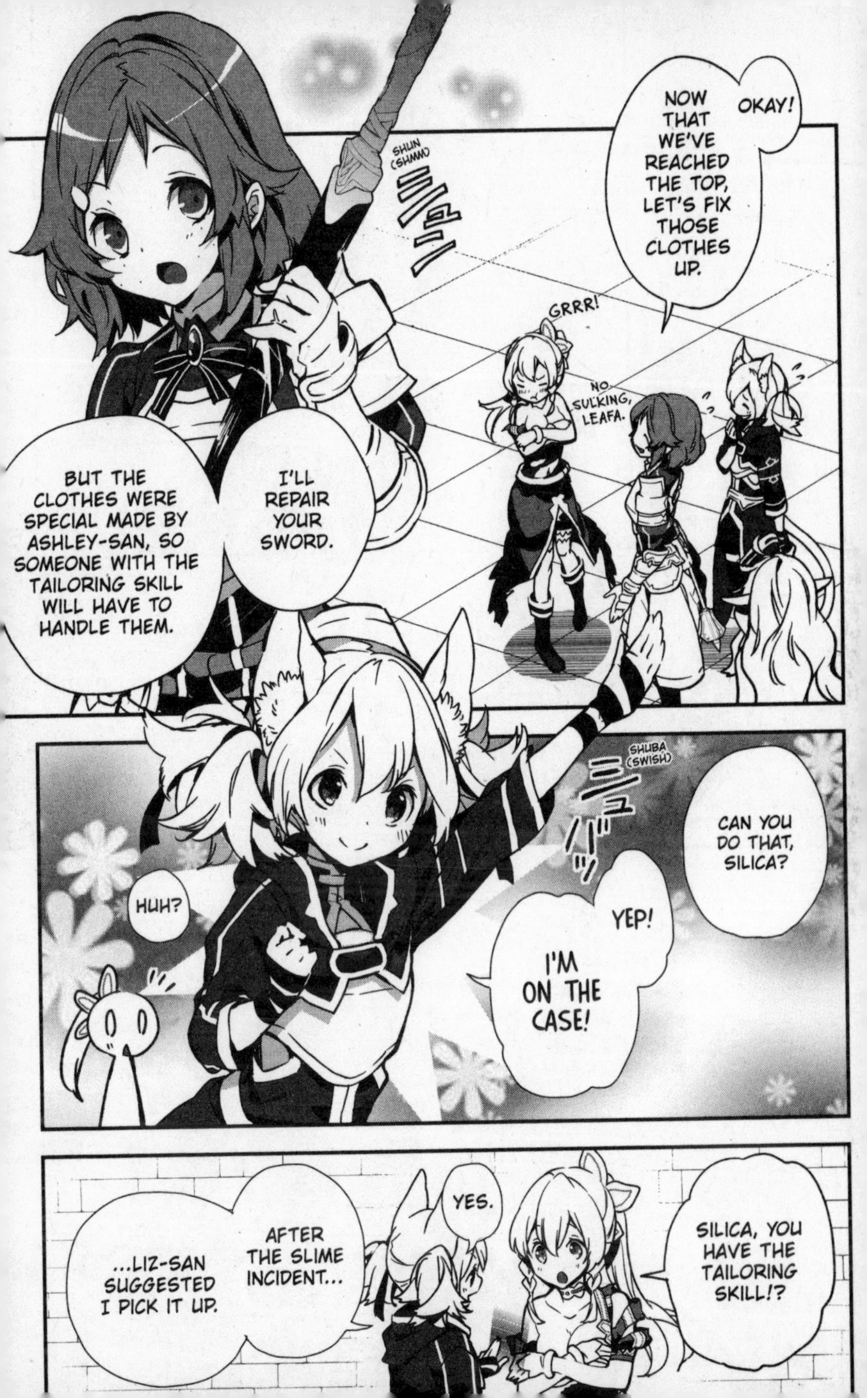
OKAY!
NOW THAT WE'VE REACHED THE TOP, LET'S FIX THOSE CLOTHES UP.
SHUN (SHMM)
GRRR!
NO SULKING, LEAFA.
I'LL REPAIR YOUR SWORD.
BUT THE CLOTHES WERE SPECIAL MADE BY ASHLEY-SAN, SO SOMEONE WITH THE TAILORING SKILL WILL HAVE TO HANDLE THEM.
CAN YOU DO THAT, SILICA?
SHUBA (SWISH)
YEP!
I'M ON THE CASE!
HUH?
SILICA, YOU HAVE THE TAILORING SKILL!?
YES.
AFTER THE SLIME INCIDENT...
...LIZ-SAN SUGGESTED I PICK IT UP.

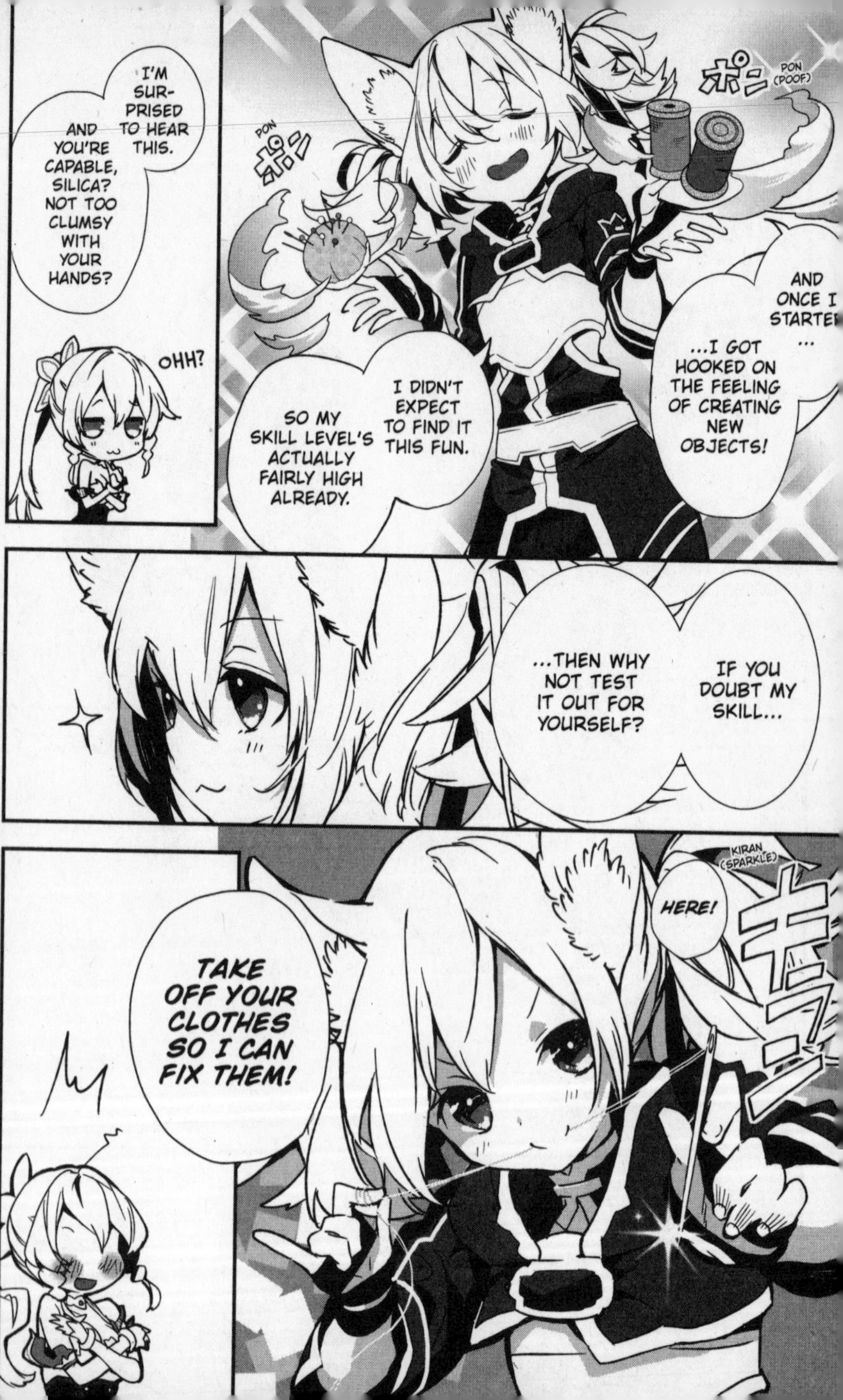
PON (POOF)
AND ONCE I STARTE...
...I GOT HOOKED ON THE FEELING OF CREATING NEW OBJECTS!
I DIDN'T EXPECT TO FIND IT THIS FUN.
SO MY SKILL LEVEL'S ACTUALLY FAIRLY HIGH ALREADY.
PON
I'M SURPRISED TO HEAR THIS.
AND YOU'RE CAPABLE, SILICA? NOT TOO CLUMSY WITH YOUR HANDS?
OHH?
IF YOU DOUBT MY SKILL...
...THEN WHY NOT TEST IT OUT FOR YOURSELF?
KIRAN (SPARKLE)
HERE!
TAKE OFF YOUR CLOTHES SO I CAN FIX THEM!

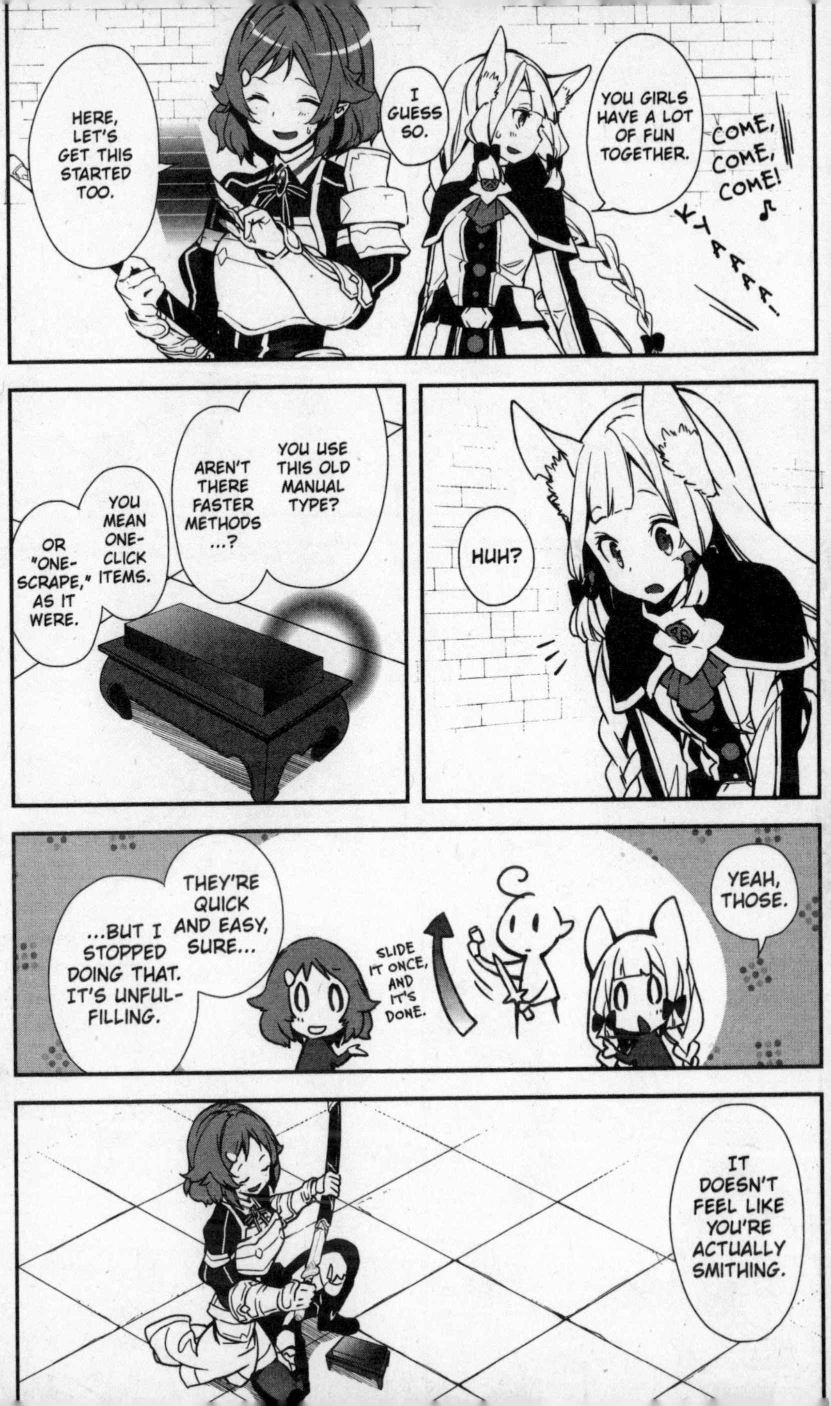
YOU GIRLS HAVE A LOT OF FUN TOGETHER.
COME, COME, COME! ♪
KTAAAA!
I GUESS SO.
HERE, LET'S GET THIS STARTED TOO.
HUH?
YOU USE THIS OLD MANUAL TYPE?
AREN'T THERE FASTER METHODS ...?
YOU MEAN ONE-CLICK ITEMS.
OR "ONE-SCRAPE," AS IT WERE.
YEAH, THOSE.
SLIDE IT ONCE, AND IT'S DONE.
THEY'RE QUICK AND EASY, SURE...
...BUT I STOPPED DOING THAT. IT'S UNFUL-FILLING.
IT DOESN'T FEEL LIKE YOU'RE ACTUALLY SMITHING.

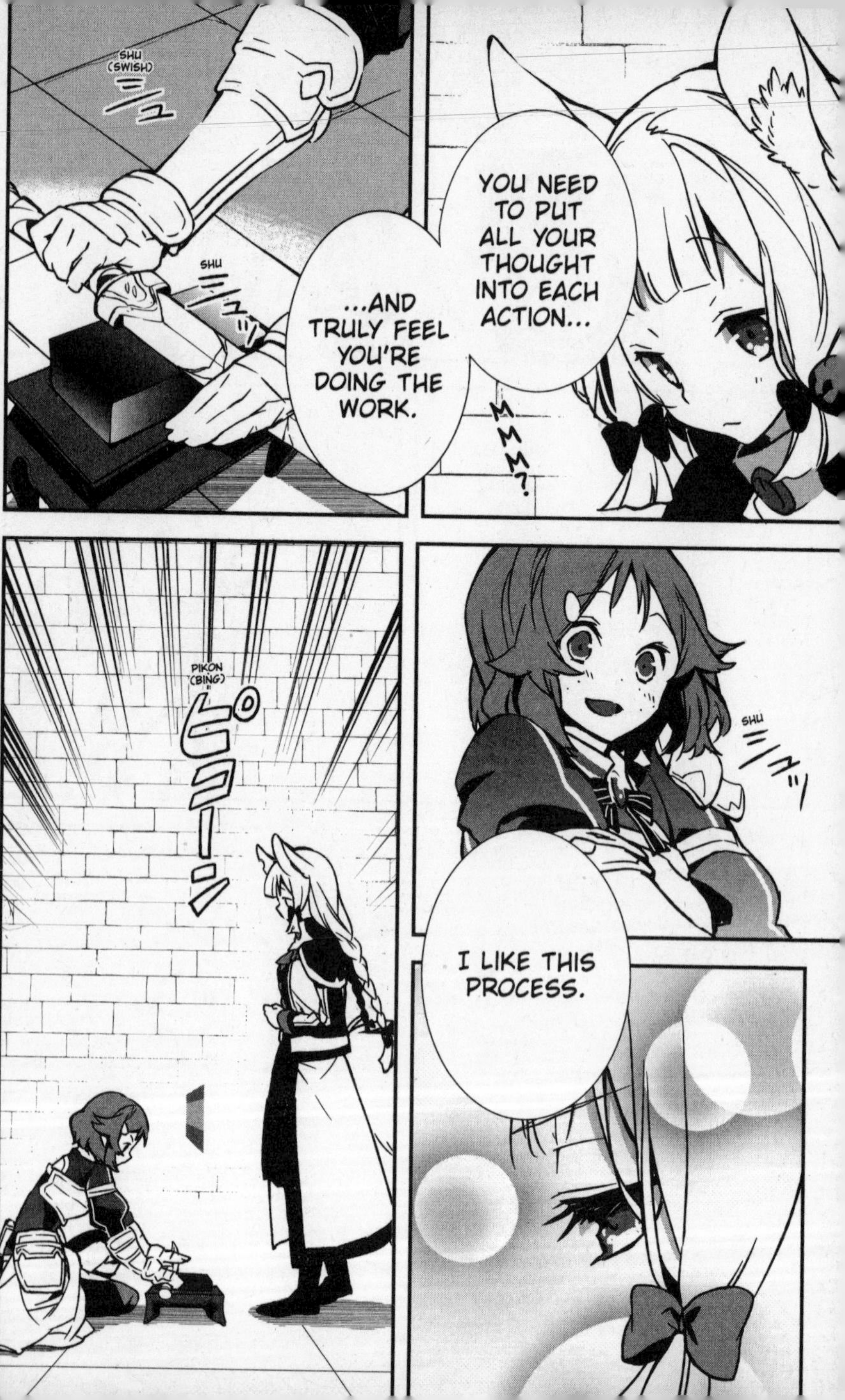
YOU NEED TO PUT ALL YOUR THOUGHT INTO EACH ACTION...
...AND TRULY FEEL YOU'RE DOING THE WORK.
MMM?
SHU (SWISH)
SHU
SHU
I LIKE THIS PROCESS.
PIKON (BING)

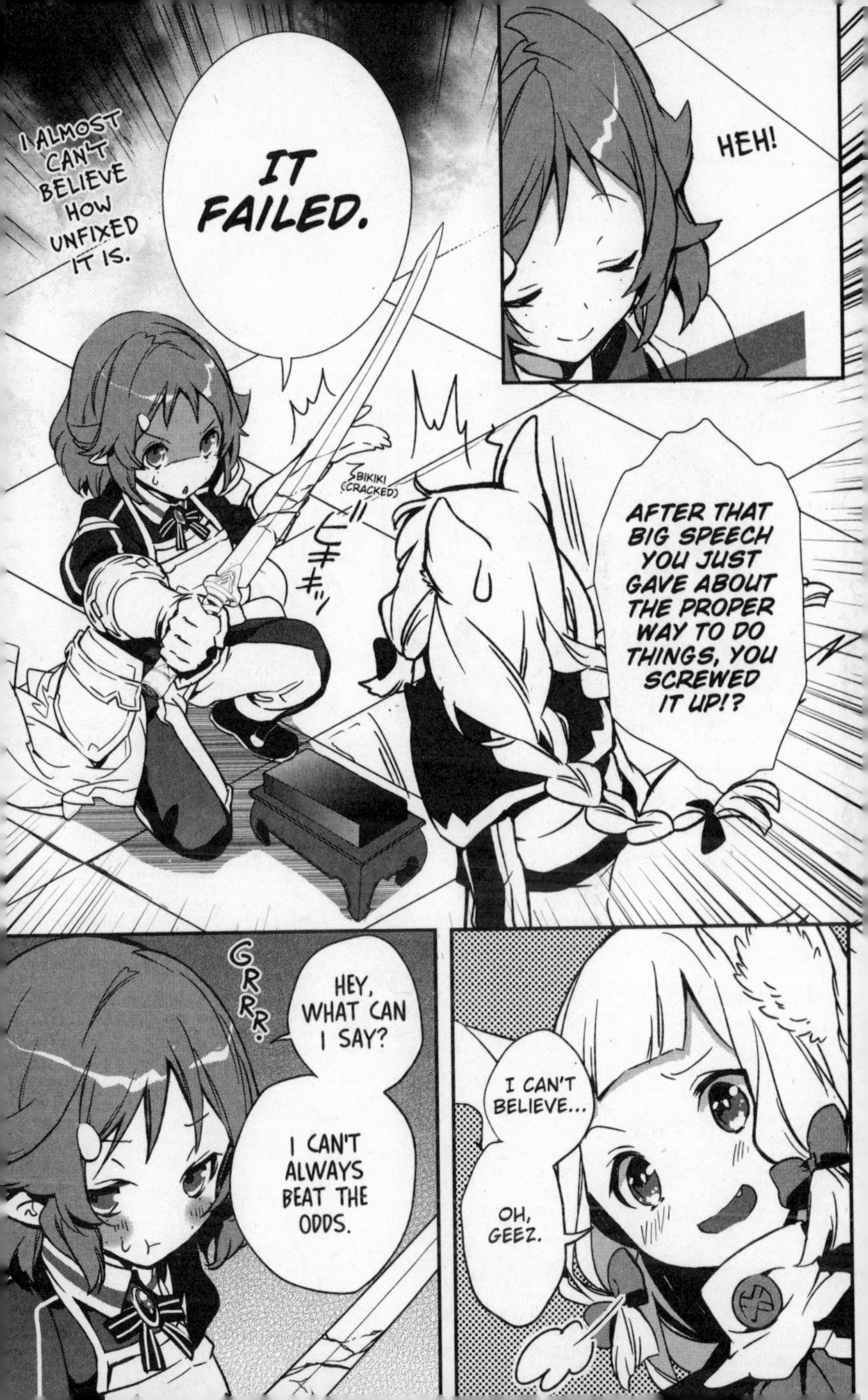
HEH!
IT FAILED.
I ALMOST CAN'T BELIEVE HOW UNFIXED IT IS.
AFTER THAT BIG SPEECH YOU JUST GAVE ABOUT THE PROPER WAY TO DO THINGS, YOU SCREWED IT UP!?
BIKIKI (CRACKED)
I CAN'T BELIEVE...
OH, GEEZ.
HEY, WHAT CAN I SAY?
GRRR.
I CAN'T ALWAYS BEAT THE ODDS.

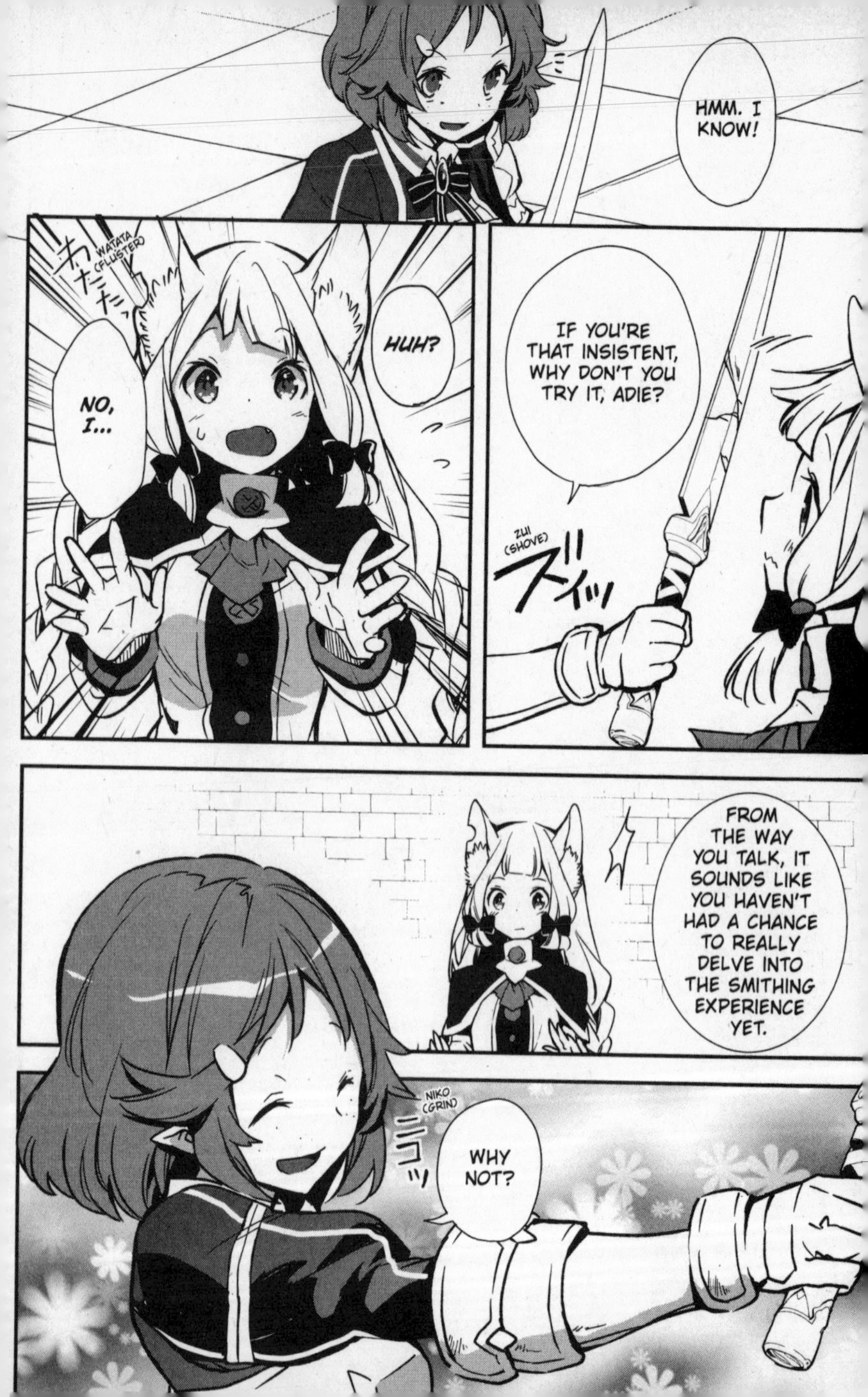
HMM. I KNOW!
IF YOU'RE THAT INSISTENT, WHY DON'T YOU TRY IT, ADIE?
ZUI (SHOVE)
HUH?
WATATA (FLUSTER)
NO, I...
FROM THE WAY YOU TALK, IT SOUNDS LIKE YOU HAVEN'T HAD A CHANCE TO REALLY DELVE INTO THE SMITHING EXPERIENCE YET.
NIKO (GRIN)
WHY NOT?

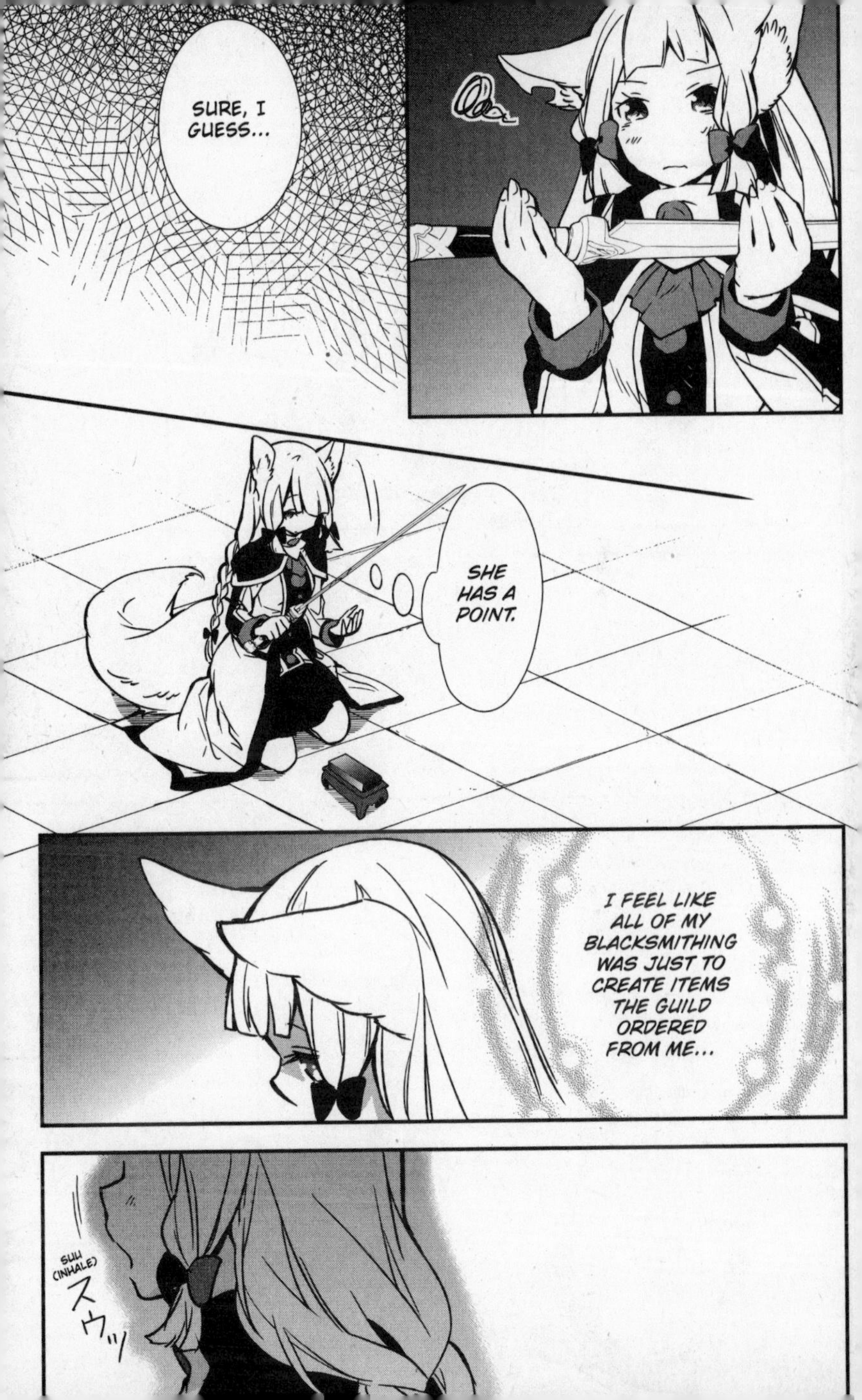
SURE, I GUESS...
SHE HAS A POINT.
I FEEL LIKE ALL OF MY BLACKSMITHING WAS JUST TO CREATE ITEMS THE GUILD ORDERED FROM ME...
SUU (INHALE)
スゥッ

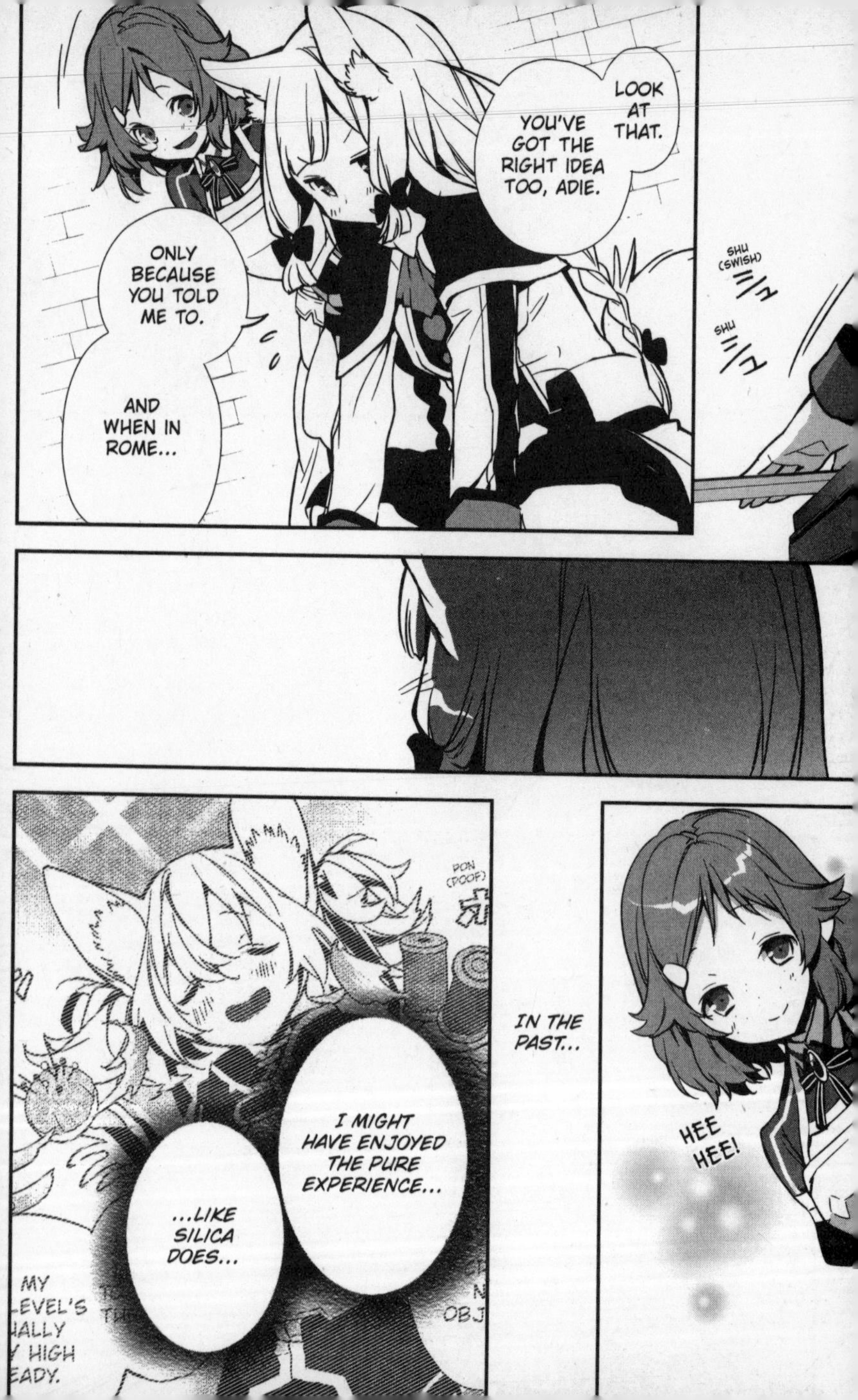
LOOK AT THAT.
YOU'VE GOT THE RIGHT IDEA TOO, ADIE.
SHU (SWISH)
SHU
ONLY BECAUSE YOU TOLD ME TO.
AND WHEN IN ROME...
HEE HEE!
IN THE PAST...
PON (POOF)
I MIGHT HAVE ENJOYED THE PURE EXPERIENCE...
...LIKE SILICA DOES...

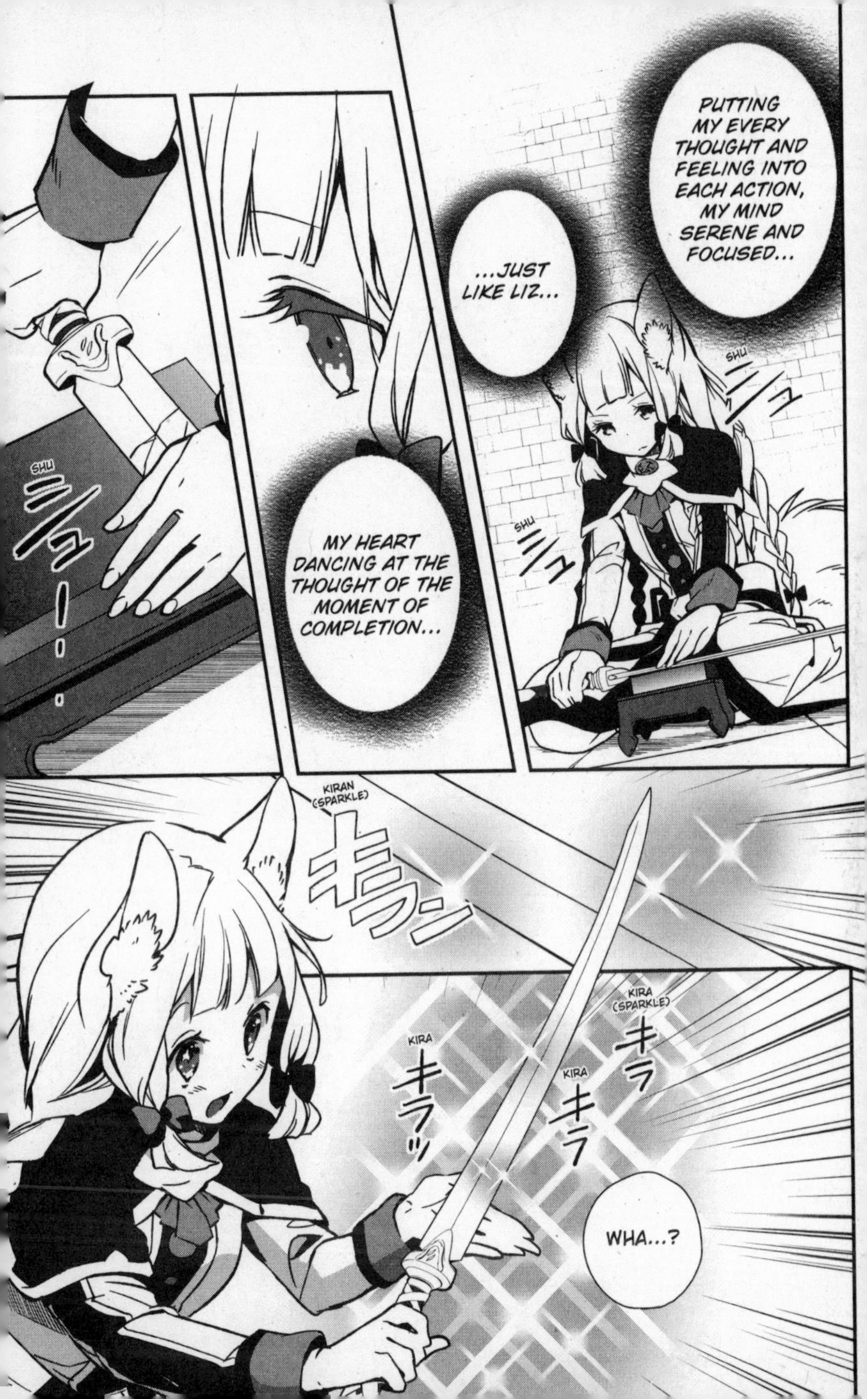
PUTTING MY EVERY THOUGHT AND FEELING INTO EACH ACTION, MY MIND SERENE AND FOCUSED...
...JUST LIKE LIZ...
SHU
シュ
SHU
シュ
MY HEART DANCING AT THE THOUGHT OF THE MOMENT OF COMPLETION...
SHU
シュー…
KIRAN (SPARKLE)
キラン
KIRA (SPARKLE)
キラ
KIRA
キラ
KIRA
キラッ
WHA...?

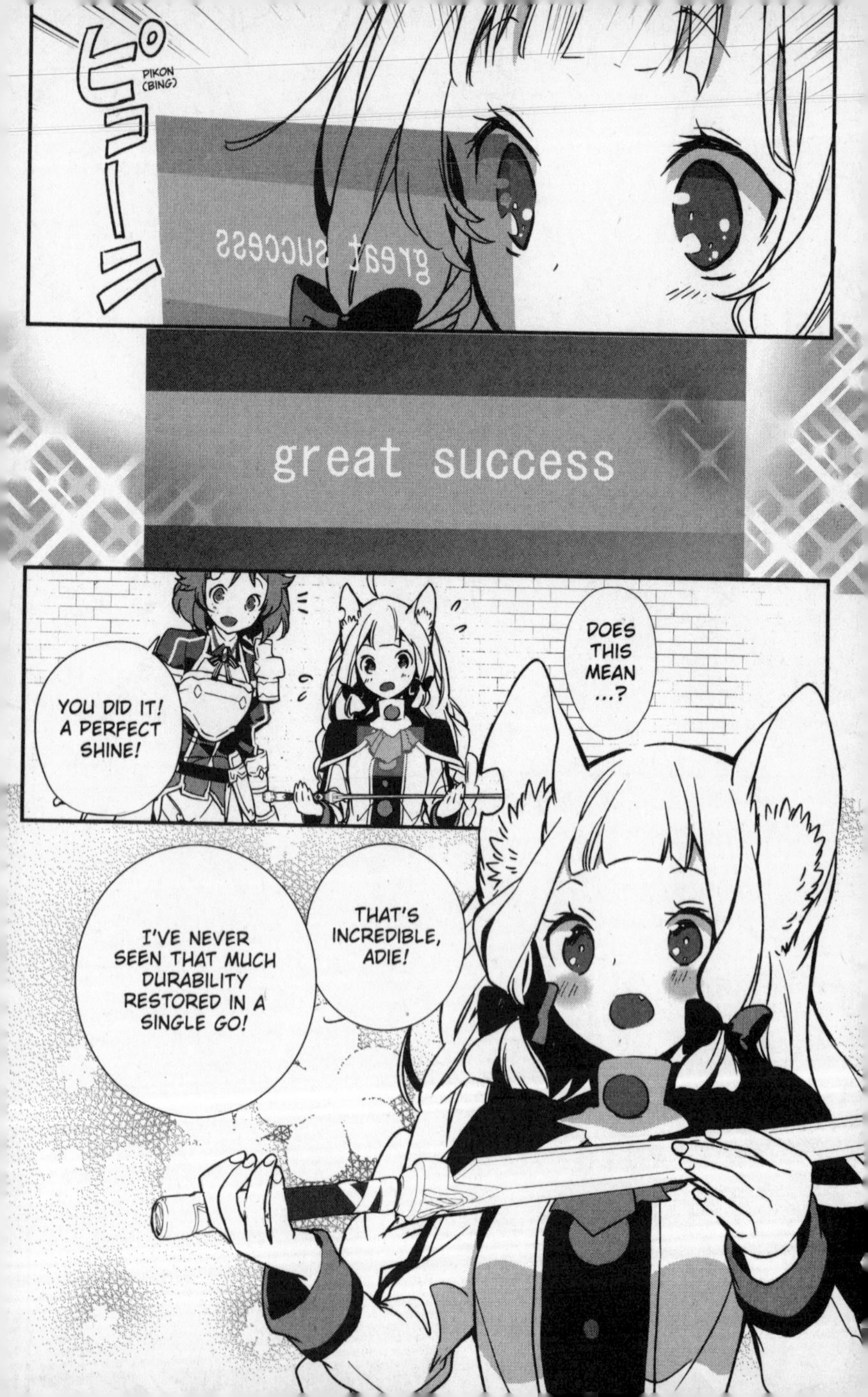
ピコーン
PIKON (BING)
great success
DOES THIS MEAN ...?
YOU DID IT! A PERFECT SHINE!
THAT'S INCREDIBLE, ADIE!
I'VE NEVER SEEN THAT MUCH DURABILITY RESTORED IN A SINGLE GO!

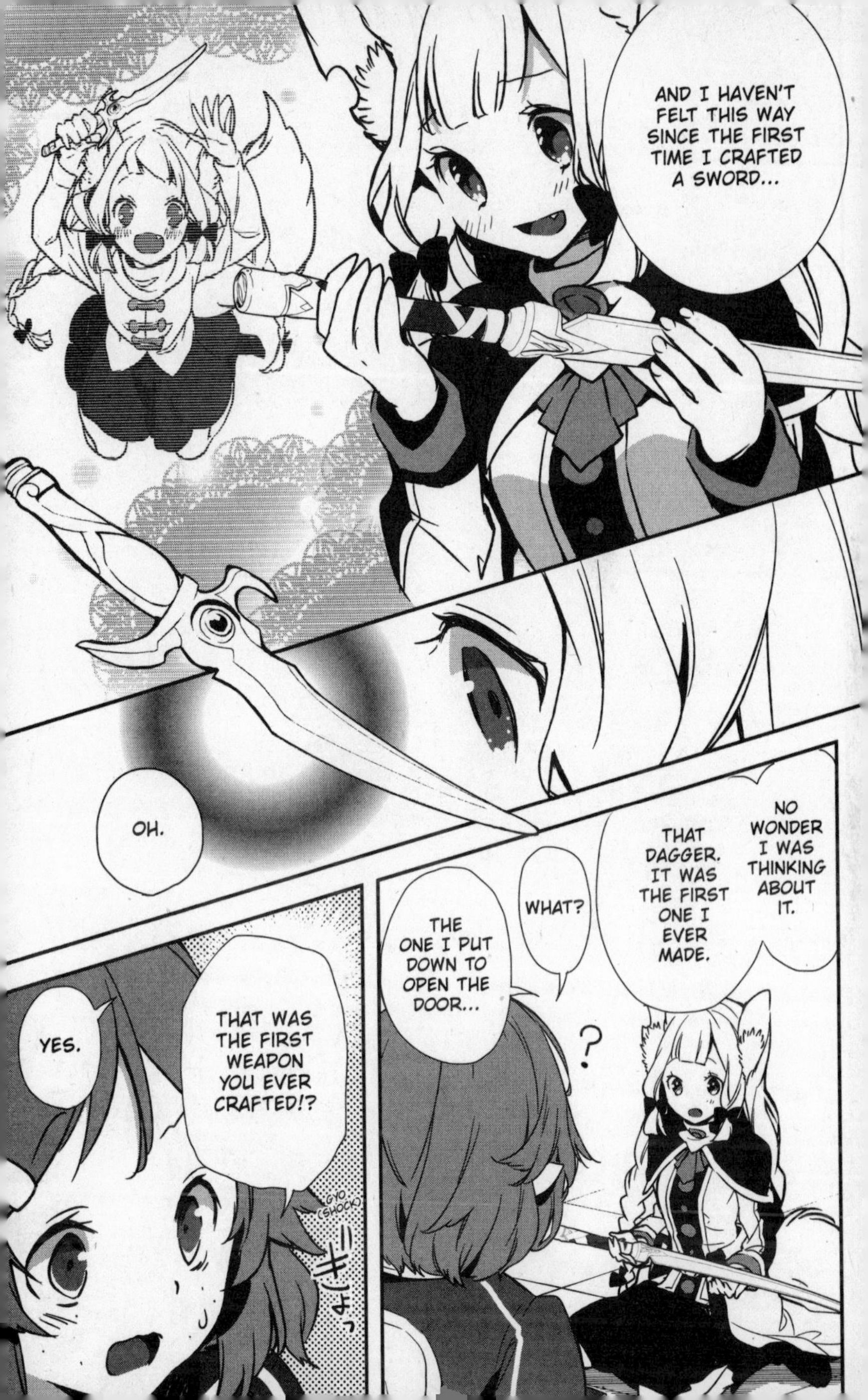
AND I HAVEN'T FELT THIS WAY SINCE THE FIRST TIME I CRAFTED A SWORD...
OH.
NO WONDER I WAS THINKING ABOUT IT.
THAT DAGGER. IT WAS THE FIRST ONE I EVER MADE.
WHAT?
THE ONE I PUT DOWN TO OPEN THE DOOR...
?
THAT WAS THE FIRST WEAPON YOU EVER CRAFTED!?
GYO (SHOCK)
YES.

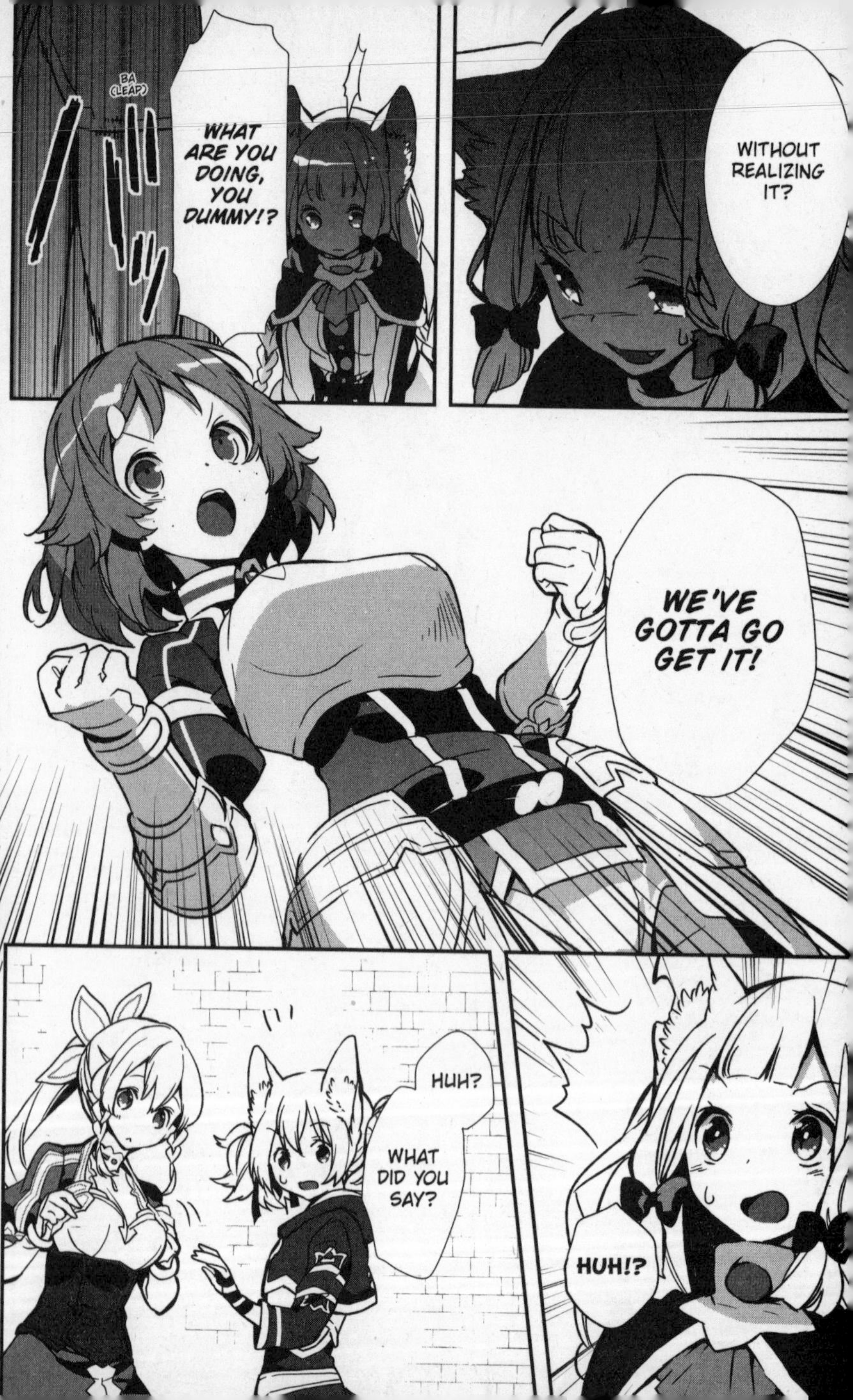
WITHOUT REALIZING IT?
BA (LEAP)
WHAT ARE YOU DOING, YOU DUMMY!?
WE'VE GOTTA GO GET IT!
HUH!?
HUH?
WHAT DID YOU SAY?

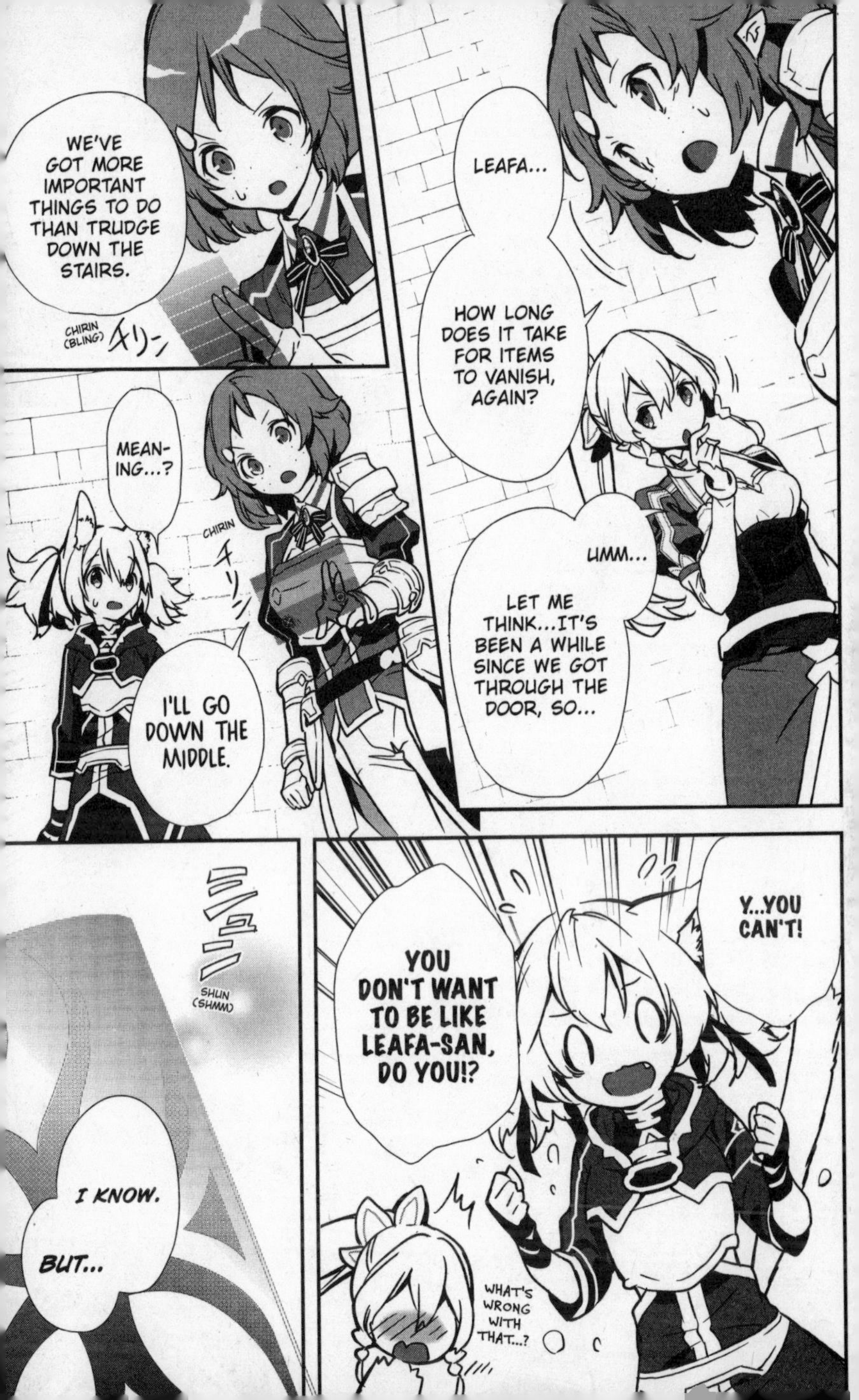
LEAFA...
HOW LONG DOES IT TAKE FOR ITEMS TO VANISH, AGAIN?
UMM...
LET ME THINK...IT'S BEEN A WHILE SINCE WE GOT THROUGH THE DOOR, SO...
WE'VE GOT MORE IMPORTANT THINGS TO DO THAN TRUDGE DOWN THE STAIRS.
CHIRIN (BLING)
チリーン
MEAN-ING...?
CHIRIN
チリーン
I'LL GO DOWN THE MIDDLE.
Y...YOU CAN'T!
YOU DON'T WANT TO BE LIKE LEAFA-SAN, DO YOU!?
WHAT'S WRONG WITH THAT...?
シュン
SHUN (SHMM)
I KNOW.
BUT...

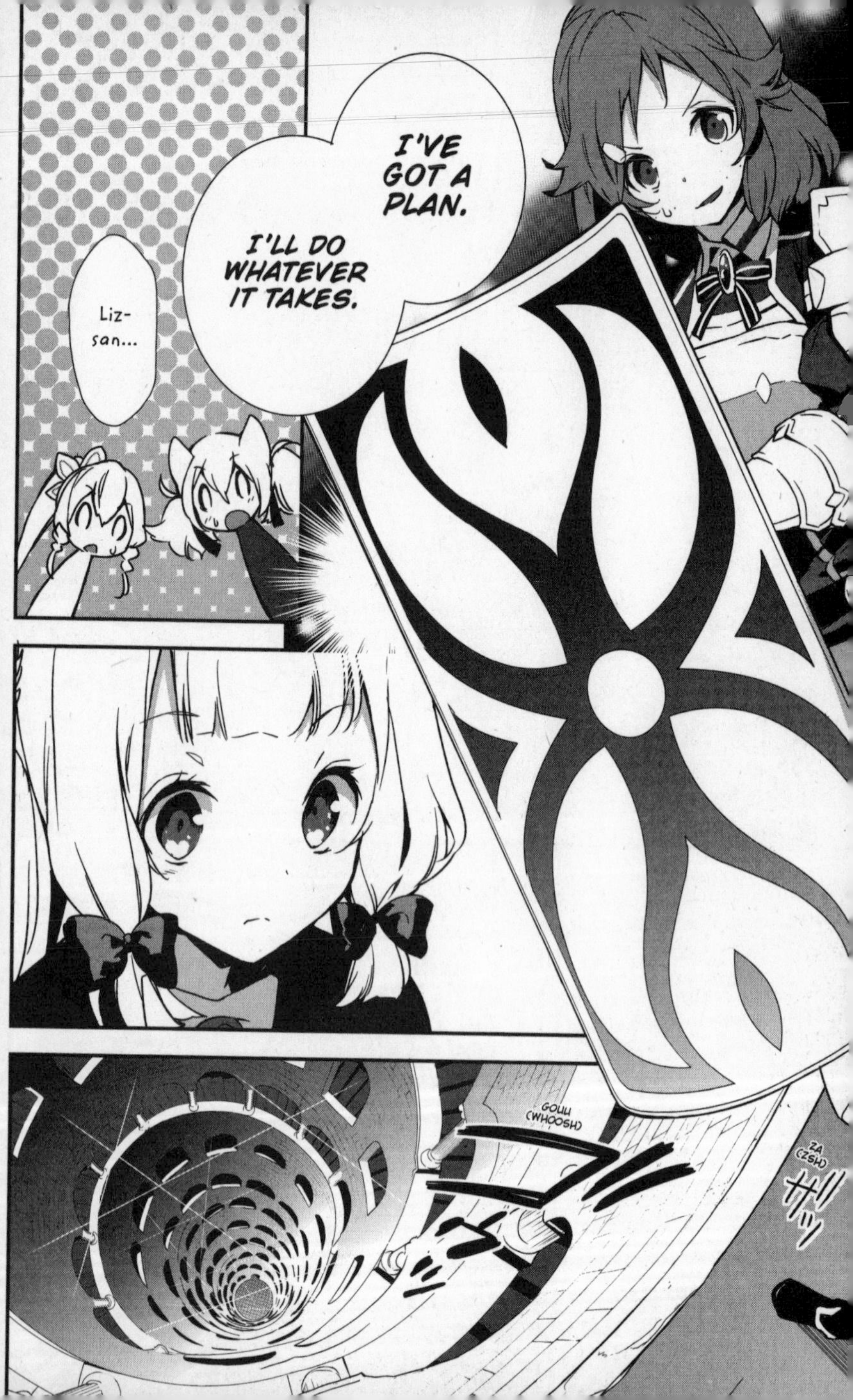
I'VE GOT A PLAN.
I'LL DO WHATEVER IT TAKES.
Liz-san...
GOUU (WHOOSH)
ZA (ZSH)

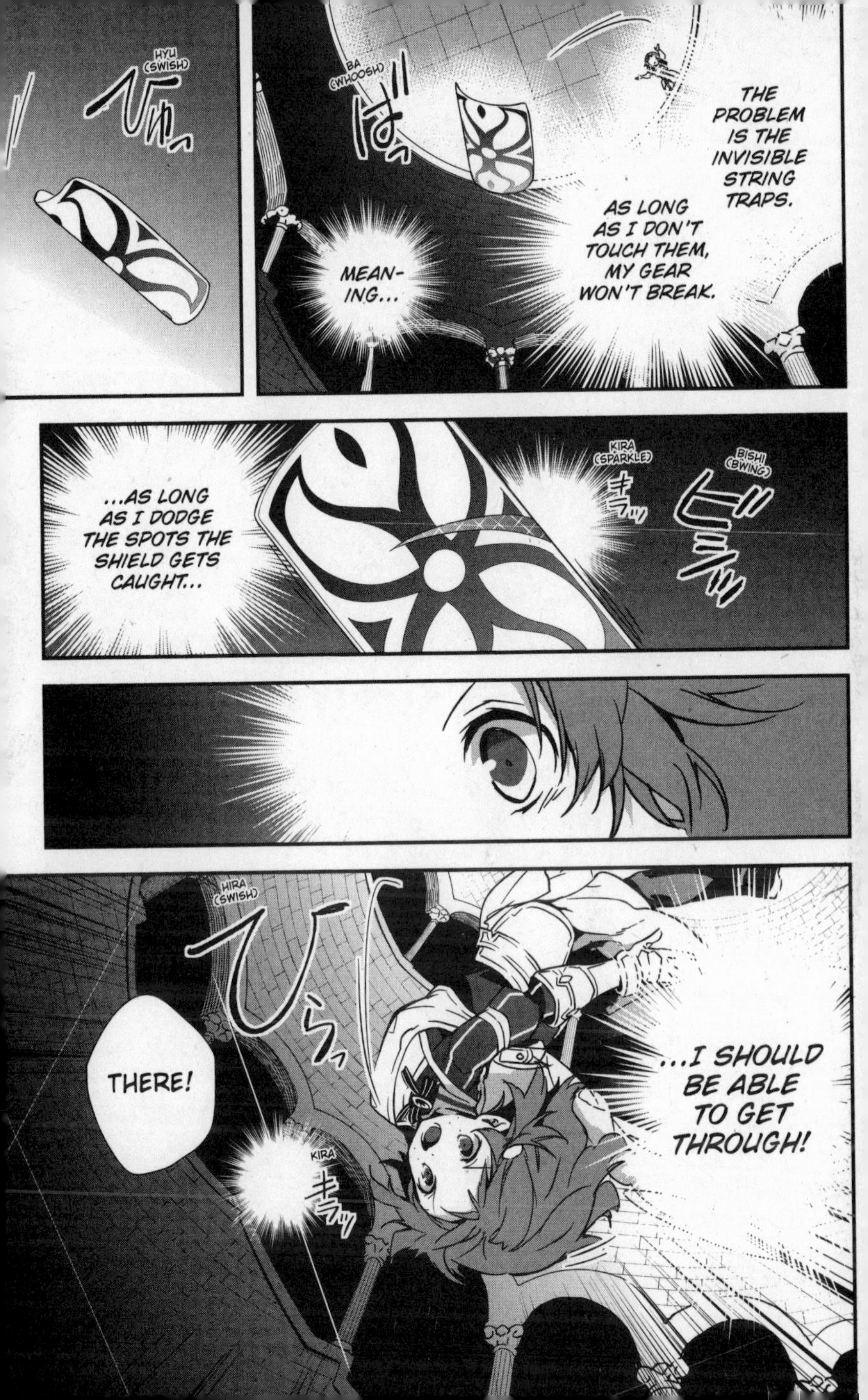
BA (WHOOSH)
THE PROBLEM IS THE INVISIBLE STRING TRAPS.
AS LONG AS I DON'T TOUCH THEM, MY GEAR WON'T BREAK.
MEAN-ING...
HYU (SWISH)
BISHI (BWING)
KIRA (SPARKLE)
...AS LONG AS I DODGE THE SPOTS THE SHIELD GETS CAUGHT...
...I SHOULD BE ABLE TO GET THROUGH!
HIRA (SWISH)
THERE!
KIRA

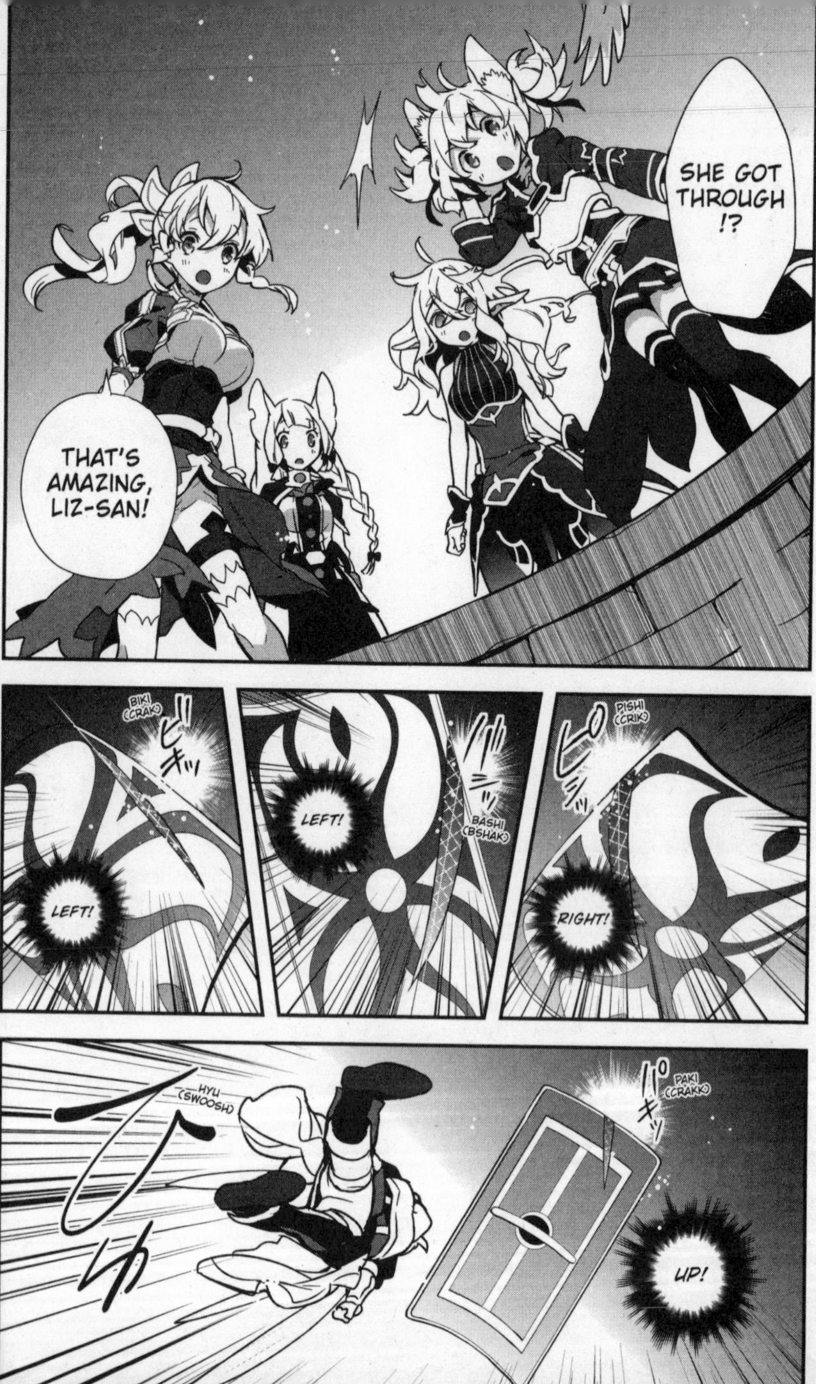
SHE GOT THROUGH!?
THAT'S AMAZING, LIZ-SAN!
PISHI (CRIK)
RIGHT!
BASHI (BSHAK)
LEFT!
BIKI (CRAK)
LEFT!
PAKI (CRAKK)
UP!
HYU (SWOOSH)

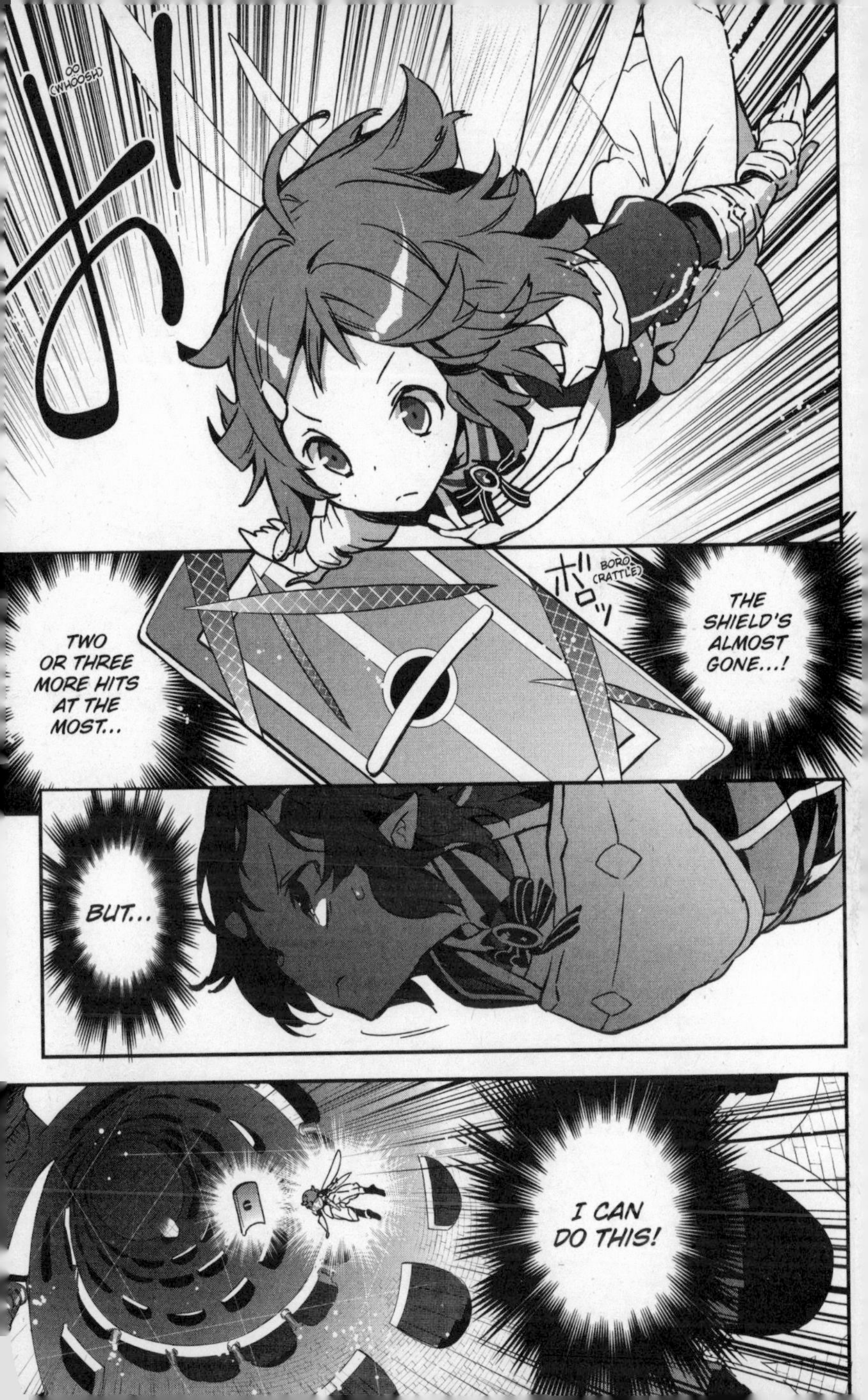
OO (WHOOSH)
ボロッ
BORO (RATTLE)
THE SHIELD'S ALMOST GONE...!
TWO OR THREE MORE HITS AT THE MOST...
BUT...
I CAN DO THIS!

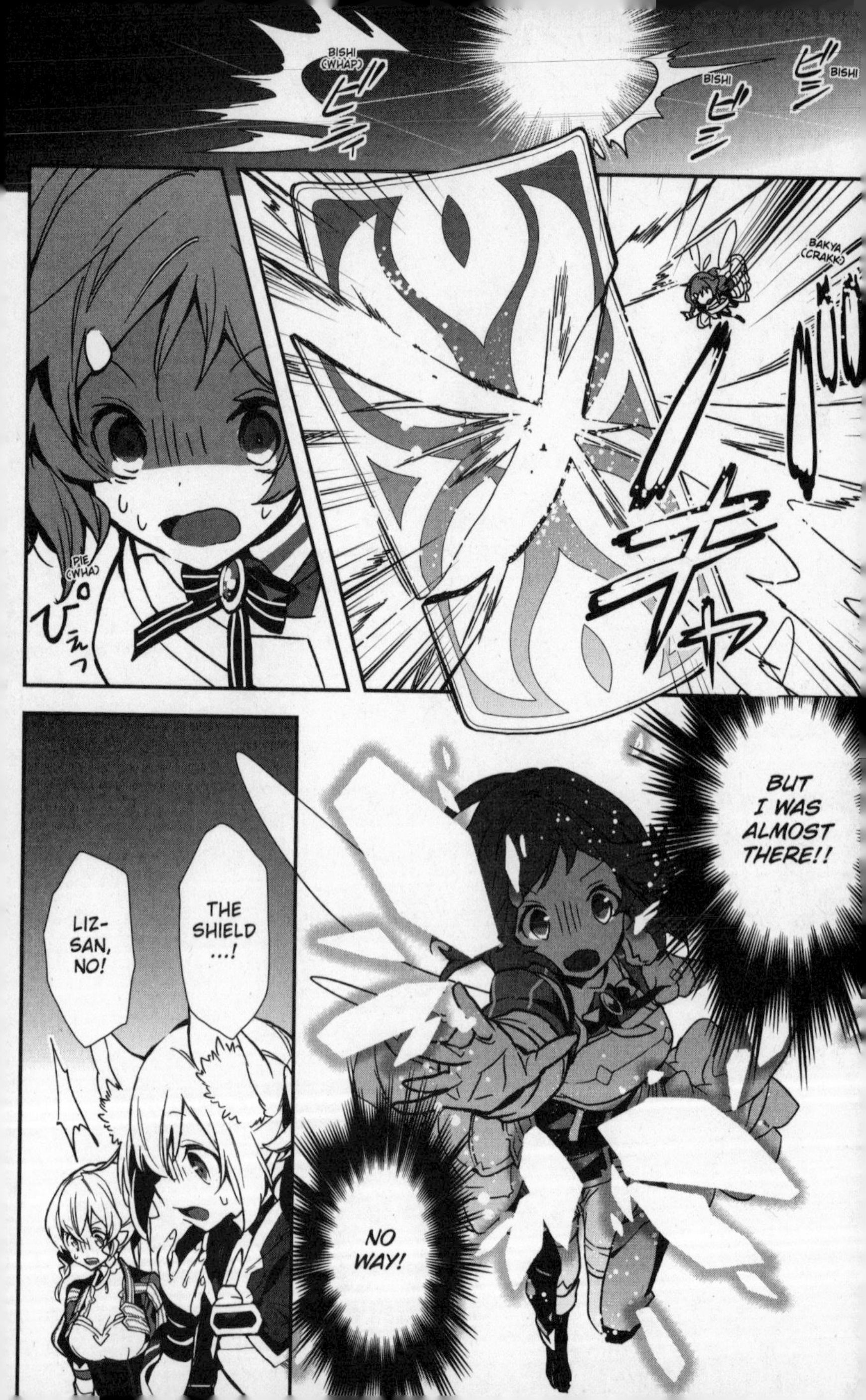

BISHI
BISHI
BISHI (WHAP)
BAKYA (CRAKK)
PIE (WHA)
BUT I WAS ALMOST THERE!!
NO WAY!
THE SHIELD ...!
LIZ-SAN, NO!

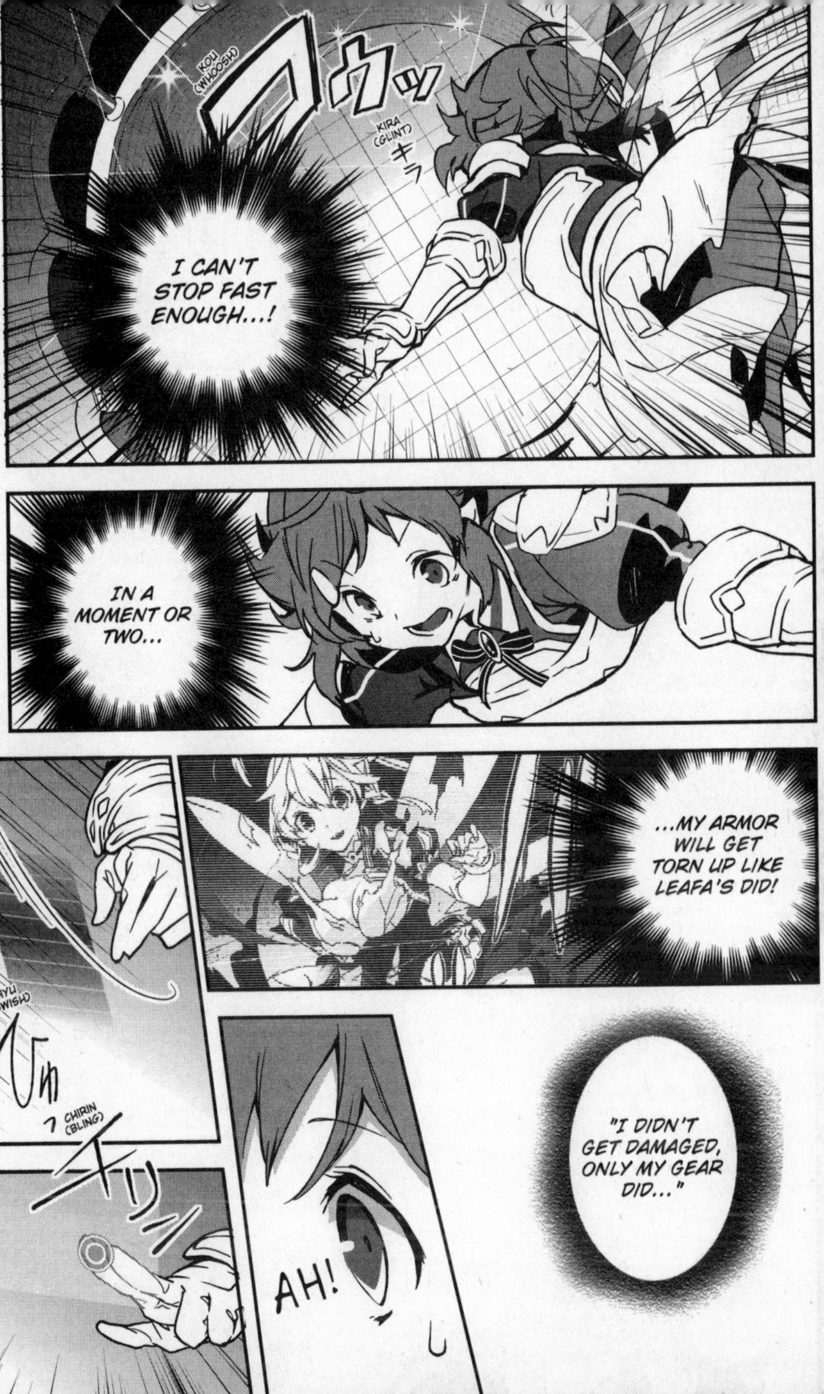
KOU (WHOOSH)
KIRA (GLINT)
I CAN'T STOP FAST ENOUGH...!
IN A MOMENT OR TWO...
...MY ARMOR WILL GET TORN UP LIKE LEAFA'S DID!
HYU (SWISH)
CHIRIN (BLING)
"I DIDN'T GET DAMAGED, ONLY MY GEAR DID..."
AH!

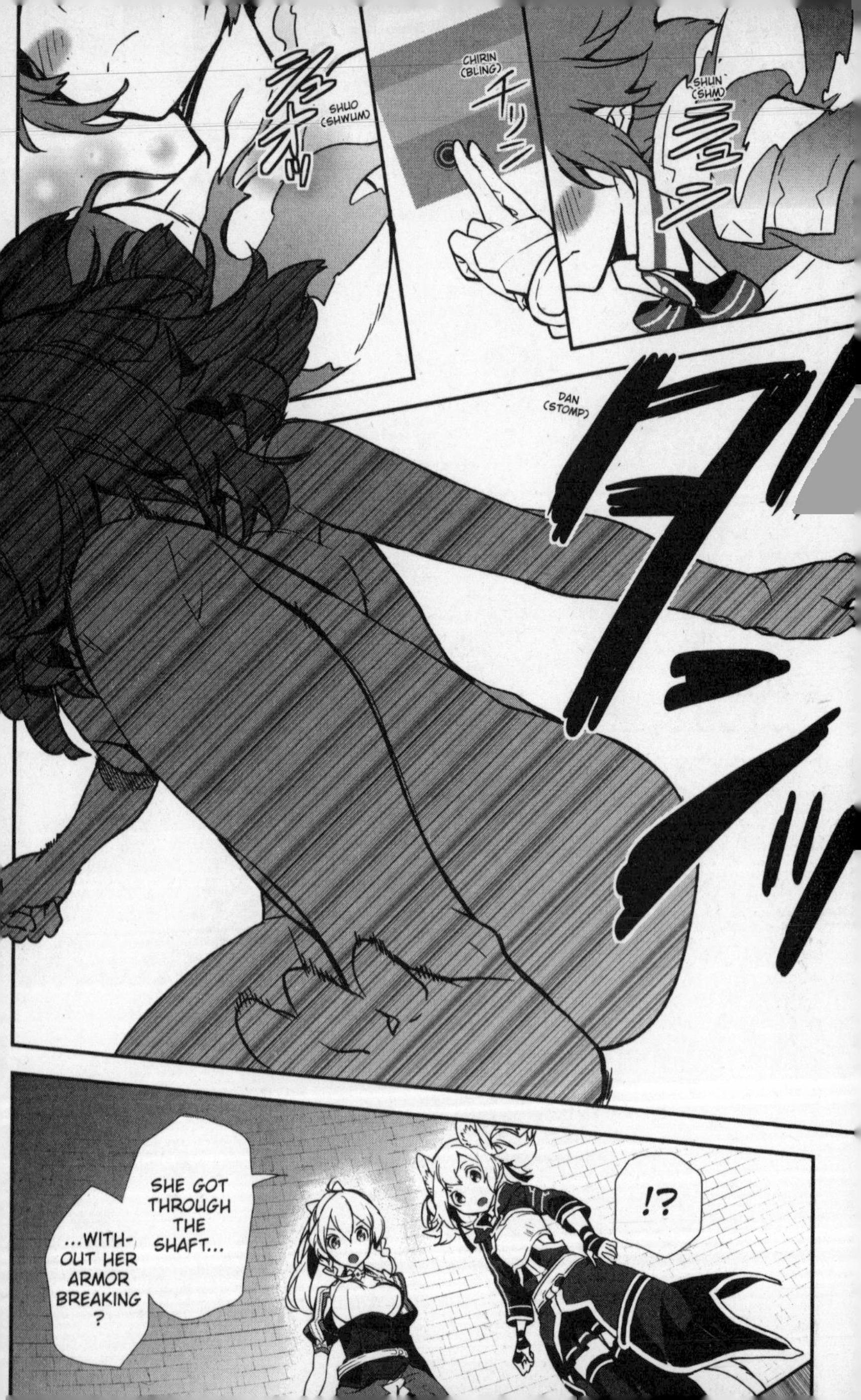
SHUN (SHM)
CHIRIN (BLING)
SHUO (SHWUM)
DAN (STOMP)
!?
SHE GOT THROUGH THE SHAFT...
...WITH-OUT HER ARMOR BREAKING?

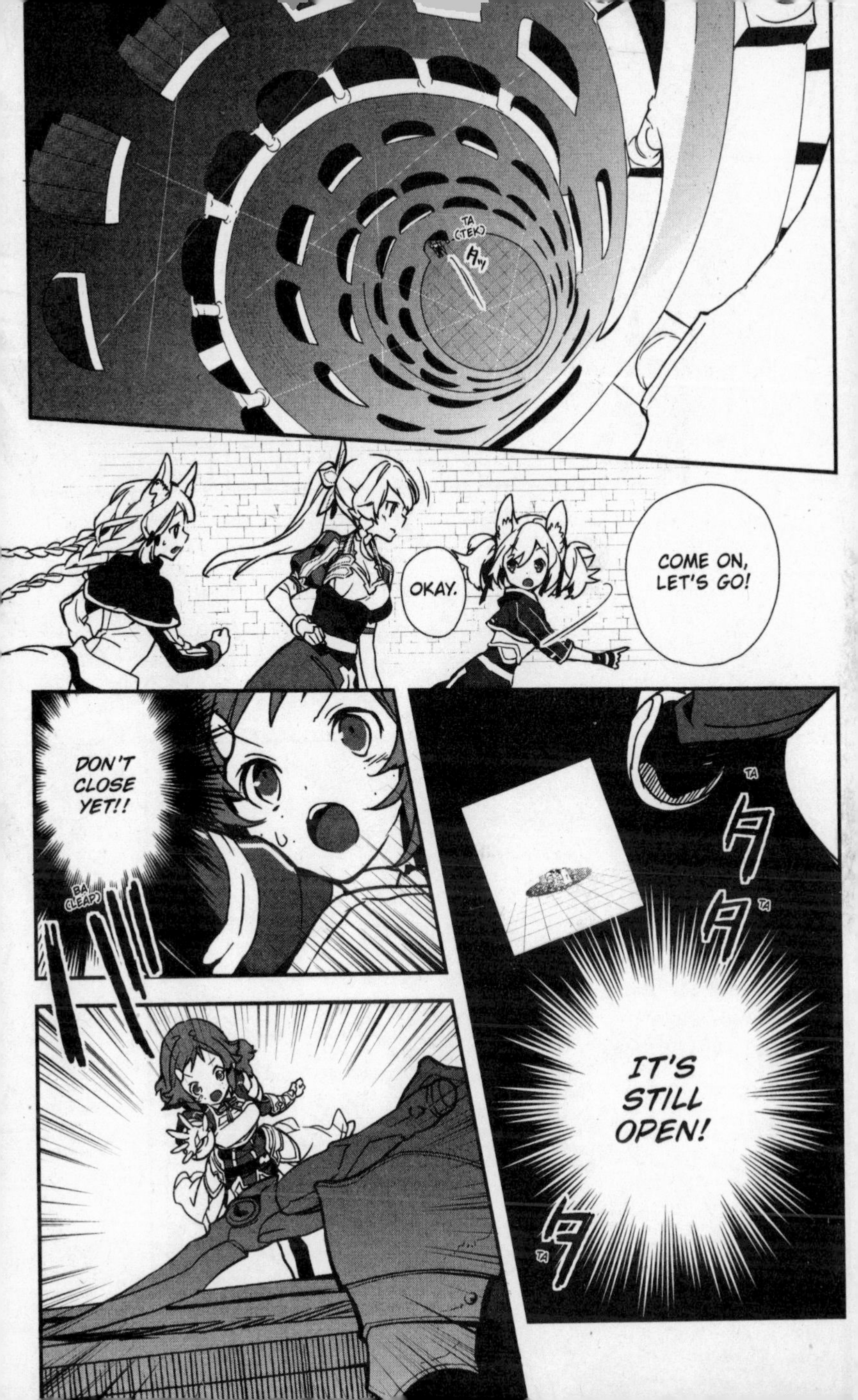
TA (TEK)
COME ON, LET'S GO!
OKAY.
TA
TA
IT'S STILL OPEN!
TA
DON'T CLOSE YET!!
BA (LEAP)

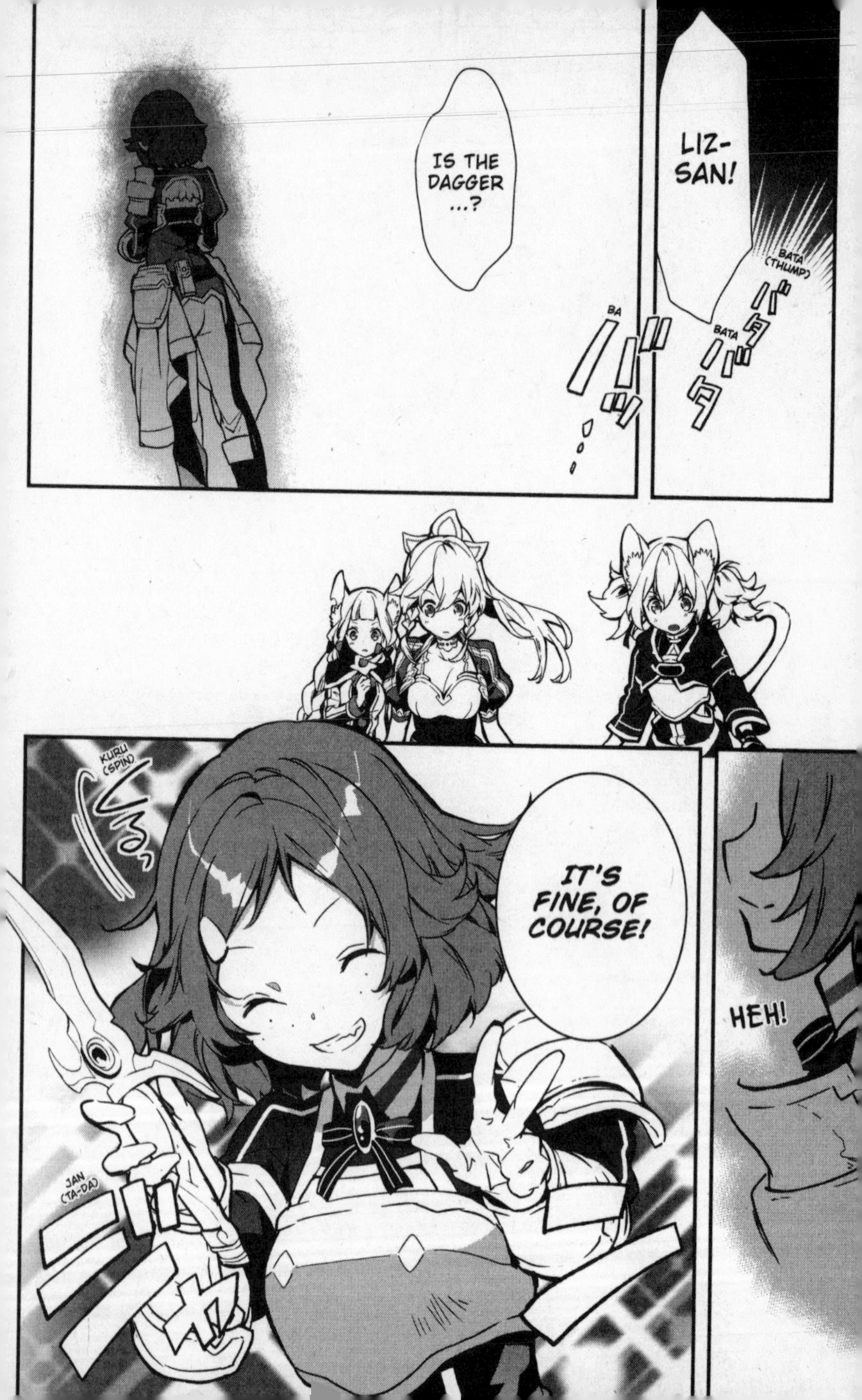
LIZ-SAN!
BATA (THUMP)
BATA
BA
IS THE DAGGER ...?
HEH!
IT'S FINE, OF COURSE!
KURU (SPIN)
JAN (TA-DA)

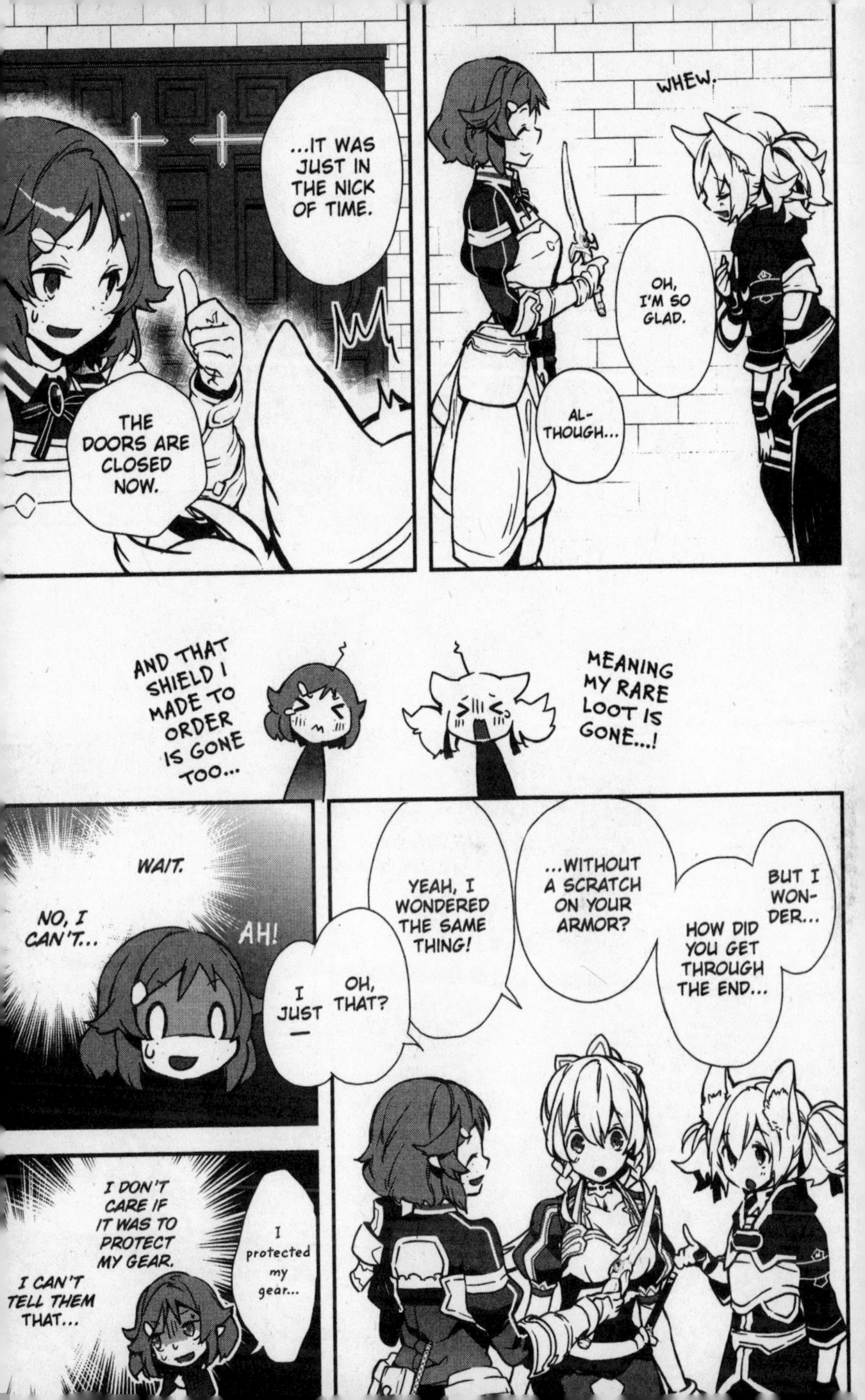
WHEW.
OH, I'M SO GLAD.
AL-THOUGH...
...IT WAS JUST IN THE NICK OF TIME.
THE DOORS ARE CLOSED NOW.
MEANING MY RARE LOOT IS GONE...!
AND THAT SHIELD I MADE TO ORDER IS GONE TOO...
BUT I WONDER...
HOW DID YOU GET THROUGH THE END...
...WITHOUT A SCRATCH ON YOUR ARMOR?
YEAH, I WONDERED THE SAME THING!
OH, THAT?
I JUST —
AH!
WAIT.
NO, I CAN'T...
I protected my gear...
I DON'T CARE IF IT WAS TO PROTECT MY GEAR.
I CAN'T TELL THEM THAT...

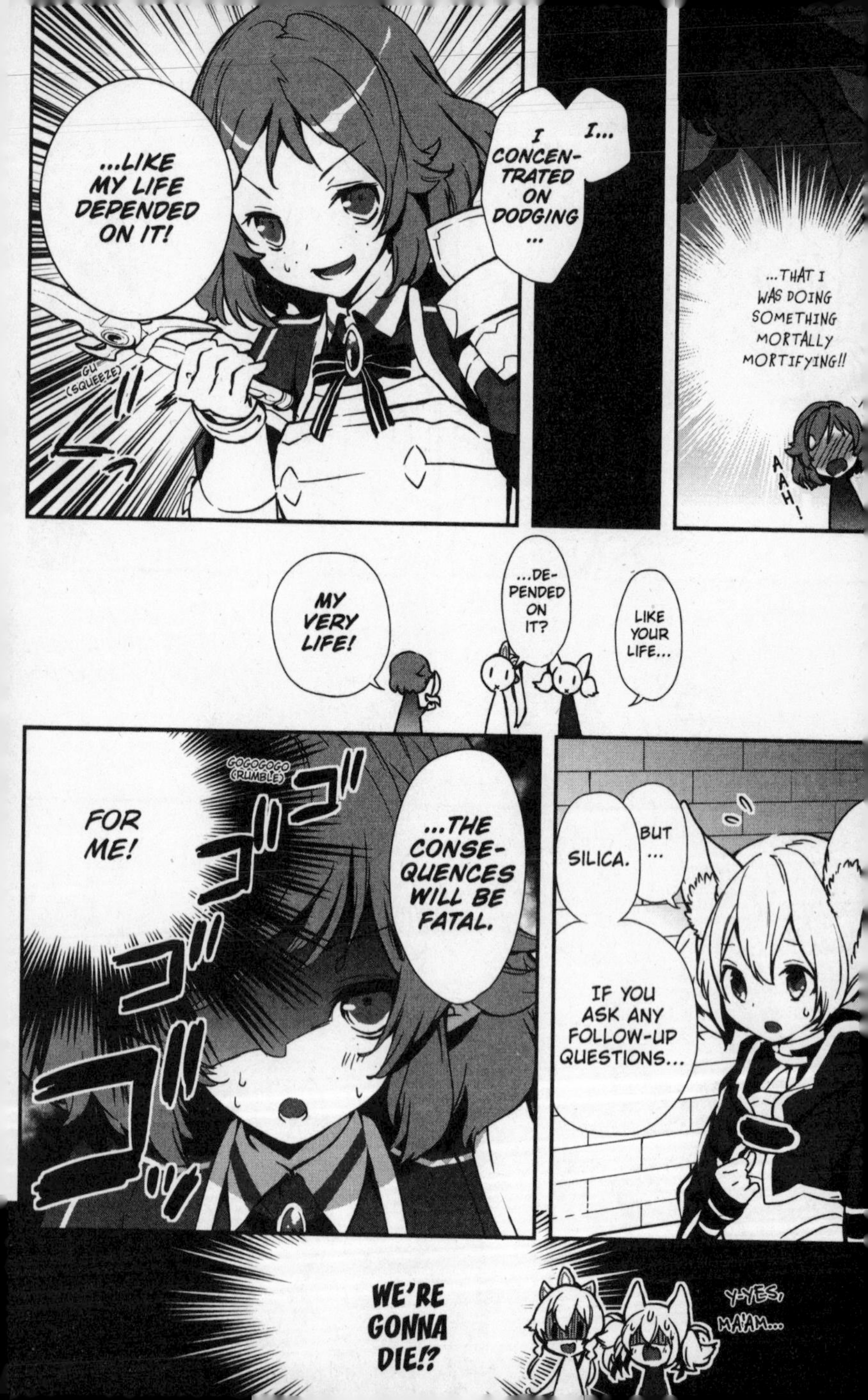
...THAT I WAS DOING SOMETHING MORTALLY MORTIFYING!!
AAH!
I...
I CONCENTRATED ON DODGING...
GU (SQUEEZE)
...LIKE MY LIFE DEPENDED ON IT!
LIKE YOUR LIFE...
...DEPENDED ON IT?
MY VERY LIFE!
BUT...
SILICA.
IF YOU ASK ANY FOLLOW-UP QUESTIONS...
GOGOGOGO (RUMBLE)
...THE CONSEQUENCES WILL BE FATAL.
FOR ME!
Y-YES, MA'AM...
WE'RE GONNA DIE!?

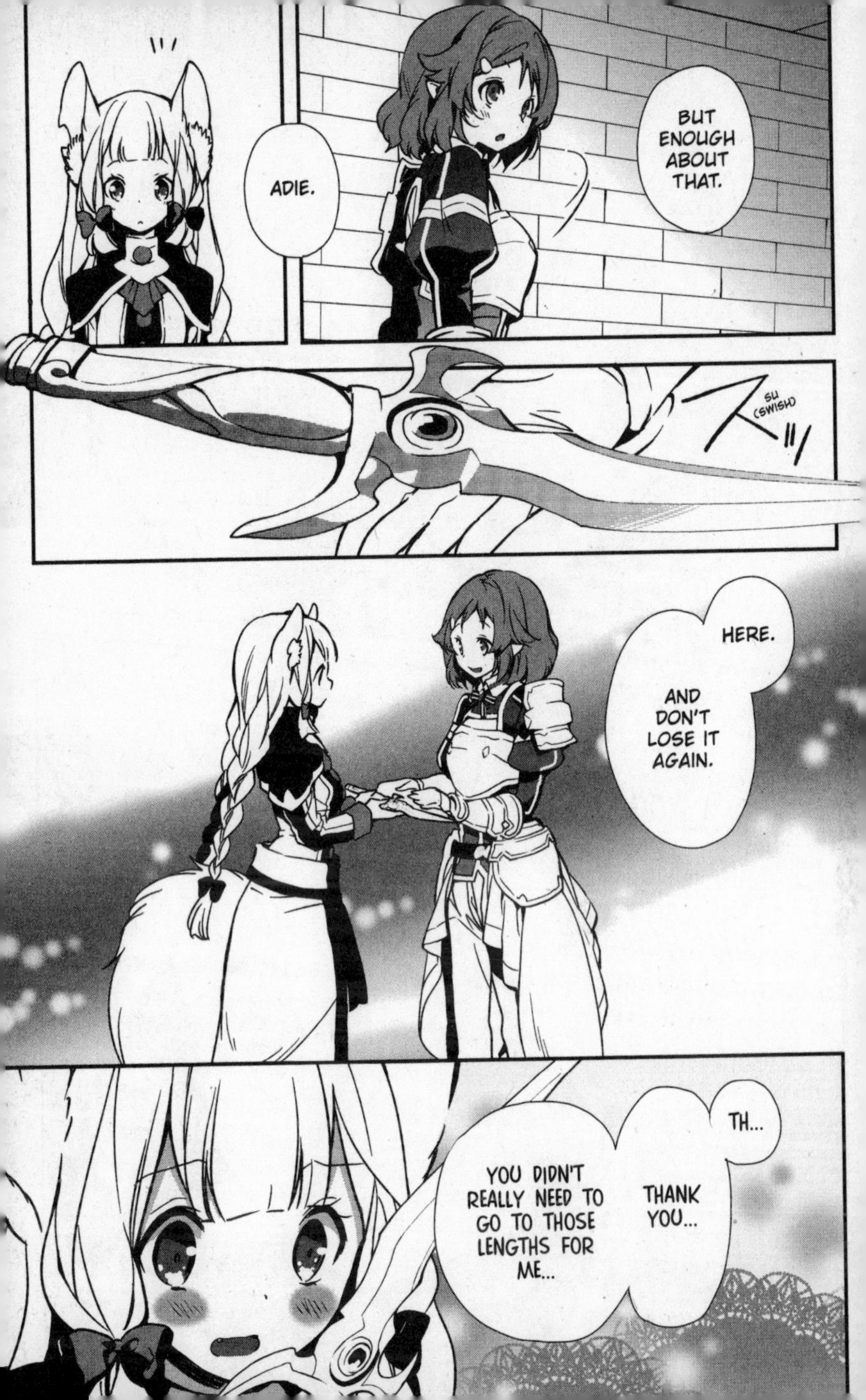
BUT ENOUGH ABOUT THAT.
ADIE.
SU (SWISH)
HERE.
AND DON'T LOSE IT AGAIN.
TH...
THANK YOU...
YOU DIDN'T REALLY NEED TO GO TO THOSE LENGTHS FOR ME...

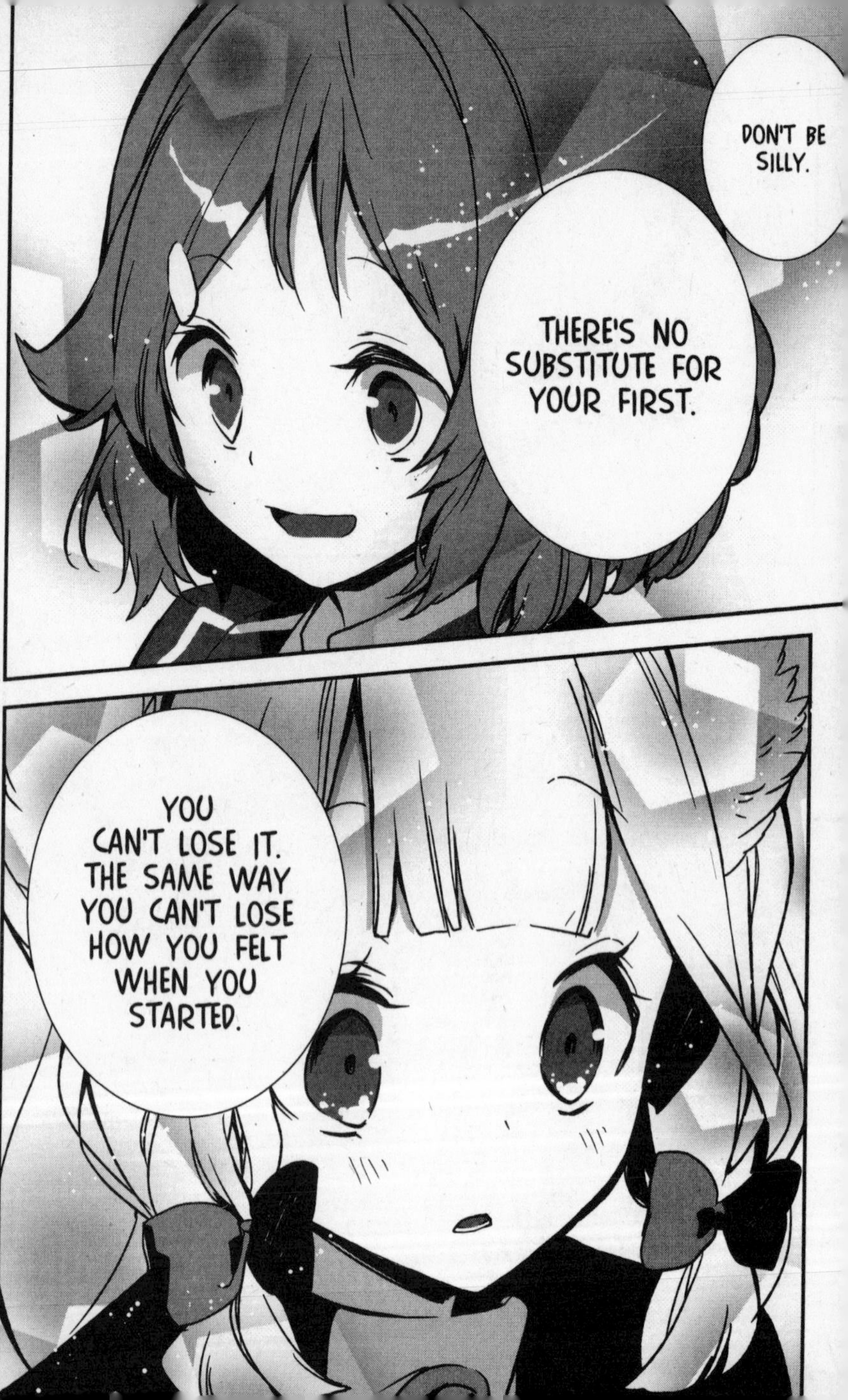
DON'T BE SILLY.
THERE'S NO SUBSTITUTE FOR YOUR FIRST.
YOU CAN'T LOSE IT. THE SAME WAY YOU CAN'T LOSE HOW YOU FELT WHEN YOU STARTED.

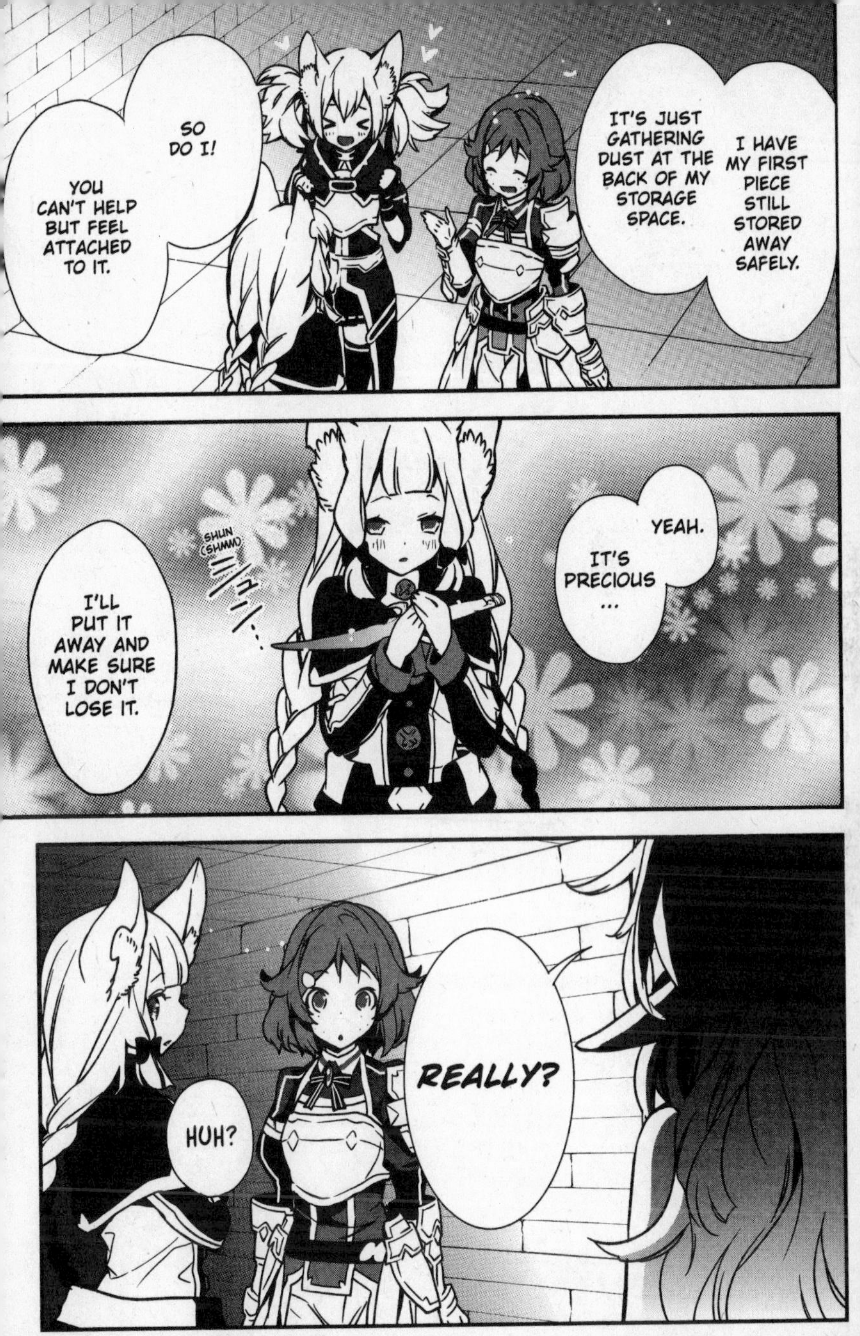
I HAVE MY FIRST PIECE STILL STORED AWAY SAFELY.
IT'S JUST GATHERING DUST AT THE BACK OF MY STORAGE SPACE.
SO DO I!
YOU CAN'T HELP BUT FEEL ATTACHED TO IT.
YEAH.
IT'S PRECIOUS ...
SHUN (SHMM)
I'LL PUT IT AWAY AND MAKE SURE I DON'T LOSE IT.
REALLY?
HUH?

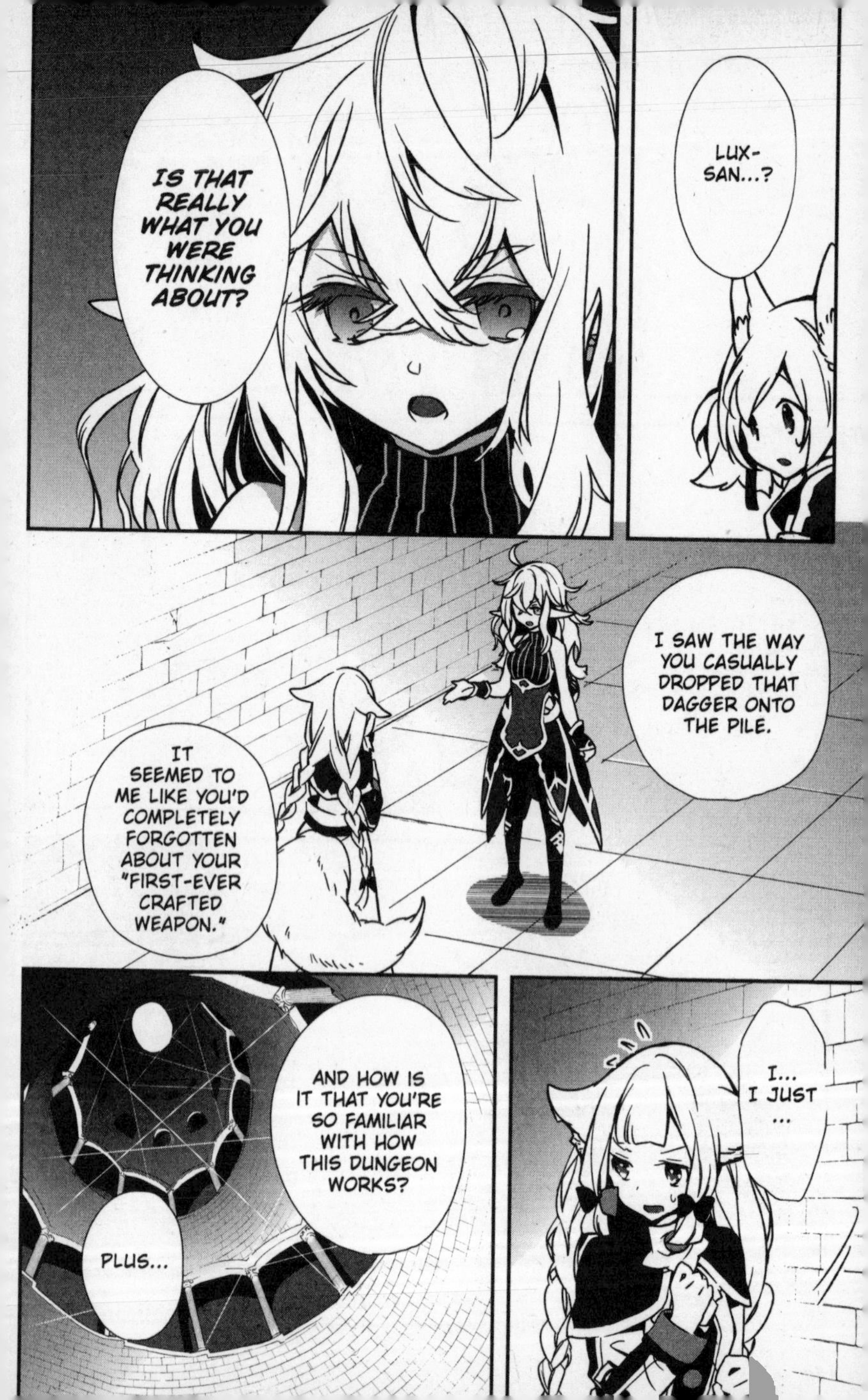
LUX-SAN...?
IS THAT REALLY WHAT YOU WERE THINKING ABOUT?
I SAW THE WAY YOU CASUALLY DROPPED THAT DAGGER ONTO THE PILE.
IT SEEMED TO ME LIKE YOU'D COMPLETELY FORGOTTEN ABOUT YOUR "FIRST-EVER CRAFTED WEAPON."
I... I JUST ...
AND HOW IS IT THAT YOU'RE SO FAMILIAR WITH HOW THIS DUNGEON WORKS?
PLUS...

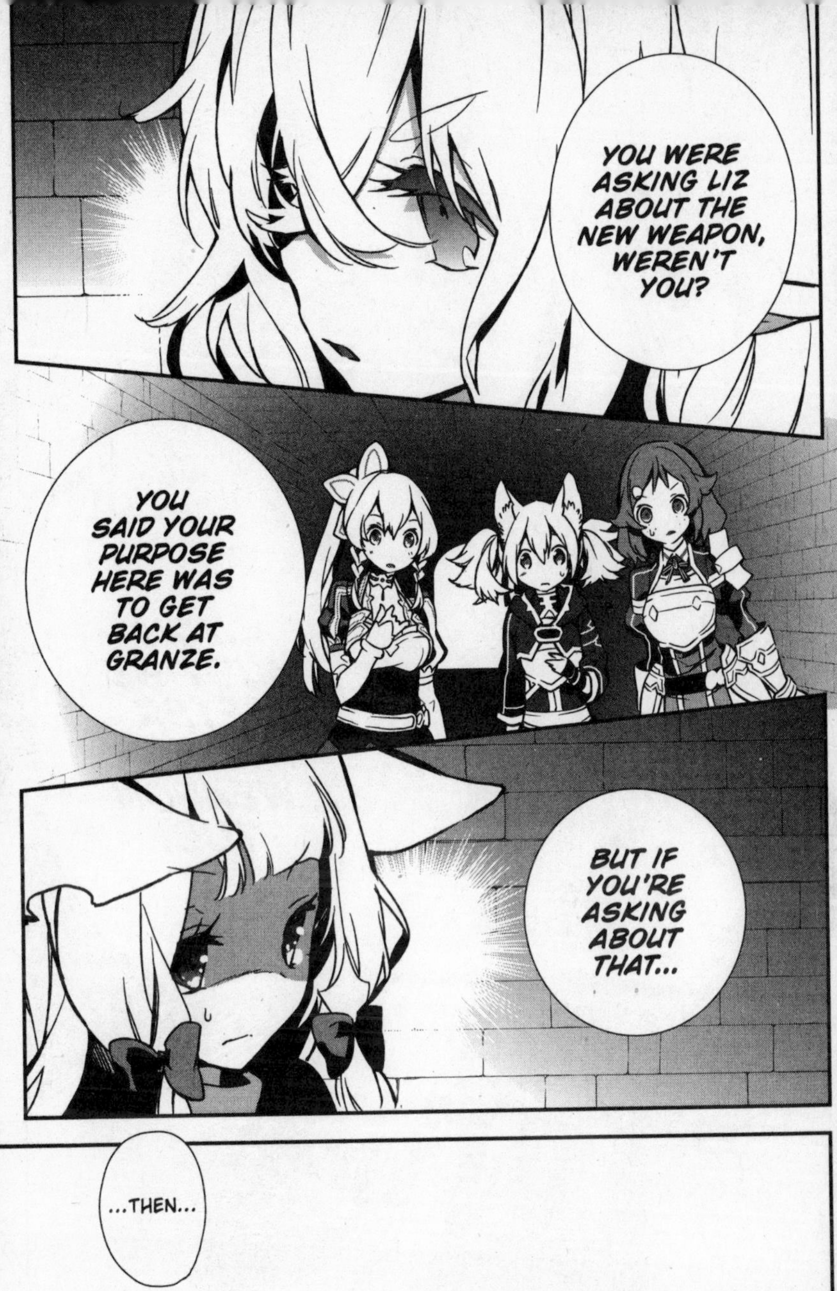
YOU WERE ASKING LIZ ABOUT THE NEW WEAPON, WEREN'T YOU?
YOU SAID YOUR PURPOSE HERE WAS TO GET BACK AT GRANZE.
BUT IF YOU'RE ASKING ABOUT THAT...
...THEN...

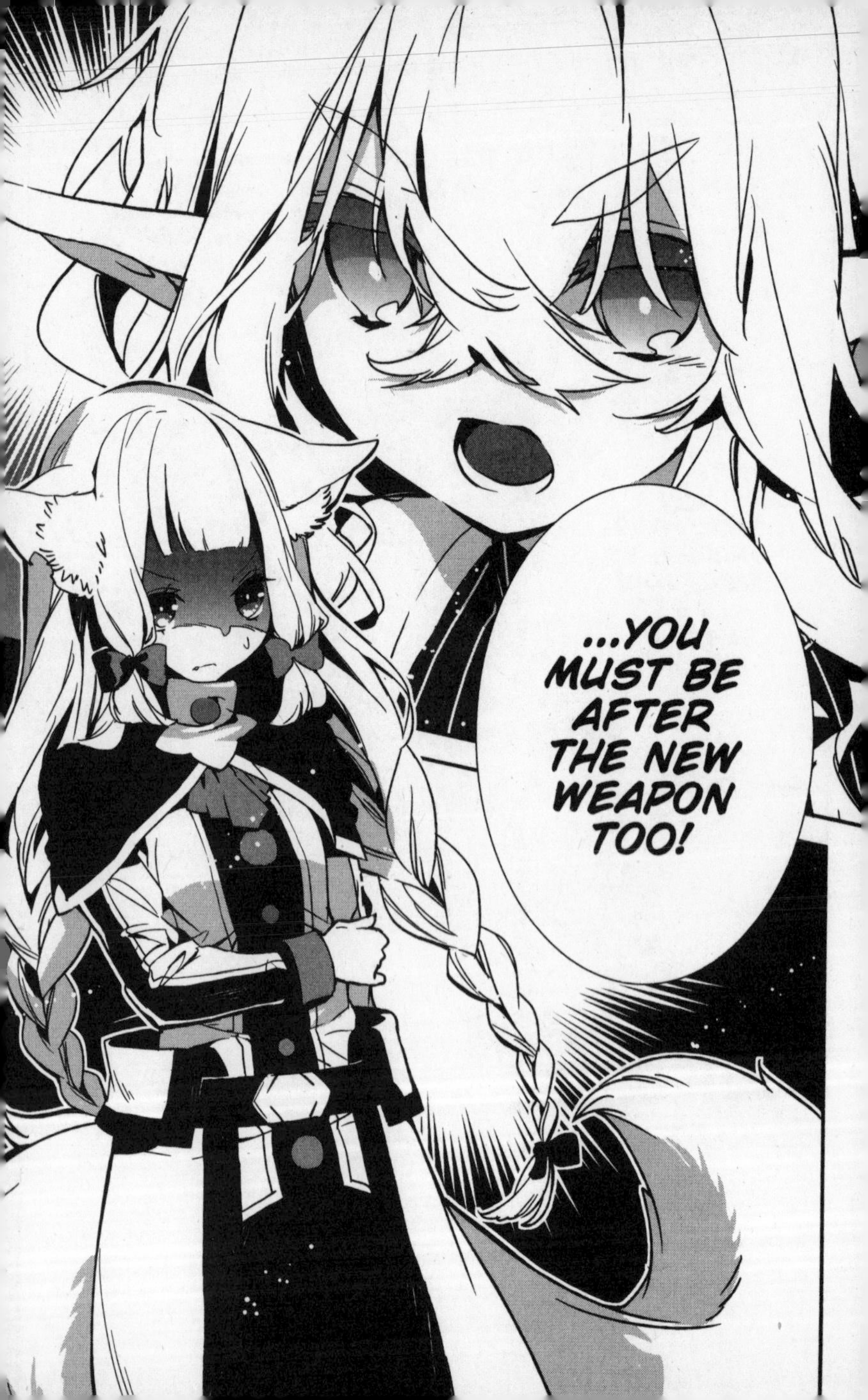
...YOU MUST BE AFTER THE NEW WEAPON TOO!

SWORD ART ONLINE
GIRLS' OPS

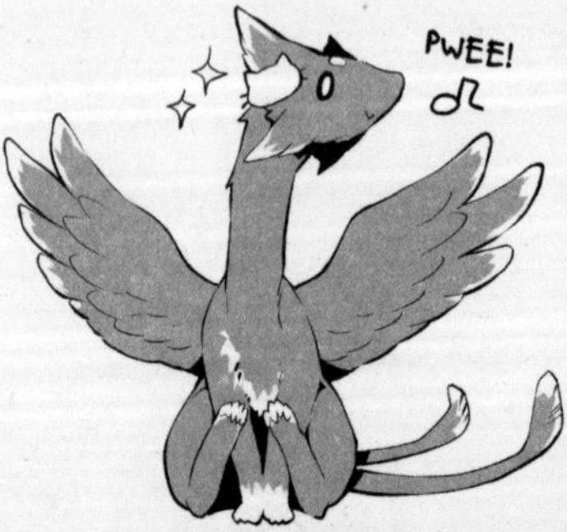
PWEE!

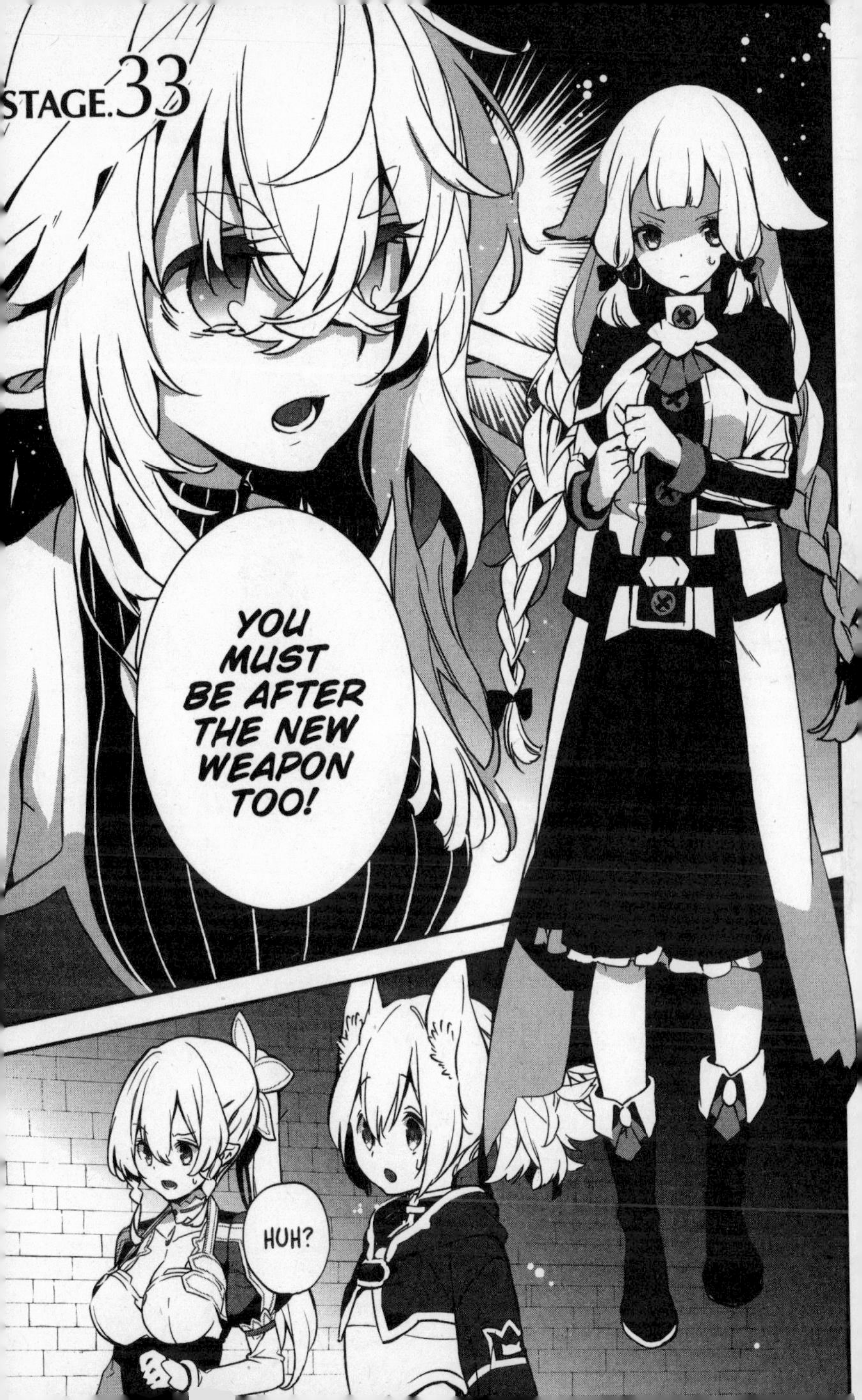
STAGE.33
YOU MUST BE AFTER THE NEW WEAPON TOO!
HUH?

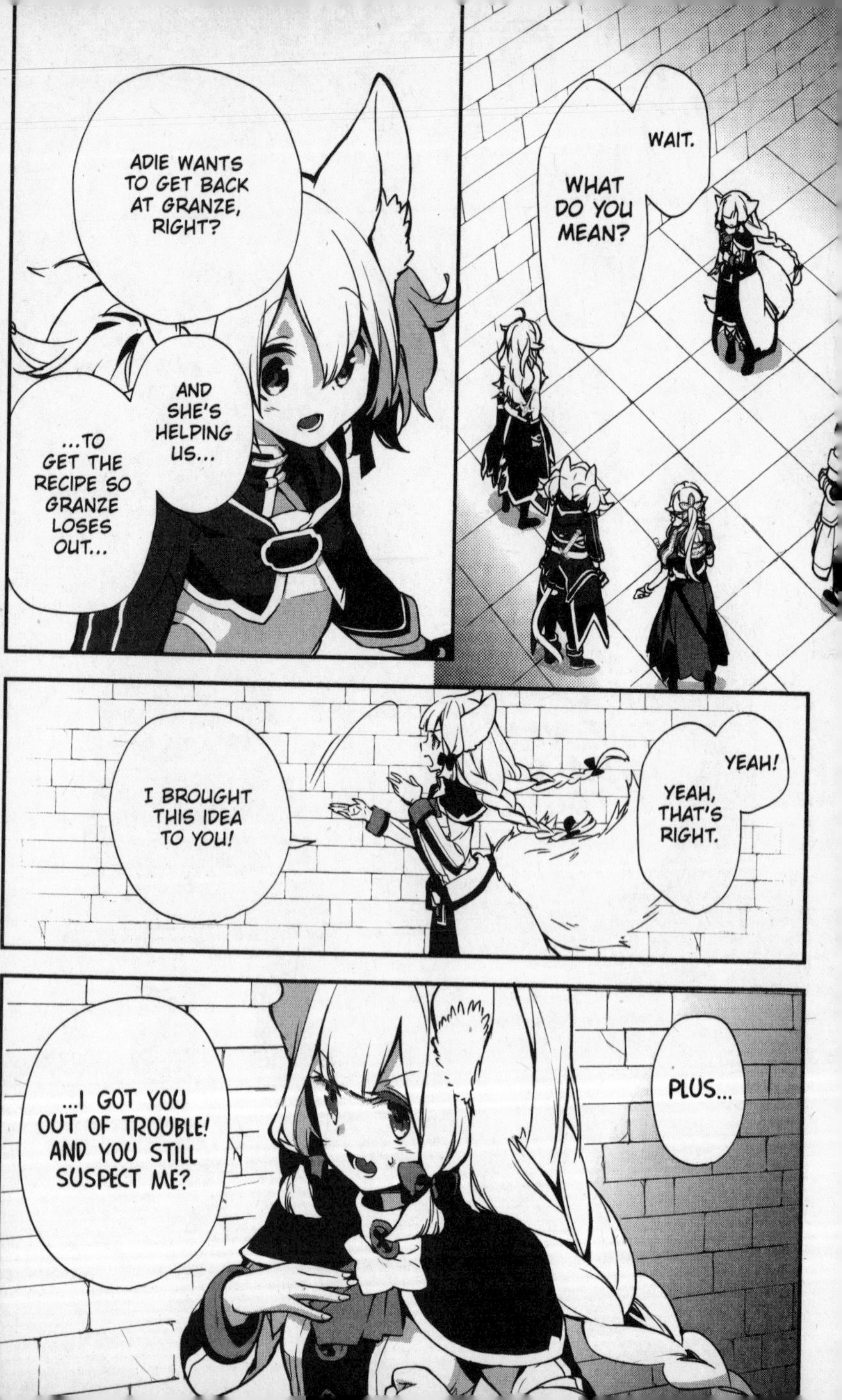
WAIT.
WHAT DO YOU MEAN?
ADIE WANTS TO GET BACK AT GRANZE, RIGHT?
AND SHE'S HELPING US...
...TO GET THE RECIPE SO GRANZE LOSES OUT...
YEAH!
YEAH, THAT'S RIGHT.
I BROUGHT THIS IDEA TO YOU!
PLUS...
...I GOT YOU OUT OF TROUBLE! AND YOU STILL SUSPECT ME?

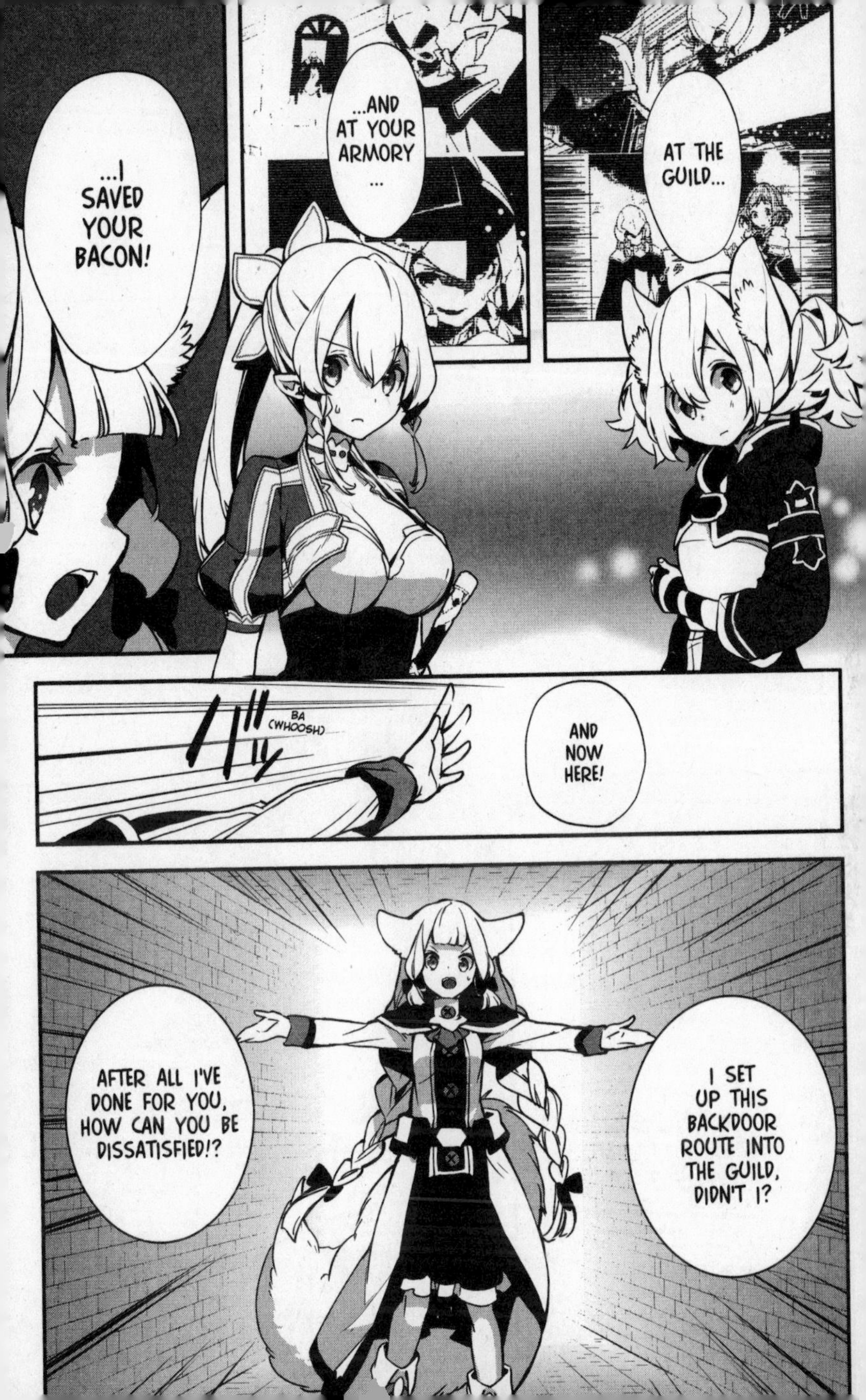
AT THE GUILD...
...AND AT YOUR ARMORY ...
...I SAVED YOUR BACON!
AND NOW HERE!
BA (WHOOSH)
I SET UP THIS BACKDOOR ROUTE INTO THE GUILD, DIDN'T I?
AFTER ALL I'VE DONE FOR YOU, HOW CAN YOU BE DISSATISFIED!?

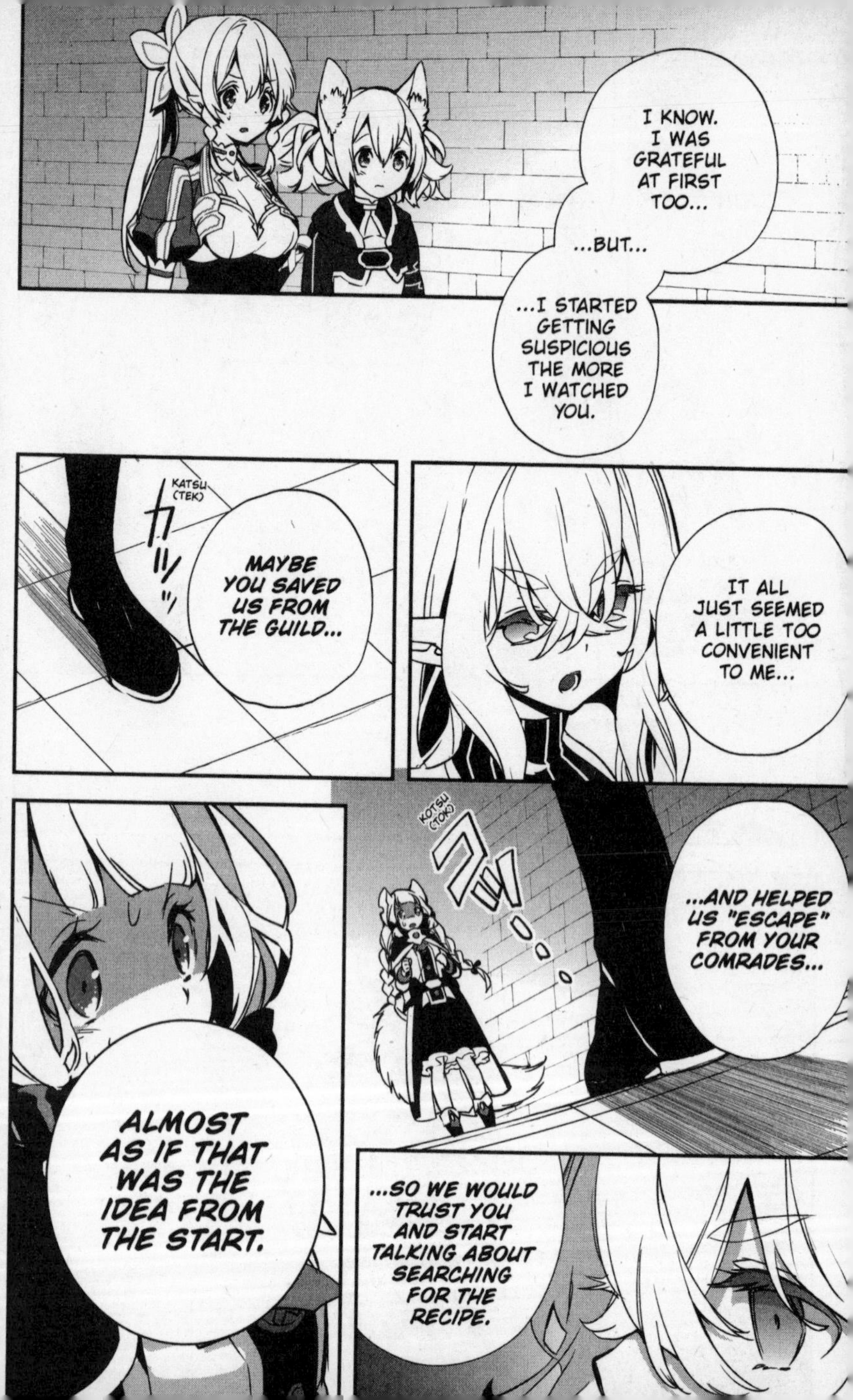
I KNOW. I WAS GRATEFUL AT FIRST TOO...
...BUT...
...I STARTED GETTING SUSPICIOUS THE MORE I WATCHED YOU.
IT ALL JUST SEEMED A LITTLE TOO CONVENIENT TO ME...
KATSU (TEK)
MAYBE YOU SAVED US FROM THE GUILD...
KOTSU (TOK)
...AND HELPED US "ESCAPE" FROM YOUR COMRADES...
...SO WE WOULD TRUST YOU AND START TALKING ABOUT SEARCHING FOR THE RECIPE.
ALMOST AS IF THAT WAS THE IDEA FROM THE START.

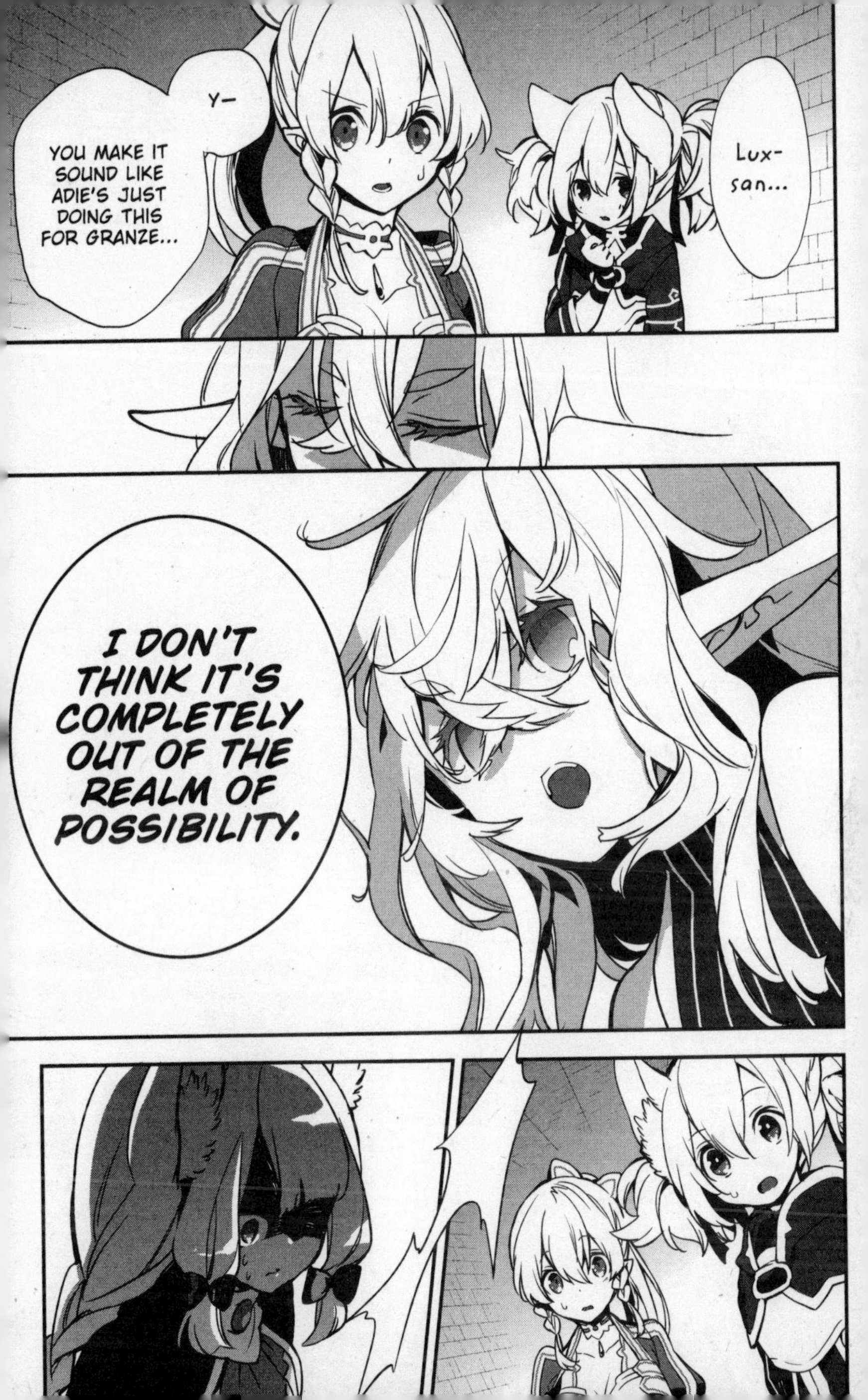
Lux-san...
Y-
YOU MAKE IT SOUND LIKE ADIE'S JUST DOING THIS FOR GRANZE...
I DON'T THINK IT'S COMPLETELY OUT OF THE REALM OF POSSIBILITY.

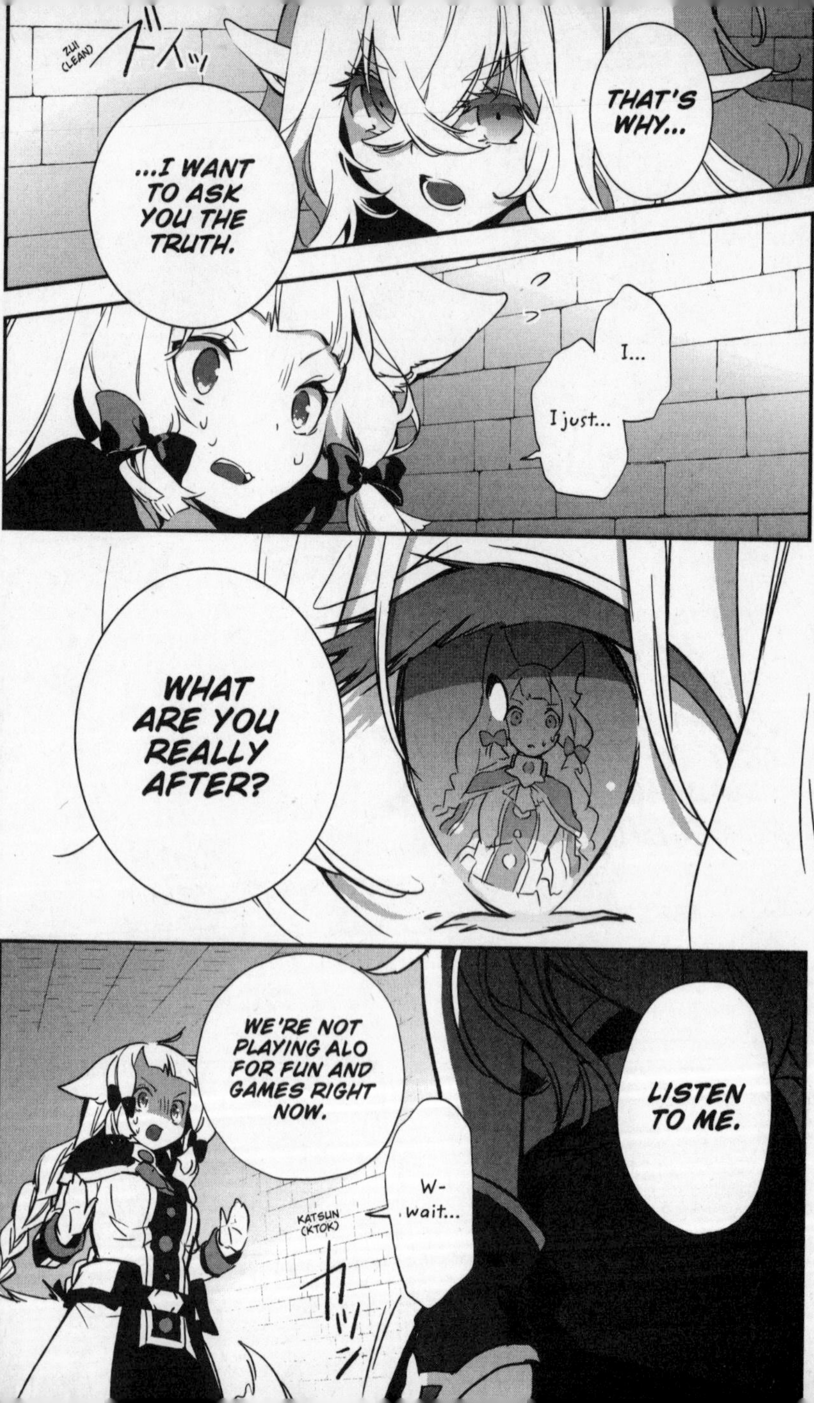
THAT'S WHY...
ZUI (LEAN)
...I WANT TO ASK YOU THE TRUTH.
I...
I just...
WHAT ARE YOU REALLY AFTER?
LISTEN TO ME.
WE'RE NOT PLAYING ALO FOR FUN AND GAMES RIGHT NOW.
W-wait...
KATSUN (KTOK)

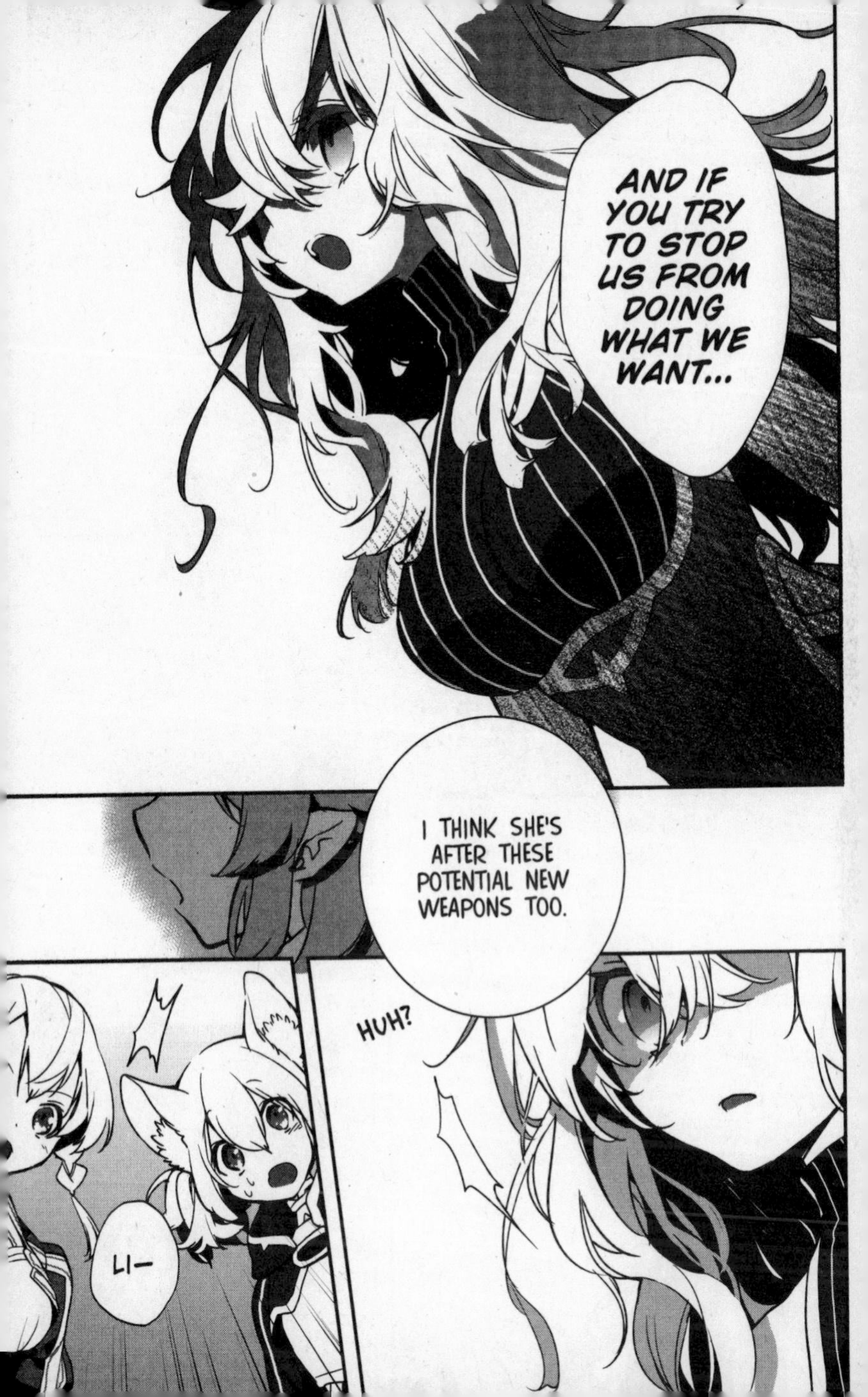
AND IF YOU TRY TO STOP US FROM DOING WHAT WE WANT...
I THINK SHE'S AFTER THESE POTENTIAL NEW WEAPONS TOO.
HUH?
LI—

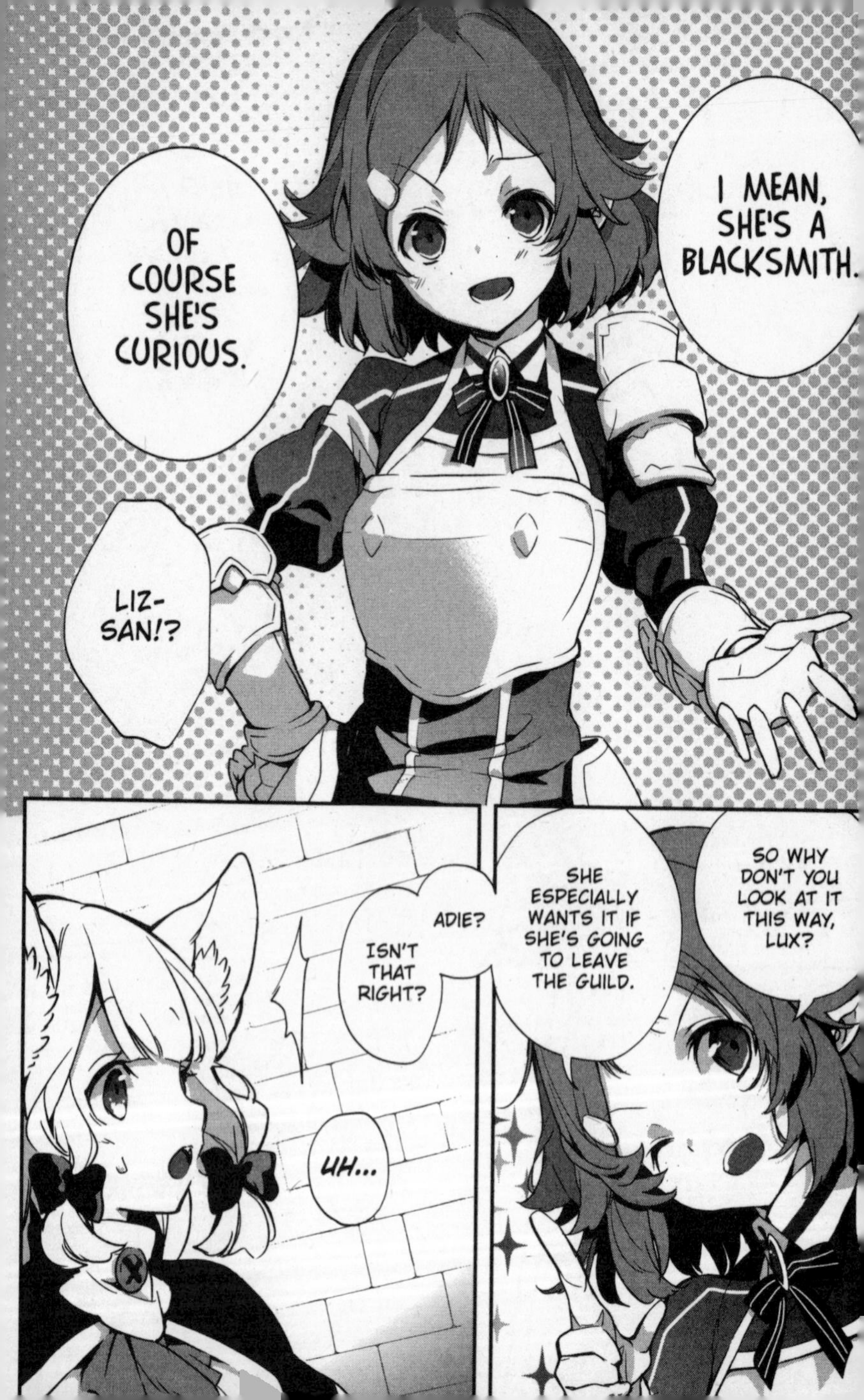
I MEAN, SHE'S A BLACKSMITH.
OF COURSE SHE'S CURIOUS.
LIZ-SAN!?
SO WHY DON'T YOU LOOK AT IT THIS WAY, LUX?
SHE ESPECIALLY WANTS IT IF SHE'S GOING TO LEAVE THE GUILD.
ADIE?
ISN'T THAT RIGHT?
UH...

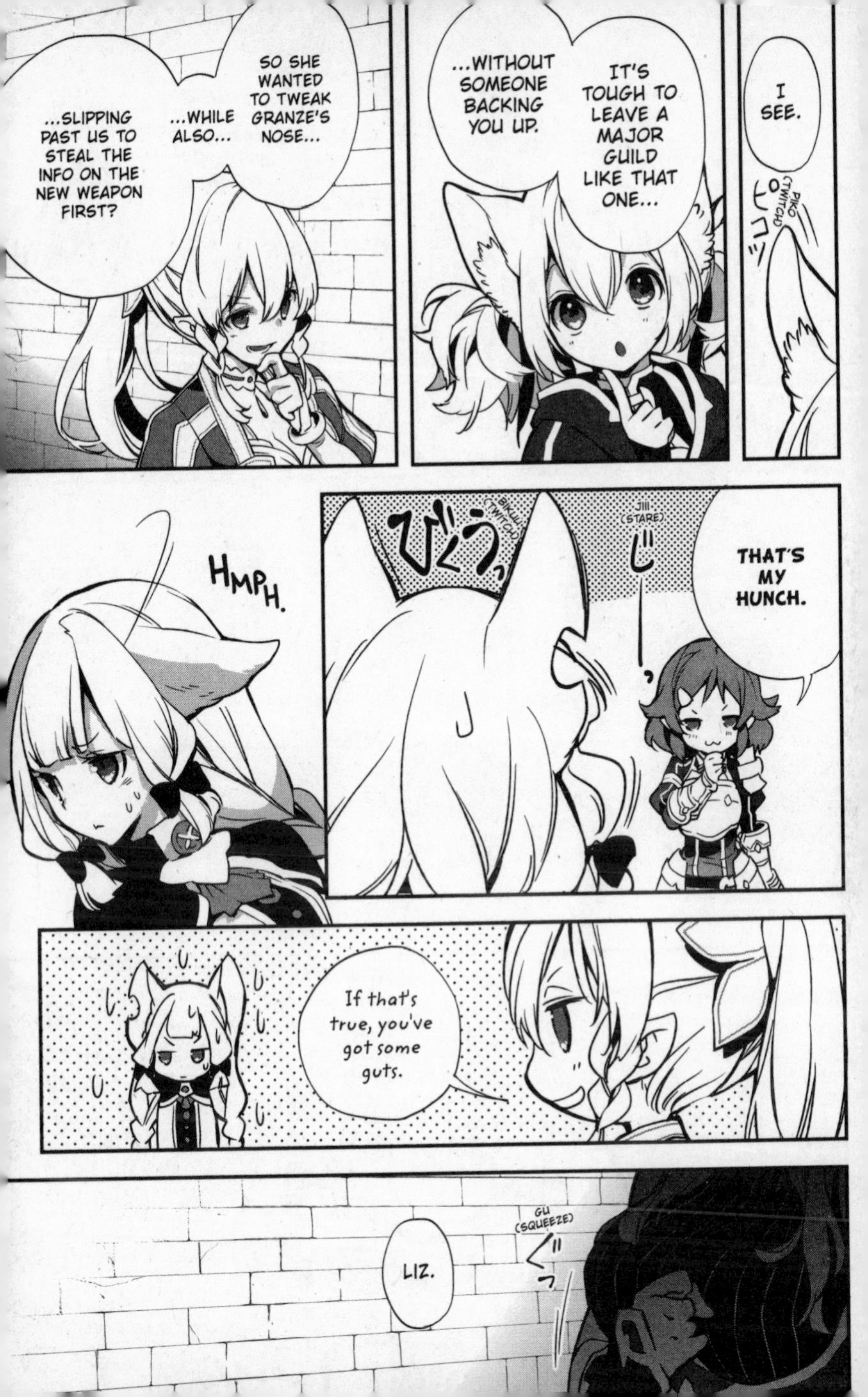
I SEE.
PIKO (TWITCH)
IT'S TOUGH TO LEAVE A MAJOR GUILD LIKE THAT ONE...
...WITHOUT SOMEONE BACKING YOU UP.
SO SHE WANTED TO TWEAK GRANZE'S NOSE...
...WHILE ALSO...
...SLIPPING PAST US TO STEAL THE INFO ON THE NEW WEAPON FIRST?
THAT'S MY HUNCH.
JIII (STARE)
BIKUH (TWITCH)
HMPH.
If that's true, you've got some guts.
GU (SQUEEZE)
LIZ.

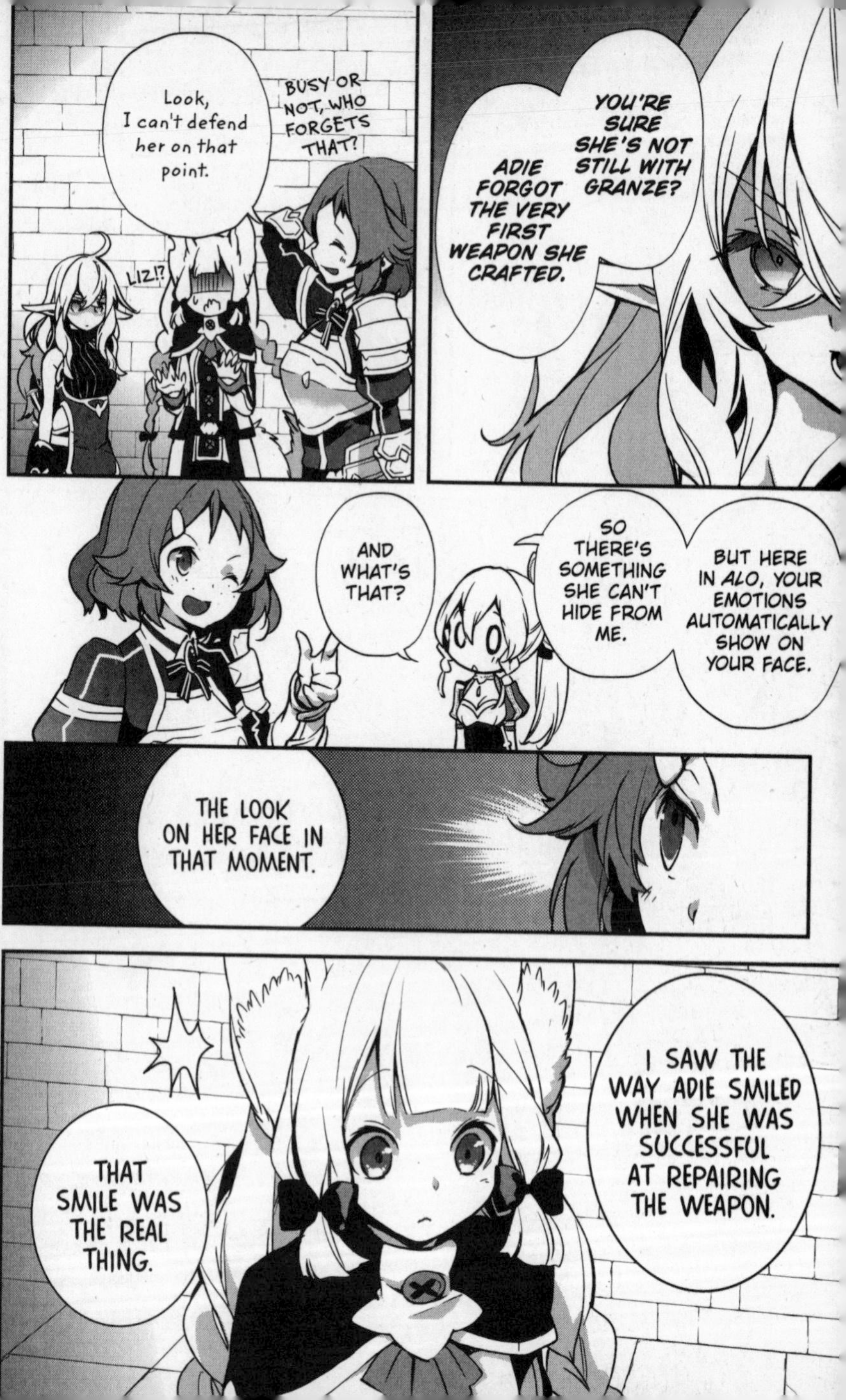
YOU'RE SURE SHE'S NOT STILL WITH GRANZE?
ADIE FORGOT THE VERY FIRST WEAPON SHE CRAFTED.
BUSY OR NOT, WHO FORGETS THAT?
Look, I can't defend her on that point.
LIZ!?
BUT HERE IN *ALO*, YOUR EMOTIONS AUTOMATICALLY SHOW ON YOUR FACE.
SO THERE'S SOMETHING SHE CAN'T HIDE FROM ME.
AND WHAT'S THAT?
THE LOOK ON HER FACE IN THAT MOMENT.
I SAW THE WAY ADIE SMILED WHEN SHE WAS SUCCESSFUL AT REPAIRING THE WEAPON.
THAT SMILE WAS THE REAL THING.

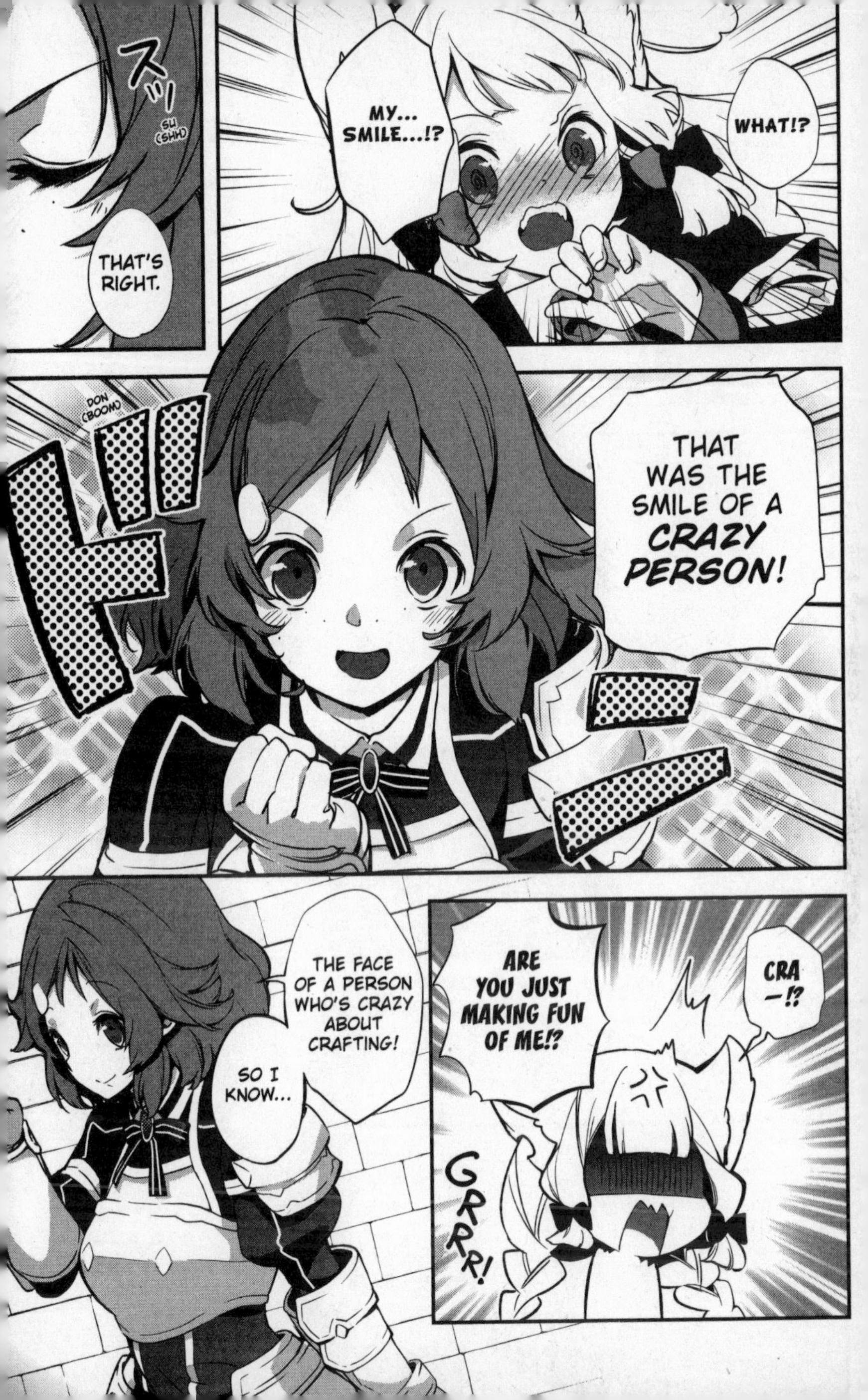
WHAT!?
MY... SMILE...!?
スッ
SU (SHH)
THAT'S RIGHT.
THAT WAS THE SMILE OF A *CRAZY PERSON*!
DON (BOOM)
CRA—!?
ARE YOU JUST MAKING FUN OF ME!?
GRRR!
THE FACE OF A PERSON WHO'S CRAZY ABOUT CRAFTING!
SO I KNOW...

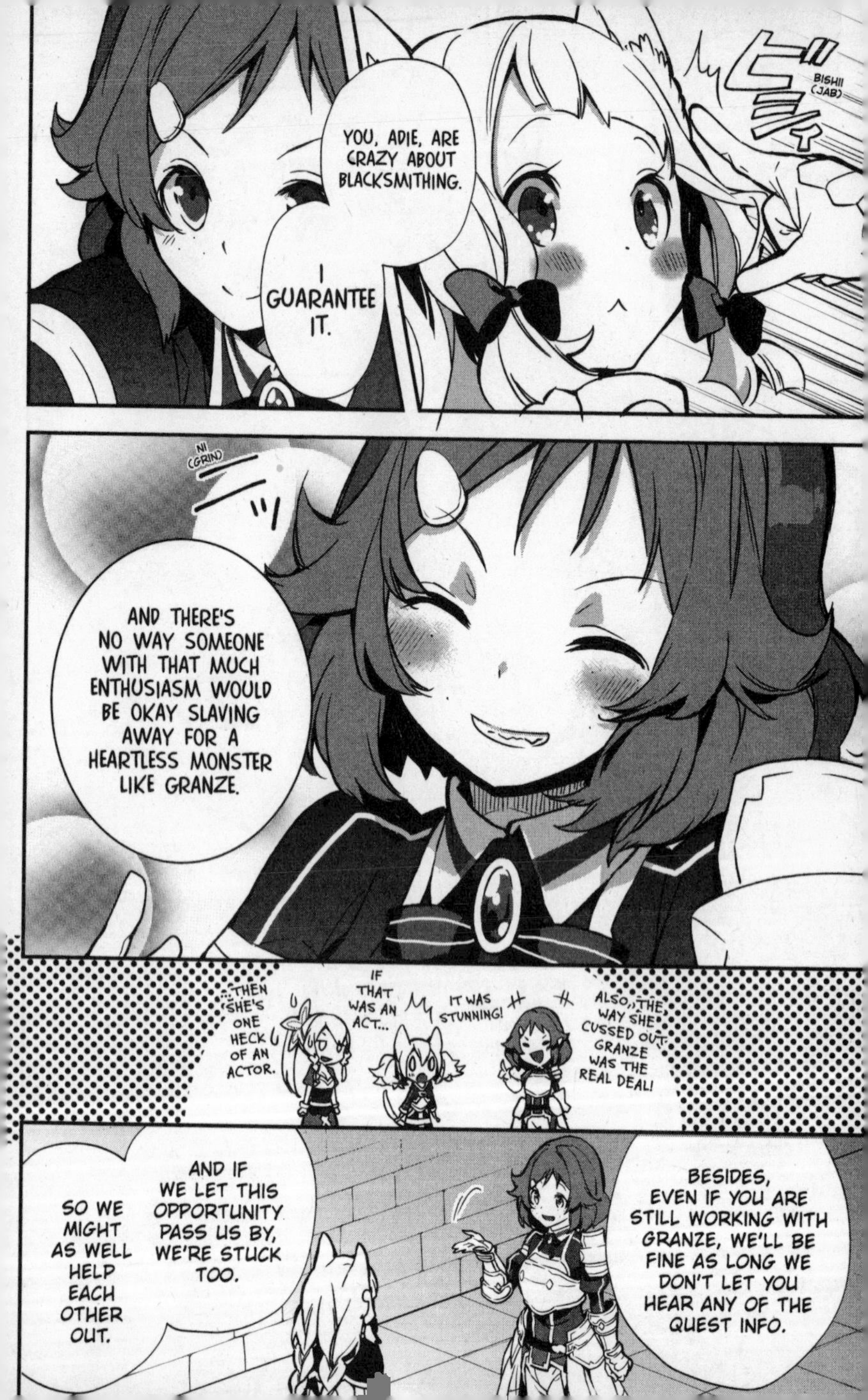
BISHI! (JAB)
YOU, ADIE, ARE CRAZY ABOUT BLACKSMITHING.
I GUARANTEE IT.
NI (GRIN)
AND THERE'S NO WAY SOMEONE WITH THAT MUCH ENTHUSIASM WOULD BE OKAY SLAVING AWAY FOR A HEARTLESS MONSTER LIKE GRANZE.
ALSO, THE WAY SHE CUSSED OUT GRANZE WAS THE REAL DEAL!
IT WAS STUNNING!
IF THAT WAS AN ACT...
...THEN SHE'S ONE HECK OF AN ACTOR.
BESIDES, EVEN IF YOU ARE STILL WORKING WITH GRANZE, WE'LL BE FINE AS LONG WE DON'T LET YOU HEAR ANY OF THE QUEST INFO.
AND IF WE LET THIS OPPORTUNITY PASS US BY, WE'RE STUCK TOO.
SO WE MIGHT AS WELL HELP EACH OTHER OUT.

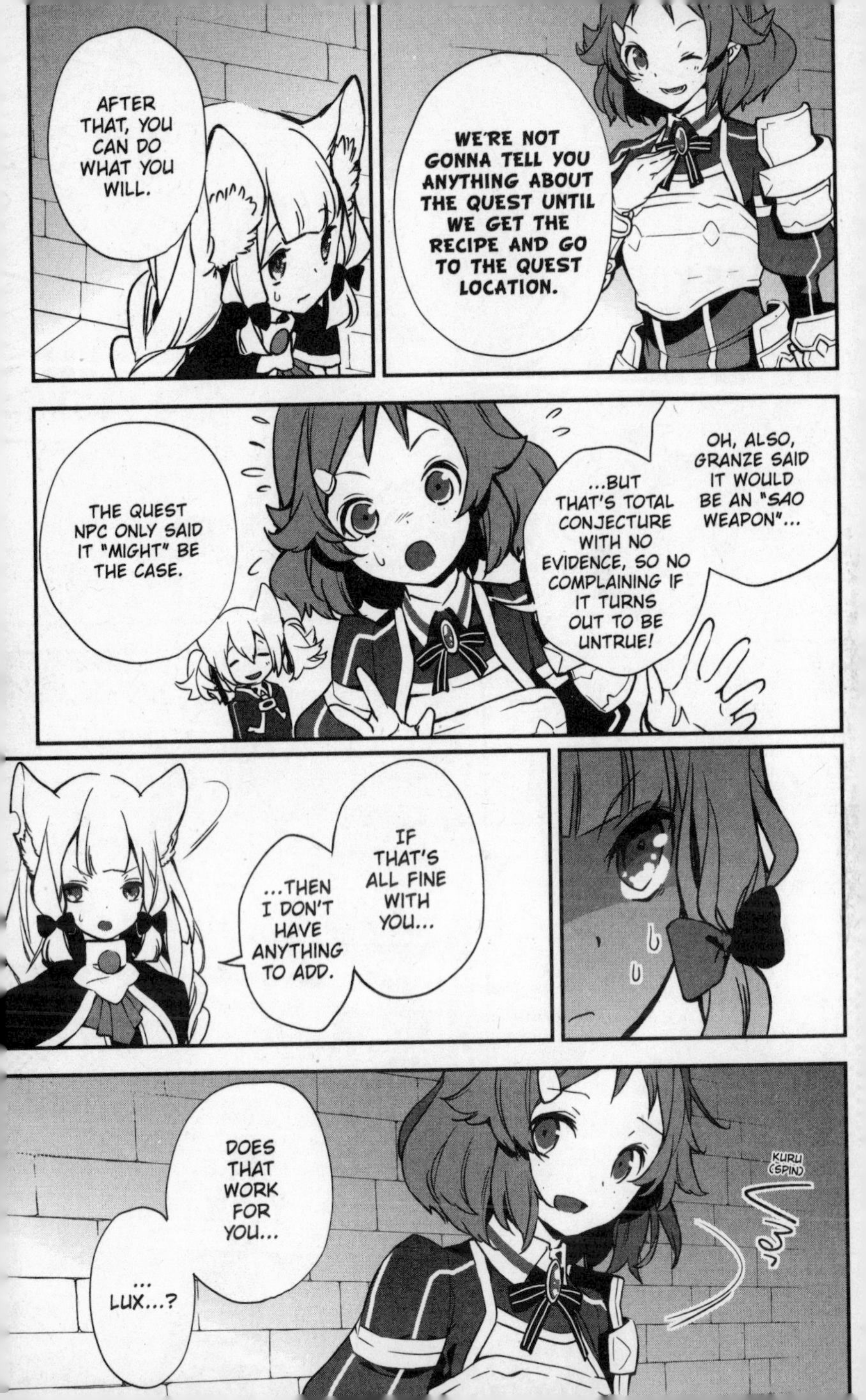
WE'RE NOT GONNA TELL YOU ANYTHING ABOUT THE QUEST UNTIL WE GET THE RECIPE AND GO TO THE QUEST LOCATION.
AFTER THAT, YOU CAN DO WHAT YOU WILL.
OH, ALSO, GRANZE SAID IT WOULD BE AN "SAO WEAPON"...
...BUT THAT'S TOTAL CONJECTURE WITH NO EVIDENCE, SO NO COMPLAINING IF IT TURNS OUT TO BE UNTRUE!
THE QUEST NPC ONLY SAID IT "MIGHT" BE THE CASE.
IF THAT'S ALL FINE WITH YOU...
...THEN I DON'T HAVE ANYTHING TO ADD.
KURU (SPIN)
DOES THAT WORK FOR YOU...
... LUX...?

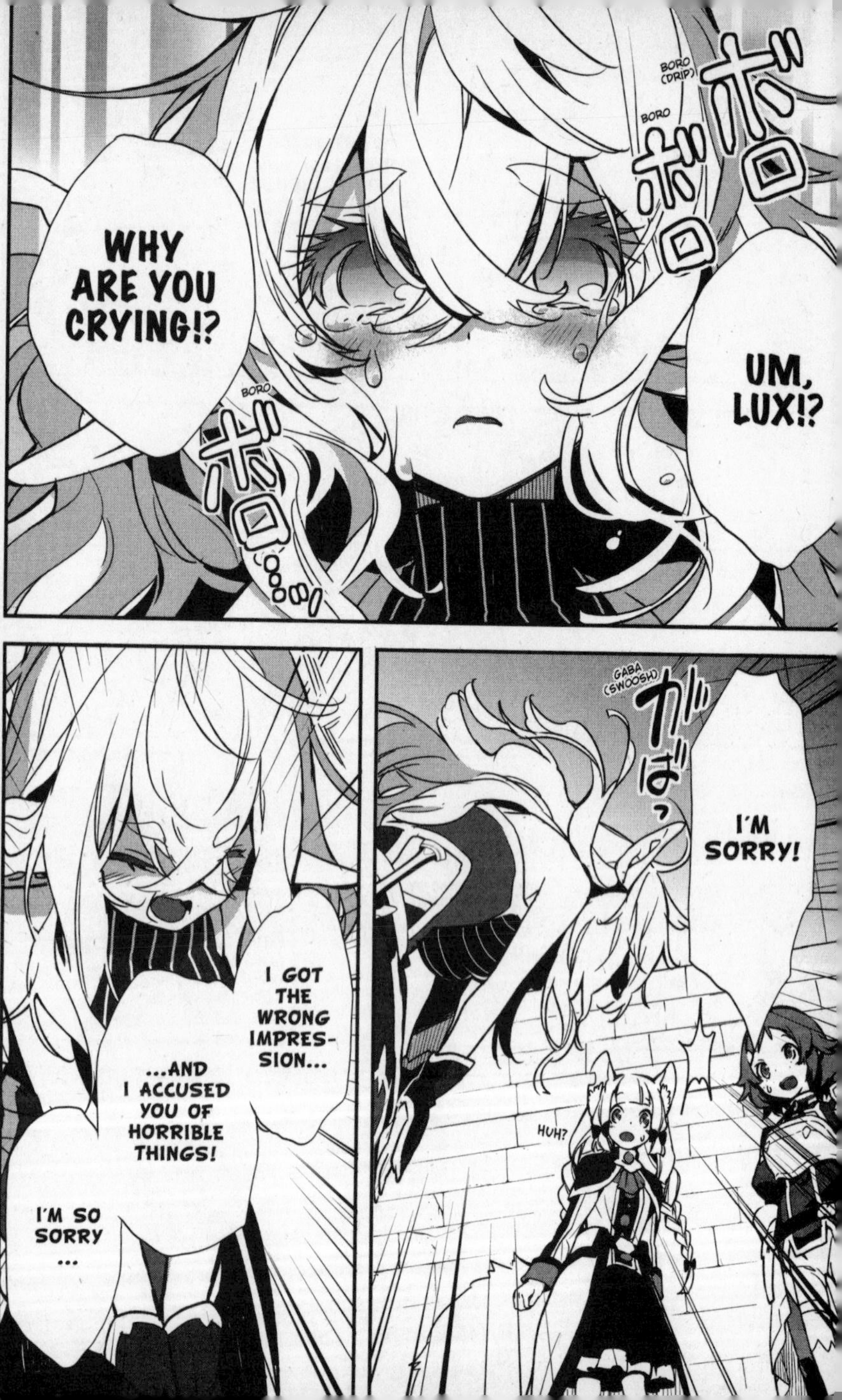

BORO (DRIP)
ボロ
BORO
ボロ
UM, LUX!?
WHY ARE YOU CRYING!?
BORO
ボロ…
GABA (SWOOSH)
がばっ
I'M SORRY!
HUH?
I GOT THE WRONG IMPRESSION...
...AND I ACCUSED YOU OF HORRIBLE THINGS!
I'M SO SORRY ...

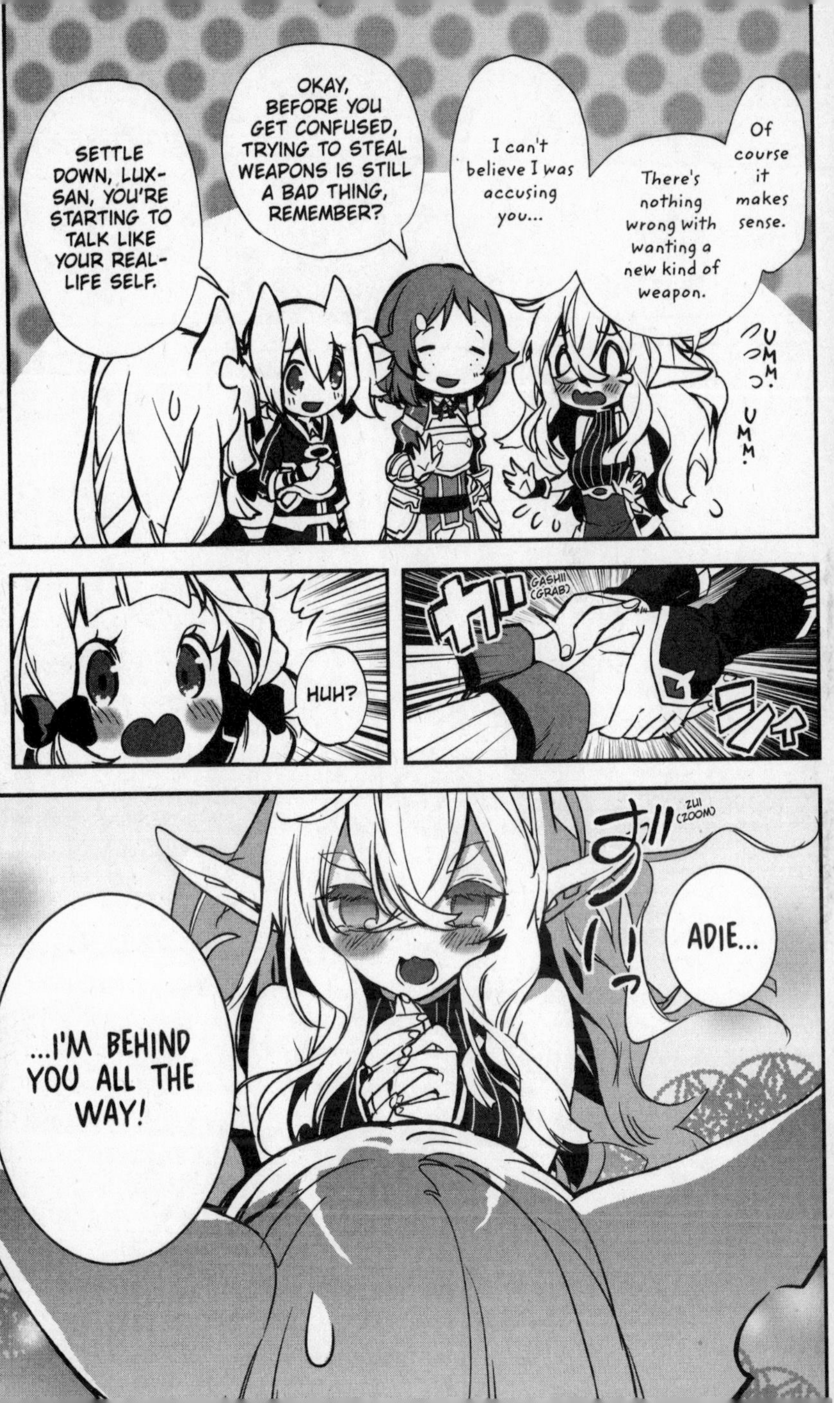
Of course it makes sense.
There's nothing wrong with wanting a new kind of weapon.
I can't believe I was accusing you...
UMM! UMM!
OKAY, BEFORE YOU GET CONFUSED, TRYING TO STEAL WEAPONS IS STILL A BAD THING, REMEMBER?
SETTLE DOWN, LUX-SAN, YOU'RE STARTING TO TALK LIKE YOUR REAL-LIFE SELF.
GASHII (GRAB)
HUH?
ZUI (ZOOM)
ADIE...
...I'M BEHIND YOU ALL THE WAY!

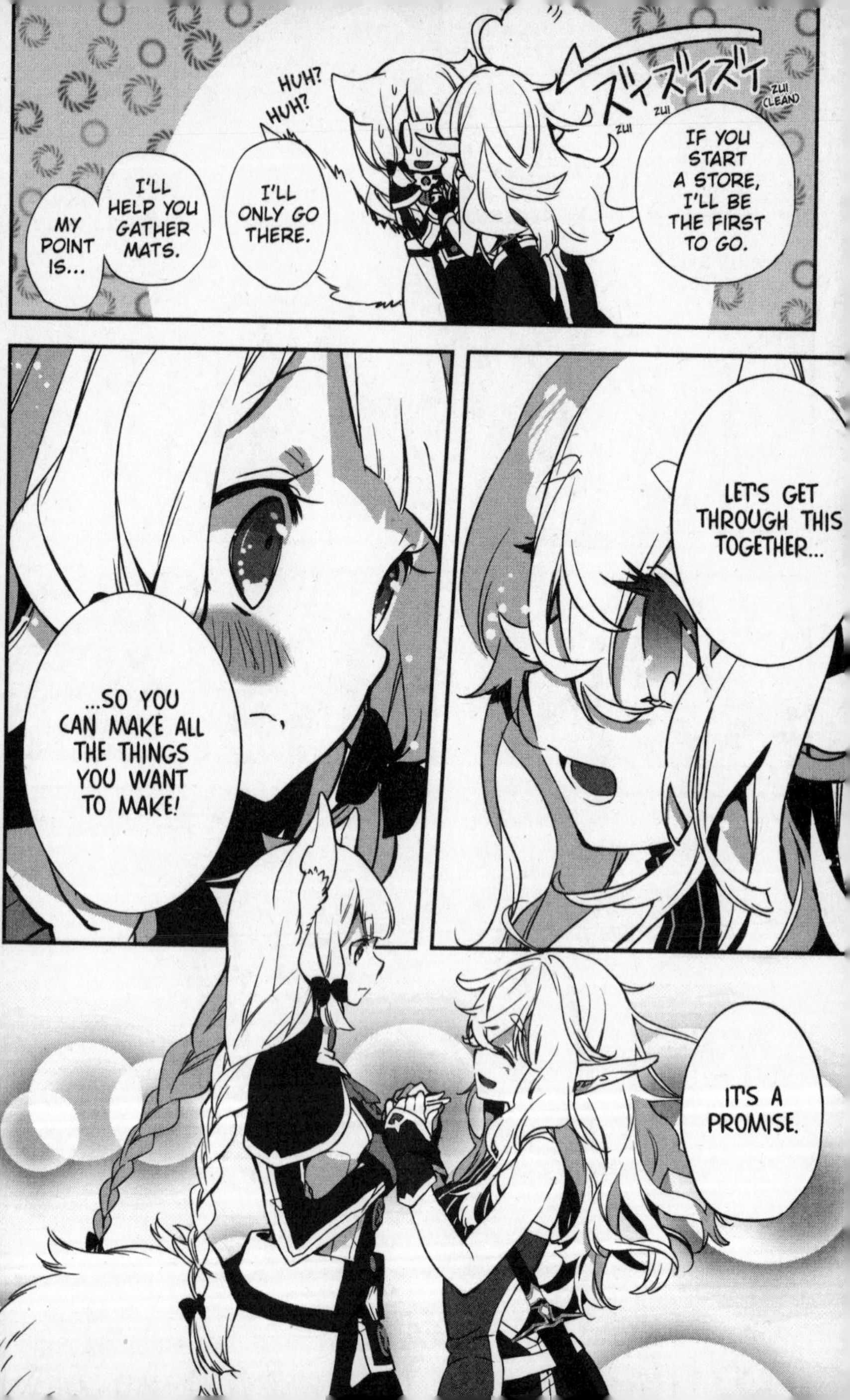
IF YOU START A STORE, I'LL BE THE FIRST TO GO.
ズィズイズイ
ZUI ZUI ZUI (CLEAN)
HUH? HUH?
I'LL ONLY GO THERE.
I'LL HELP YOU GATHER MATS.
MY POINT IS...
LET'S GET THROUGH THIS TOGETHER...
...SO YOU CAN MAKE ALL THE THINGS YOU WANT TO MAKE!
IT'S A PROMISE.

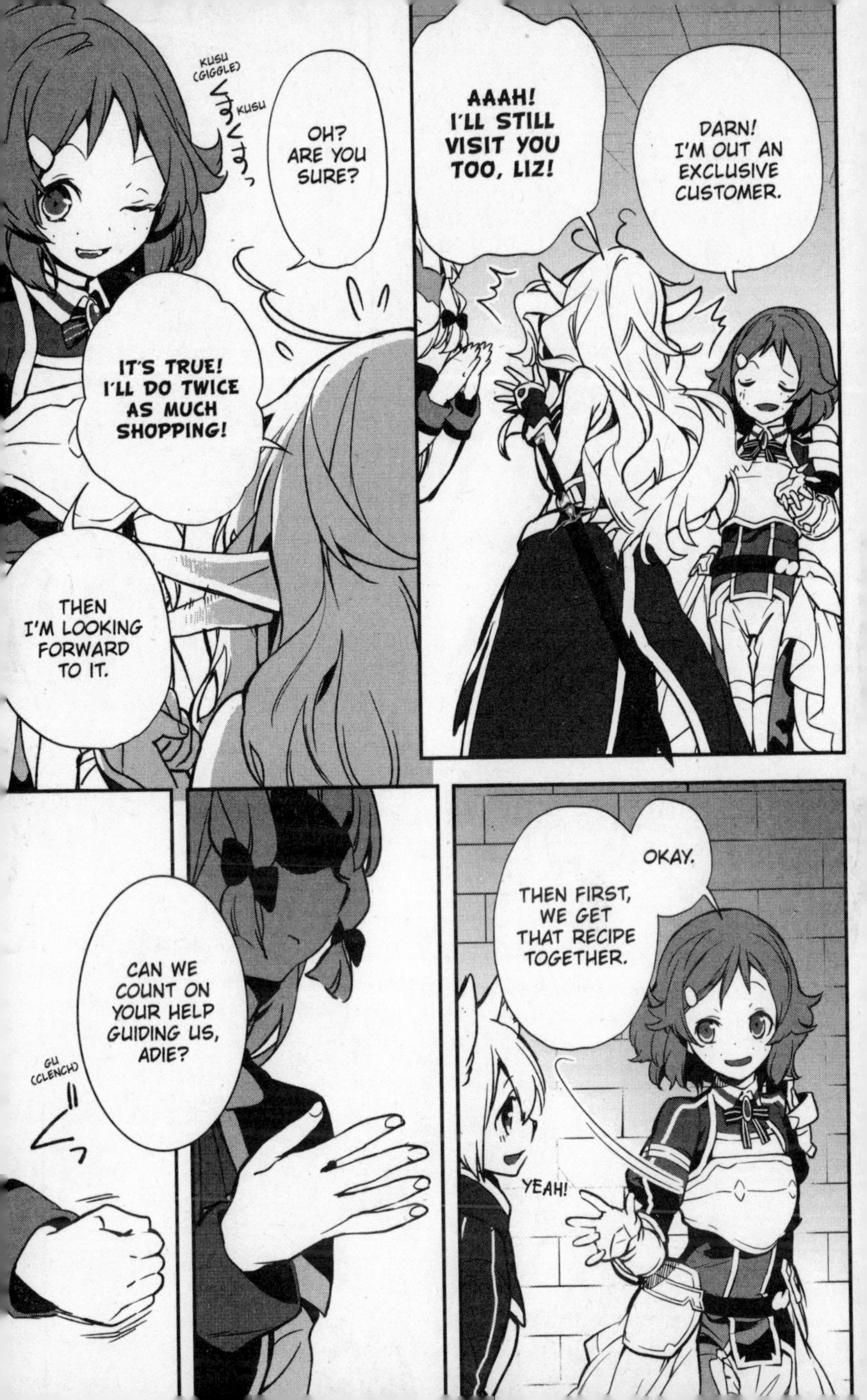
DARN! I'M OUT AN EXCLUSIVE CUSTOMER.
AAAH! I'LL STILL VISIT YOU TOO, LIZ!
KUSU (GIGGLE) KUSU
OH? ARE YOU SURE?
IT'S TRUE! I'LL DO TWICE AS MUCH SHOPPING!
THEN I'M LOOKING FORWARD TO IT.
OKAY.
THEN FIRST, WE GET THAT RECIPE TOGETHER.
YEAH!
CAN WE COUNT ON YOUR HELP GUIDING US, ADIE?
GU (CLENCH)

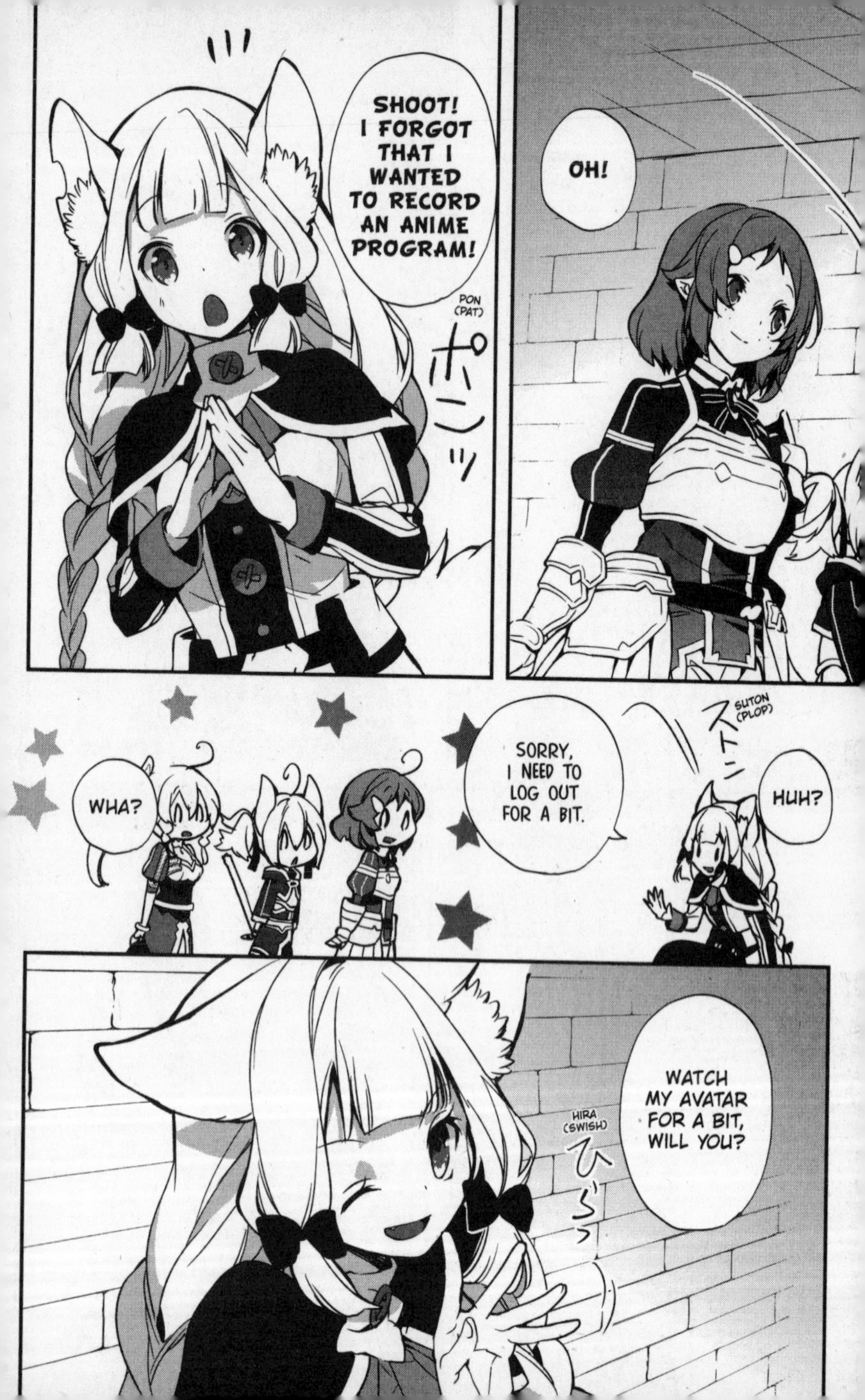
OH!
SHOOT! I FORGOT THAT I WANTED TO RECORD AN ANIME PROGRAM!
PON (PAT)
SUTON (PLOP)
HUH?
SORRY, I NEED TO LOG OUT FOR A BIT.
WHA?
WATCH MY AVATAR FOR A BIT, WILL YOU?
HIRA (SWISH)

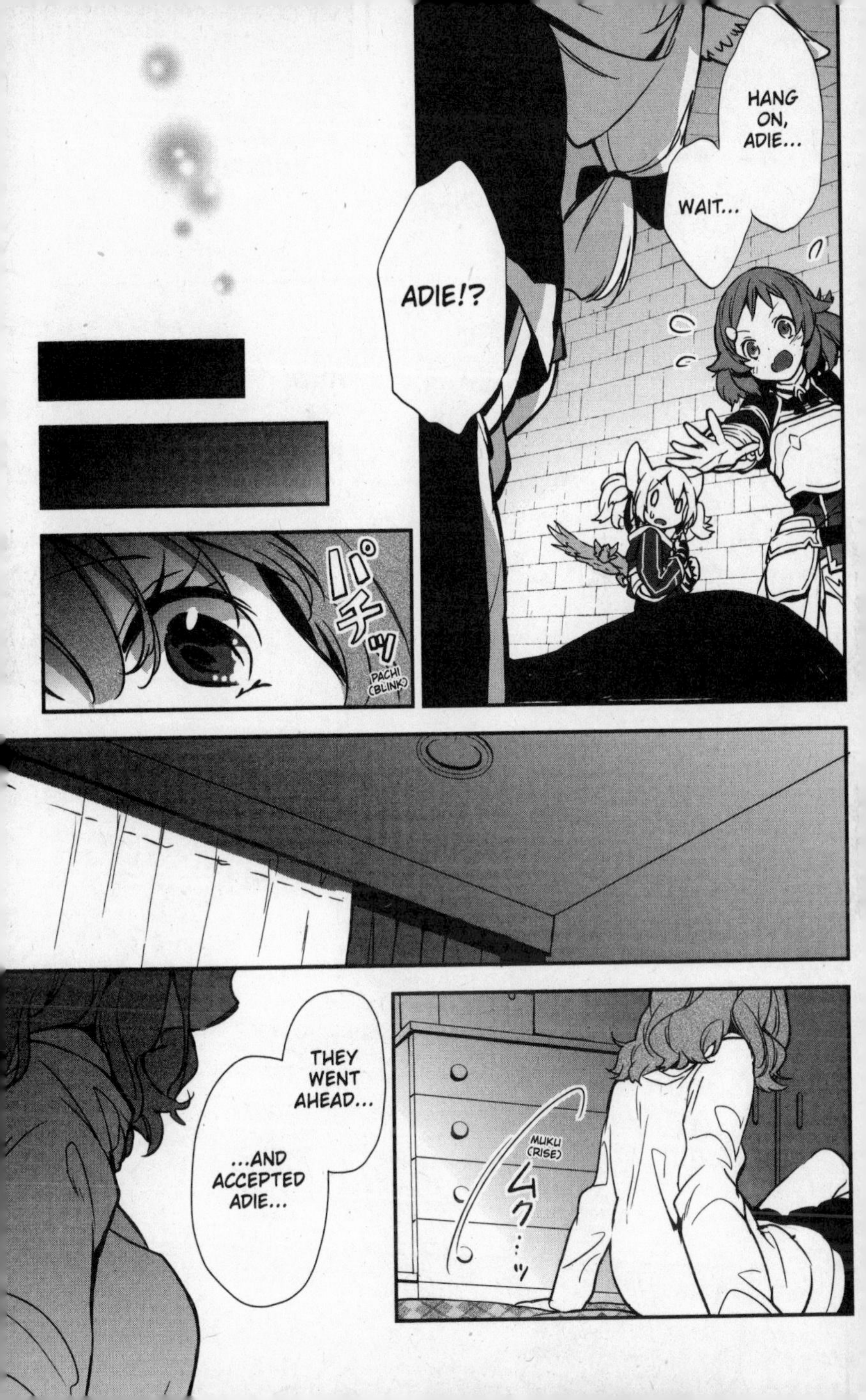
HANG ON, ADIE...
WAIT...
ADIE!?
パチッ
PACHI (BLINK)
ムク…ッ
MUKU (RISE)
THEY WENT AHEAD...
...AND ACCEPTED ADIE...

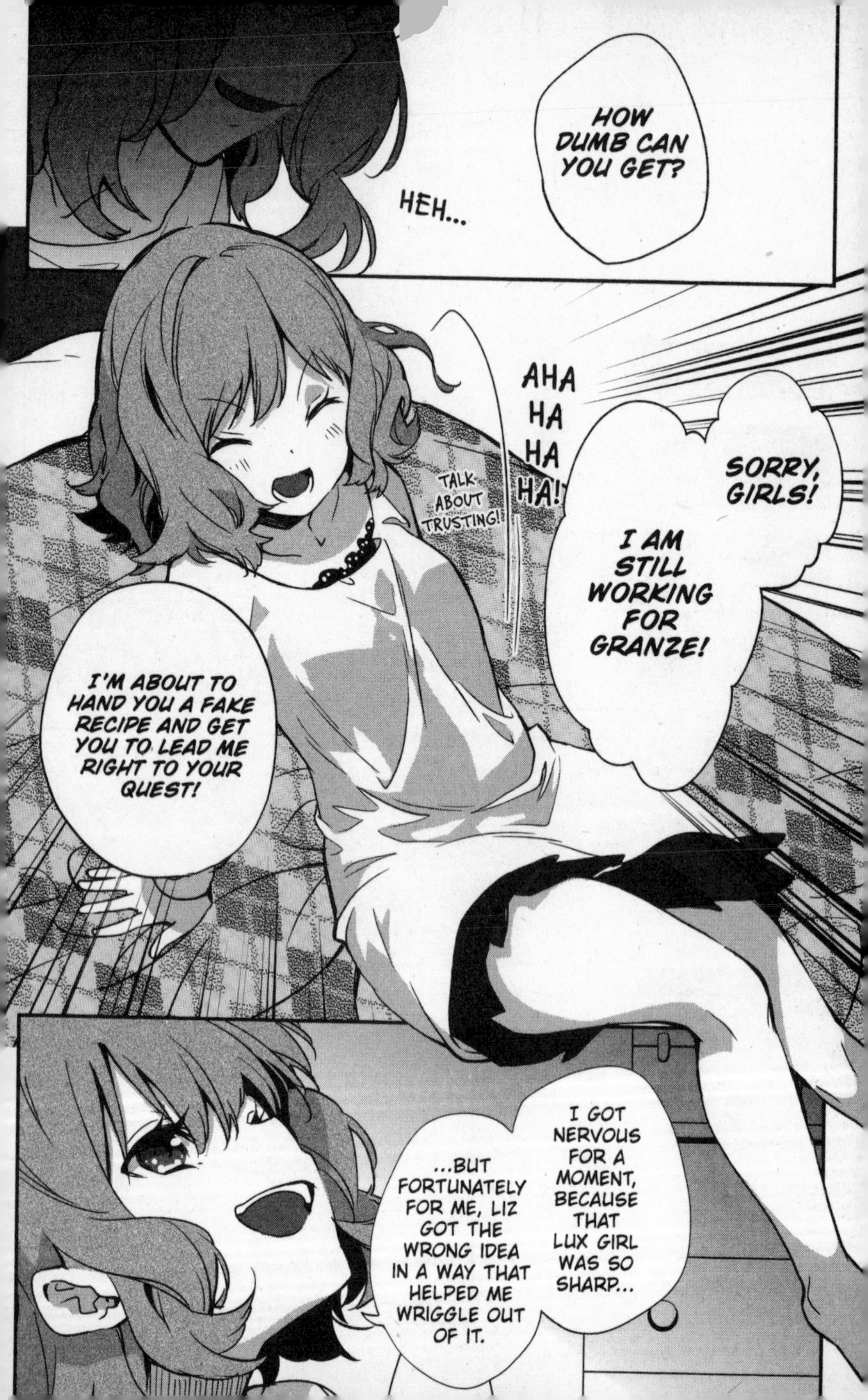
HOW DUMB CAN YOU GET?
HEH...
SORRY, GIRLS!
I AM STILL WORKING FOR GRANZE!
AHA HA HA HA!
TALK ABOUT TRUSTING!
I'M ABOUT TO HAND YOU A FAKE RECIPE AND GET YOU TO LEAD ME RIGHT TO YOUR QUEST!
I GOT NERVOUS FOR A MOMENT, BECAUSE THAT LUX GIRL WAS SO SHARP...
...BUT FORTUNATELY FOR ME, LIZ GOT THE WRONG IDEA IN A WAY THAT HELPED ME WRIGGLE OUT OF IT.

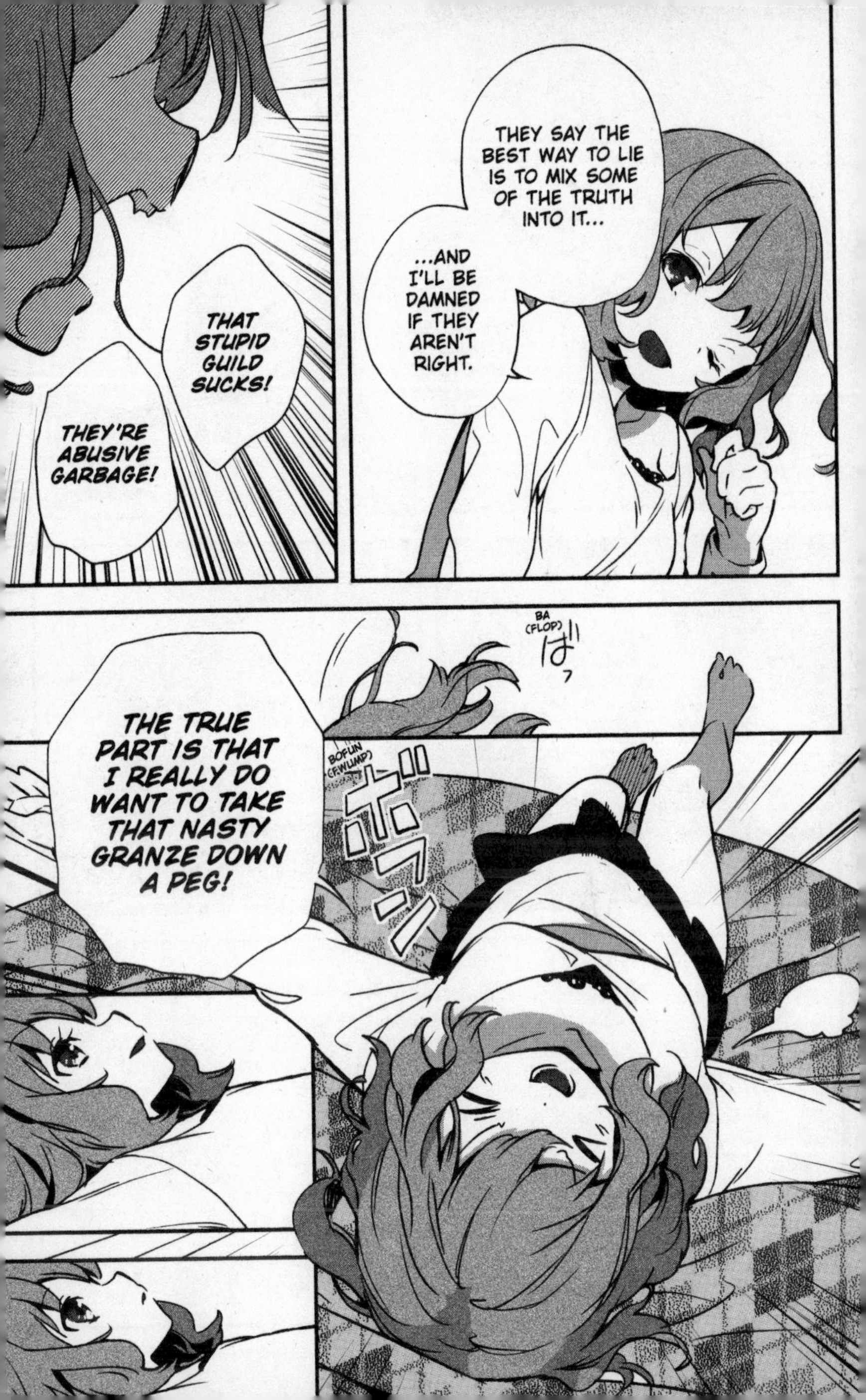
THEY SAY THE BEST WAY TO LIE IS TO MIX SOME OF THE TRUTH INTO IT...
...AND I'LL BE DAMNED IF THEY AREN'T RIGHT.
THAT STUPID GUILD SUCKS!
THEY'RE ABUSIVE GARBAGE!
BA (FLOP)
ばっ
BOFUN (F-WUMP)
ボフン
THE TRUE PART IS THAT I REALLY DO WANT TO TAKE THAT NASTY GRANZE DOWN A PEG!

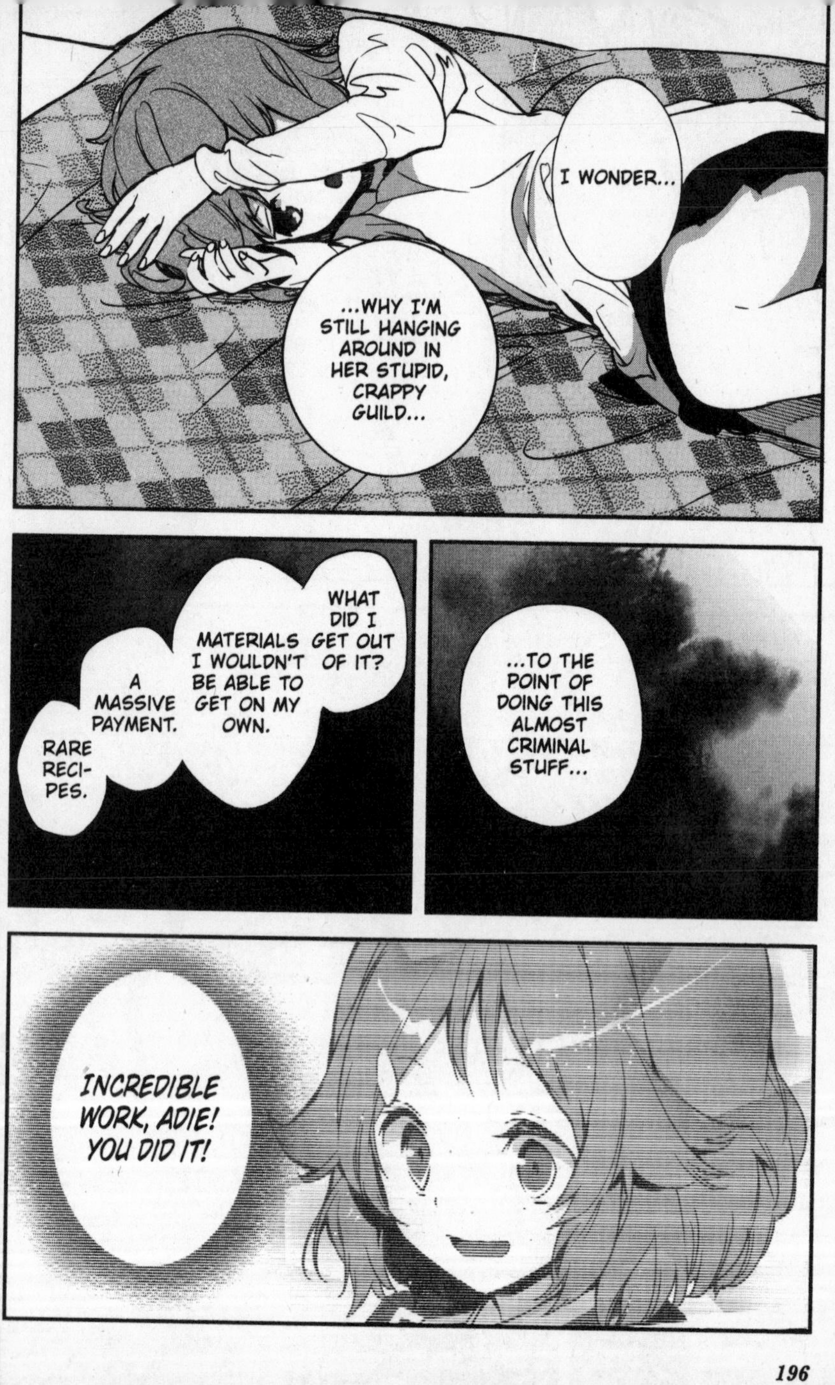
I WONDER...
...WHY I'M STILL HANGING AROUND IN HER STUPID, CRAPPY GUILD...
...TO THE POINT OF DOING THIS ALMOST CRIMINAL STUFF...
WHAT DID I GET OUT OF IT?
MATERIALS I WOULDN'T BE ABLE TO GET ON MY OWN.
A MASSIVE PAYMENT.
RARE RECI-PES.
INCREDIBLE WORK, ADIE! YOU DID IT!

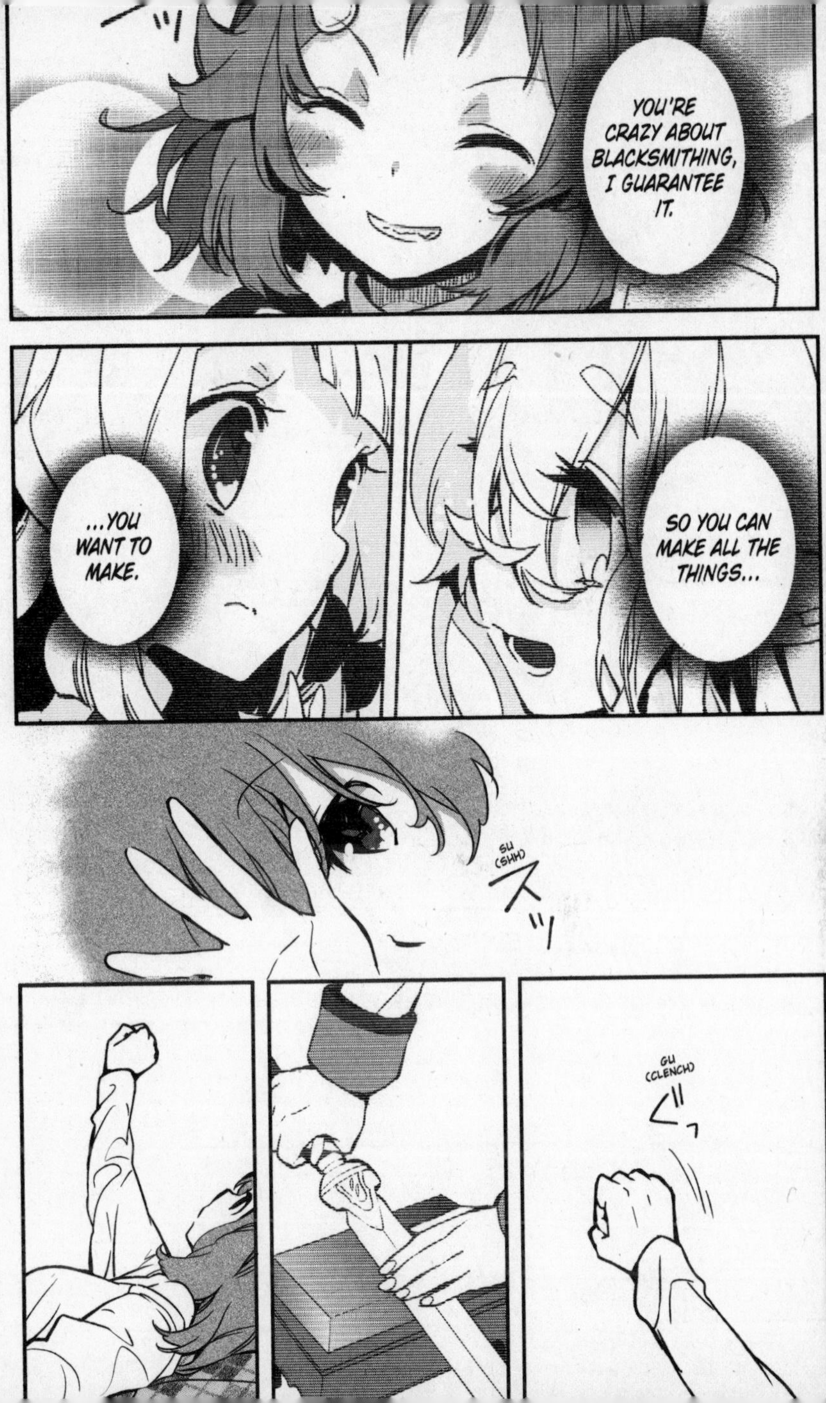
YOU'RE CRAZY ABOUT BLACKSMITHING, I GUARANTEE IT.
SO YOU CAN MAKE ALL THE THINGS...
...YOU WANT TO MAKE.
SU (SHHH)
GU (CLENCH)

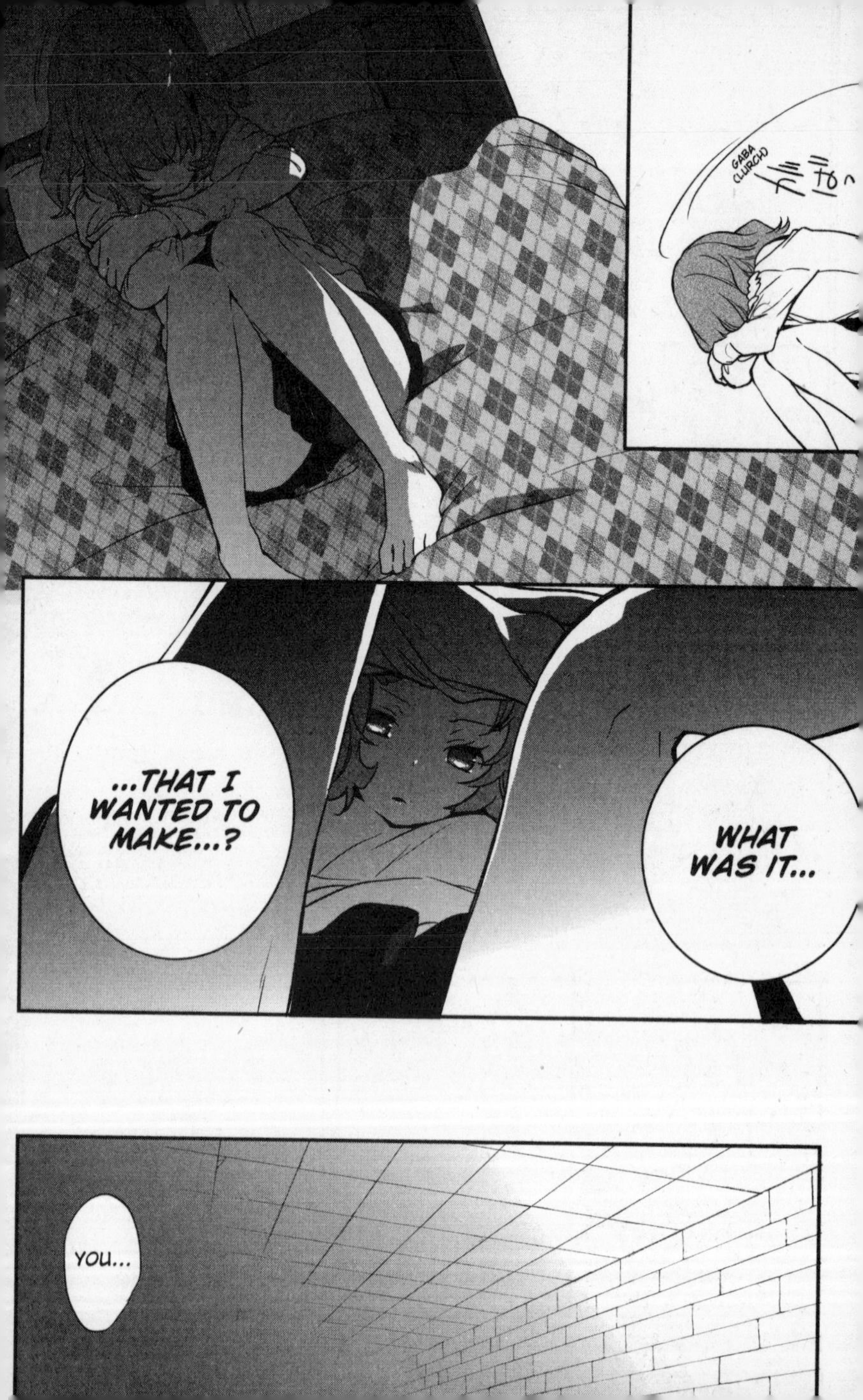
GABA (CLURCH)
WHAT WAS IT...
...THAT I WANTED TO MAKE...?
YOU...

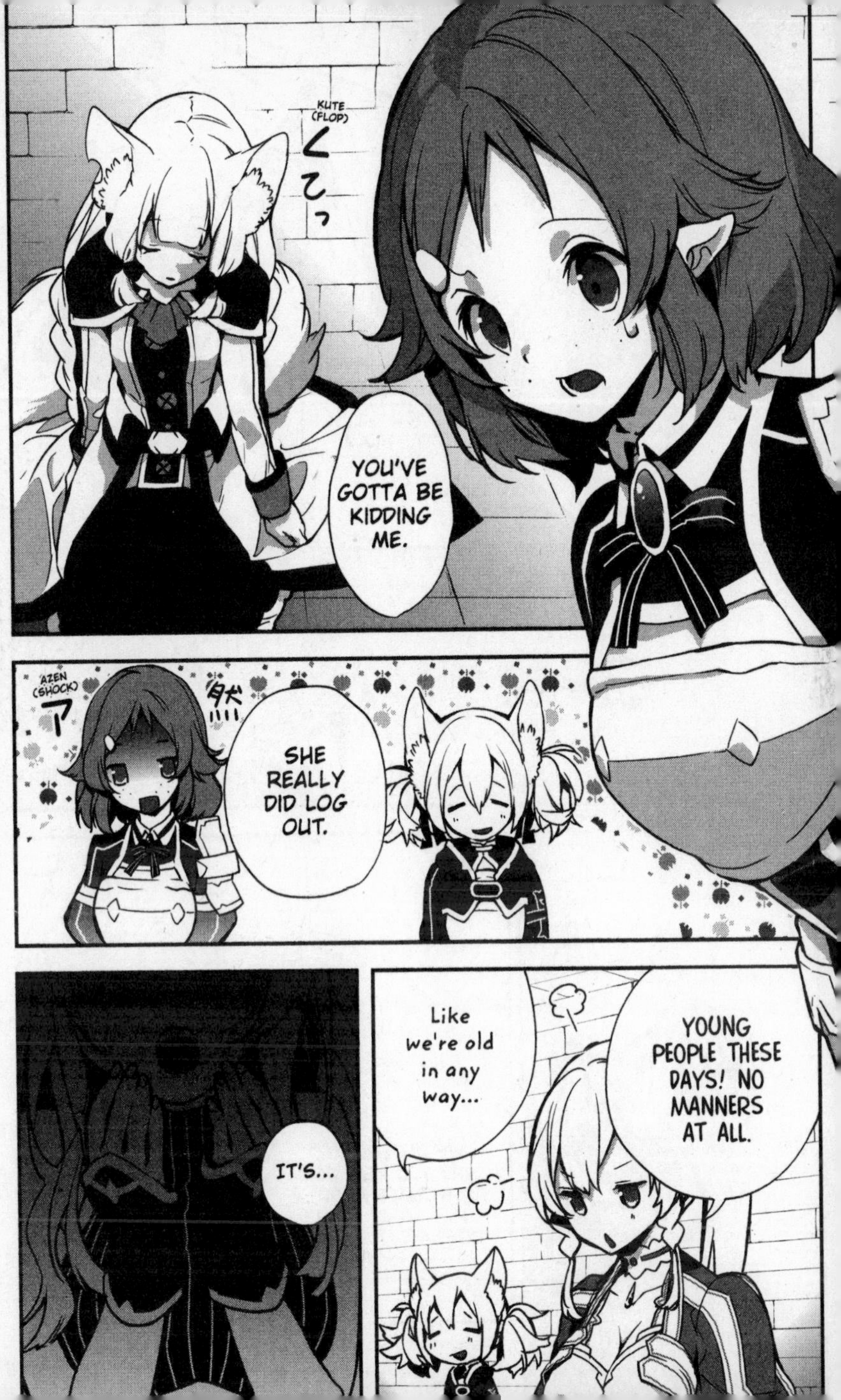
KUTE (FLOP)
くてっ
YOU'VE GOTTA BE KIDDING ME.
SHE REALLY DID LOG OUT.
AZEN (SHOCK)
ア
YOUNG PEOPLE THESE DAYS! NO MANNERS AT ALL.
Like we're old in any way...
IT'S...

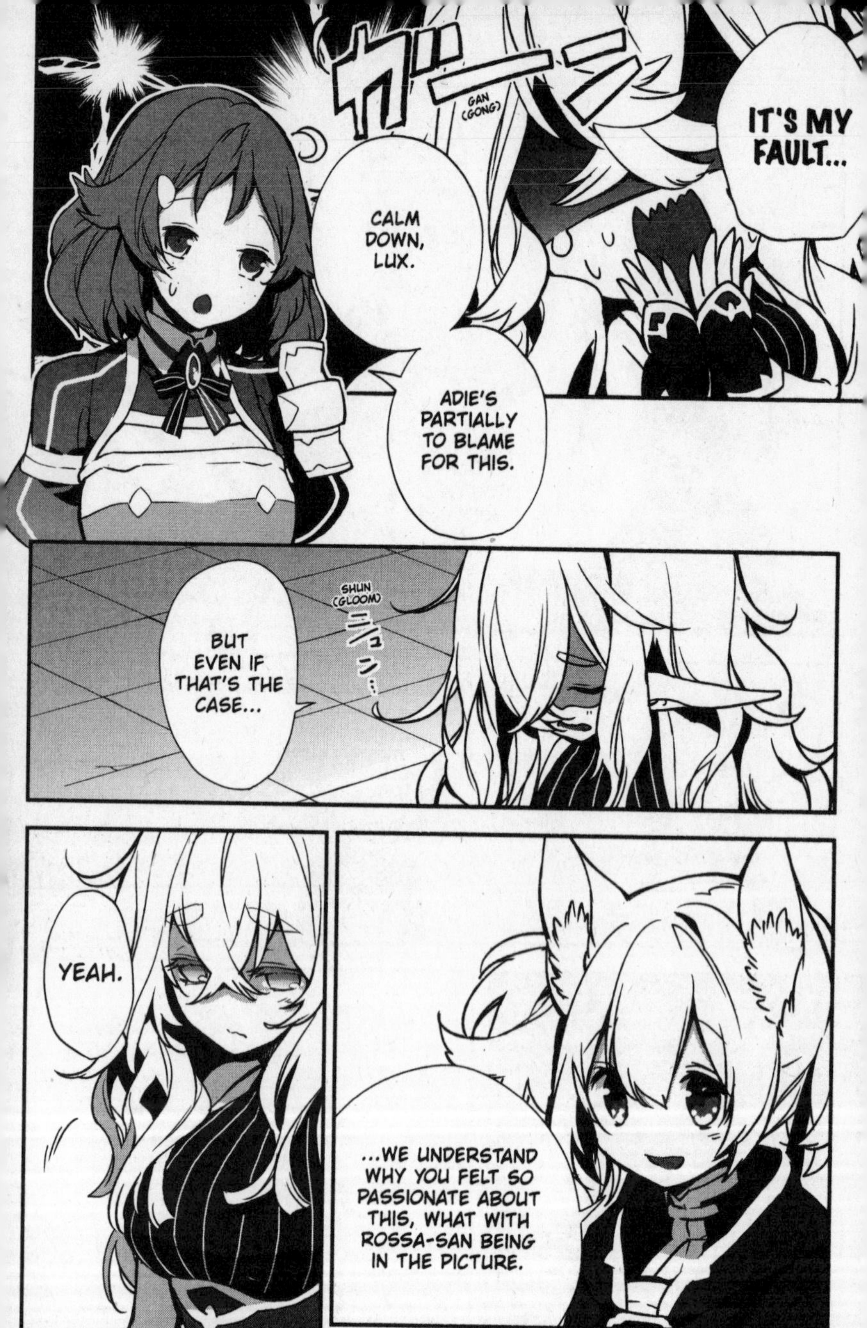
GAN (GONG)
IT'S MY FAULT...
CALM DOWN, LUX.
ADIE'S PARTIALLY TO BLAME FOR THIS.
SHUN (GLOOM)
BUT EVEN IF THAT'S THE CASE...
...WE UNDERSTAND WHY YOU FELT SO PASSIONATE ABOUT THIS, WHAT WITH ROSSA-SAN BEING IN THE PICTURE.
YEAH.

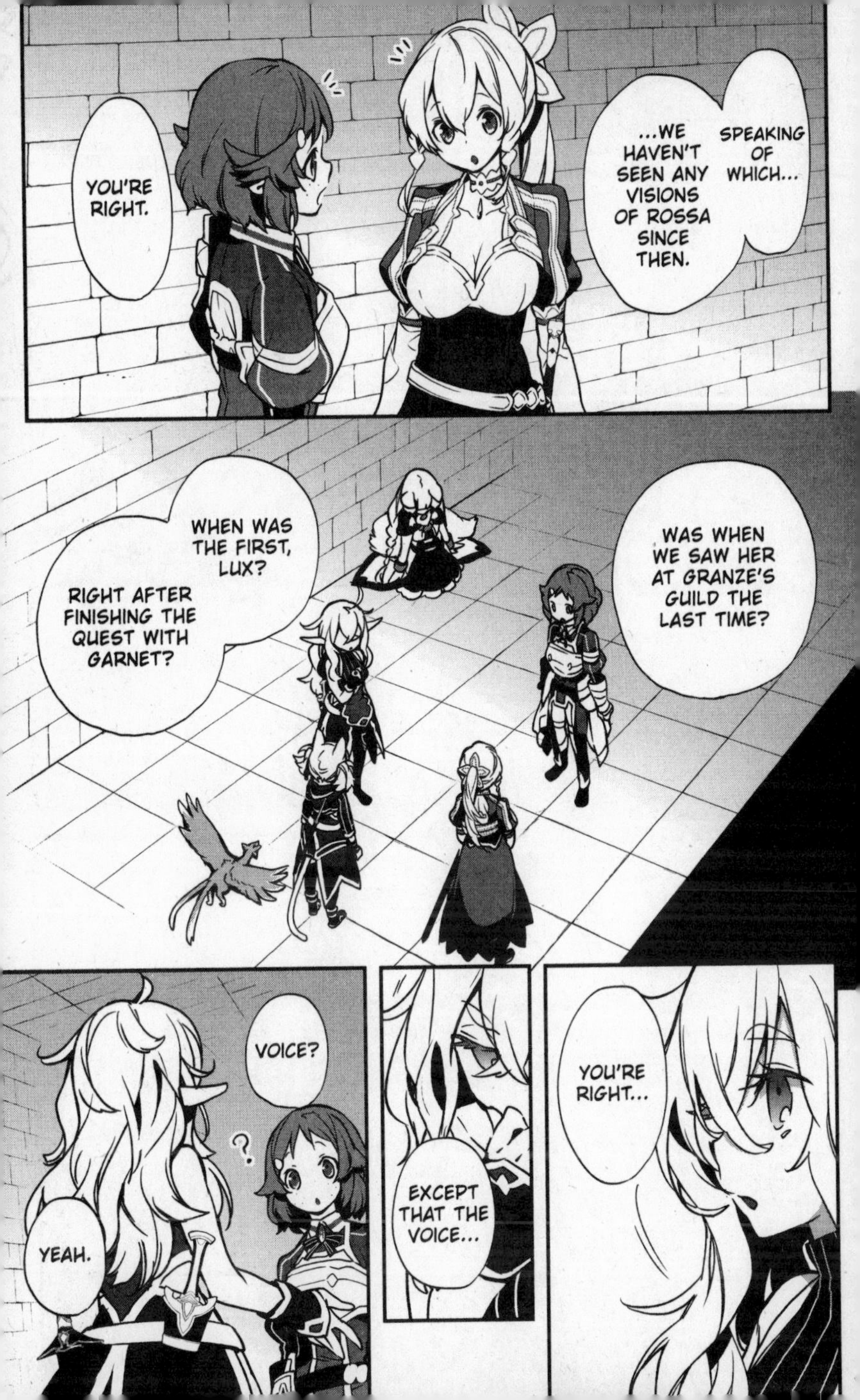
SPEAKING OF WHICH...
...WE HAVEN'T SEEN ANY VISIONS OF ROSSA SINCE THEN.
YOU'RE RIGHT.
WAS WHEN WE SAW HER AT GRANZE'S GUILD THE LAST TIME?
WHEN WAS THE FIRST, LUX?
RIGHT AFTER FINISHING THE QUEST WITH GARNET?
YOU'RE RIGHT...
EXCEPT THAT THE VOICE...
VOICE?
YEAH.

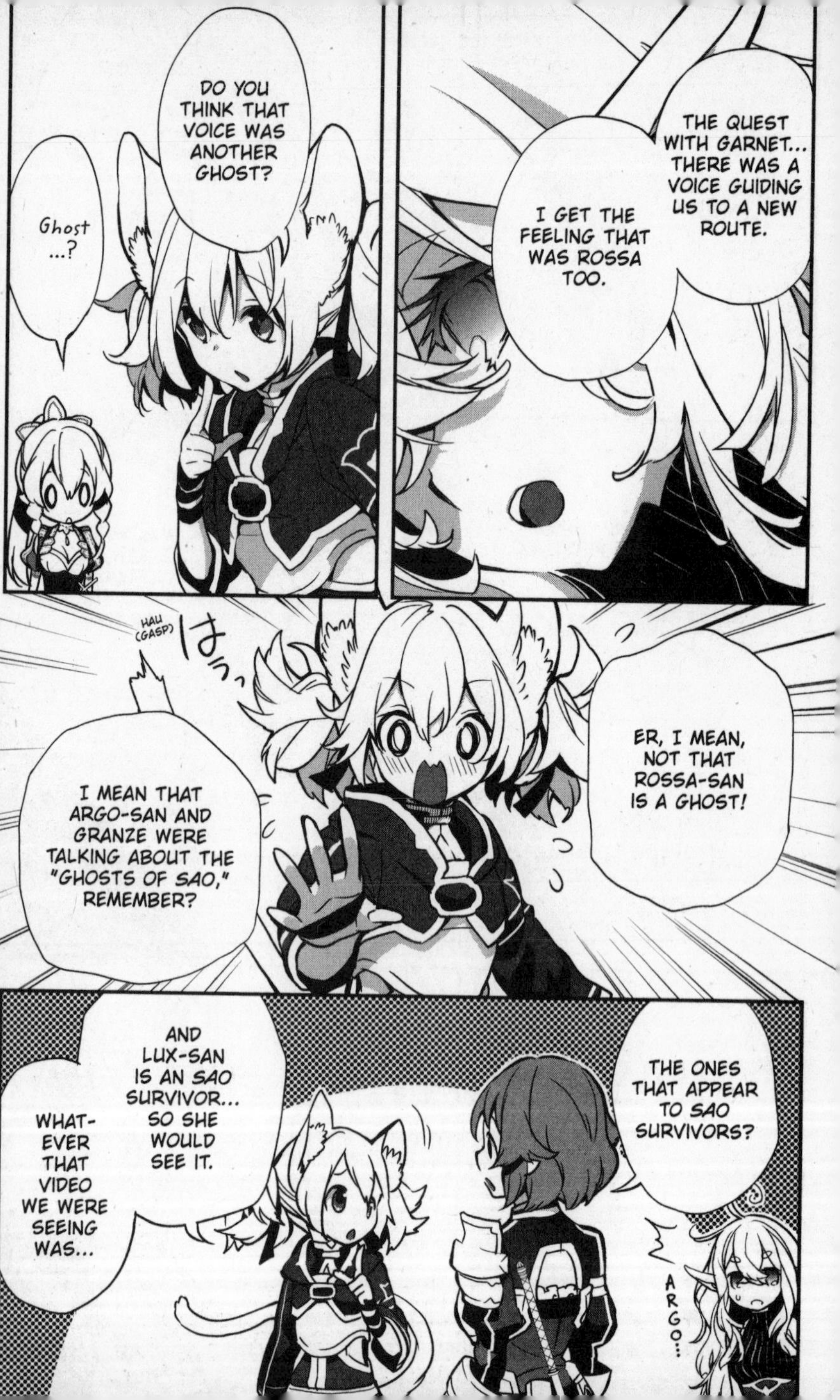
THE QUEST WITH GARNET... THERE WAS A VOICE GUIDING US TO A NEW ROUTE.
I GET THE FEELING THAT WAS ROSSA TOO.
DO YOU THINK THAT VOICE WAS ANOTHER GHOST?
Ghost ...?
HAU (GASP)
ER, I MEAN, NOT THAT ROSSA-SAN IS A GHOST!
I MEAN THAT ARGO-SAN AND GRANZE WERE TALKING ABOUT THE "GHOSTS OF SAO," REMEMBER?
THE ONES THAT APPEAR TO SAO SURVIVORS?
ARGO...
AND LUX-SAN IS AN SAO SURVIVOR... SO SHE WOULD SEE IT.
WHAT-EVER THAT VIDEO WE WERE SEEING WAS...

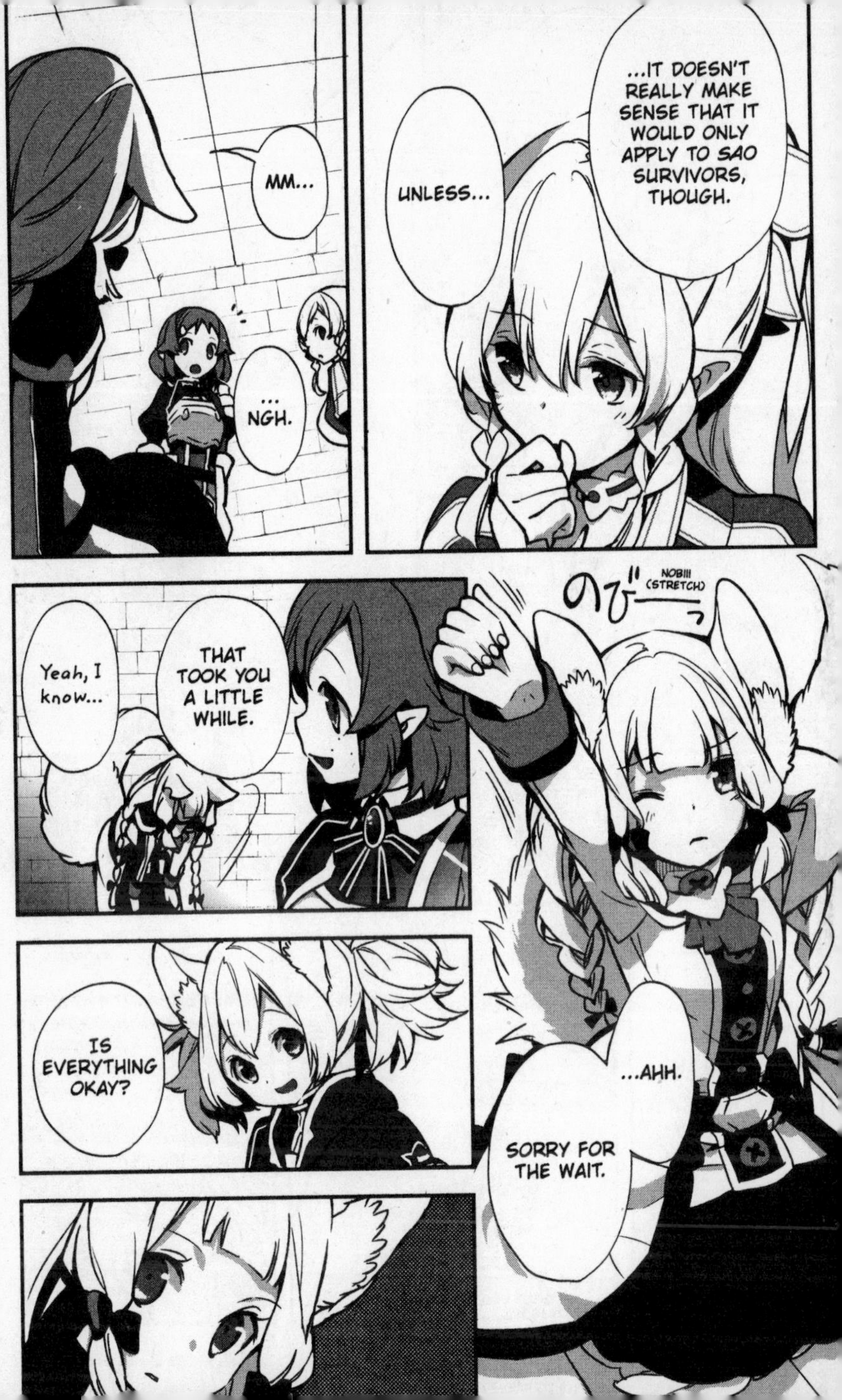
...IT DOESN'T REALLY MAKE SENSE THAT IT WOULD ONLY APPLY TO SAO SURVIVORS, THOUGH.
UNLESS...
MM...
... NGH.
のび
NOBIII (STRETCH)
...AHH.
SORRY FOR THE WAIT.
THAT TOOK YOU A LITTLE WHILE.
Yeah, I know...
IS EVERYTHING OKAY?

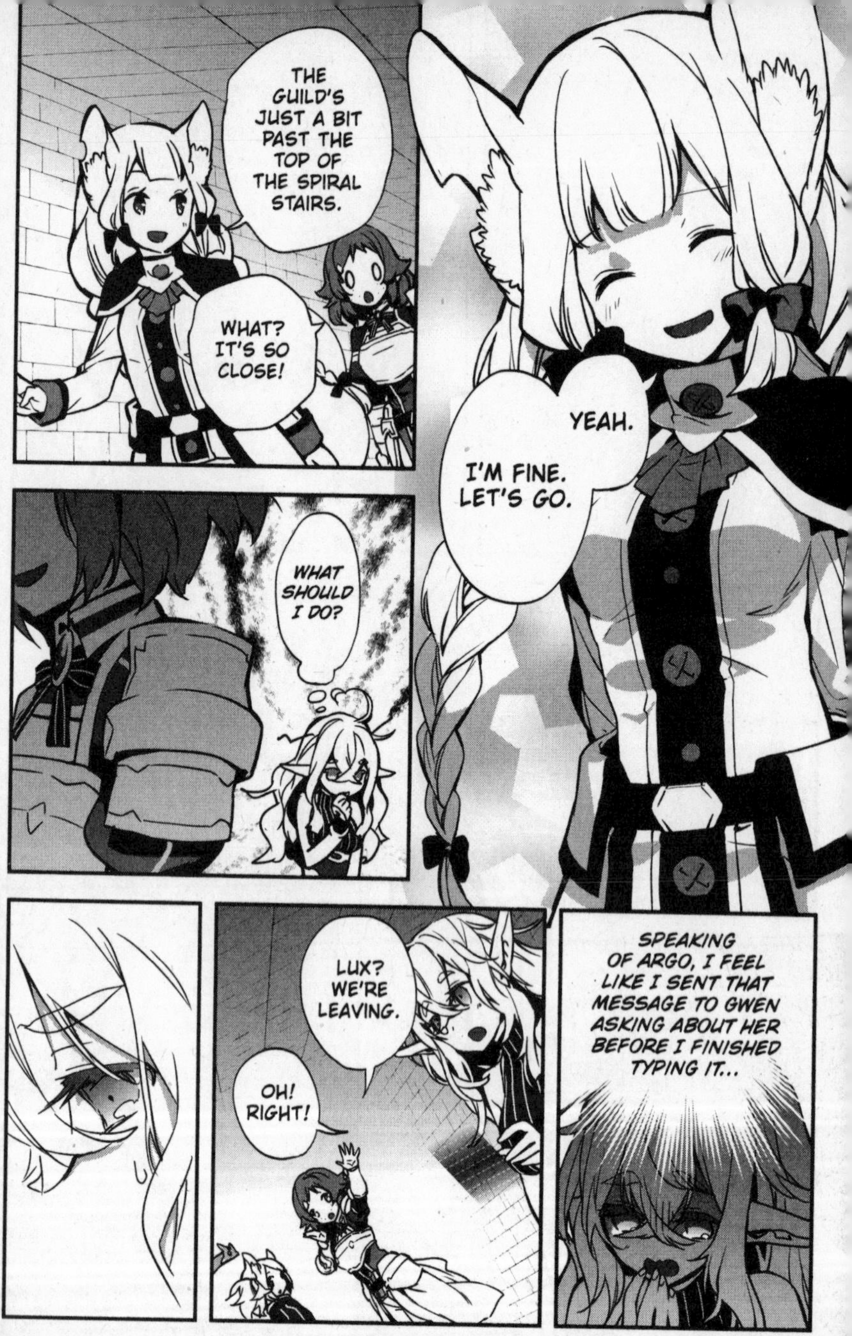
YEAH.
I'M FINE. LET'S GO.
THE GUILD'S JUST A BIT PAST THE TOP OF THE SPIRAL STAIRS.
WHAT? IT'S SO CLOSE!
WHAT SHOULD I DO?
SPEAKING OF ARGO, I FEEL LIKE I SENT THAT MESSAGE TO GWEN ASKING ABOUT HER BEFORE I FINISHED TYPING IT...
LUX? WE'RE LEAVING.
OH! RIGHT!

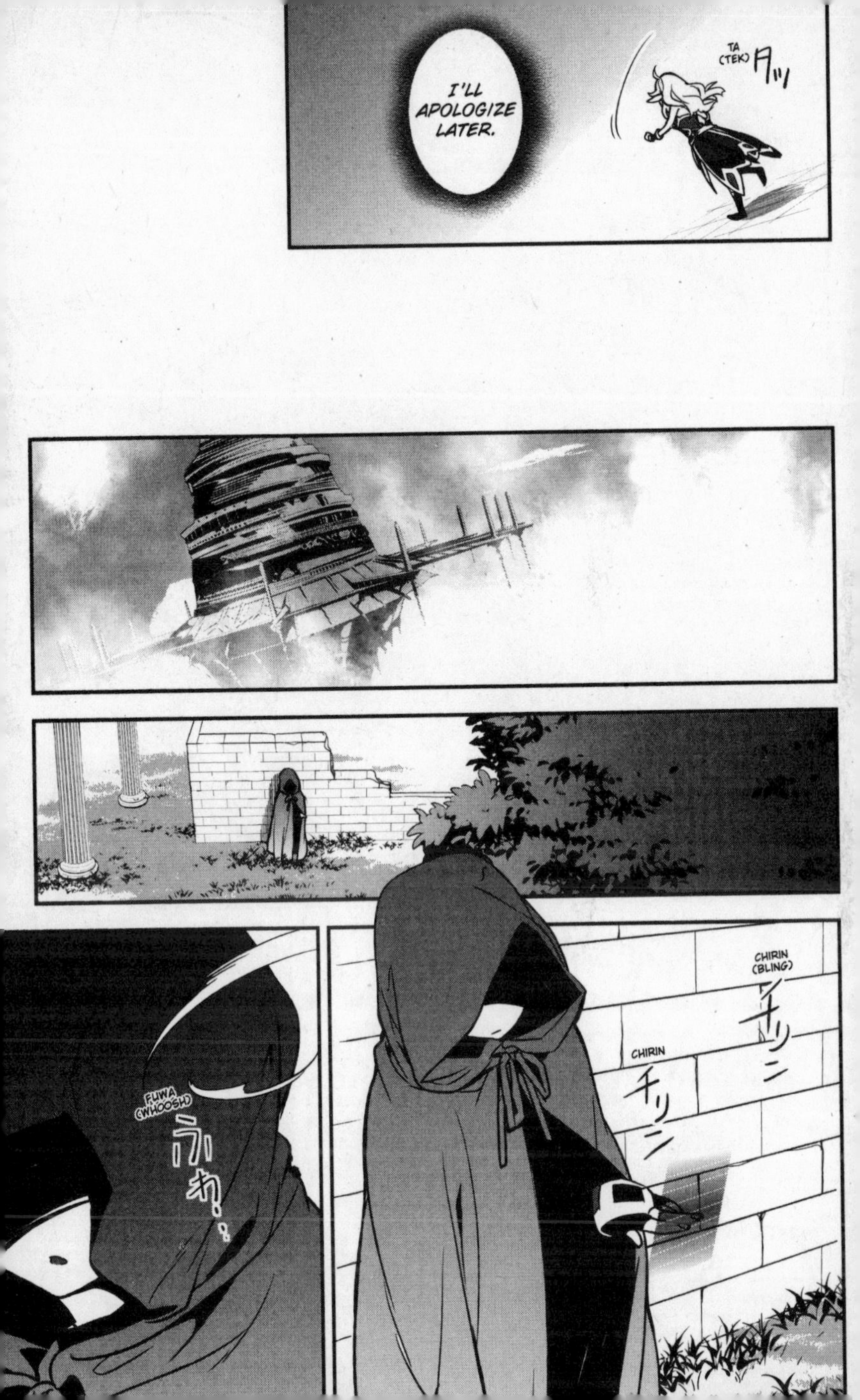
TA (TEK)
I'LL APOLOGIZE LATER.
CHIRIN (BLING)
CHIRIN
FUWA (WHOOSH)

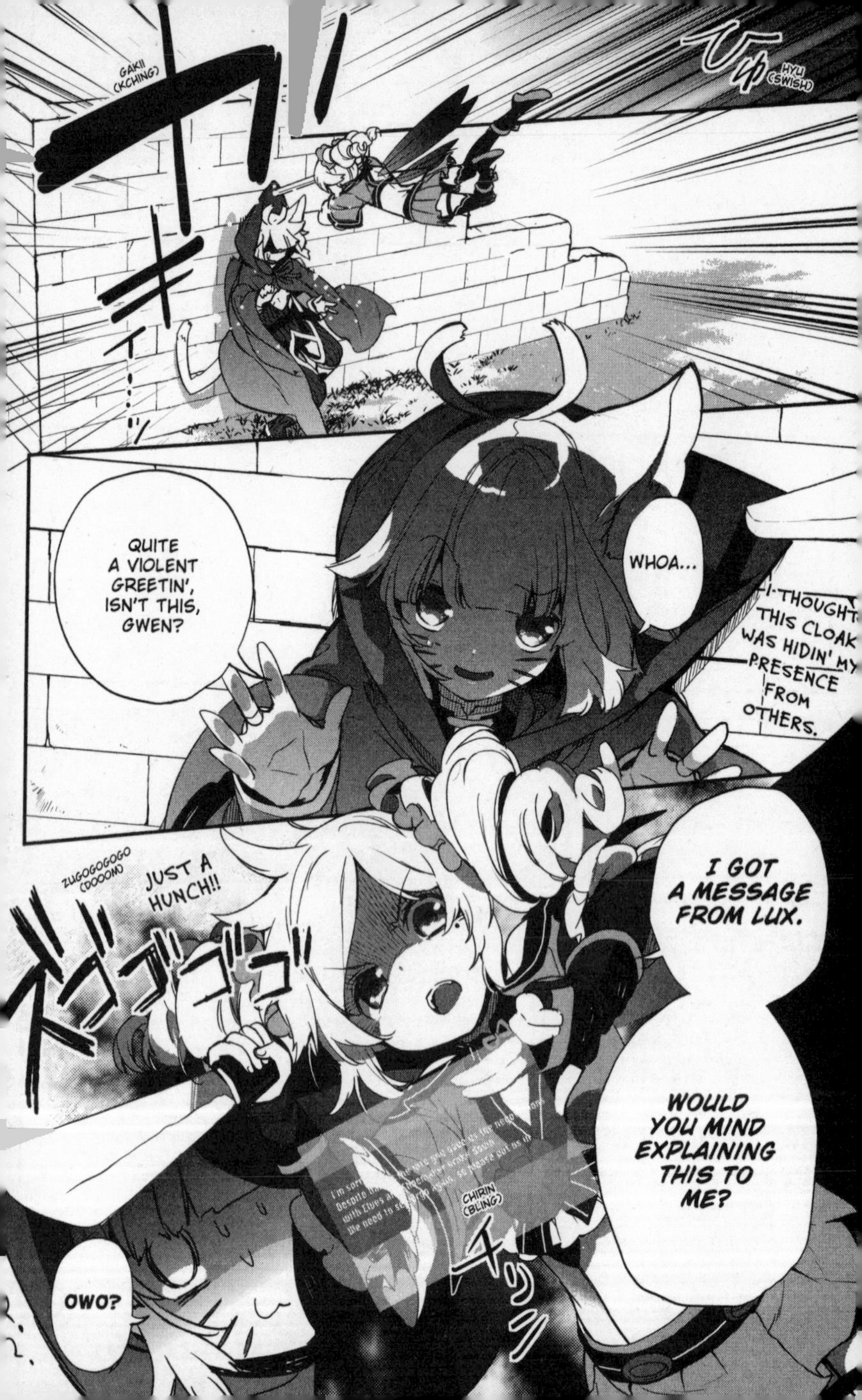
HYU (SWISH)
GAKII (KCHING)
WHOA...
I THOUGHT THIS CLOAK WAS HIDIN' MY PRESENCE FROM OTHERS.
QUITE A VIOLENT GREETIN', ISN'T THIS, GWEN?
I GOT A MESSAGE FROM LUX.
WOULD YOU MIND EXPLAINING THIS TO ME?
CHIRIN (BLING)
JUST A HUNCH!!
ZUGOGOGOGO (DOOOM)
OWO?

IT'S SO
SPARKLY.

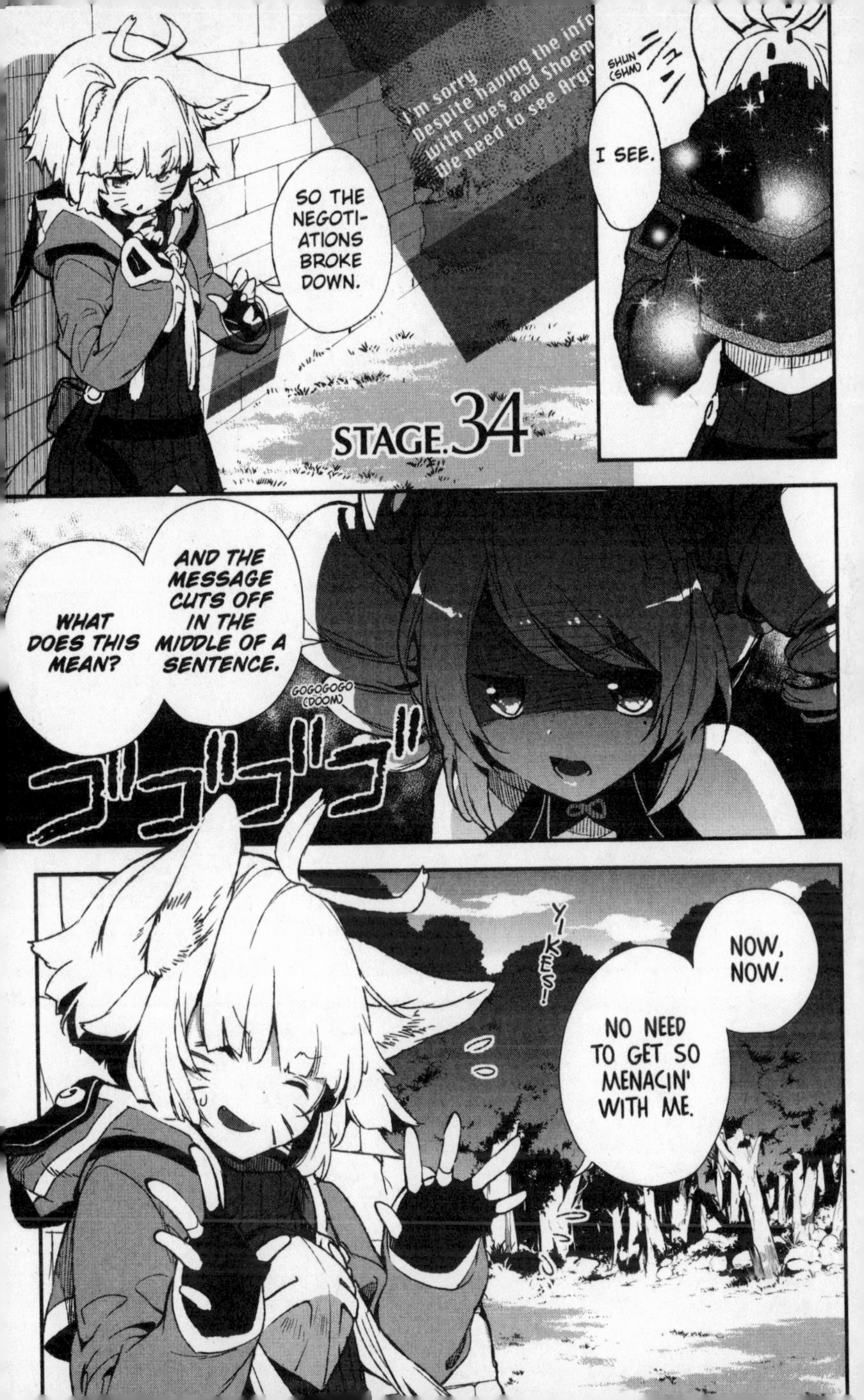
SHUN (SHM)
I SEE.
I'm sorry
Despite having the info
with Elves and Shoem
We need to see Argo
SO THE NEGOTIATIONS BROKE DOWN.
STAGE.34
AND THE MESSAGE CUTS OFF IN THE MIDDLE OF A SENTENCE.
WHAT DOES THIS MEAN?
GOGOGOGO (DOOM)
NOW, NOW.
NO NEED TO GET SO MENACIN' WITH ME.
YIKES!

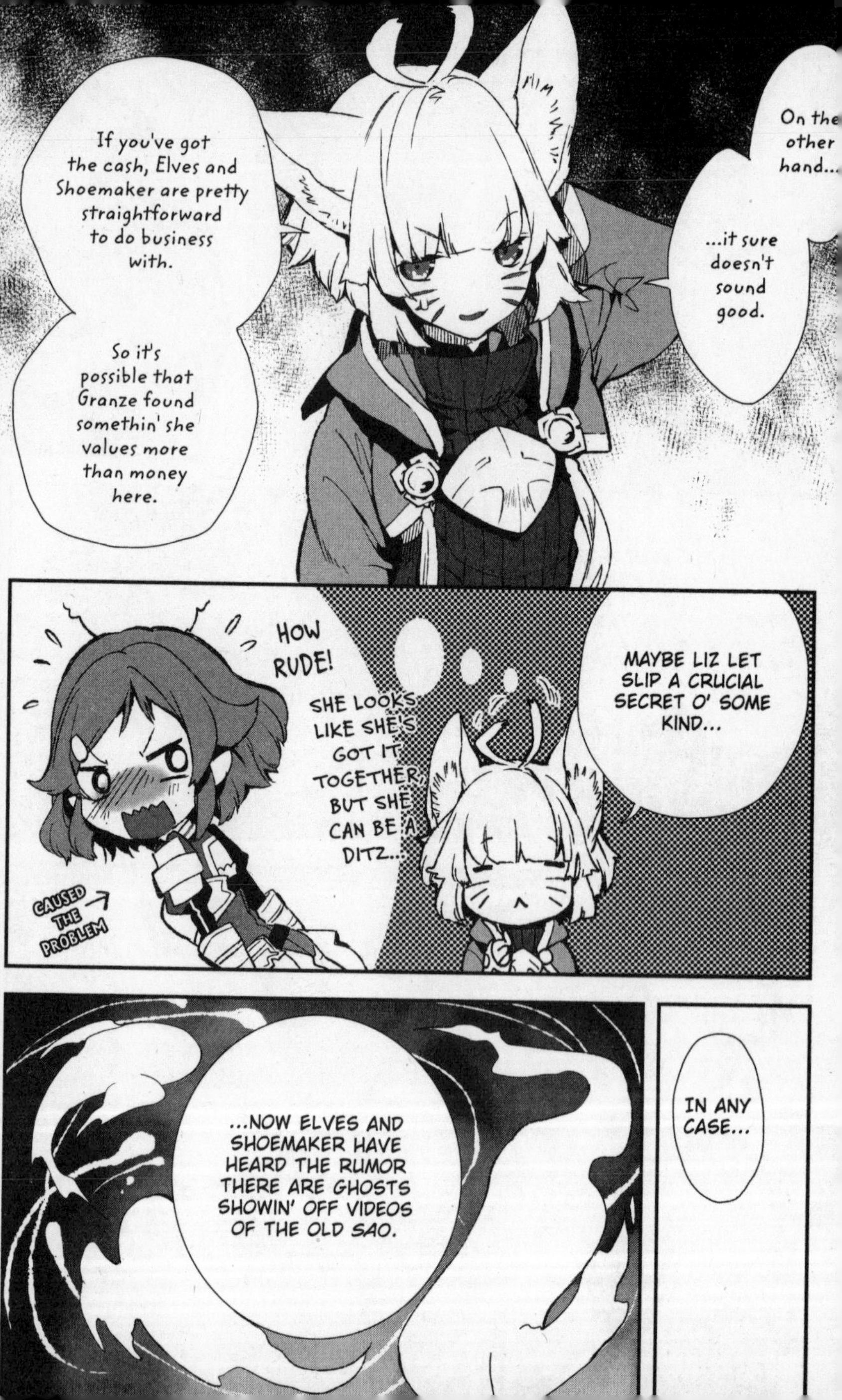
If you've got the cash, Elves and Shoemaker are pretty straightforward to do business with.
So it's possible that Granze found somethin' she values more than money here.
On the other hand...
...it sure doesn't sound good.
MAYBE LIZ LET SLIP A CRUCIAL SECRET O' SOME KIND...
SHE LOOKS LIKE SHE'S GOT IT TOGETHER, BUT SHE CAN BE A DITZ...
HOW RUDE!
CAUSED THE PROBLEM
IN ANY CASE...
...NOW ELVES AND SHOEMAKER HAVE HEARD THE RUMOR THERE ARE GHOSTS SHOWIN' OFF VIDEOS OF THE OLD SAO.

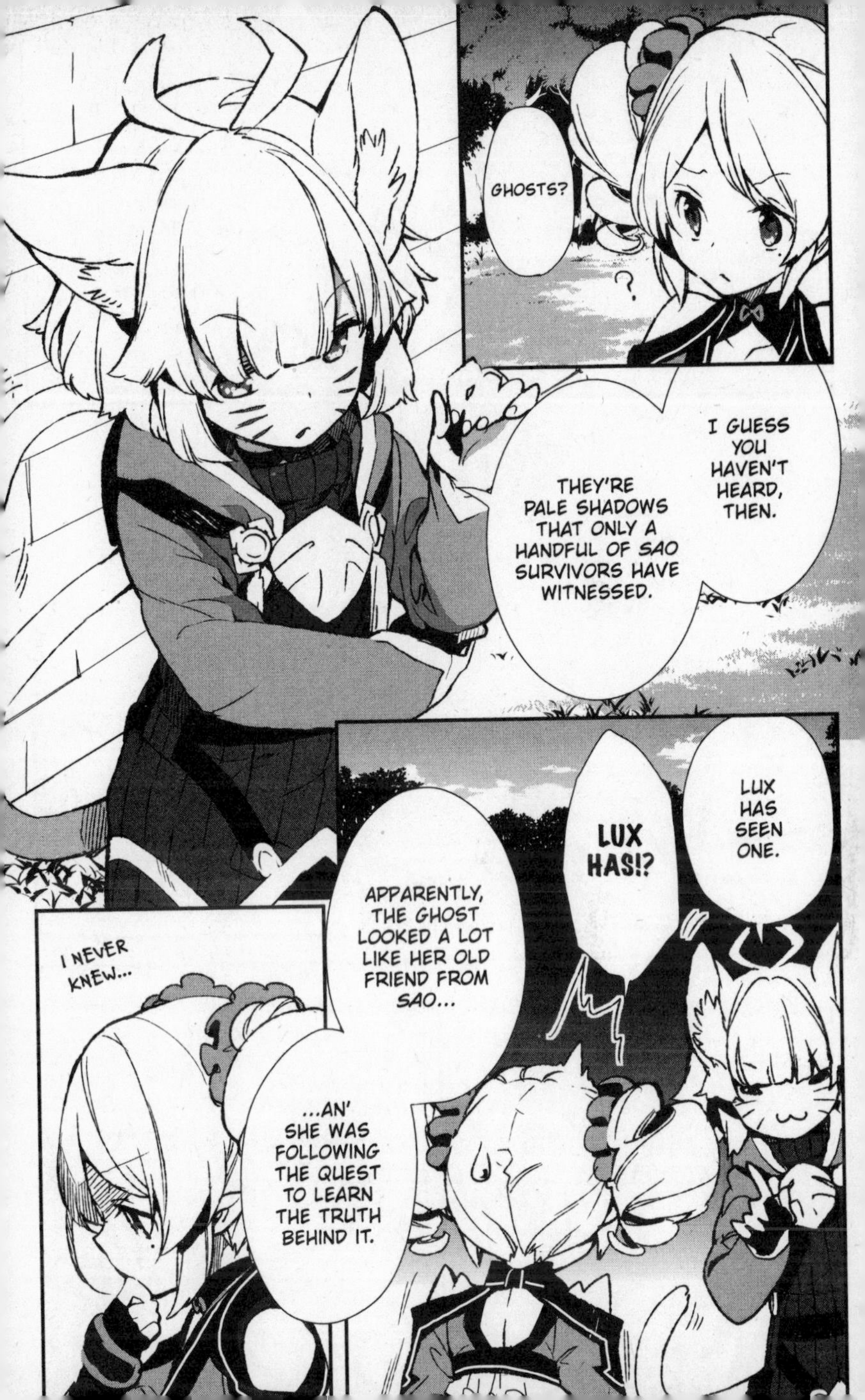
GHOSTS?
I GUESS YOU HAVEN'T HEARD, THEN.
THEY'RE PALE SHADOWS THAT ONLY A HANDFUL OF SAO SURVIVORS HAVE WITNESSED.
LUX HAS SEEN ONE.
LUX HAS!?
APPARENTLY, THE GHOST LOOKED A LOT LIKE HER OLD FRIEND FROM SAO...
...AN' SHE WAS FOLLOWING THE QUEST TO LEARN THE TRUTH BEHIND IT.
I NEVER KNEW...

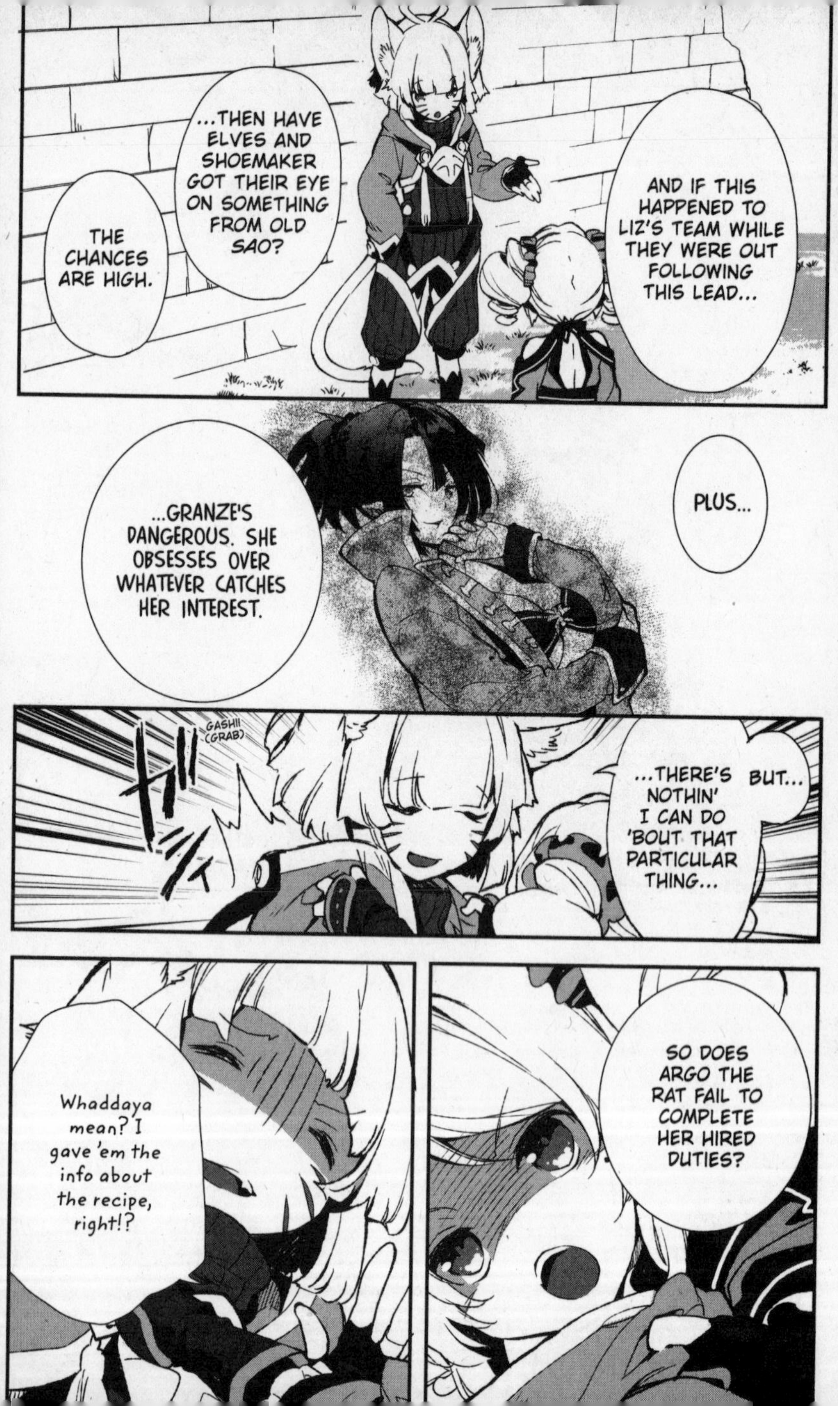
AND IF THIS HAPPENED TO LIZ'S TEAM WHILE THEY WERE OUT FOLLOWING THIS LEAD...
...THEN HAVE ELVES AND SHOEMAKER GOT THEIR EYE ON SOMETHING FROM OLD SAO?
THE CHANCES ARE HIGH.
PLUS...
...GRANZE'S DANGEROUS. SHE OBSESSES OVER WHATEVER CATCHES HER INTEREST.
BUT...
...THERE'S NOTHIN' I CAN DO 'BOUT THAT PARTICULAR THING...
GASHI! (GRAB)
SO DOES ARGO THE RAT FAIL TO COMPLETE HER HIRED DUTIES?
Whaddaya mean? I gave 'em the info about the recipe, right!?

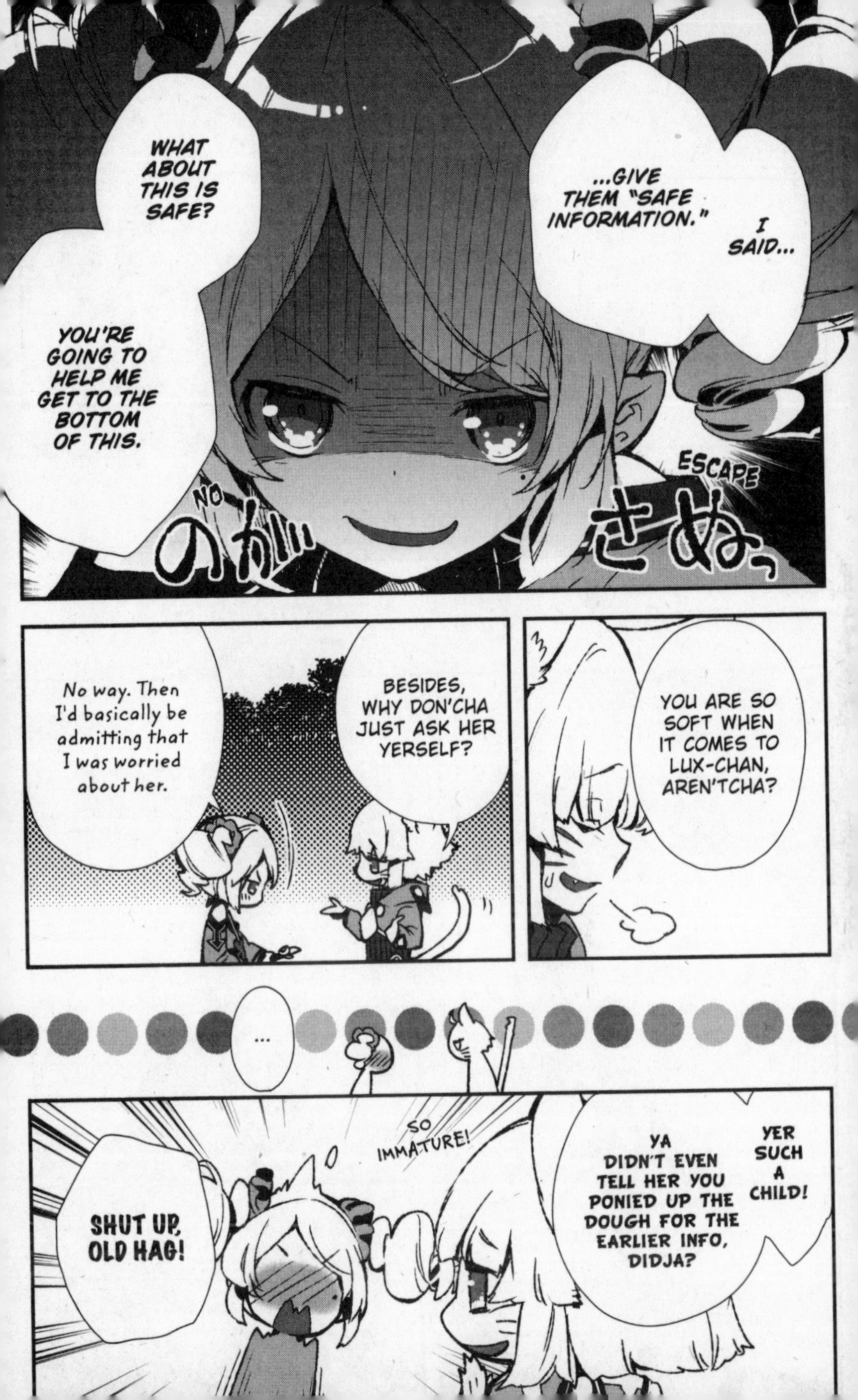
I SAID...
...GIVE THEM "SAFE INFORMATION."
WHAT ABOUT THIS IS SAFE?
YOU'RE GOING TO HELP ME GET TO THE BOTTOM OF THIS.
ESCAPE
さぬっ
NO
のわ
YOU ARE SO SOFT WHEN IT COMES TO LUX-CHAN, AREN'TCHA?
BESIDES, WHY DON'CHA JUST ASK HER YERSELF?
No way. Then I'd basically be admitting that I was worried about her.
...
YER SUCH A CHILD!
YA DIDN'T EVEN TELL HER YOU PONIED UP THE DOUGH FOR THE EARLIER INFO, DIDJA?
SO IMMATURE!
SHUT UP, OLD HAG!

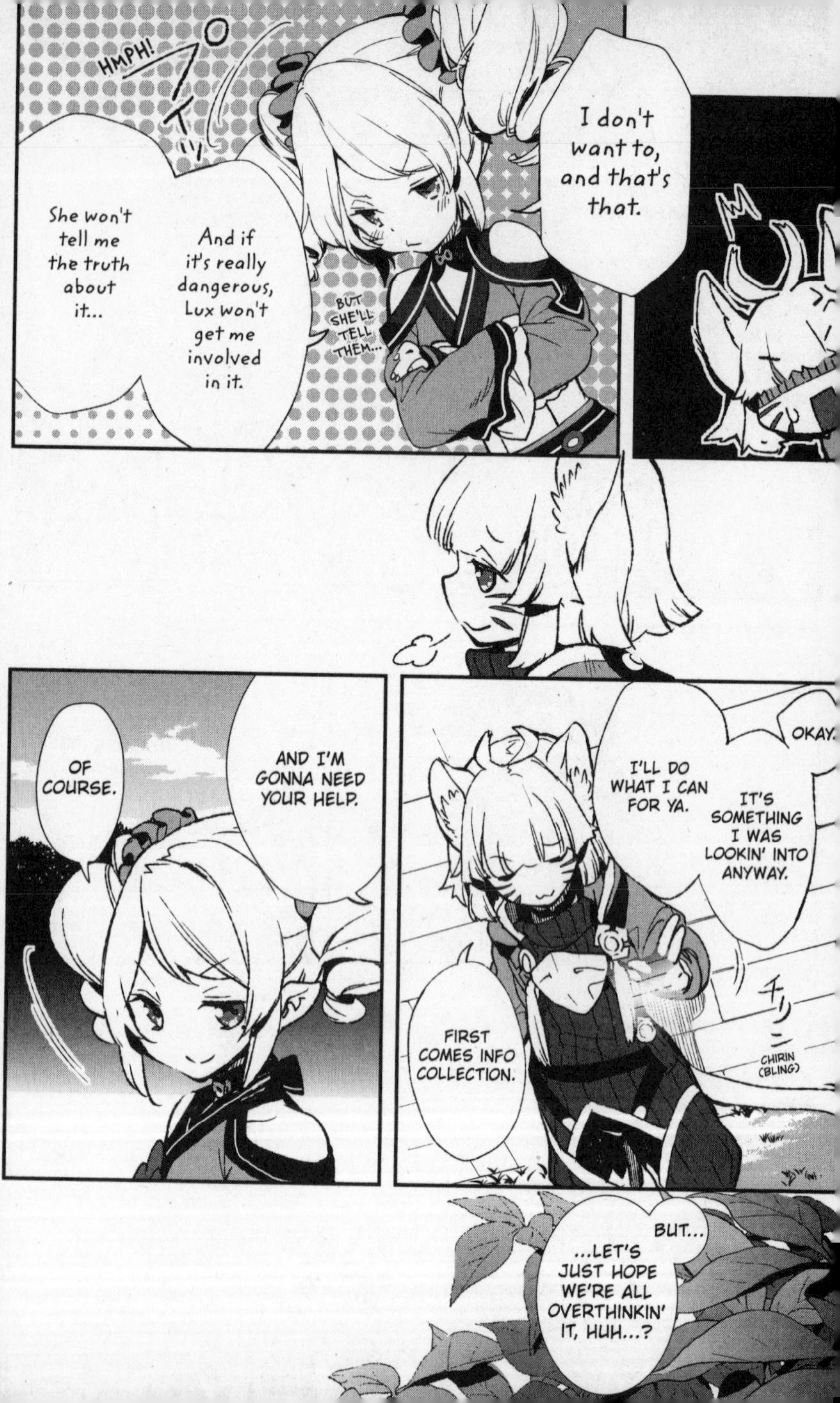
I don't want to, and that's that.
HMPH!
She won't tell me the truth about it... And if it's really dangerous, Lux won't get me involved in it.
BUT SHE'LL TELL THEM...
OKAY.
IT'S SOMETHING I WAS LOOKIN' INTO ANYWAY.
I'LL DO WHAT I CAN FOR YA.
CHIRIN (BLING)
FIRST COMES INFO COLLECTION.
AND I'M GONNA NEED YOUR HELP.
OF COURSE.
BUT...
...LET'S JUST HOPE WE'RE ALL OVERTHINKIN' IT, HUH...?

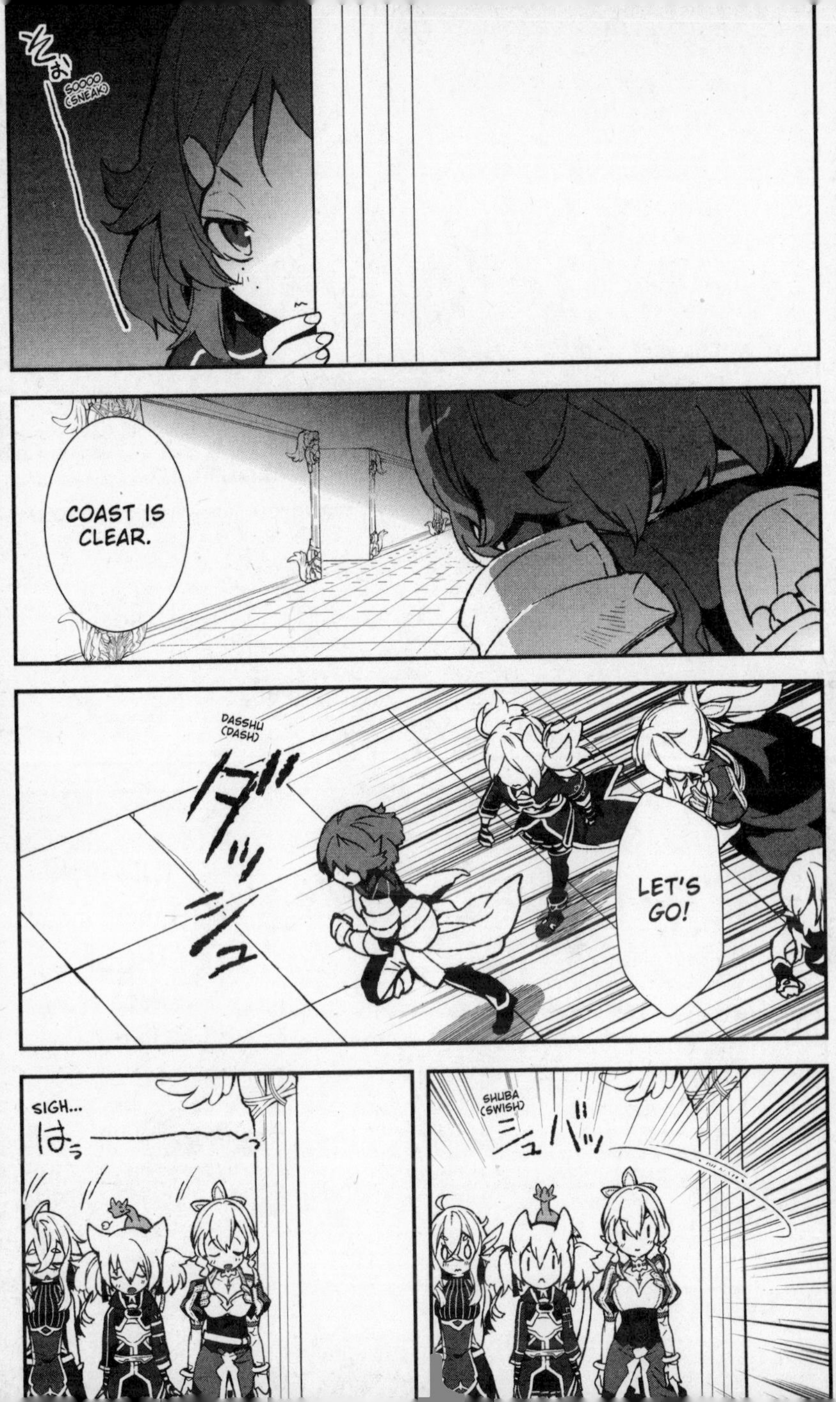
そぉ
SOOOO (SNEAK)
COAST IS CLEAR.
DASSHU (DASH)
ダッシュ
LET'S GO!
SHUBA (SWISH)
シュバッ
SIGH...
はっ

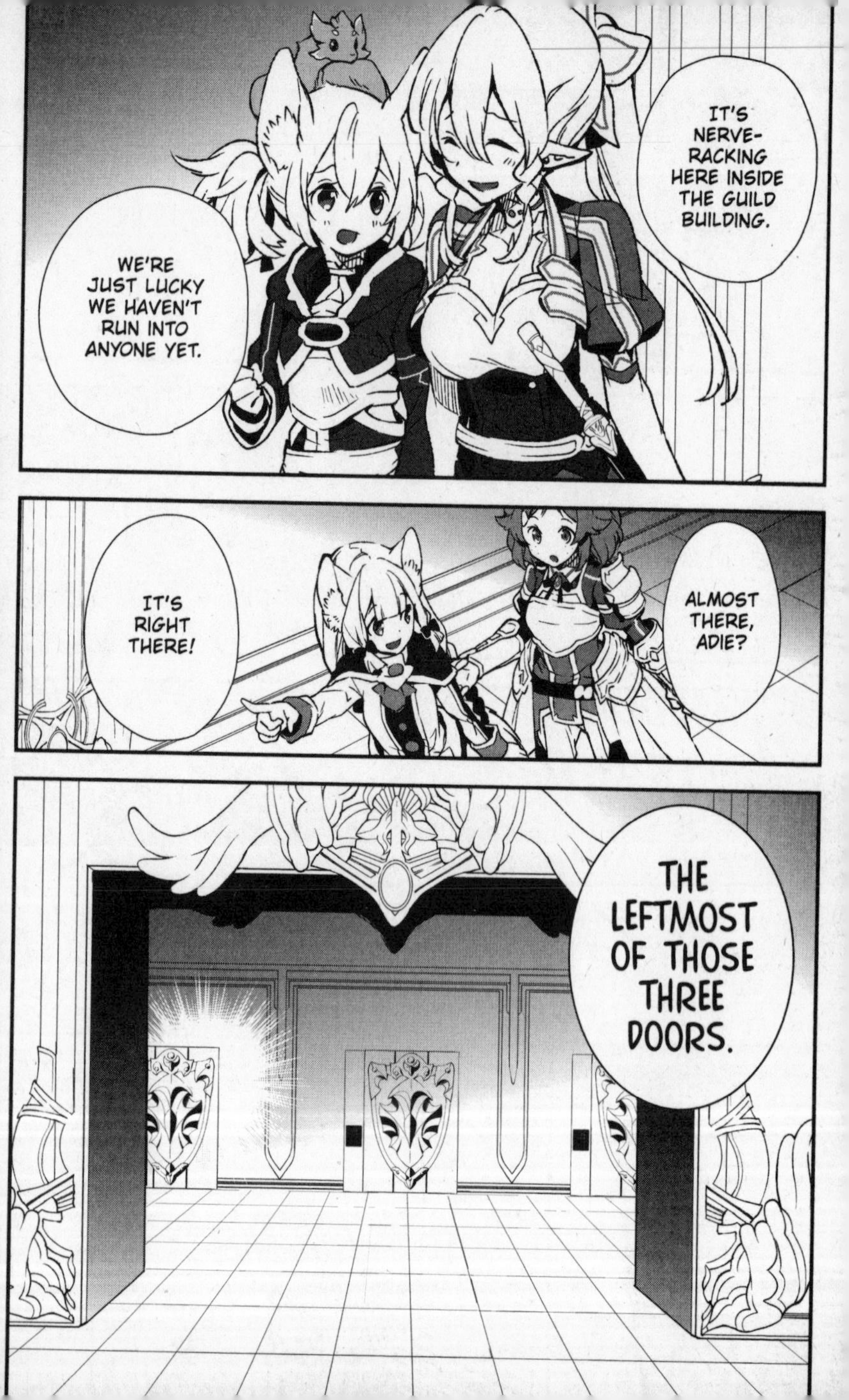
IT'S NERVE-RACKING HERE INSIDE THE GUILD BUILDING.
WE'RE JUST LUCKY WE HAVEN'T RUN INTO ANYONE YET.
ALMOST THERE, ADIE?
IT'S RIGHT THERE!
THE LEFTMOST OF THOSE THREE DOORS.

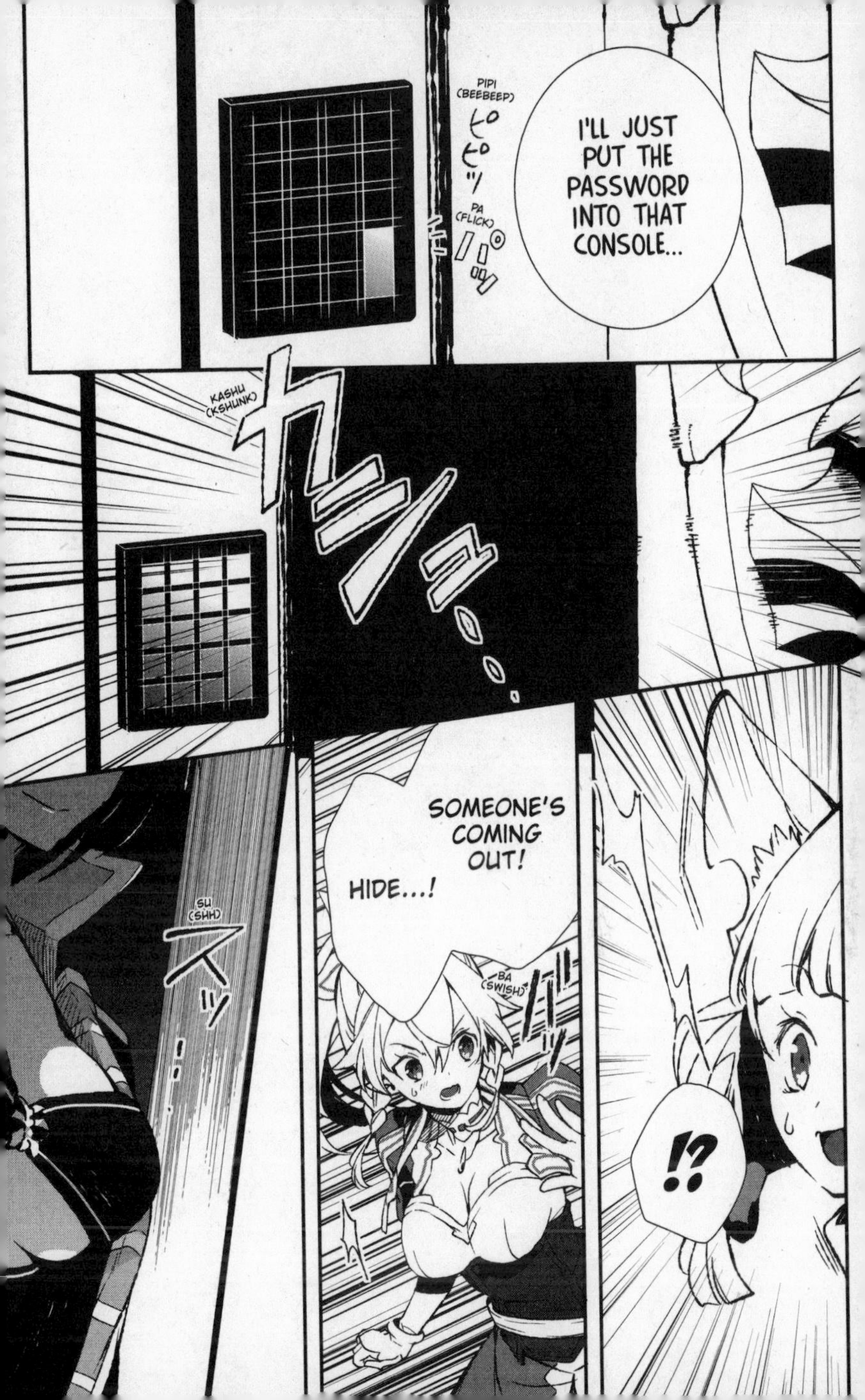
I'LL JUST PUT THE PASSWORD INTO THAT CONSOLE...
PIPI (BEEBEEP)
PA (FLICK)
KASHU (KSHUNK)
!?
SOMEONE'S COMING OUT!
HIDE...!
BA (SWISH)
SU (SHH)

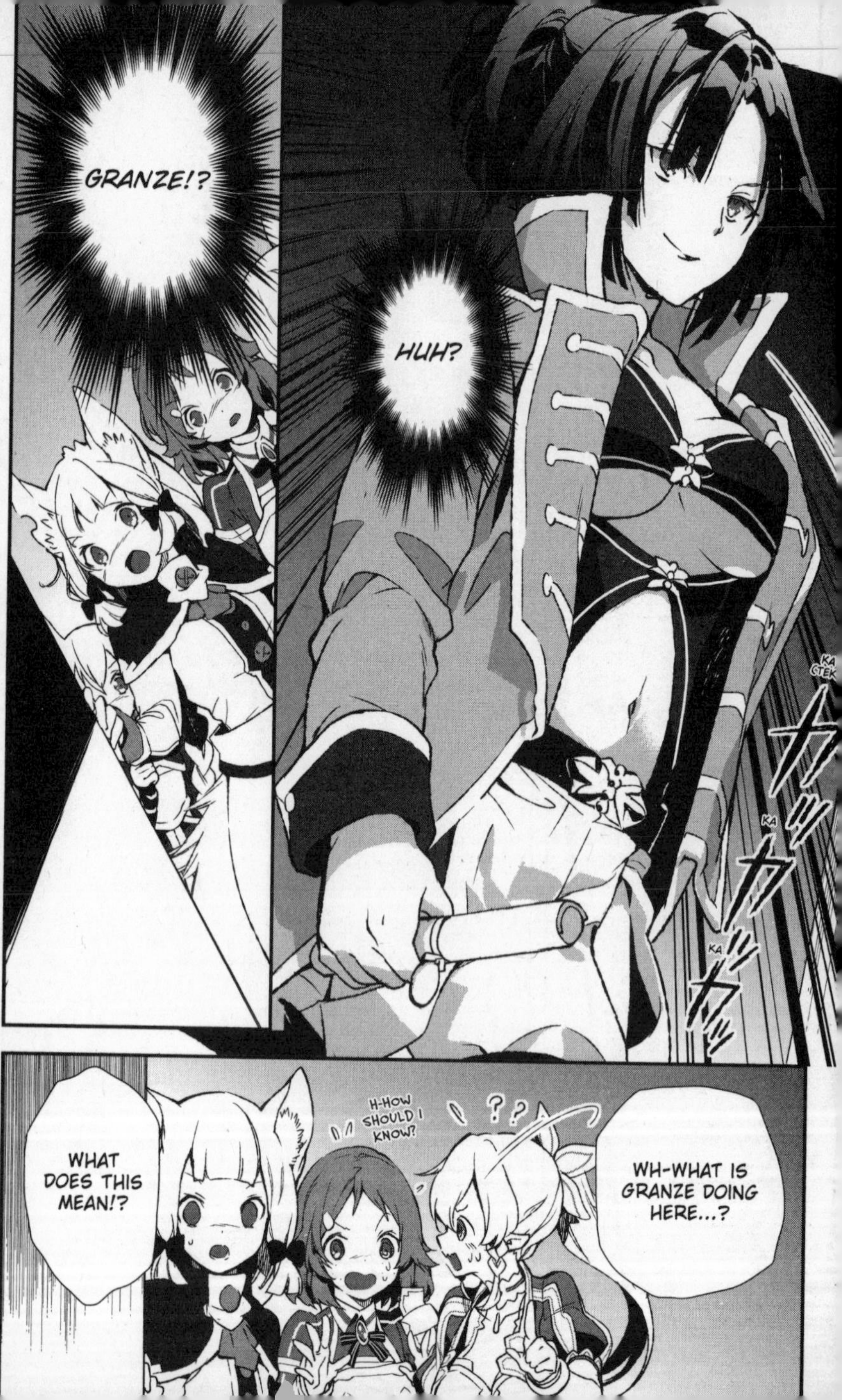
HUH?
KA CTEK
KA
KA
GRANZE!?
WH-WHAT IS GRANZE DOING HERE...?
! ??
H-HOW SHOULD I KNOW?
WHAT DOES THIS MEAN!?

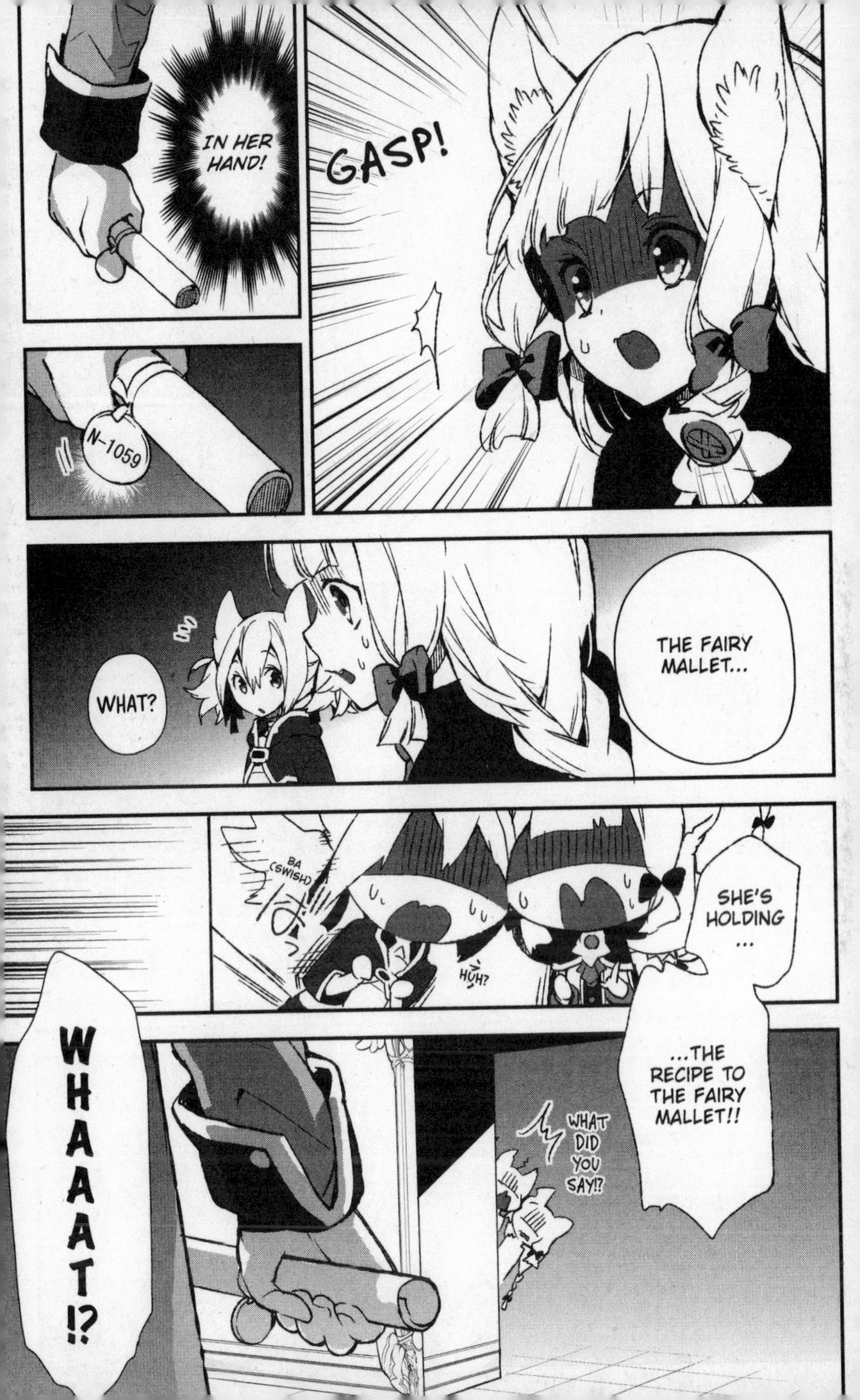
GASP!
IN HER HAND!
N-1059
THE FAIRY MALLET...
WHAT?
SHE'S HOLDING ...
HUH?
BA (SWISH)
...THE RECIPE TO THE FAIRY MALLET!!
WHAT DID YOU SAY!?
WHAAAAT!?

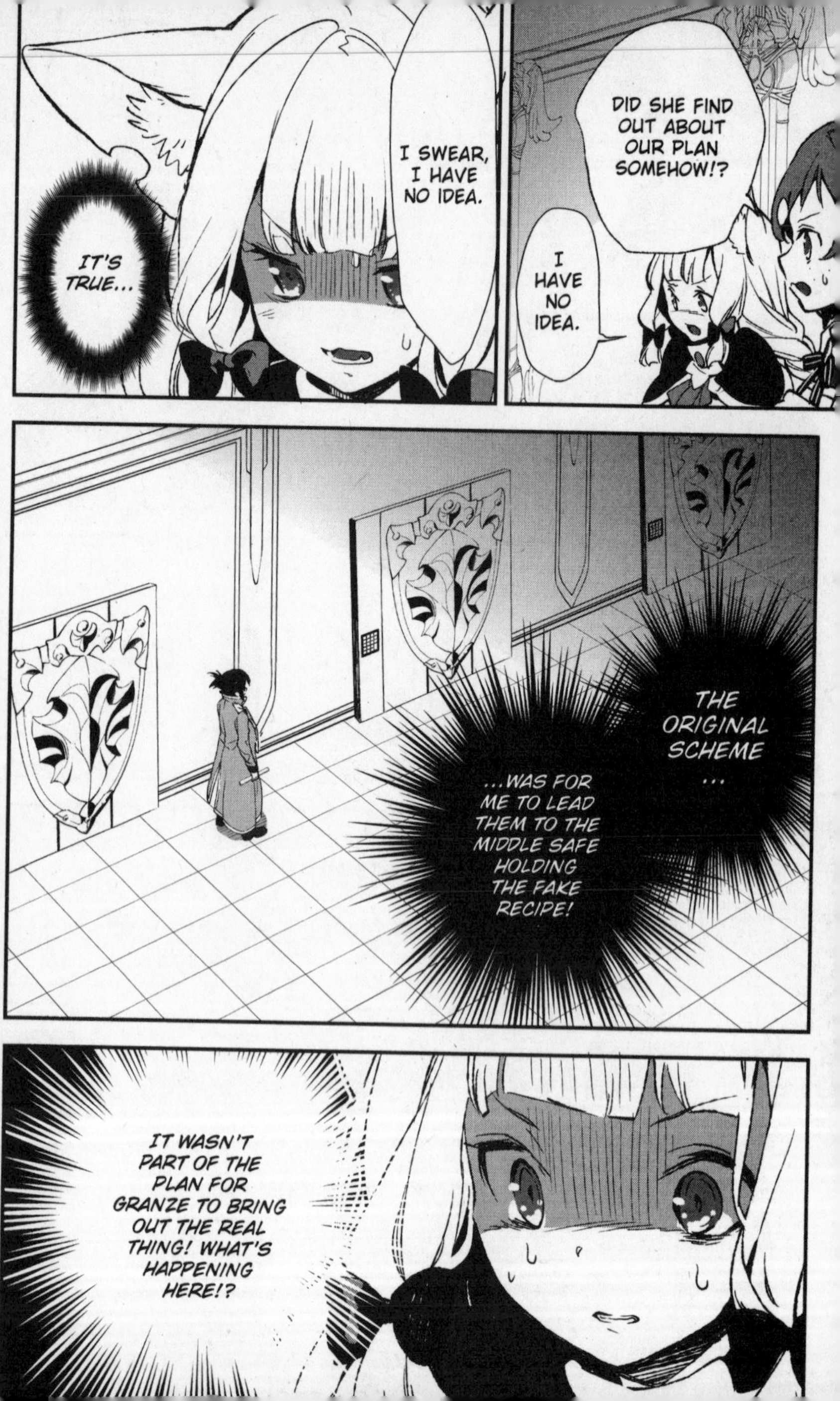
DID SHE FIND OUT ABOUT OUR PLAN SOMEHOW!?
I HAVE NO IDEA.
I SWEAR, I HAVE NO IDEA.
IT'S TRUE...
THE ORIGINAL SCHEME...
...WAS FOR ME TO LEAD THEM TO THE MIDDLE SAFE HOLDING THE FAKE RECIPE!
IT WASN'T PART OF THE PLAN FOR GRANZE TO BRING OUT THE REAL THING! WHAT'S HAPPENING HERE!?

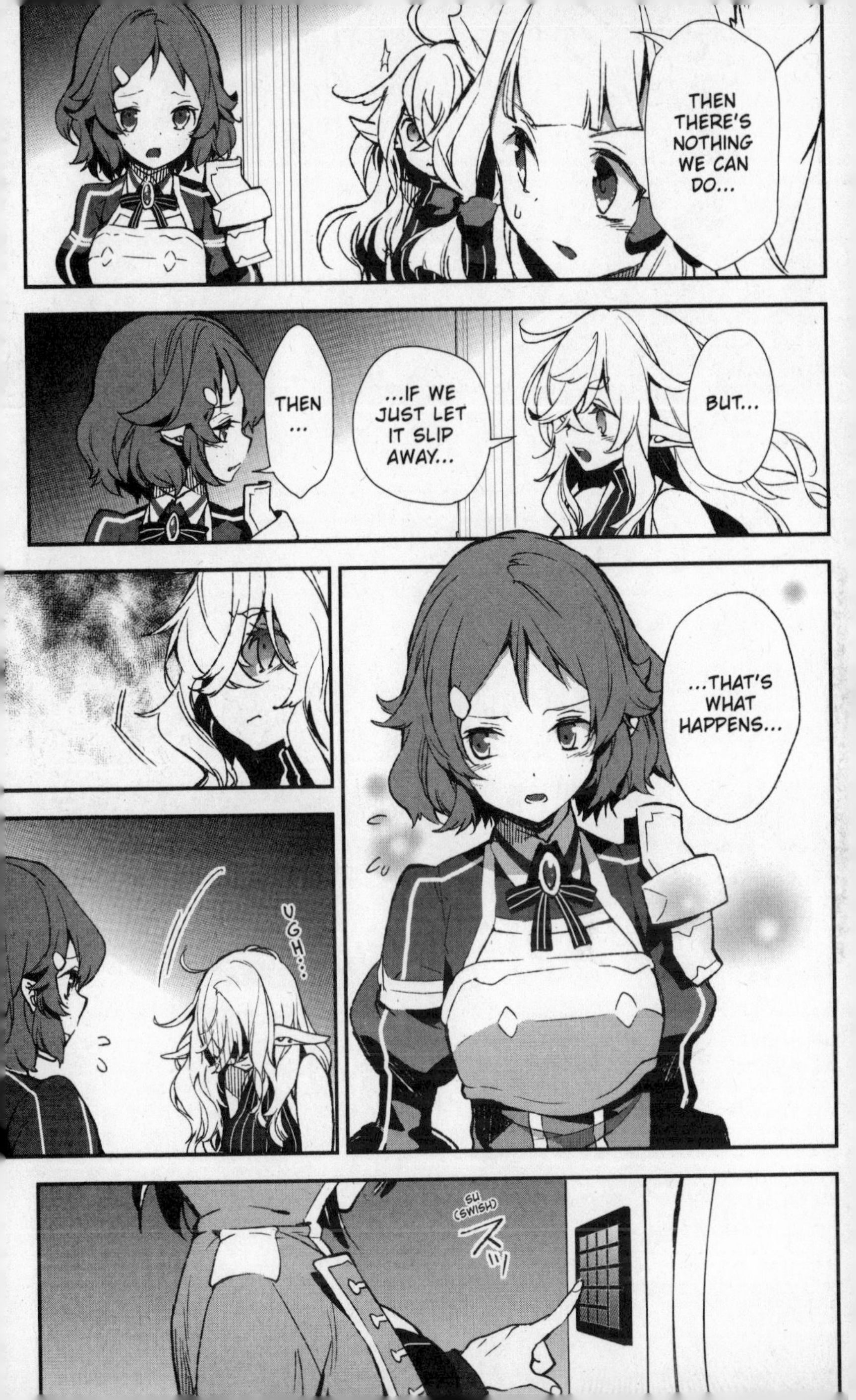
THEN THERE'S NOTHING WE CAN DO...
BUT...
...IF WE JUST LET IT SLIP AWAY...
THEN ...
...THAT'S WHAT HAPPENS...
UGH...
SU (SWISH)

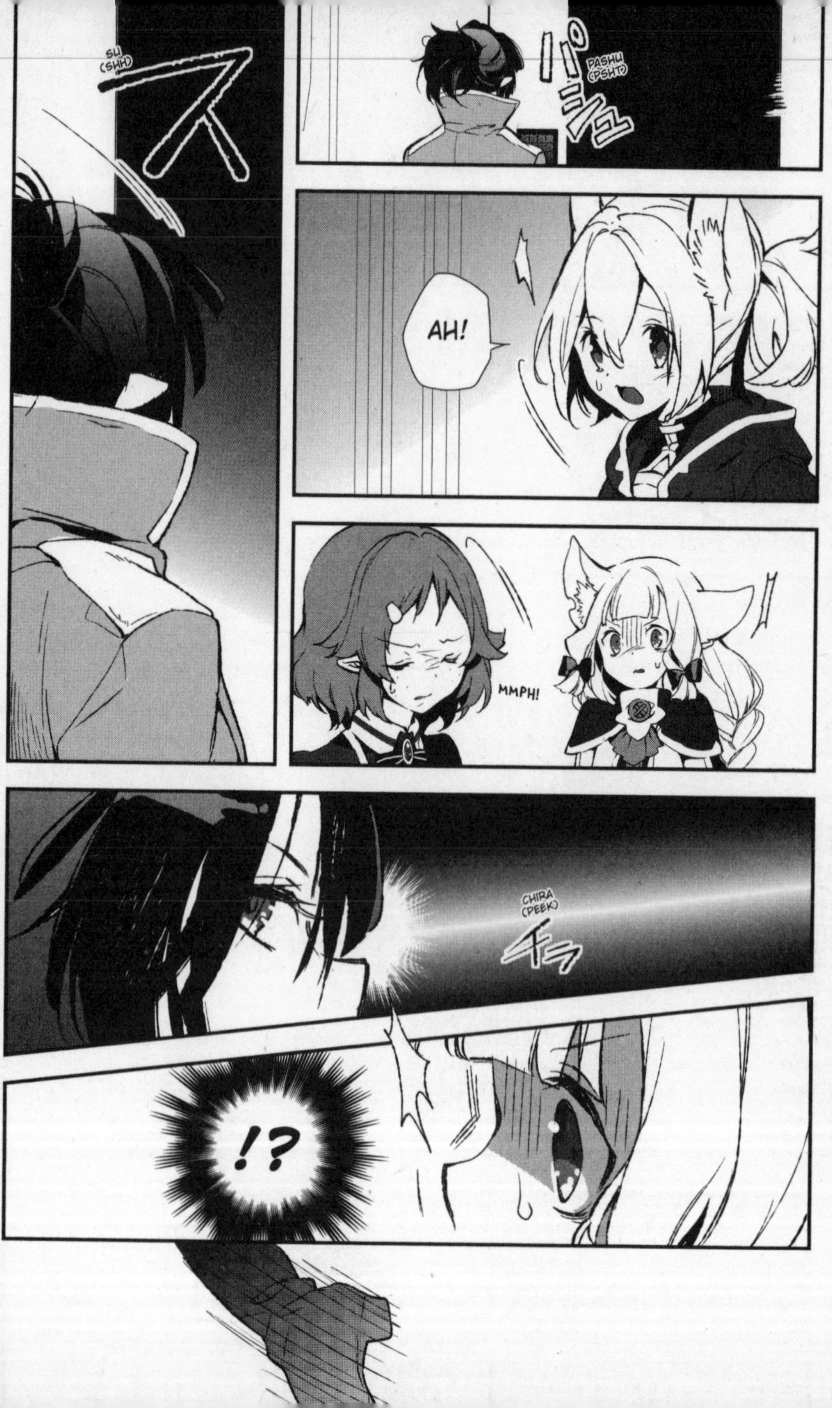
PASHU (PSHT)
AH!
MMPH!
SU (SHH)
CHIRA (PEEK)
!?

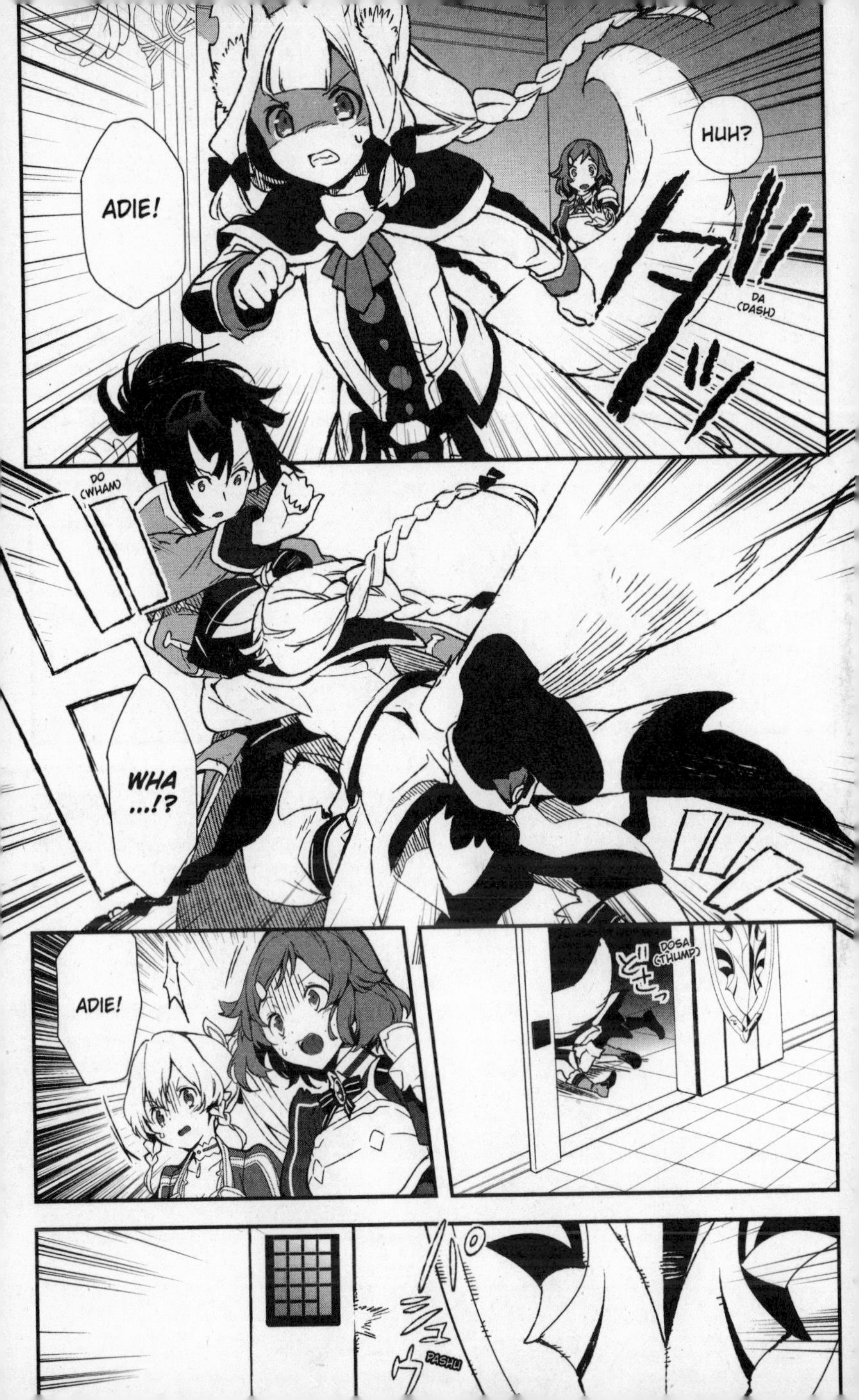
HUH?
DA
(DASH)
ADIE!
DO
(WHAM)
WHA
...!?
DOSA
(THUMP)
ADIE!
PASHU

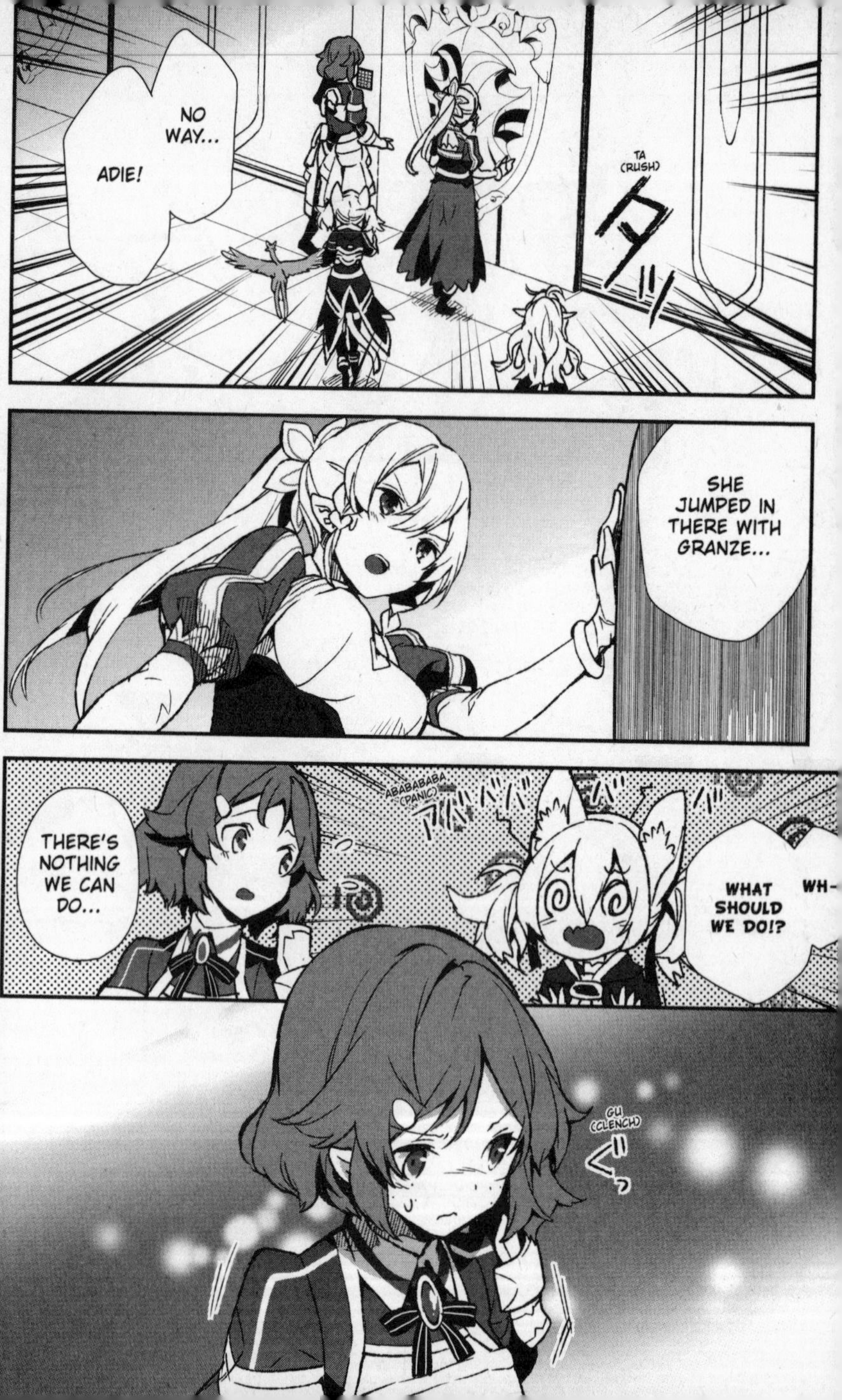
TA (RUSH)
NO WAY...
ADIE!
SHE JUMPED IN THERE WITH GRANZE...
WH- WHAT SHOULD WE DO!?
ABABABABA (PANIC)
THERE'S NOTHING WE CAN DO...
GU (CLENCH)

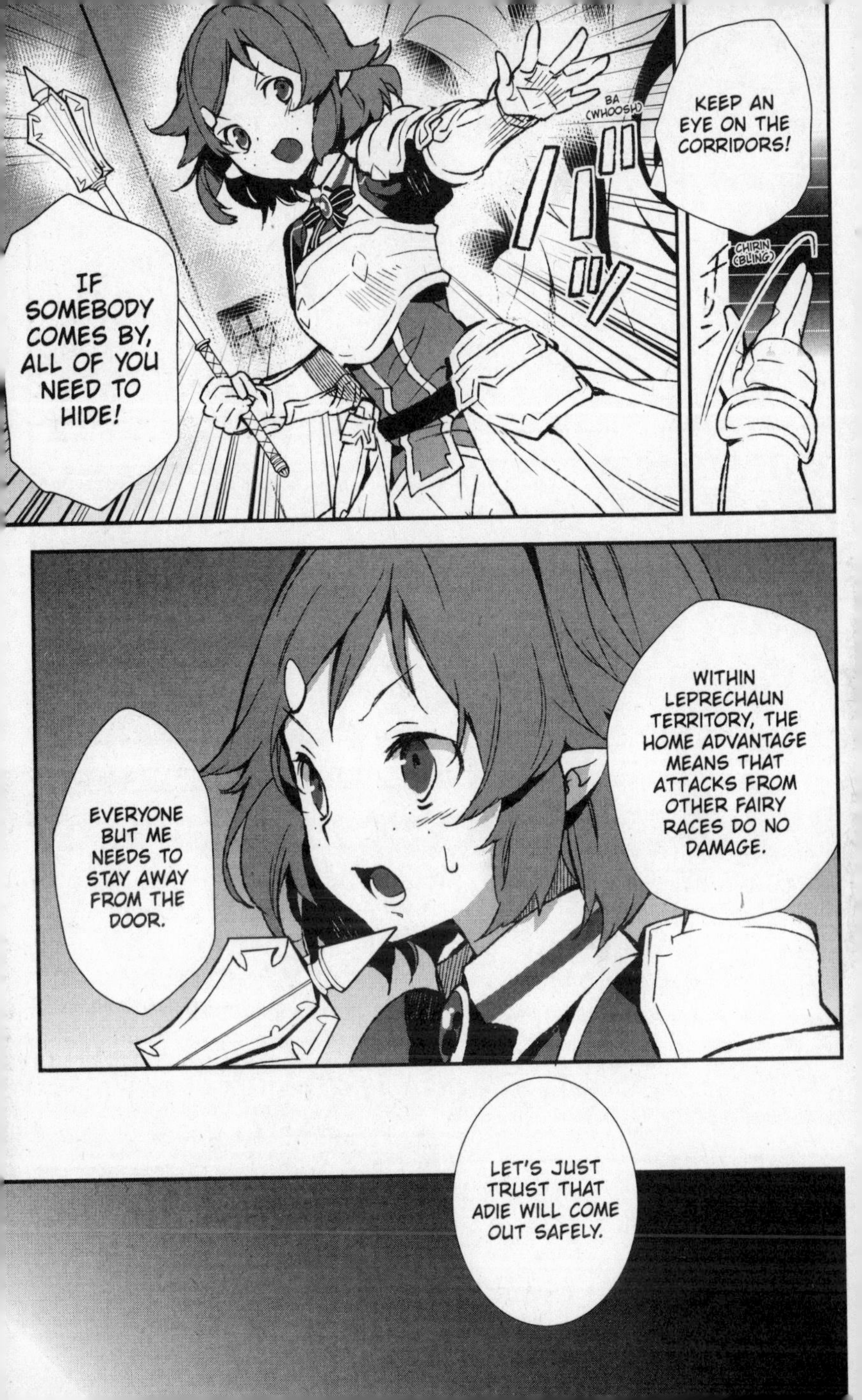
KEEP AN EYE ON THE CORRIDORS!
CHIRIN (BLING)
BA (WHOOSH)
IF SOMEBODY COMES BY, ALL OF YOU NEED TO HIDE!
WITHIN LEPRECHAUN TERRITORY, THE HOME ADVANTAGE MEANS THAT ATTACKS FROM OTHER FAIRY RACES DO NO DAMAGE.
EVERYONE BUT ME NEEDS TO STAY AWAY FROM THE DOOR.
LET'S JUST TRUST THAT ADIE WILL COME OUT SAFELY.

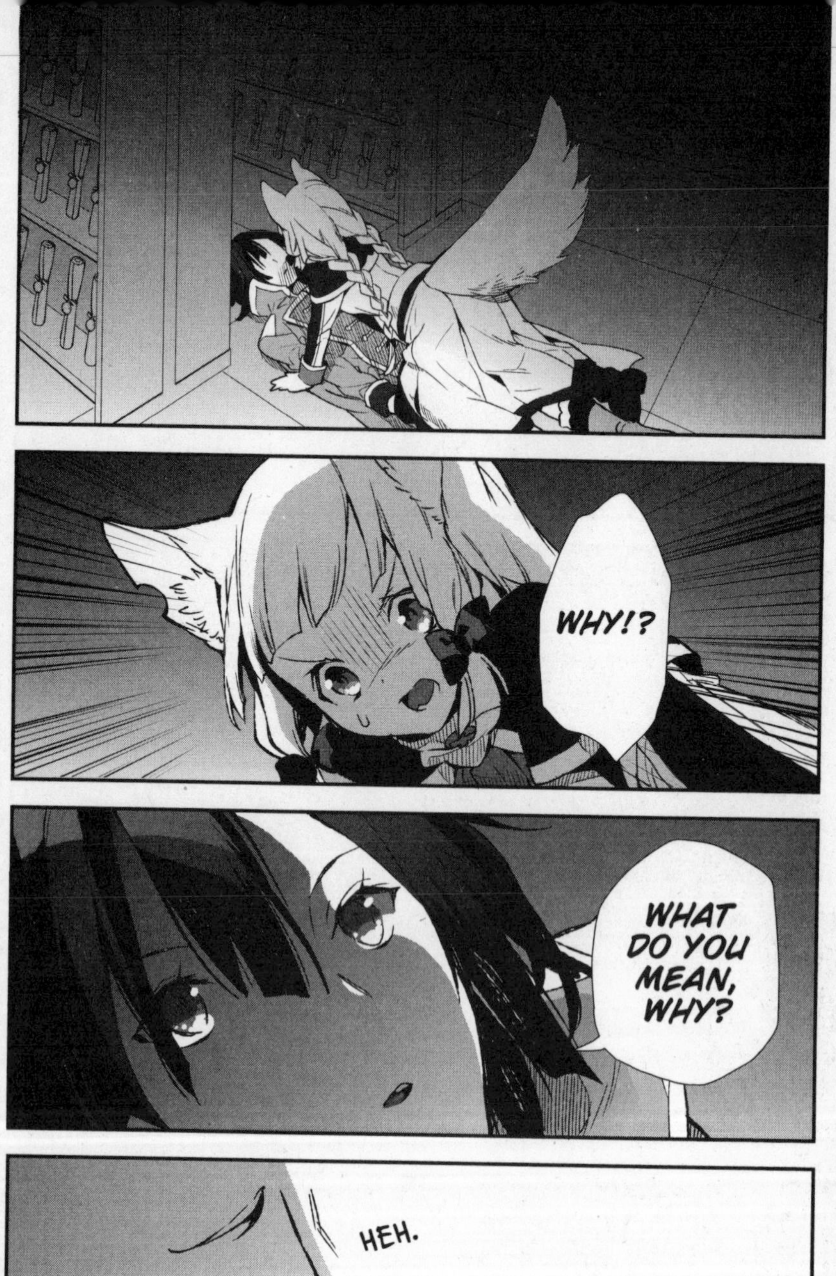
WHY!?
WHAT DO YOU MEAN, WHY?
HEH.

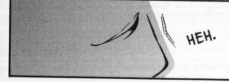

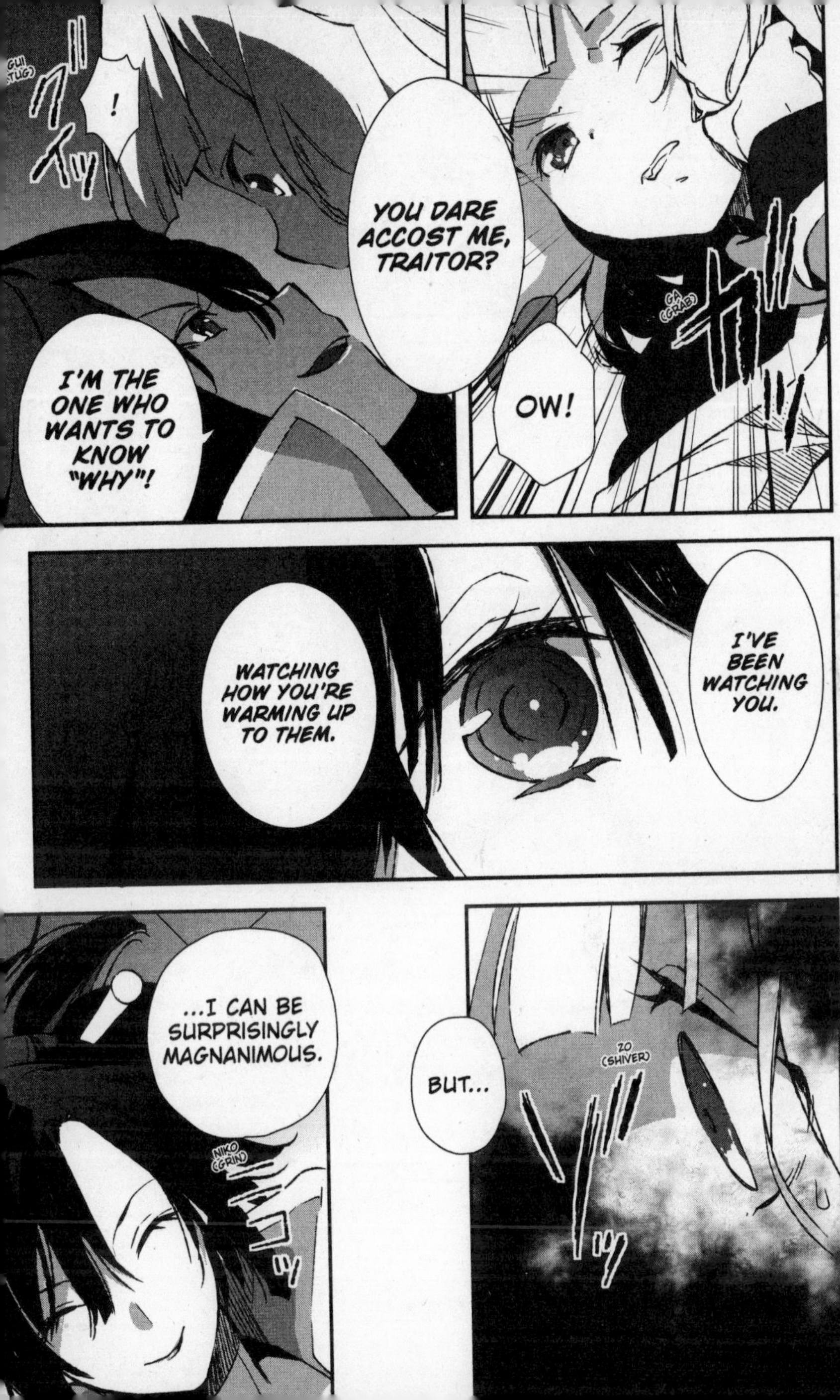
YOU DARE ACCOST ME, TRAITOR?
GA (GRAB)
OW!
GUI (TUG)
!
I'M THE ONE WHO WANTS TO KNOW "WHY"!
I'VE BEEN WATCHING YOU.
WATCHING HOW YOU'RE WARMING UP TO THEM.
BUT...
ZO (SHIVER)
...I CAN BE SURPRISINGLY MAGNANIMOUS.
NIKO (GRIN)

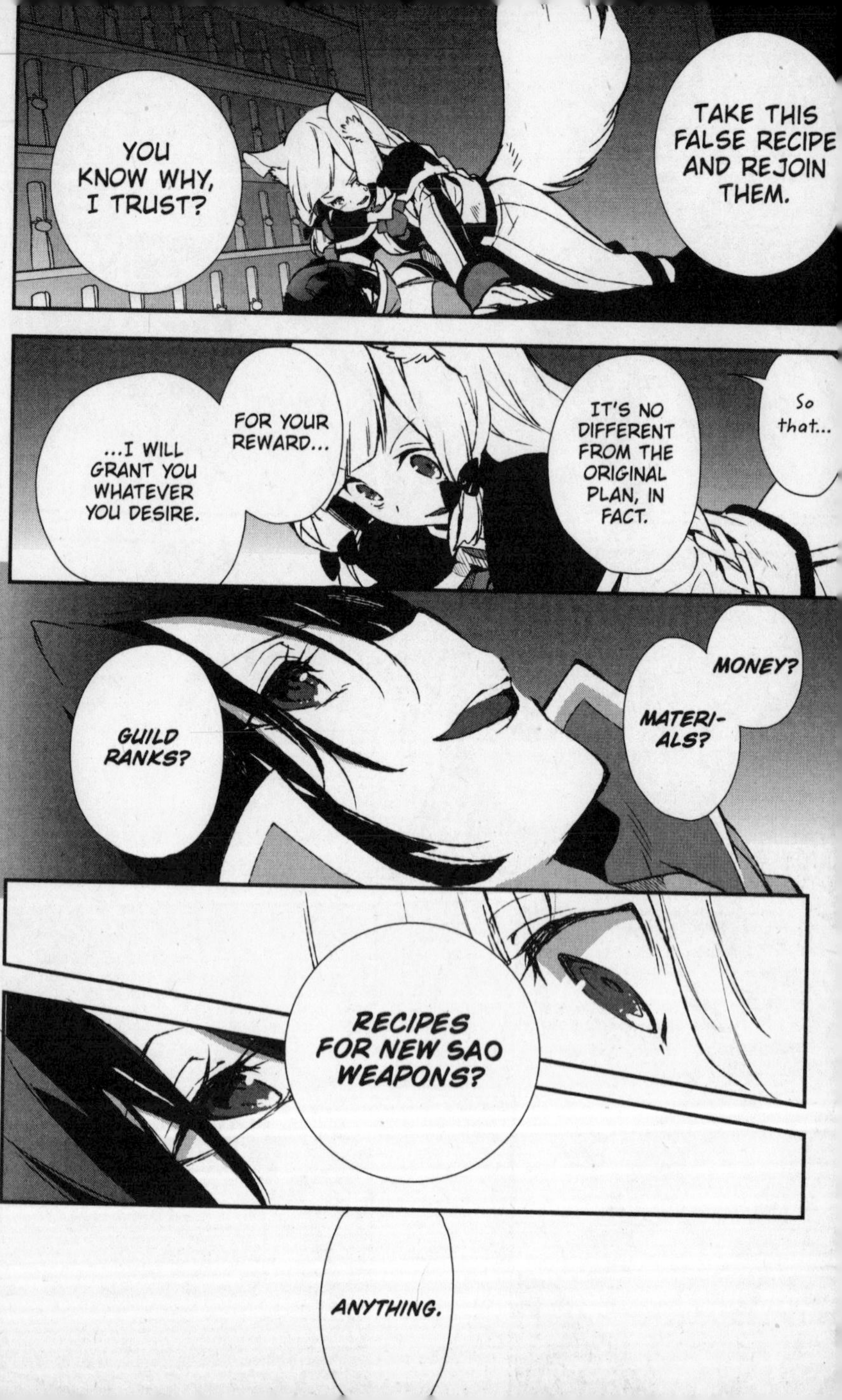
TAKE THIS FALSE RECIPE AND REJOIN THEM.
YOU KNOW WHY, I TRUST?
So that...
IT'S NO DIFFERENT FROM THE ORIGINAL PLAN, IN FACT.
FOR YOUR REWARD...
...I WILL GRANT YOU WHATEVER YOU DESIRE.
MONEY?
MATERI-ALS?
GUILD RANKS?
RECIPES FOR NEW SAO WEAPONS?
ANYTHING.

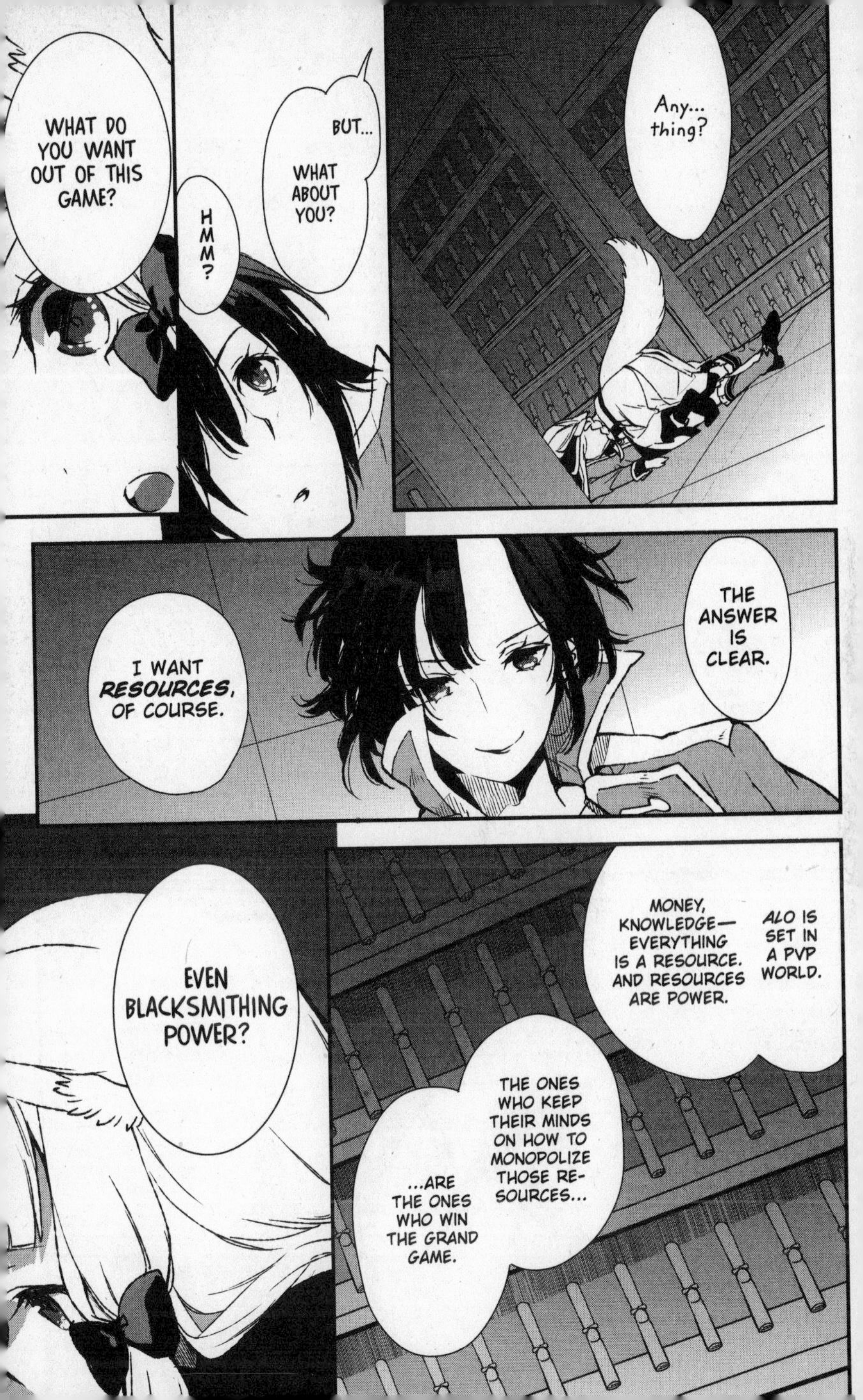
Any... thing?
BUT... WHAT ABOUT YOU?
HMM?
WHAT DO YOU WANT OUT OF THIS GAME?
THE ANSWER IS CLEAR.
I WANT *RESOURCES*, OF COURSE.
ALO IS SET IN A PVP WORLD.
MONEY, KNOWLEDGE—EVERYTHING IS A RESOURCE. AND RESOURCES ARE POWER.
THE ONES WHO KEEP THEIR MINDS ON HOW TO MONOPOLIZE THOSE RE-SOURCES...
...ARE THE ONES WHO WIN THE GRAND GAME.
EVEN BLACKSMITHING POWER?

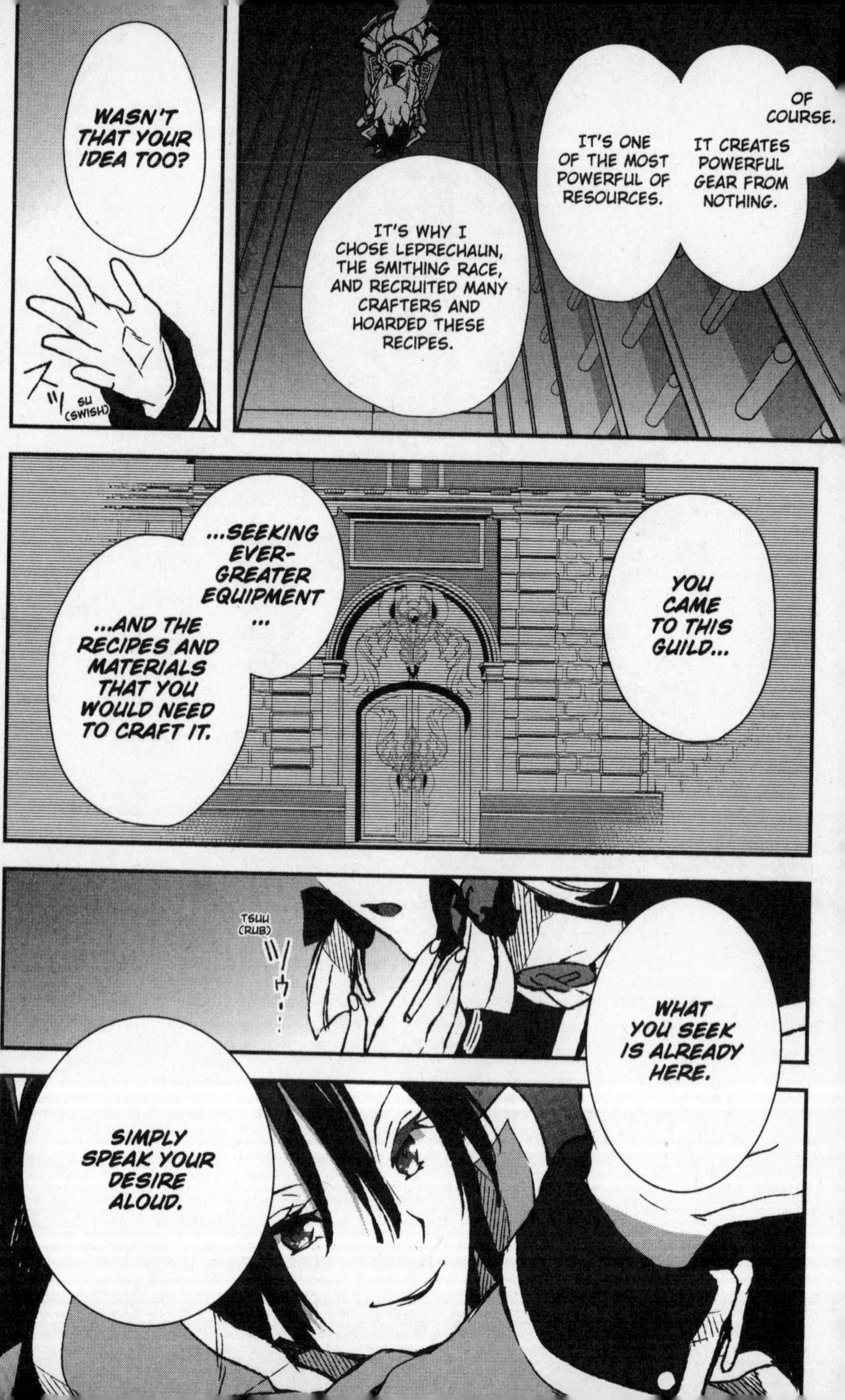
OF COURSE.
IT CREATES POWERFUL GEAR FROM NOTHING.
IT'S ONE OF THE MOST POWERFUL OF RESOURCES.
IT'S WHY I CHOSE LEPRECHAUN, THE SMITHING RACE, AND RECRUITED MANY CRAFTERS AND HOARDED THESE RECIPES.
WASN'T THAT YOUR IDEA TOO?
SU (SWISH)
YOU CAME TO THIS GUILD...
...SEEKING EVER-GREATER EQUIPMENT...
...AND THE RECIPES AND MATERIALS THAT YOU WOULD NEED TO CRAFT IT.
TSUU (RUB)
WHAT YOU SEEK IS ALREADY HERE.
SIMPLY SPEAK YOUR DESIRE ALOUD.

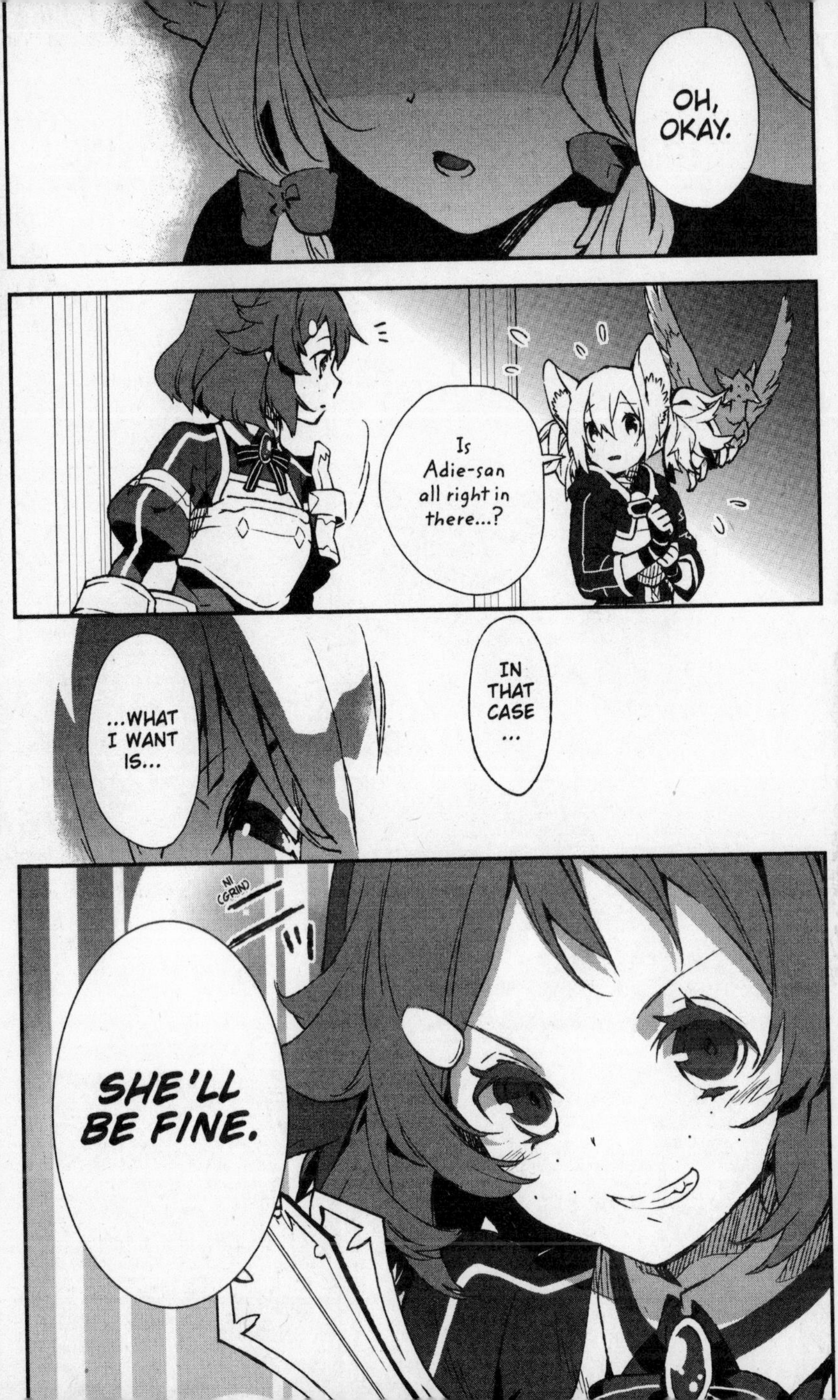
OH, OKAY.
Is Adie-san all right in there...?
IN THAT CASE...
...WHAT I WANT IS...
NI (GRIN)
SHE'LL BE FINE.

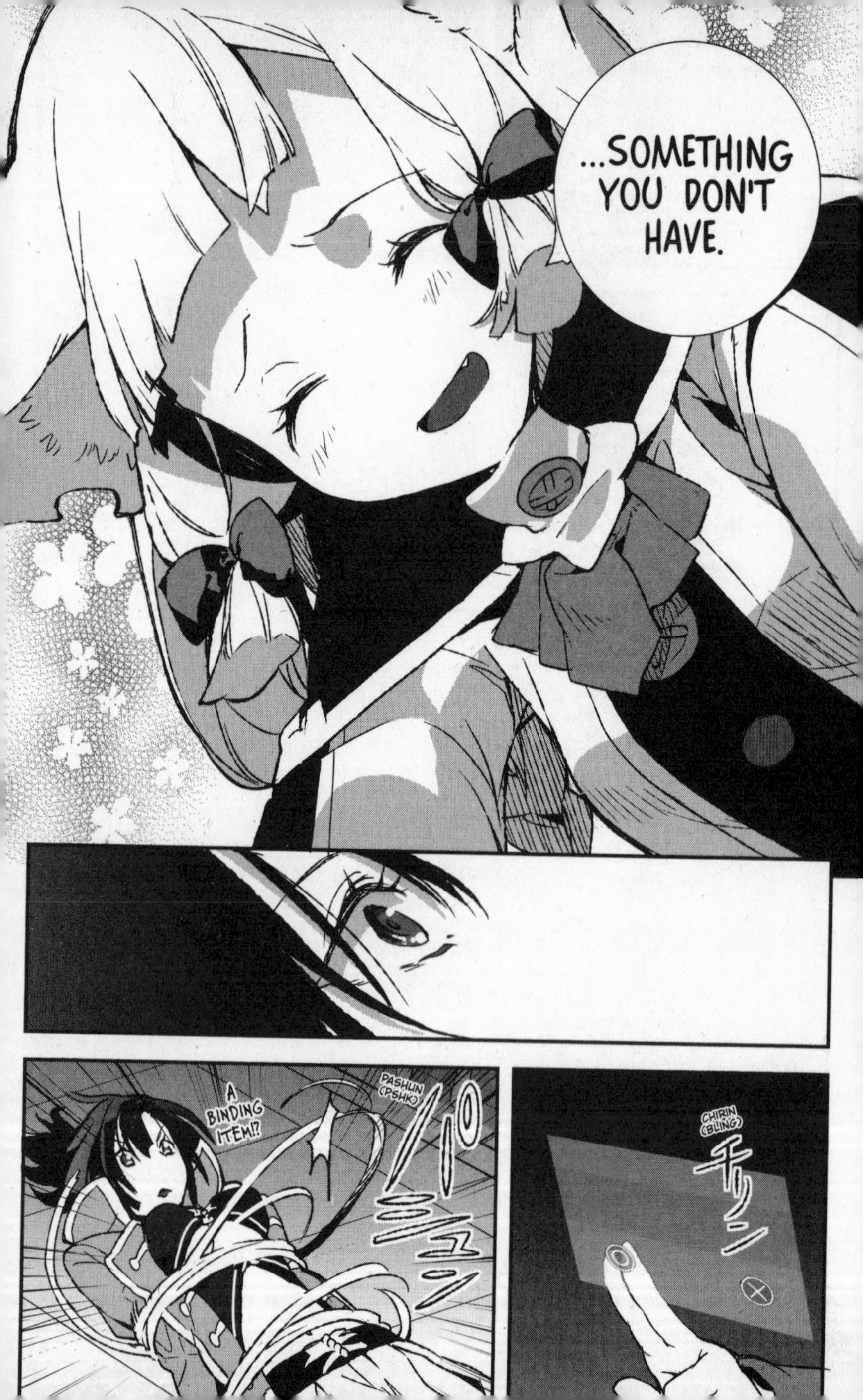
...SOMETHING YOU DON'T HAVE.
CHIRIN (BLING)
チリーン
PASHUN (PSHK)
パシュン
A BINDING ITEM!?

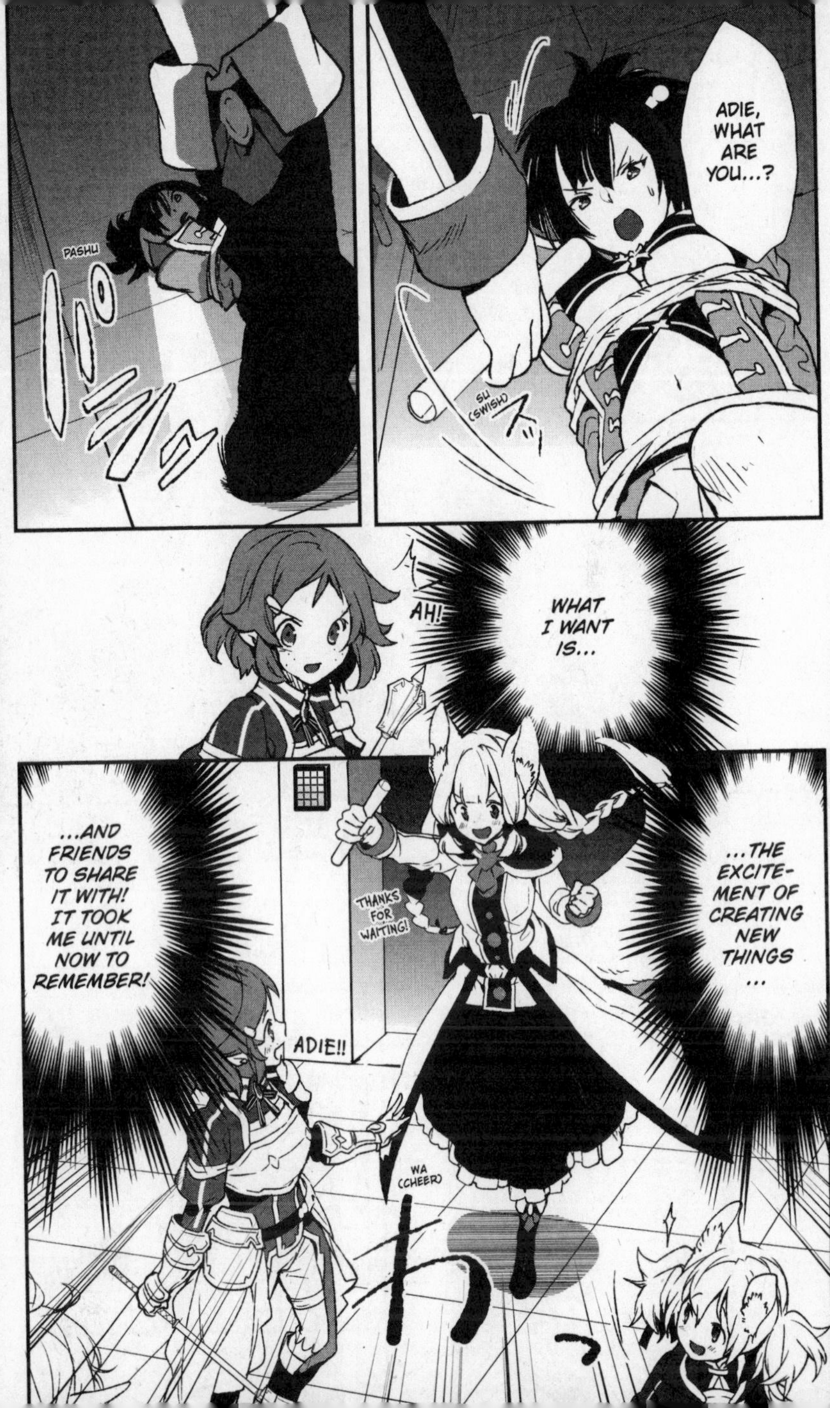
ADIE, WHAT ARE YOU...?
SU (SWISH)
PASHU
AH!
WHAT I WANT IS...
...THE EXCITEMENT OF CREATING NEW THINGS...
...AND FRIENDS TO SHARE IT WITH! IT TOOK ME UNTIL NOW TO REMEMBER!
THANKS FOR WAITING!
ADIE!!
WA (CHEER)

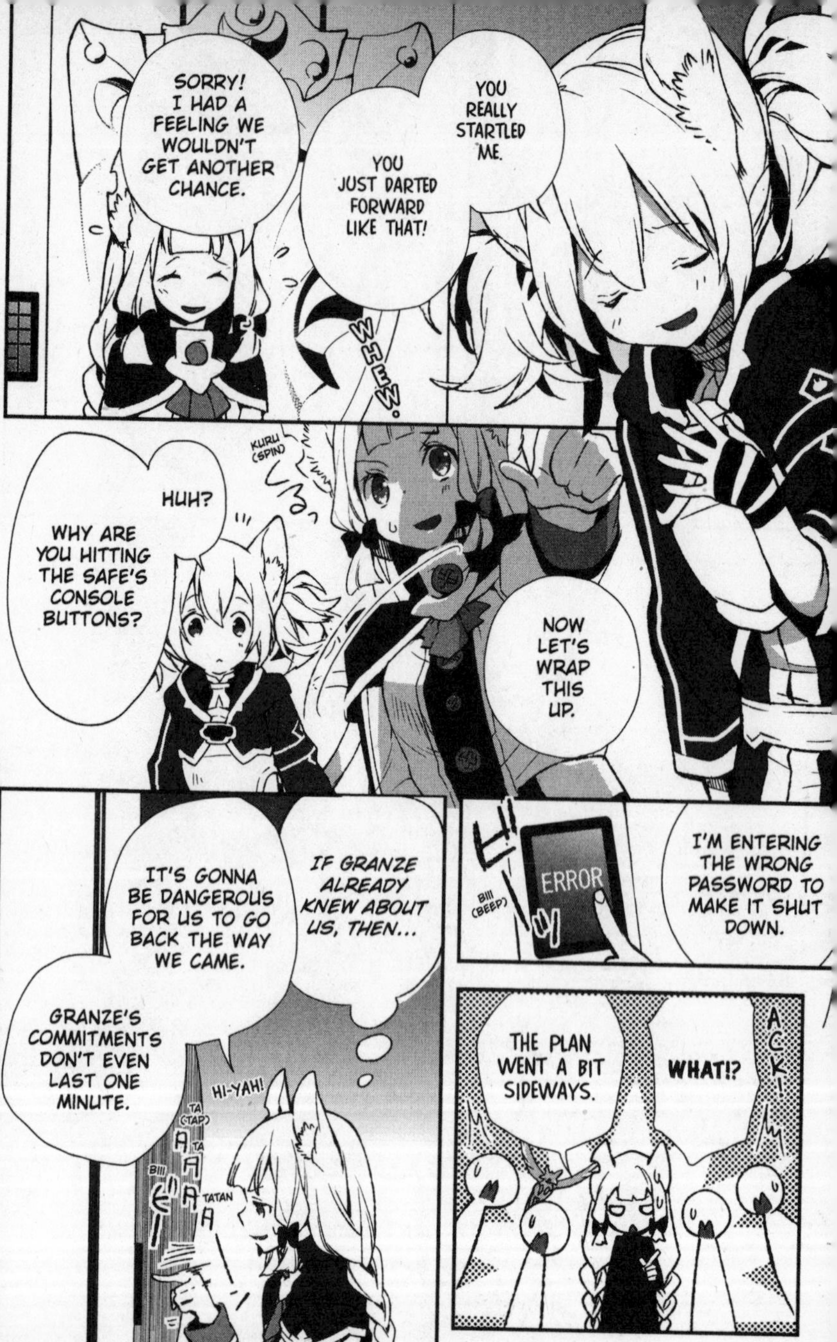
YOU REALLY STARTLED ME.
YOU JUST DARTED FORWARD LIKE THAT!
WHEW.
SORRY! I HAD A FEELING WE WOULDN'T GET ANOTHER CHANCE.
NOW LET'S WRAP THIS UP.
KURU (SPIN)
HUH?
WHY ARE YOU HITTING THE SAFE'S CONSOLE BUTTONS?
I'M ENTERING THE WRONG PASSWORD TO MAKE IT SHUT DOWN.
ERROR
BIII (BEEP)
ACK!
WHAT!?
THE PLAN WENT A BIT SIDEWAYS.
IF GRANZE ALREADY KNEW ABOUT US, THEN...
IT'S GONNA BE DANGEROUS FOR US TO GO BACK THE WAY WE CAME.
GRANZE'S COMMITMENTS DON'T EVEN LAST ONE MINUTE.
HI-YAH!
TA (TAP) TA
BIII
TATAN

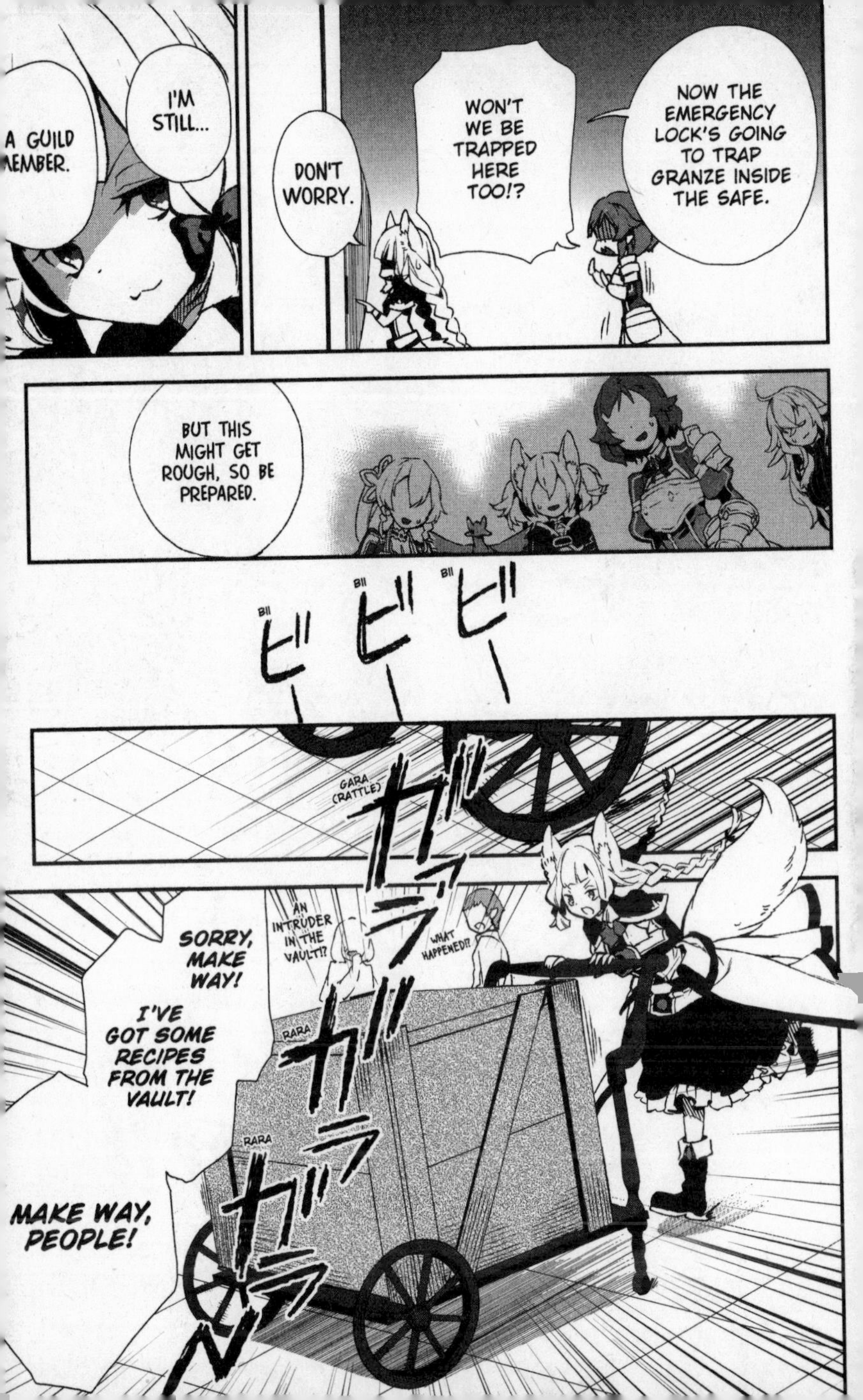
NOW THE EMERGENCY LOCK'S GOING TO TRAP GRANZE INSIDE THE SAFE.
WON'T WE BE TRAPPED HERE TOO!?
DON'T WORRY.
I'M STILL...
A GUILD MEMBER.
BUT THIS MIGHT GET ROUGH, SO BE PREPARED.
BII
BII
BII
GARA (RATTLE)
WHAT HAPPENED!?
AN INTRUDER IN THE VAULT!?
SORRY, MAKE WAY!
I'VE GOT SOME RECIPES FROM THE VAULT!
RARA
RARA
MAKE WAY, PEOPLE!

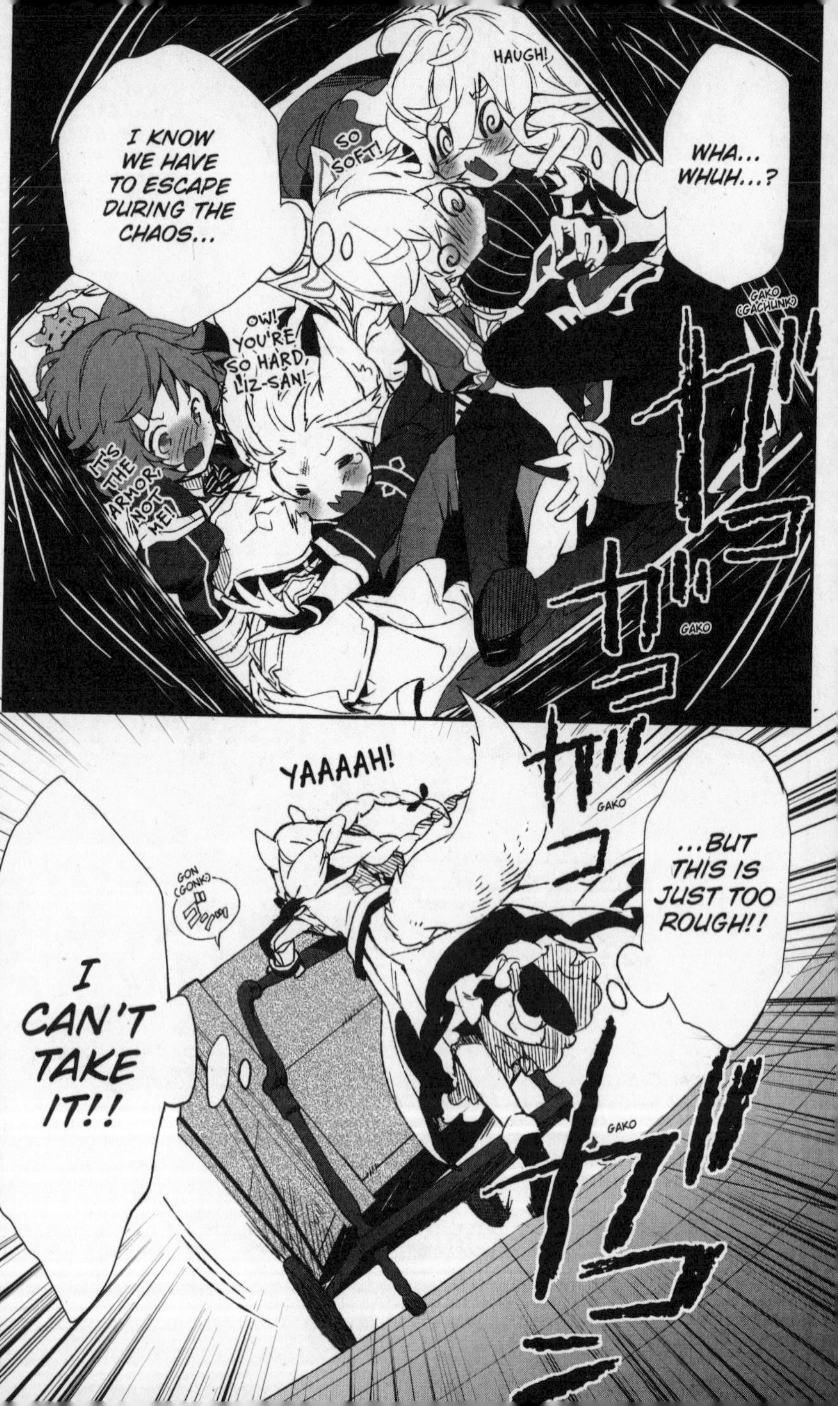
HAUGH!
WHA... WHUH...?
SO SOFT!
I KNOW WE HAVE TO ESCAPE DURING THE CHAOS...
GAKO (GACHUNK)
OW! YOU'RE SO HARD, LIZ-SAN!
IT'S THE ARMOR, NOT ME!
GAKO
...BUT THIS IS JUST TOO ROUGH!!
GAKO
YAAAAH!
GON (GONK)
I CAN'T TAKE IT!!
GAKO

SWORD ART ONLINE
GIRLS' OPS

SWORD ART ONLINE
GIRLS' OPERATIONS

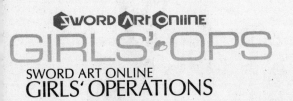

To be continued in the next volume!

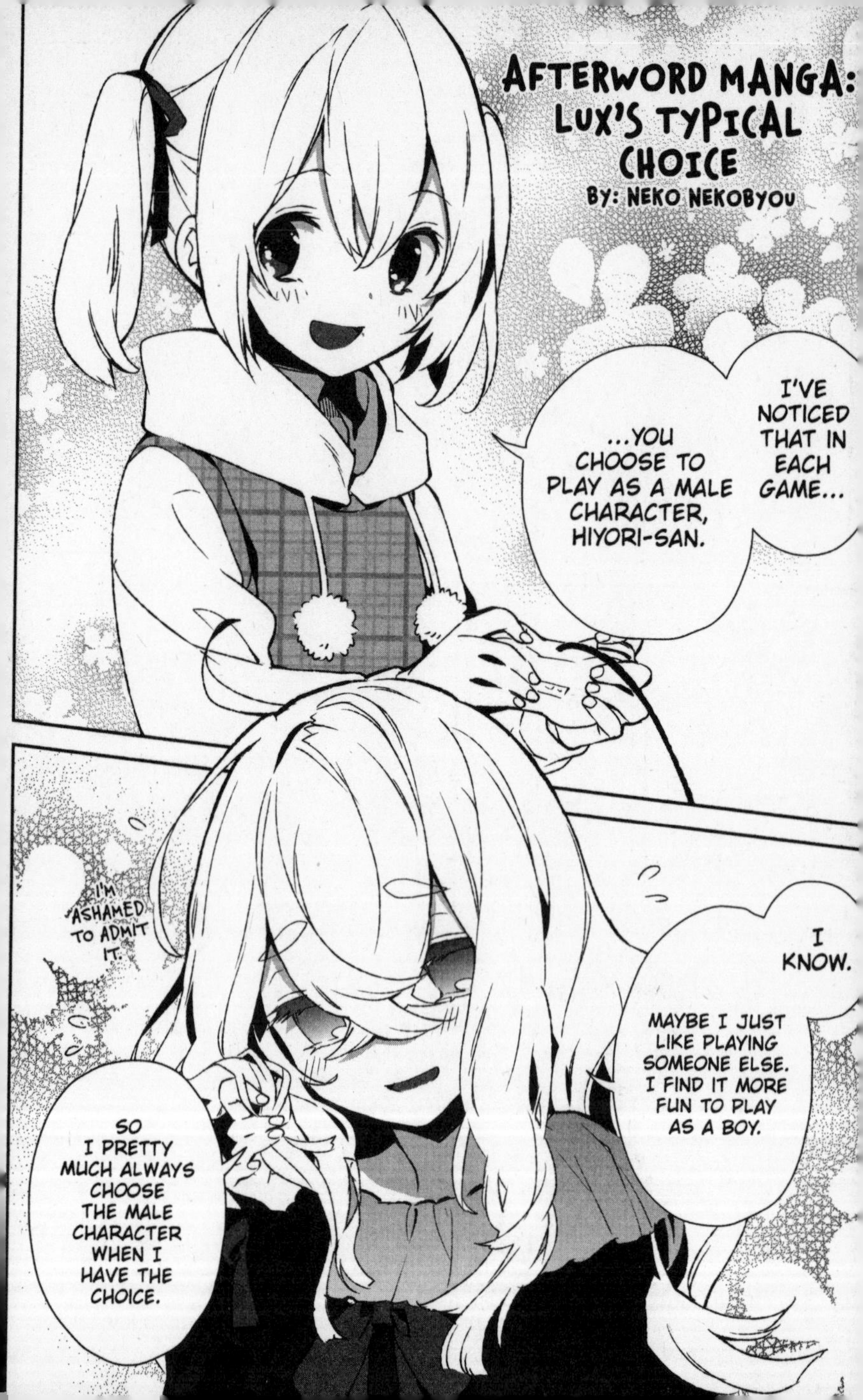
AFTERWORD MANGA: LUX'S TYPICAL CHOICE
BY: NEKO NEKOBYOU
I'VE NOTICED THAT IN EACH GAME...
...YOU CHOOSE TO PLAY AS A MALE CHARACTER, HIYORI-SAN.
I KNOW.
MAYBE I JUST LIKE PLAYING SOMEONE ELSE. I FIND IT MORE FUN TO PLAY AS A BOY.
SO I PRETTY MUCH ALWAYS CHOOSE THE MALE CHARACTER WHEN I HAVE THE CHOICE.
I'M ASHAMED TO ADMIT IT.

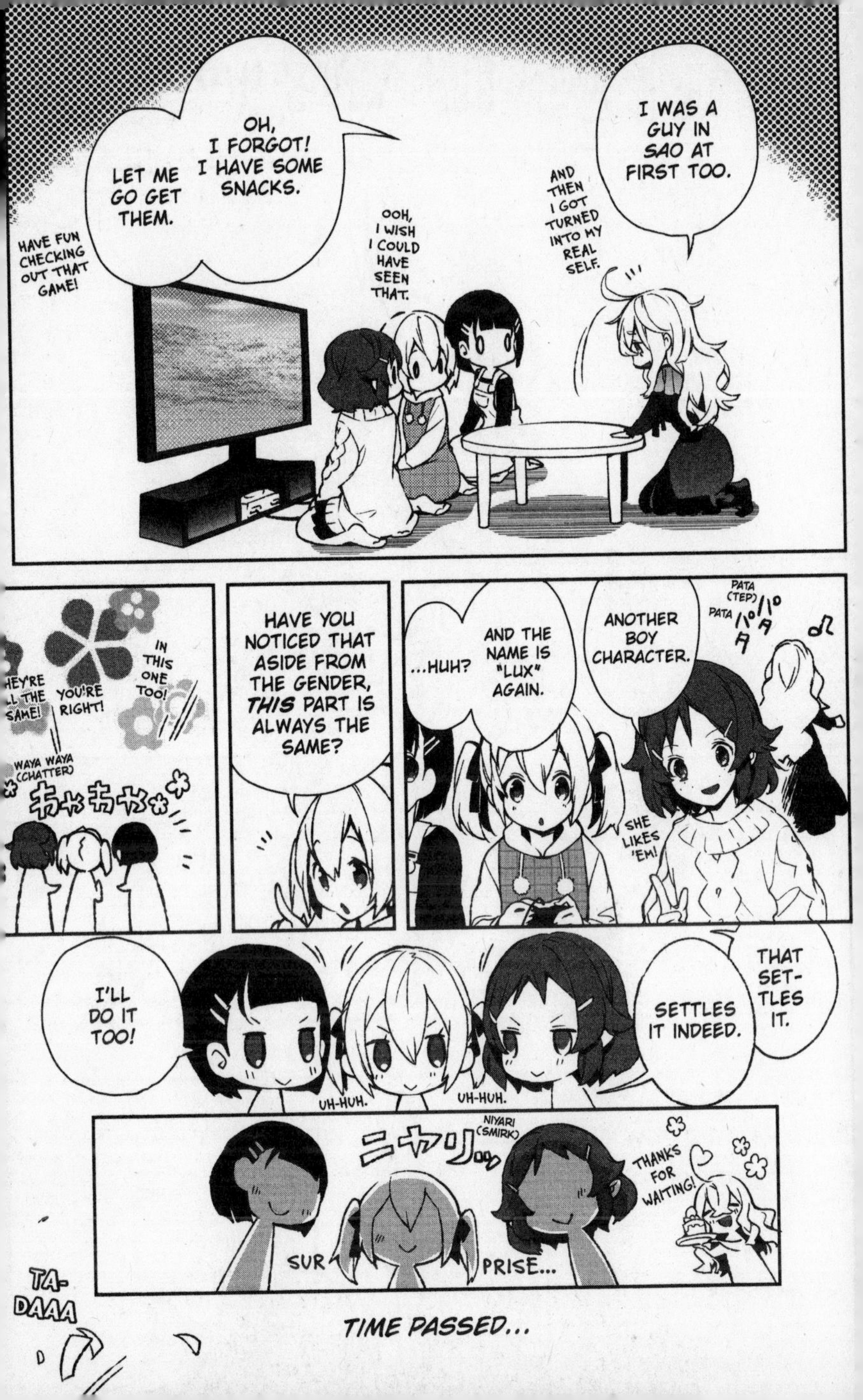
I WAS A GUY IN SAO AT FIRST TOO.
AND THEN I GOT TURNED INTO MY REAL SELF.
OOH, I WISH I COULD HAVE SEEN THAT.
OH, I FORGOT! I HAVE SOME SNACKS.
LET ME GO GET THEM.
HAVE FUN CHECKING OUT THAT GAME!
PATA PATA (TEP)
ANOTHER BOY CHARACTER.
SHE LIKES 'EM!
AND THE NAME IS "LUX" AGAIN.
...HUH?
HAVE YOU NOTICED THAT ASIDE FROM THE GENDER, *THIS* PART IS ALWAYS THE SAME?
IN THIS ONE TOO!
YOU'RE RIGHT!
HEY'RE LL THE SAME!
WAYA WAYA (CHATTER)
THAT SETTLES IT.
SETTLES IT INDEED.
UH-HUH.
UH-HUH.
I'LL DO IT TOO!
THANKS FOR WAITING!
NIYARI (SMIRK)
SUR
PRISE...
TA-DAAA
TIME PASSED...

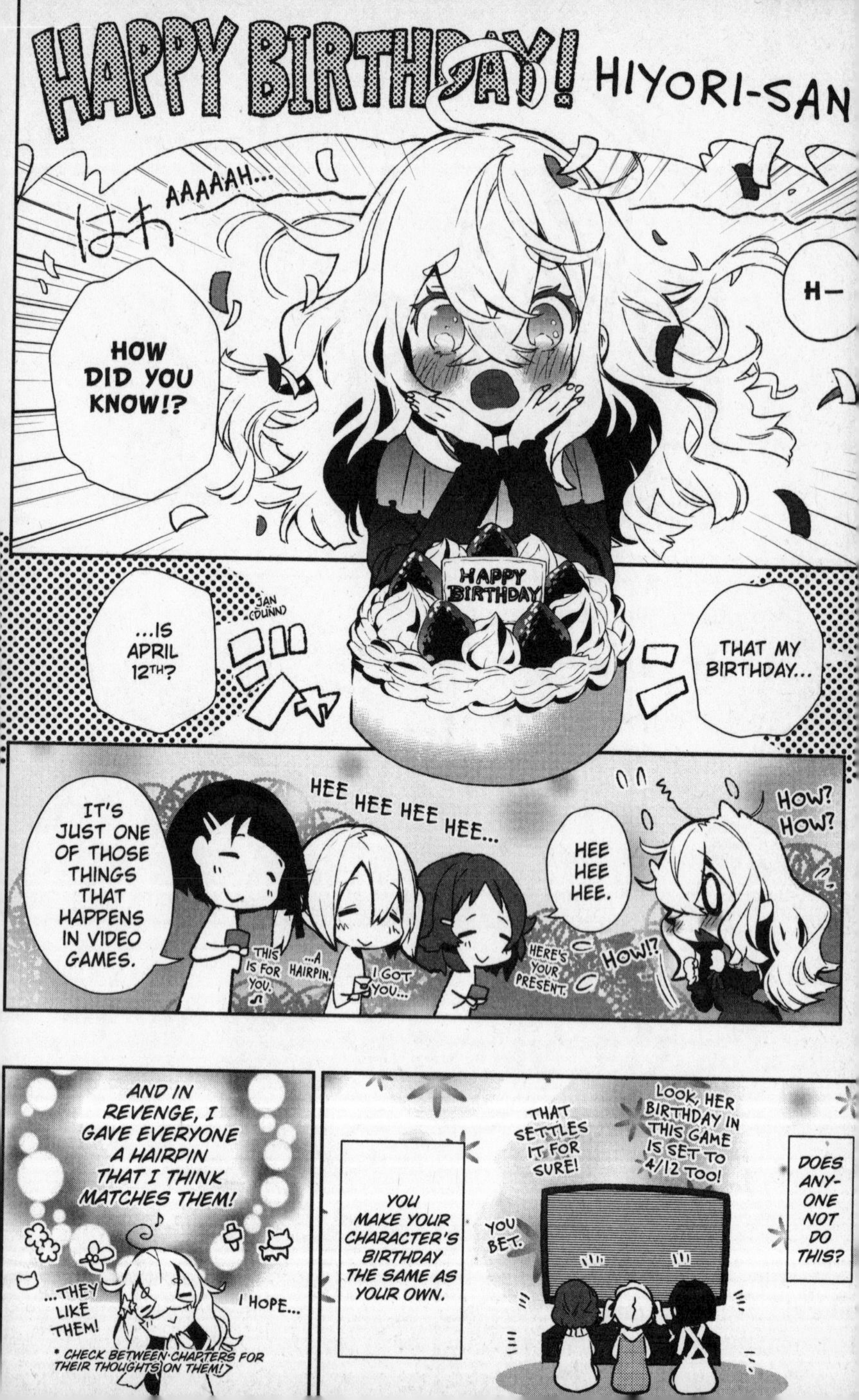
HAPPY BIRTHDAY! HIYORI-SAN
H—
はわ AAAAAH...
HOW DID YOU KNOW!?
THAT MY BIRTHDAY...
JAN (DUNN)
...IS APRIL 12TH?
HOW? HOW?
HEE HEE HEE.
HOW!?
HERE'S YOUR PRESENT.
I GOT YOU...
...A HAIRPIN.
THIS IS FOR YOU. ♫
HEE HEE HEE HEE...
IT'S JUST ONE OF THOSE THINGS THAT HAPPENS IN VIDEO GAMES.
DOES ANY-ONE NOT DO THIS?
LOOK, HER BIRTHDAY IN THIS GAME IS SET TO 4/12 TOO!
THAT SETTLES IT FOR SURE!
YOU BET.
YOU MAKE YOUR CHARACTER'S BIRTHDAY THE SAME AS YOUR OWN.
AND IN REVENGE, I GAVE EVERYONE A HAIRPIN THAT I THINK MATCHES THEM!
I HOPE...
...THEY LIKE THEM!
* CHECK BETWEEN-CHAPTERS FOR THEIR THOUGHTS ON THEM!

SPecial Thanks!

YAJI

CHISATO MINAMI-SAN

REKI KAWAHARA-SENSEI

ABEC-SENSEI

SHINGO NAGAI-SENSEI

KAZUMI MIKI-SAMA

TOMOYUKI TSUCHIYA-SAMA

EVERYONE WHO
READ THIS
BOOK!

SWORD ART ONLINE: GIRLS' OPS 6

ART: NEKO NEKOBYOU
ORIGINAL STORY: REKI KAWAHARA
CHARACTER DESIGN: abec

Translation: Stephen Paul
Lettering: Phil Christie

SWORD ART ONLINE: GIRLS' OPS
© REKI KAWAHARA/NEKO NEKOBYOU 2019
First published in Japan in 2019 by KADOKAWA CORPORATION, Tokyo.
English translation rights arranged with KADOKAWA CORPORATION, Tokyo, through Tuttle-Mori Agency, Inc., Tokyo.

English translation © 2019 by Yen Press, LLC

Yen Press
150 West 30th Street, 19th Floor
New York, NY 10001

Visit us at yenpress.com
facebook.com/yenpress
twitter.com/yenpress
yenpress.tumblr.com
instagram.com/yenpress

First Yen Press Edition: September 2019

Yen Press is an imprint of Yen Press, LLC.
The Yen Press name and logo are trademarks of Yen Press, LLC.

The publisher is not responsible for websites (or their content) that are not owned by the publisher.

Library of Congress Control Number: 2015952589

ISBNs: 978-1-9753-3220-4 (paperback)
       978-1-9753-8646-7 (ebook)

10 9 8 7 6 5 4 3 2 1

WOR

Printed in the United States of America